Political Behavior *in* America

New Directions

Edited, with an Introduction and Notes, by

Heinz Eulau *Stanford University*

RANDOM HOUSE *New York*

First Printing

 Published in New York by Random House, Inc. and simultaneously in Toronto, Canada, by Random House of Canada Limited
Library of Congress Catalog Card Number: 66-23283
Manufactured in the United States of America
by The Hadden Craftsmen, Inc., Scranton, Pennsylvania

To the Memory of V. O. KEY, *Jr.*

For whom politics was not end but beginning

Contents

Political Behavior *in* America
New Directions

Introduction

V. O. Key once told all of us—and, I think, in telling us he was telling himself—to beware of taking politics out of the study of political behavior. If he were still with us, I believe that he would have approved of the "new directions" that political behavior studies have taken in the last few years. His approval would have been tentative, for he always maintained a measured skepticism about innovations. But he was ever encouraging—a note here, a comment there that would mean a good deal. "I'm greatly obliged to you for having your publisher send me a copy of your book," he once wrote me; "it interests me very much; I often wish that I could write a short book; I seem never to be able to accomplish that difficult feat." V. O. will live in our memory for a long time. It is for what he did for us that this volume is dedicated to his memory.

In the last ten years, the "behavioral movement" in political science has grown so much that one of its most eminent members, Robert A. Dahl, did not hesitate to write an "epitaph for a monument to a successful protest."* In a little book, *The Behavioral Persuasion in Politics,* I tried to present, in a light vein, the variety of conceptual approaches that have been taken, the complexities involved in behavioral research, the difficulties that stand in the way of linking behavioral research with the traditional global concerns of political science, and the promises of the future. The favorable reception of

*Robert A. Dahl, "The Behavioral Approach in Political Science: Epitaph for a Monument to a Successful Protest," *American Political Science Review,* 55 (December, 1961), 763–772.

the book suggested a volume of readings that would serve as a companion to illustrate at least some of the arguments presented there. This is what the present volume is designed to do.

When planning this book of readings, I intended to reprint in it the full text of *The Behavioral Persuasion.* I have decided against that because, in view of the abundance of excellent research materials that deserved to be included, to do so would have been to make this volume bulkier than it should be. Nevertheless, I envisage this book as being read and used alongside *The Behavioral Persuasion,* although it can of course be used quite independently. And I do not propose to repeat, in this Introduction or in the later Introductory Notes, what I have written elsewhere about the behavioral orientation in political science.*

The organization of this volume follows the three central chapters of *The Behavioral Persuasion.* This does not mean that alternate schemes would not have been serviceable. The material could have been presented within the conventional institutional categories of analysis—electoral behavior, legislative behavior, party behavior, and so on. Or the material could have been organized in terms of theoretical categories —power, decision-making, elite and mass, communication, and so on. But my purpose in classifying the materials as I have is to underline the interdisciplinary orientation of political behavior research. The great bulk of this research is still largely conducted on the social level of analysis. This is probably as it should be, for most of the variances in political behavior can be explained in purely social terms. But unex-

*In addition to *The Behavioral Persuasion in Politics,* the student might wish to consult the following: "Segments of Political Science Most Susceptible to Behavioristic Treatment," in James C. Charlesworth, ed., *The Limits of Behavioralism in Political Science* (Philadelphia: American Academy of Political and Social Science, 1962), pp. 26–48; in Bert F. Hoselitz, ed., "Political Science," *A Reader's Guide to the Social Sciences* (New York: Free Press, 1959), pp. 89–127; the prefaces to volumes one to six of the *International Yearbook of Political Behavior Research,* edited by Morris Janowitz (1961), Dwaine Marvick (1961), Samuel P. Huntington (1962), Glendon Schubert (1963), David E. Apter (1964), and J. David Singer (1966), all published by Free Press; and Part V, "Maps for a Science of Politics," of *Journeys in Politics* (Indianapolis: Bobbs-Merrill, 1963), pp. 229–293.

For other references to behavioral studies in political science, see the bibliography at the end of this volume.

plained residues remain, and these suggest the need for analysis in terms of culture and personality. In fact, skillful treatment of political behavior from the perspectives of culture and personality remains a challenge. It is very likely that American studies of American politics are more culture-bound than we admit when we look at political behavior in its social dimensions alone. And political behavior research from the vantage point of personality or personality-related factors is still in its infancy.

Most of the selections deal with aspects of political behavior in the United States. Only two of the studies make cross-national comparisons. There is a very simple reason for this; the term "new directions" in the book's title gives a hint of it. My purpose is not merely to illustrate the kinds of research that are being done on the social, cultural, and personal aspects of political behavior. I also want to give the reader an inkling of the exciting theoretical, methodological, and technical developments in contemporary political behavior research. And the fact is that these developments have, with a few exceptions—notably in comparative research on underdeveloped areas and in the study of international politics—largely taken place in the American field.

What, then, are these "new directions"? In the first place —and V. O. Key would certainly have placed it first—most of the studies included here are representative of the efforts to make behavioral research *relevant to explaining the functioning of political systems.* Most of the earlier studies of political behavior were concerned with describing and explaining individual behavior, regardless of its consequences for larger structures. But, in the long run, it is not only the behavior of individual political actors but the political process as a whole that interests the political scientist. Behavioral studies of politics have come a long way in this respect, and in a surprisingly short period of time. This is not to say that the problem of linking individual and collective patterns of behavior has been solved. A good deal of the linkage is inferred rather than established from the data. But there is lively concern with the question of how studies of political behavior that take the individual person as the unit of analysis can be made significant from the perspective of the political system.

As a result, the questions that are asked of behavioral

research have changed. Some of the studies in this volume deal with such questions as these: What are the consequences for democratic government of different styles of representational behavior? What is the impact of group integration on the effectiveness of legislative decision-making? What are the consequences of different degrees of class polarization for cleavage and consensus in the political party system? What effect does the uneven utilization of political resources have on the achievement of political goals? What are the consequences for political stability of the presence or absence of cross-pressures? What is the significance for public policy outcomes of different conceptions of "interest"? What are the consequences of childhood socialization experiences for the acceptance of authority? What are the implications for party strategies of political alienation? What are the consequences of anomy for the viability of political ideologies?

These and many other questions are now asked by the practitioners of the behavioral persuasion in politics and by asking them, they have given new directions to political research. In redirecting research to the answering of these kinds of questions, the behavioral approaches have greatly expanded the range of politically relevant considerations.

Second, there are the attempts to *build empirical investigations explicitly on theoretical propositions.* Typical of these efforts are the work of Eulau and his associates on representational behavior, which derives from Edmund Burke's notions about the role of the representative; Fenno's study of the House Appropriations Committee, which it influenced by Talcott Parsons' concept of integration as a functional requisite of any social system; Smith's analysis of community politics, which is indebted to Norton Long's metaphor of politics as an ecology of games; Verba's cross-national study of organizational membership and democratic consensus, which examines hypotheses derived from group theory; and Wilson and Banfield's study of "public-regardingness" in voting choices, which is related to the "rational self-interest" model of man in Anthony Downs' economic theory of democracy. These studies do not seek so much to test particular hypotheses—though they sometimes do—as to apply broad theoretical formulations to concrete research questions that, in turn, may lead to reformulations of the original theory.

Closely related is another set of studies, which uses empirical data *to develop new theoretical propositions.* Representative of this type of inquiry are Dahl's conception of participation as political resource utilization and his theory of "political strata;" Eldersveld's notion of the political party as a "motivationally complex and pluralistic structure;" Wilson and Banfield's hypothesis about "public-regardingness" as an independent cultural variable in political decision-making; Fiellin's explication of the latent functions performed by informal groups in the legislative process; and McClosky and Schaar's reformulation of the theory of political anomy.

Connected with both these types of approach is a group of studies which, *through theoretical reconceptualization, extend the range of empirical research.* Among these studies are McMurray and Parsons' effort to look at representation from the perspective of the electorate, an attempt which contributes to theoretical closure, as does, to an even greater extent, Miller and Stokes' analysis of reciprocal attitudes of congressmen and their constituents. One also might include here Friedman's re-examination of the urban-rural hypothesis and Greenstein's study of children's feelings about political authority. Moreover, some of these studies are geared toward *making empirical research findings more cumulative for the purpose of ascertaining their theoretical validity.* For instance, Francis' application of probability calculations to the findings of Eulau and his associates contributes to this objective. Similarly, Salisbury and Black probe, through the use of census and election statistics, the relationship between social classes and political parties previously investigated in survey research. Kornberg's study of the "rules of the game" in the Canadian House of Commons, in replicating the work of Wahlke and others, is able to examine the validity of relevant propositions about the legislature as a subculture. And the research by Flinn and Wirt on Ohio party leaders follows up on McClosky's earlier study of issue conflict and consensus among national party activists.

All these studies, then, are vitally concerned with theoretical problems, and no hard and fast line can be drawn between them. They differ only in the accents they place on different aspects of the interchange between political theory and empirical research, and in several of the studies several different accents occur. All the studies, however, attest to the growing maturity of political behavior research. The striving toward theoretical sophistication, the testing of propositions, the replication of analyses, and the cumulation of research findings are as symptomatic of the "new directions" in the behavioral study of politics as is the quest to make behavioral research relevant to the macro-analysis of political phenomena.

A third major tendency indicative of "new directions" is the increased effort to *develop more rigorous research designs through the introduction of quasi-experimental,* post factum *controls,* and to bring to the analysis of political behavior the most advanced research techniques available in the social sciences. None of the studies included in this volume is experimental in the classical sense, but many of them, either through comparative analysis or through the introduction of control variables, seek to maximize the reliability of inferences and to minimize spurious conclusions. One way of doing this is by means of the formalization of models; this process, apart from whatever theoretical advantages can be derived from it, contributes to the ordering of reality. Francis' invention of a probability model for representation, Smith's use of coalition theory, and Levin and Eden's application of the Downs model of rational political action exemplify this approach. Of a somewhat different nature are Friedman's *post factum* experimental design of legislative attitudes toward "daylight-saving time," Salisbury and Black's comparison of the role of class and party in partisan and nonpartisan elections, and, above all, Miller and Stokes' clever design, linking constituency preferences and representatives' perceptions and attitudes, as well as their behavior on legislative roll-calls, within a single analytical schema.

The control of variables through statistical techniques, long practiced in psychology and sociology, has only recently been introduced in the study of politics. Many of the studies included in this volume are indicative of this trend. I hope they will convince the young student that competence in the use of statistics is as necessary nowadays as competence in political theory. For instance, McMurray and Parsons use factorial techniques to identify and isolate related attitudes; both Francis and Smith employ rank order correlations; Salisbury and Black treat their data with the aid of partial and multiple correlation measures; Kornberg employs chi square to appraise statistical significance; Wilson and Banfield illustrate correlations with scatter diagrams; Flinn and Wirt use analysis of variance; and McClosky and Schaar develop a variety of unidimensional scales. Many of the studies employ multivariate tables for handling individual data, typologies, and other notational devices of "the language of social research." In general, political science has not been innovative in the development of techniques for data handling. The one exception, perhaps, is the contribution that political scientists have made to "bloc analysis," the identification of people with similar attitudes or attributes in interacting aggregates. Grumm's extension of bloc analysis beyond the earlier work of Rice, Beyle, and Truman, and its preparation for computer treatment, is a truly innovative departure.

A great variety of data serve the needs of political behavior analysis—census data, aggregate election returns, survey interview data, mail questionnaire data, roll-call data, documentary and direct observational data. All these types of data are found in this volume; all have both advantages and drawbacks. To discuss these in detail here would lead me too far from the main theme of this essay. The point I wish to make is that data are not necessarily "givens"; they can be "made." The creation of new data must be high on the agenda of political research.

The practitioners of the behavioral persuasion in politics are sometimes criticized for not orienting their work more purposefully toward helping cure the world's personal and social ills; the critics demand that political behavior research be placed unequivocally in the service of human needs and wants. The goal, of course, is man. But I strongly disagree with those who would transform behavioral science into an ideology—a program for social and political action.

Students of political behavior may have failed to articulate with sufficient candor some of the dilemmas in regard to the relationship between facts and values, for which—at least at present—no ready solutions exist. But because they have failed to do so, it does not follow that political behaviorists are insensitive to values, as has been charged. And I think it is a mistake to say that this alleged insensitivity is the consequence of their commitment to "value neutrality." I think the problem is quite the other way round: it is not that students of political behavior are insensitive to values, but that, on becoming increasingly involved in questions of public policy, they have become hypersensitive to values. No student of political behavior any longer believes that his work is "value-free." And it is not denied that his work, no matter how remote it may appear to be from immediate actualities, must serve some socially useful purpose.

Values enter behavioral research in politics at many points and in many forms: in the selection and formulation of problems for research, in the choice of what are considered to be the significant variables, in the interpretation of research findings, and in the application of findings to questions of public policy, as standards of professional conduct, as cultural determinants of meanings, as substantive topics in their own right, and last but not least, as biases.

But it does not follow that no difficulties exist, or that they can be readily turned into blessings. For instance, "value bias" remains a perennial danger in scientific work on political behavior. Of course, only a scientist who was not devoted to truth and objectivity would consciously and purposefully cultivate biases that stemmed from prior commitment to the interests of race, class, religion, nation, or ideology. Yet such biases have a way of being smuggled into scientific research, at least unconsciously. It is utopian to assume that value bias can be readily eliminated by some act of scientific will.

On the other hand, the term "value neutrality" may be useful in that it calls attention to just that function that the term "neutrality" implies: that we seek to "neutralize" biases and to treat them as "errors" that can be isolated and discounted, just as we allow for the other errors—of observation, sampling, measurement, or inference—that are characteristic of all scientific work. In this sense, then, "value neutrality" does not mean self-deception that value biases do not exist or that they can be easily eliminated; it does suggest, however, the need for techniques that will enable us to neutralize our biases and to increase the level of confidence in the results of political behavior research.

Value neutralization must not be confused with value neutralism. Scientific indifference to values is not only impossible; it would be, in fact, undesirable. For such value neutralism is just the opposite of the kind of sensitivity to values that the quest for neutralization implies. Indifference to values is indeed counter to the ideals of science. Yet rejection of neutralism cannot be taken as meaning that behavioral research is, or must be, somehow subservient to values. Judicious appraisal of the relationship between facts and values is a norm of scientific conduct that must always guide the the scientist's conduct in the research process—and, as I shall suggest, in the interpretation and application of research findings.

Judiciousness in this respect is, of course, only one among many norms in the culture of science. Truth, objectivity, honesty, and integrity are values that scientists try to live by, just as they must insist on freedom of inquiry if they wish to function effectively as scientists. These are not self-fulfilling values, and though they have been maintained by the scientific community with remarkable success, it is by no means impossible to violate them. Judiciousness as a norm in the appraisal of the relationship between facts and values is certainly of the same order.

Values such as truth or objectivity are accepted by the scientific community as norms of professional conduct because they prove to be useful in the task of discovery. They are not absolute ends in themselves or articles of faith, but instrumental links in the chain of means and ends that has no ultimate ends, links that are, indeed, sometimes treated as means and sometimes as ends. Truth and objectivity are values that are instrumental in the scientist's search for knowledge.

"Value neutrality," only in the sense of a judicious attitude toward values, is similarly instrumental. It is not and cannot be some ultimate, absolute end, which has to be either embraced altogether or rejected altogether. If it were so treated, it would be an abstraction that could not serve any good purpose and should for that reason be banned from discourse about the ethics of science. But if it is treated instrumentally as a norm of scientific conduct, it enjoins us to undertake just those intellectual operations that enable us to clarify the relationship between facts and values. Our attention becomes focused on the functions of values, and their functions point to the context in which values guide political research.

The context in which neutrality as a norm of scientific conduct must be activated is just that point where the process of inquiry reaches its (always tentative) termination—the point, in other words, at which the findings of behavioral research come within the purview of the public, indeed become "public property." At this point, the behavioral scientist faces two dilemmas at once. First, he may come to realize that his findings contravene the values that guided his inquiry, and possibly even values that are widely cherished by the public. And second, as I said in *The Behavioral Persuasion in Politics,* he may discover that there is nothing in his work to prevent its being used for political purposes of which he disapproves.

Those who attack "neutrality" as if it were an absolute end not only tend to ignore such dilemmas; they also ignore the context in which these dilemmas arise. It is as if the dilemmas could be ruled out of existence by some kind of preventive mental therapy of good intentions, on the assumption that "right" values can be derived from the very processes of behavior that behavioral science investigates. Once derived, so the argument seems to go, these values have such compelling force that they cannot but be accepted by all men—at least by all men of good will. Rejection can be due only to lack of perception of the benefits that behavioral science, as the new dispensation, can bring to mankind. To buttress the argument, certain "fundamental human needs," discoverable if not already discovered, are posited as the ultimate criteria for choosing topics of research that will lead to correct social action. The satisfaction of these needs becomes a self-evident proposition, and a "scientific ideology of political behavior" is thereby created.

I cannot here dissect in detail the faultiness of this argument. Suffice it to say that, even if the technical problems of deriving values from human needs could be solved, there is at present little agreement among behavioral scientists about just what human needs are "fundamental," and there is a good deal of disagreement about the priority of particular needs—a priority that is likely to change from time to time. The difficulty is, of course, that any ordering of needs is impossible without some prior preference ordering of values.

By way of medical analogy, diagnosis (of which behavioral science is quite capable) is one thing, but therapy is quite another. Even if there were consensus on the nature of "social diseases" (it is difficult to obtain, but not impossible), there is unlikely to be similar agreement on the steps that should be taken to remedy or prevent these diseases, or on the order in which these steps might be taken. The notion that behavioral science can provide the criteria for a program of social or political therapy is utopian.

In the context of reality in which scientific findings may be abused to implement values of which the researcher disapproves, the resultant dilemmas cannot be solved by magic formulas of "human needs." But it is also within this context alone that the notion of neutrality—referring to judicious appraisal of the relationship between facts and values—can be given useful meaning. I think that the notion of neutrality serves to sensitize the behavioral scientist and to make him faithful to two sets of values—social values *and* scientific values. These are not mutually contradictory demands on the scientist. For his commitment to social purposes can best be implemented, if he serves well the demands of science, and he can best serve the demands of science by demonstrating judicious restraint in regard to the diverse uses to which his scientific knowledge may be put.

These views are my own, of course, and should not be attributed to any of the contributors to this volume, who may well disagree with me in these philosophical matters. I doubt, however, that our disagreement would seriously interfere with our work: it is perhaps the supreme virtue of science that scientists can disagree on values and yet agree on facts. I feel truly indebted to my colleagues for permitting me to include their work in this volume. Their creativity alone made this volume possible. In that sense, it is more their book than mine.

HEINZ EULAU

Stanford University
June, 1966

Part 1. The Social Matrix of Political Behavior

Political behavior is social behavior. Human behavior is social when at least two persons confront each other, are related to each other, make demands upon each other, or entertain expectations concerning each other's conduct. The relationship is one of mutuality and interdependence. The concept that most economically expresses the interpersonal relationship is "role." If we know the roles that actors take toward one another, we know a good deal about the nature of the relationship between them and the behavior of each in the relationship.

Moreover, if we say that people are friends, or colleagues, or legislators, and so on, we imply that their interactions are structured in a particular way—in this case, that they are horizontally patterned, and that these patterned interactions make for the existence of a "group." On the other hand, if we designate one person as leader and another as follower, we imply that their relationship is vertically structured, that each belongs to a different "stratum" in the social order. Very simple considerations such as these make it convenient to think of the "social matrix" of political behavior as a system of relationships that can be effectively analyzed in terms of the roles people take, the groups to which they belong or relate, and the patterns of equality or inequality that characterize their interactions.

In politics, perhaps no set of relationships is of greater interest than that between the "representative" and the "represented." In "The Role of the Representative: Some Empirical Observations on the Theory of Edmund Burke," Heinz Eulau and his associates show how, through careful re-examination

NOTE: At this point, the student is referred to Chapter Two of *The Behavioral Persuasion in Politics,* which develops the view of a social matrix of political behavior.

of Burke's classical theory of representation from the perspective of role analysis, it is possible to extend the range of political research. Empirical findings at odds with theory forced the re-examination of theory, and theoretical explication, in turn, served to explain the empirical data. In making the theoretical distinction between the "style" and the "focus" of representation, and in harnessing their data accordingly, the authors paved the way to further theoretical development and empirical research.

Roles can be analyzed from a variety of observational standpoints. In the study by Eulau and his colleagues, the actor's self-definitions of his role served the purposes of analysis. Carl D. McMurray and Malcolm B. Parsons, in "Public Attitudes Toward the Representational Roles of Legislators and Judges," concentrate on constituents' perceptions of and attitudes toward their representatives. In trying to answer the question of whether public attitudes are consonant with legislators' self-definitions of their representational roles, the authors, through factor-analytical procedures, identify four rather than three constituent orientations. Perhaps because the public's orientations toward representational roles are characterized by a good deal of attitudinal confusion, McMurray and Parsons do not attempt to give their findings theoretical significance. But they suggest that popular attitudes toward the "delegate" role are less favorable than was previously supposed, and that attitudinal confusion concerning representational styles may well be the result of representatives' failure to enlighten their constituents about the facts of modern legislative life.

A further inference may be drawn from the McMurray and Parsons study. They find that the "trustee" role is more likely to be favored by that sector of the population that is well-educated, has a higher income and higher occupational status, and is politically more participant. This is precisely the grouping in the population from which most representatives are recruited. It would seem that, in taking the trustee role more frequently than any other, representatives find in the high-status, high-participant sector among their constituents those "significant others" whose expectations may, in fact, determine their own role orientations.

A criticism sometimes made of role analysis is that it relies on orientations and expectations rather than on actual conduct in the performance of roles, and that it is incapable of predicting behavior in specific situations. This criticism is largely erroneous, for if roles were reconstructed from behavior, the resultant definition would inevitably be tautological; in any case, role analysis does not aspire to predicting individual behavior in every conceivable situation. It merely assumes that most persons do behave in most situations in predictable ways.

Wayne L. Francis' study, "The Role Concept in Legislatures: A Probability Model and a Note on Cognitive Structure," explicates the probabilistic nature of representational roles. In building on the work of Eulau and associates, Francis' analysis is a good example of how knowledge can be cumulated, validated, and extended. By relating representational role types to independently secured indices of political behavior, Francis is able to demonstrate that, while the correlation between role and behavior was not perfect, the correspondence was statistically close enough to confirm the viability of the role types.

But Francis' study is of interest for another reason. By attaching probability calculations to the distributions of individual role orientations, Francis is able to present "summary profiles" of four representational systems. This adroit use of the probability calculus not only permits closing the gap between micro- and macro-analysis, but it also facilitates more genuinely comparative analysis of larger political structures. The study demonstrates the utility of role formulations of political behavior for both individual and institutional analysis.

Indeed, most political roles are institutionalized roles—that is, they are taken within more or less permanent social groups, which shape the expectations and behavior of their members. The number and diversity of groups that constitute the universe of politics, or that are politically relevant, is enormous—ranging from the nuclear family to the inclusive nation-state. What these groups do to people and what, in turn, people do to groups provides an infinitely rich source of empirical investigations. The study of political groups, both as determinants of individual political behavior and as collective actors in their own right, is the task of group theory and analysis. For the purposes of this volume, I have chosen studies of three types of groups, all of which are themselves located in a larger institutionalized group—the legislature. This makes it possible to examine not only what the group does for its members or for itself, but also what effects it has on the larger system of which it is a part.

Alan Fiellin's "The Functions of Informal Groups in Legislative Institutions" is a study of New York City's Democratic delegation in the United States House of Representatives. This informal group was not only central in the political behavior of its members, but had consequences, both of a manifest and latent sort, for the legislature as a whole, as well as for party leaders and constituents in New York. Two types of behavioral pattern are identified—interactions that are group properties, such as the organization of the group and its network of communication, and individual behavior patterns that are common to the members of the group but are not group-structured. Although this is a case study, with all the limitations of a case study, the author offers a series of interesting hypotheses about the functions of informal groups in the legislative setting.

Not the least advantage to be derived from a study of infra-structures, as exemplified by Fiellin's research, is that institutional research, subjected to functional analysis, can be made more manageable. The legislature turns out to be neither so simple as one might believe after one has treated it as a kind of indivisible macro-unit, nor so complex as one might assume if one sees it only as composed of a great many individual members. Rather, as Fiellin demonstrates, its informal subgroups are important intervening structures; they provide channels for information exchange, negotiation, and bargaining that link the individual legislators to each other and, through the functioning of the group, to the larger political system of which the group is a part.

Functional analysis is also the strategy employed by Richard F. Fenno in his study of a formal legislative group, "The House Appropriations Committee as a Political System: The Problem of Integration." The legislative committee, Fenno shows, is not simply a micro-replica of the legislature as a whole. Rather, the committee is a discrete group, faced with functional problems of its own that it must solve in order to achieve its goals and maintain itself. Integration—one of Talcott Parsons' functional imperatives of any social system—is a necessary response to differentiation among subgroups and roles, for only if integration is achieved can conflict be minimized and norms evolved, and the existence of control mechanisms such as the socialization of group members guaranteed.

Fenno's research not only demonstrates the theoretical utility of conceiving of the group as a "system," but in pursuing a particular problem—that of group integration—the author is able to consider the consequences of success or failure in integration for the larger system of which the group is a part. He presents a series of hypotheses (in principle testable) that would confirm the crucial role of group integration as a key variable in the study of legislative politics. As he rightly points out, only comparative analysis can answer some of the problems raised in this case study.

A quite different type of group is the "voting bloc" in a legislature. Whether or not it can be called a group depends largely on the degree of confidence one has in the assumption that, because certain legislators vote together over a series of issues, some prior interaction must have taken place among them. Nevertheless, the very notion that there exist "cohesive" voting blocs implies the existence of at least temporarily cohesive coalitions, even if we do not know, from bloc analysis alone, just how these coalitions have come about. The major interest of voting-bloc analysts has been the identification of coalitions as at least a first step to further analysis. As John G. Grumm shows in his "Voting Blocs in Legislative Behavior: A Systematic Analysis," the specification of a voting bloc's boundaries is difficult and requires considerable methodological finesse. Grumm, building critically yet creatively on earlier techniques of bloc analysis, demonstrates that this method of identifying voting units can be highly useful in accounting for causes of variance in legislative behavior.

Like interaction groups, voting blocs evidently play a role in linking the individual legislator to the legislature as a whole. Relatively simple statistical procedures make it possible to achieve maximum objectivity in the identification of blocs and to relate bloc behavior on the part of individual legislators to hypothetically related independent variables. The fact that the procedure proposed by Grumm can be handled easily by modern computing equipment opens up new possibilities for the study of political groups generally.

While I conceive of the social matrix as being horizontally structured by virtue of people's group memberships, group identifications, or reference group behavior, it is conventional to think of social structure as being vertically patterned as a result of the super- and sub-ordination of a group's or society's members. And there is good reason to believe that stratification—the assignment of individuals to "higher" and "lower" rankings in the continuum of recognizable superior and inferior positions—has determinable consequences both for individual political behavior and for the character of a political system. Rankings are possible in terms of almost all those values that are recognized as being scarce—for example, prestige, wealth, knowledge, power, or wisdom. Whether status differentiation is or is not a universal characteristic of all social systems, or whether strata or classes are real, need not concern us here. The fact is that, from Aristotle on, the relationship between a group's or a society's stratification system and its political system has been recognized as one of the most intriguing problems of political analysis.

Under modern democratic conditions, it is the relationship between social classes, however defined, and political parties that has fascinated political scientists. Both class and party function as sources of cleavage and consensus in the political system. It is generally assumed that polarization—as when parties appeal only to particular social strata in the population—is likely to threaten the stability of political systems. Polarization is, of course, a matter of degree. But just as pure "class parties" would seem to endanger the viability of a political system, so the existence of parties entirely unrelated to class differentiation is likely to make the political battleground void of issues—and of meaning.

These speculations are relevant to placing Robert H. Salisbury and Gordon Black's "Class and Party in Partisan and Non-Partisan Elections" within an appropriate theoretical perspective. The authors use party registration and a class index based on housing as independent variables in order to measure their effect on the direction of the vote and the size of turnout in partisan and non-partisan elections. While the effect of class was relatively constant, traditional party affiliation was more highly correlated with the direction of the vote than was class in both types of elections. But in non-partisan contests the effect of party varied more widely than in partisan elections, apparently in response to the intensity of the municipal campaign that was being waged. Finally, the authors show that class is significantly related to participation, while party affiliation is not.

A quite different problem is tackled by Robert A. Dahl in "The Utilization of Political Resources: Variations on a Theme." In this selection from his classical study of New Haven politics, Dahl shows that differential political participation on the part of individuals who belong to different population strata has significant consequences for the kinds of rewards they reap in the political system. While Dahl's raw data merely confirm what is generally known about the effects on political behavior of differences in socio-economic position, his theoretical exploitation of the findings is both novel and ingenious. He draws a suggestive picture of how the differential utilization of their political resources (as he conceptualizes different types of citizen participation) affects not only the distribution of payoffs, but also how the existence of a cadre of highly active citizens—the "professionals"—is a source both of stability and instability in the political system.

A. *Role as a Basic Unit of Analysis*

1 *The Role of the Representative: Some Empirical Observations on the Theory of Edmund Burke**

by Heinz Eulau, John C. Wahlke, William Buchanan, and LeRoy C. Ferguson

The problem of representation is central to all discussions of the functions of legislatures or the behavior of legislators. For it is commonly taken for granted that, in democratic political systems, legislatures are both legitimate and authoritative decision-making institutions, and that it is their representative character which makes them authoritative and legitimate. Through the process of representation, presumably, legislatures are empowered to act for the whole body politic and are legitimized. And because, by virtue of representation, they participate in legislation, the represented accept legislative decisions as authoritative. But agreement about the meaning of the term "representation" hardly goes beyond a general consensus regarding the context within which it is appropriately used. The history of political theory is studded

Reprinted from *American Political Science Review,* 53 (September, 1959), 742–756, by permission of the authors and the publisher.

*This study was made possible by grants from the Political Behavior Committee of the Social Science Research Council. Neither the Committee nor the Council is responsible for what we have written.

with definitions of representation,[1] usually embedded in ideological assumptions and postulates which cannot serve the uses of empirical research without conceptual clarification.[2]

I

Many familiar formulations treat representation in a nonfunctional fashion, viewing it as something valuable in itself, as an ultimate end, and seek to discover or specify its "nature" or "essence." Functional theory, on the other hand, deals with representation from the point of view of the political system as a whole or its component units. Herman Finer, for instance, has suggested that "responsibility is the chief and wider aim, and representativeness merely a convenient means to attain this. . . . The desire for responsible government is paramount; people not merely wish to represent their views, but actually to make and unmake governments."[3] But while functional formulations treat representation as a means for the attainment of some other political objective, failure to test functional propositions by way of empirical research leaves the problems raised by theory in the realm of hypothesis rather than reliable knowledge. In connection with Finer's proposition, for example, there has been little, if any, empirical analysis of the extent to which the represented do, in fact, want to enforce political responsibility, and how capable they are, under modern conditions, of exercising the necessary control. Nevertheless, once relevant concepts are clarified, a functional formulation of representation can open up areas of research which, in turn, may contribute to theoretical cumulation.

The relationship between the representative and the represented is at the core of representational theory. The term "representation" directs attention, first of all, to the attitudes, expectations and behaviors of the represented—to their acceptance of representatives' decisions as legitimate and authoritative for themselves. More particularly, representation concerns not the mere fact that they do accept such decisions, but rather the reasons they have for doing so, their rationalizations of the legitimacy and authority of the decisions made by their representatives.

Sometimes the adjective "representative" denotes nothing more than the publicly approved process by which representatives are to be chosen—as when a distinction is made between a "representative body" (meaning a group of men elected by specific modes of popular election) and a "non-representative body" (meaning a group of men selected by royal or executive appointment, entailed inheritance, or some other non-electoral process). Such usage implies that citizens' attitudes and expectations include, and may extend no farther than, the belief that representatives' decisions must be accepted as legitimate and authoritative *if* the representatives have been selected in the approved manner. In other words, elected officials are called "representatives" primarily because of the way they have been chosen. Even in a looser usage an appointed commission may be approvingly called a body of "representative" citizens, or may be attacked as "unrepresentative," depending on whether its members might conceivably have been chosen had they been subject to election rather than appointment; and their views will correspondingly be accorded or denied a measure of authority and legitimacy.

But the appropriate process of selecting public decision-makers has never been the really fundamental question for theories of representation. Behind every proposal for altering the method of selecting officials is some assumption, at least, about the effect of such changes on what decision-makers or decision-making institutions do, and how they do it. Proposals for reform must assume or show that the proposed change will bring it about that *what* representatives decide and *the way* they reach decisions is more nearly in accord with expectations and demands of the represented than has been in the case under the system to be reformed. The various defenses of existing systems of selection which postulate "virtual representation" have in common some shading of the belief that the process of selection is not of major significance in determining what representatives do or how they do it, or that decisions made by representatives can be brought in harmony with public expectations, without altering whatever process of selection is being defended by the advocacy of virtual representation.

The relationship between the process of selection of legislators and the modes and consequences of legislative behavior, or the relationship between public expectations and legislative decisions, offer wide and fertile fields for empirical research. Our purpose here, however, is less ambitious than a full-scale investigation of such relationships. It is to eliminate those particular ambiguities in the concept of representation which concern the actions or behavior of representatives, by use of the concept of "role," and to demonstrate the utility of this approach for further research relevant to the theory of representation.

II

A convenient and useful starting point in theoretical clarification is Edmund Burke's theory of representation. For, in following his classic argument, later theorists have literally accepted Burke's formulation and ignored its contextual basis and polemical bias. Burke ingeniously combined two notions which, for analytical purposes, should be kept distinct. In effect, he combined a conception of the *focus* of representation with a conception of the *style* of representation. Parliament, Burke said in a famous passage,[4]

> is not a *congress* of ambassadors from different and hostile interests; which interests each must maintain, as an agent and advocate, against other agents and advocates; but parliament is a *deliberative* assembly of *one* nation, with *one* interest, that of the whole; where, not local purposes, not local prejudices ought to guide but the general good, resulting from the general reason of the whole.

The sentence indicates that Burke postulated two possible foci of representation: local, necessarily hostile interests, on the one hand; and a national interest, on the other hand. He rejected the former as an improper and advocated the latter as the proper focus of the representative's role. But in doing so, he also linked these foci of representation with particular representational styles. If the legislature is concerned with only one interest, that of the whole, and not with compromise among diverse interests, it follows that the representative cannot and must not be bound by instructions, from whatever source, but must be guided by what Burke called "his unbiased opinion, his mature judgment, his enlightened conscience." Moreover, Burke buttressed his argument by emphasizing the deliberative function of the legislature—presumably in contrast to its representational function. Yet if one rejects his notion of the legislature as only a deliberative body whose representational focus is the whole rather than its constituent parts, the logic of Burke's formulation is no longer necessary or relevant.

Today, many "publics" constitute significant foci of orientation for the representative as he approaches his legislative task. Under the conditions of a plural political and social order, these foci of representation may be other than geographical interests, be they electoral districts or the larger commonwealth. The modern representative faces similar choices concerning the style of his representational role not only *vis-à-vis* his constituency or state and nation, but *vis-à-vis* other clienteles, notably political parties, pressure groups and administrative agencies. From an analytical point of view—though not, of course, from an empirical standpoint—the style of the representative's role is neutral as far as these different foci of representation are concerned. Regardless of his focus of representation—a geographical unit, a party, a pressure group, or an administrative organization—he is not committed to take either the role of free agent, following his own convictions, or the role of delegate, bound by instructions. In other words, Burke's linkage of a particular areal focus of representation with a particular representational style constitutes only a special case in a generic series of empirically viable relationships between possible and different foci of representation and appropriate styles of representation.

Of course, different foci of representation need not be mutually exclusive. They may occur simultaneously, and appropriate role orientations may be held simultaneously. For instance, a party may be so strong in a district that, in the representative's mind, the interests of district and party are identical. Or a pressure group may have such pervasive influence—as, for example, the Farm Bureau in a predominantly agricultural constituency, or the AFL-CIO in a predominantly working class district—that, again, the interests of district and pressure group become identified. Moreover, it is possible that different focal role orientations are activated *seriatim* as circumstances require. In particular one may assume that on matters of no relevance to the representative's district, roles oriented towards party or lobby as foci of representation may serve as major premises of choice.

The generic extension of Burke's special case, broken down into analytic components, suggests that the focal and stylistic dimensions of representation must be kept separate in empirical research. Burke combined them for polemical reasons: he was writing in opposition to the idea of mandatory representation which had much popular support in the middle of the eighteenth century.[5] The result of this polemical commitment was that the problem of *how* the representative should behave *vis-à-vis* his clienteles became a substantive problem—*what* he should do for the clienteles. But the fact that a representative sees himself as reaching a decision by following his own convictions or judgment does not mean that the content of his decisions is necessarily oriented towards a general rather than a particular interest, just as his acceptance of instructions from a clientele group does not necessarily mean that he is oriented towards a special rather than the public interest. A representative may base his decisions on his own conscience or judgment, but the cause he promotes may be parochial. Or he may follow instructions, but the mandate may be directed towards the realization of the general welfare.

The distinction between the focal and stylistic dimensions of the representative's role allows us to suggest that representation is not concerned with what decisions should be made, but with how decisions are to be made. Now, it is axiomatic that decisions made in institutional contexts, such as legislatures provide, are made in terms of a set of premises which guide the behavior of decision-makers. The notion—explicit in Burke and other traditional formulations—that legislative decisions can be purely rational is not tenable in view of the fact that rationality, while not altogether absent, is invariably bounded by the legislature's institutional environment.[6] One of these boundaries is the representational fabric of the legislature. The representative system provides the representative with some of the assumptions in terms of which he defines his role. The roles he takes, in turn, whether in the focal or stylistic dimensions of representation, provide the premises for decision.

Premises underlying decisions made by legislatures, then, may be of two kinds: (1) they may be premises relevant to the focus of representation; and (2) they may be relevant to the style of representation. With regard to the first kind, for instance, a representative may be guided by premises such as that legislation should benefit either his district or the state, that it should be "liberal" or "conservative," that it should or should not favor special interests, that it should or should not be in performance of his party's campaign pledges, and so on. With regard to the second kind of premises, the representative's choices may be circumscribed by his stylistic role orientation, whether he sees himself following his own conscience or instructions. In this dimension the premises involved in his decisional behavior refer not to the focus but to the style of his role as representative.

III

The issue of styles of representation—free agency versus mandate—has been confounded by the fact that the enabling source of a representative's power is the electorate of a geographical district. Representation of geographical areas introduces a certain amount of ambiguity into the relationship between representative and represented which is likely to be absent under schemes of proportional or vocational representation.[7] Part of this ambiguity is the widely held expectation, contested by Burke but shared by many citizens and politicians alike, that the representative is a spokesman of the presumed "interests" of the area from which he has been elected. Of course, implicit in this expectation is the assumption that a geographical unit has interests which are distinct and different from those of other units, and which should be represented in public decision-making. This assumption has been challenged on a variety of grounds: that the geographical area as such, as an electoral unit, is artificial; that it cannot and does not generate interests shared by its residents; that it has no unique interests; and so on. Schemes of proportional or vocational representation have been advanced to make possible the representation of allegedly more "natural" interest groupings, such as minority groups, skill groups or economic groups.[8]

The assumption that geographical districts have particular characteristics—such as population attributes and industrial, agricultural or commercial properties—and, hence, unique interests which are, or ought to be, factors influencing the direction of public decisions continues to be shared not only by voters, politicians and others involved in policy-making, but also by scientific students of the political process. It underlies many studies which seek to relate legislative roll-call votes to the socio-economic characteristics of electoral districts,[9] as well as those studies which analyze the socio-economic composition of legislatures.[10]

It is a further assumption of these studies that legislators, having lived in their districts for all or substantial parts of their lives, share the values, beliefs, habits and concerns of the people who elected them and whom they presumably represent. Indeed, a literal interpretation of "represent" is to make something present that is not actually present. But this interpretation is most tenuous under modern conditions. Electoral districts tend to be so heterogeneous in population attributes, so pluralistic in the character of their group life, so diverse in the kinds of values and beliefs held, that whatever measures of central tendency are used to classify a district are more likely to conceal than to reveal its real character. The notion that elections are held as a method to discover persons whose attributes and attitudes mirror those most widely shared by people in their district appears to be of dubious validity.

This does not mean, of course, that the geographical district is dysfunctional from the point of view of maintaining the political system. The very circumstance of heterogeneity in the district tends to free the representative from being readily bound by a mandate, to make for discretion and political responsibility, and to enable him to integrate conflicting demands. The function of representation in modern political systems is not to make the legislature a mathematically exact copy of the electorate.

But the difficulty of finding an identity between representative and represented does not also mean that a representative's point of reference in making decisions cannot be his district. It may or may not be, and whether it is or not is a matter of empirical inquiry. We merely doubt that what orients a representative towards his district rather than some other focus of attention is the similarity between his district's characteristics and his own. We cannot assume, therefore, that even if a representative incorporates in himself the characteristics of his district—which, for argument's sake, may be admitted when he comes from a relatively homogeneous area—he will be more oriented towards the district than a representative who, from the point of view of district characteristics, is a deviant. In fact, the latter may be more concerned with his district and seek to discover its "interests," if they are discoverable, than the former. And if a district interest, so-called, can be specifically singled out, it is more likely to be the interest of a politically salient group in the district than of the district as an undifferentiated entity.

In so far as the district rather than some other unit, such as the entire commonwealth, is at the representative's focus of attention, it is more likely to be a function of political than of demographic or socio-economic variables. The problem is one of discovering under what conditions the representative can afford to disregard the district and still hope to maintain the confidence of his constituents. We might speculate, for instance, that in so far as he cherishes the position of power he holds, he is unlikely to ignore his district. We should expect, therefore, that representatives from districts where competition between the parties is keen are more district-oriented than representatives from one-party districts. Yet, we also know that competitive districts are more likely to be found in the heterogeneous metropolitan areas where district "interests" are difficult to ascertain.[11] In other words, what tends to orient the representative towards his district is likely to be the mechanism of political responsibility effectuated by political competition. District-oriented representatives from metropolitan areas where party competition is strong are, therefore, likely to rely on their own judgment, for a mandate must yield here to discretion to satisfy the demands of political responsibility. Discretion, of course, does not mean that the representative is wholly free to act as he pleases. On the contrary, it means that he will have due regard for all the considerations relevant in the making of legislative decisions. And among these considerations, certainly, the "interests" of his electorate or segments of the electorate, as well as his own estimate of the limits which these interests set to his actions, are important. As Burke admitted,

> it ought to be the happiness and glory of a representative to live in the strictest union, the closest correspondence, and the most unreserved communication with his constituents. Their wishes ought to have great weight with him; their opinion high respect, their business unremitted attention. . . .

Though analytically the foci and the style of the representative's role are distinct, they can be expected to be related empirically in a system of mutually interpenetrating orientations. In other words, just as we need not assume that a commitment to district invariably involves the representative's following instructions from his district (the role orientation of Delegate), or that a commonweal-oriented representative is invariably a free agent (the role orientation of Trustee), so also we need not assume that the foci of a representative's role are invariably unrelated to his representational style. In fact, it is the functionally related network of roles which makes for a representational *system.* We can assume, for instance, that a representative who is highly sensitive to the conflict of pressure groups, but not committed to any one, is more likely to be a Trustee in his representational role than the representative who feels close to a particular group and, consequently, is more likely to be a Delegate. Similarly, we might expect that a representative not strongly attached to a party, but not independent of it, is likely to shift between his own judgment and instructions (the role orientation of Politico).

IV

An opportunity to test the validity of the theoretical distinction here made, between the focus and style of representation, as well as of the representative's role, was afforded in connection with a comparative research project undertaken by the authors during the 1957 sessions of the state legislatures in California, New Jersey, Ohio and Tennessee.[12] State legislators in these four states were asked the following question, among others: "How would you describe the job of being a legislator—what are the most important things you should do here?" Of the 474 respondents, 295 gave answers relevant to the stylistic dimension of the representative's role, and 197 of these gave additional answers referring to the areal focus of their role.[13]

Responses concerning the stylistic dimension yielded three major representational role types: Trustee, Delegate, and Politico.[14] These types may be described as follows:

1. *Trustee.* This role finds expression in two major conceptions which may occur separately or jointly. First, a moral-

istic interpretation: the representative is a free agent, he follows what he considers right or just—his convictions or principles, the dictates of his conscience. Second, a rational conception: he follows his own judgments based on an assessment of the facts in each case, his understanding of the problems involved, his thoughtful appraisal of the sides at issue.

The orientation of Trustee derives not only from a purely normative definition, but is often grounded in conditions which make it functionally necessary. The represented may not have the information to give intelligent instructions; the representative is unable to discover what his clienteles want; preferences remain unexpressed; there is no need for instructions because of a presumed harmony of interests between representative and represented—all of these circumstances may be cited as sources of the role orientation of Trustee.

2. *Delegate.* Just as the Trustee is by no means an empirically pure type, the orientation of Delegate allows for a number of conceptions. All Delegates are, of course, agreed that they should *not* use their independent judgment or convictions as criteria of decision-making. But this does not mean that they feel equally committed to follow instructions, from whatever clientele. Some merely speak of consulting their constituents, though implying that such consultation will have a mandatory effect on their behavior. Others frankly acknowledge their direct dependence on instructions and accept them as a necessary or desirable premise for their decisions. Some may even follow instructions counter to their own judgment or principles. In other words, the possibility of conflict in role orientations is clearly envisaged and resolved in favor of subordinating one's independence to what is considered a superior authority.

3. *Politico.* The classical dichotomization of the concept of representation in terms of free agency and mandate was unlikely to exhaust the possibilities of representational styles. Depending on circumstances, a representative may hold the Trustee orientation at one time, and the Delegate orientation at another time. Or he might seek to reconcile both in terms of a third. One can think of representation as a continuum, with the Trustee and Delegate orientations as poles, and a midpoint where the orientations tend to overlap and, within a range, give rise to a third role. Within this middle range the roles may be taken simultaneously, possibly making for

conflict, or they may be taken serially, one after another as conditions call for.

Because the data do not permit sharp discrimination between the two possibilities, we shall speak of representatives who express both orientations, either simultaneously or serially, as Politicos. In general, then, the Politico as a representational role type differs from both the Trustee and the Delegate in that he is more sensitive to conflicting alternatives in role assumption, more flexible in the way he resolves the conflict of alternatives, and less dogmatic in his representational style as it is relevant to his decision-making behavior.

The spell of the Burkean formulation on the interpretation of representation tended to create reactions which, it seems, are almost as arbitrary as Burke's formula itself. In particular, the functional notion, itself quite realistic under modern conditions, that the legislature is an agency for the coordination and integration of diverse social, economic and political interests makes apparent the simple-mindedness of Burke's theory, now as then. Carl J. Friedrich, for instance, has pointed out that "the pious formula that representatives are not bound by mandate, that they are subject only to their conscience and are supposed to serve the common weal, which is repeated in so many European constitutions, while significant as a norm, may lead to differentiating as well as to integrating results."[15] Yet, in concentrating on the multiplicity of potential representational foci, Friedrich went too far in his rejection of Burke. For, once the distinction is made between the style of the representative's role and its focus, Burke's "pious formula" is still relevant. Both the focus and the style are likely to be influenced by the character of politics at a given time and by the demands of contemporary political circumstances on the representative as a decision-maker. Functional analysis cannot limit itself to the foci of representation alone, but must also pay attention to those political requirements which may be relevant to the representative's style.

Our hypothesis may be stated as follows: the exigencies of modern government, even on the relatively low level of state government, are exceedingly complex. Taxation and finance, education and public welfare, legal reform, licensing and regulatory problems, transportation, and so on, are topics more often than not, beyond the comprehension of the average citizen. Unable to understand their problems and helpless to cope with them, people are likely to entrust the affairs of government to the elected representatives who, presumably, are better informed than their constituents. People may pay lip service to the notion that a representative should *not* use his independent judgment,[16] but in fact they are unable, or do not care, to give him instructions as may once have been possible when the tasks of government were comparatively simpler. It is likely, therefore, that the representative has become less and less a Delegate and more and more a Trustee as the business of government has become more and more intricate and technical. Rather than being a "pious formula," the role orientation of Trustee may be a functional necessity, and one should expect it to be held by state legislators more frequently than that of Politico, and the latter more frequently than that of Delegate.

Table I. ***Distribution of Representational Role Orientations in Four States***

Representational Role Orientation	Calif. (N =49)	N.J. (N =54)	Ohio (N =114)	Tenn. (N =78)	Total (N =295)
Trustee	55%	61%	56%	81%	63%
Politico	25	22	29	13	23
Delegate	20	17	15	6	14
Total	100%	100%	100%	100%	100%

A test of this general proposition is possible by way of comparative analysis of the distribution of representational role styles in the four states. As Table I indicates the role orientation of Trustee is held by a greater number of legislators than that of either Politico or Delegate. In all four states it appears more frequently, and significantly more frequently, than the other two. Moreover, the Politico appears somewhat more frequently in all states than the Delegate.

The Trustee orientation appears significantly more frequently in Tennessee than in the other three states, a fact that seems to contradict the proposition that the orientation of Trustee varies with the complexity of governmental affairs. As Tennessee is less urbanized and industrialized than the other states, one should expect Tennessee legislators to be less often Trustees and more often Delegates than legislators in California, New Jersey or Ohio. But it may also be that "complexity" is a function of perceptions, regardless of the real situation. If so, then to Tennesseans the relatively less complex character of socio-economic life may appear more complex than it actually is, compared with the other states. The more frequent appearance of the Trustee orientation there may only be symptomatic of an even greater feeling of helplessness and inefficacy on the part of people *vis-à-vis* governmental problems, as it is perceived by state representatives. Such perceptions may be a reflection of the lower educational level in Tennessee; but to demonstrate this is beyond the limits of this analysis.[17]

V

If, as suggested earlier, a representative's areal-focal orientation does not automatically derive from ascertainable district interests or from personal characteristics he may share with his constituents, the question arises where such orientations do come from, and how they intrude on the representative's conception of his role. For the purposes of this study, it was possible to delineate three areal-focal orientations which may be described as follows:

1. *District-orientation.* District-oriented representatives had essentially two alternatives: either they could simply mention their districts or counties as being relevant in their conception of their jobs, or they could explicitly place their districts as being above the state as an important factor in their legislative behavior. Among the former, the most frequent responses suggested that it is the representative's job to take care of his district's needs and pass legislation which will benefit his district or county. Others emphasized the policy problems involved in legislation and the necessity to protect what they considered district interests from the policy point of view. Or the emphasis was on the services which these representatives think they are expected to render for their district. Another group of district-oriented representatives specifically pointed to the importance of placing the interests of their district above those of the state, though they usually admitted that state concerns should also be given consideration.

2. *State-orientation.* As in the case of the district-oriented respondents, state-oriented representatives may either mention the state alone as the salient focus, or they may also mention the district, but clearly tend to place state above district. Some emphasized the need of state policy or state programs as an overriding consideration. A second group pointed to both state and district as relevant foci, but tended to give the benefit of doubt to the state. Finally, some state-oriented representatives explicitly emphasized the desirability of overcoming parochial considerations in favor of the state.

3. *District-and-state-orientation.* A third major group of respondents who spontaneously concerned themselves with the areal focus of their role mentioned both district and state, but, apparently, did not envisage a possibility of conflict and thought that they could attend to both foci without undue difficulty. Yet, the generality of the responses given in this connection may be deceptive, and coding them under this rubric may have been somewhat arbitrary in a number of cases. Though the actual language used tended in the direction of the state as the focus of role orientation, the tone often appeared to be more indicative of a latent district orientation. One should expect these hyphenated representatives to resemble district- more than state-oriented representatives.

Areal role orientations may be assumed to be a function of the dynamics of the democratic political system with its emphasis on the responsibility of the representatives to the represented. Political responsibility—a set of relationships in which the elected are sensitive to the power of the electors over them, and in which the elected are aware of the sanctions which make responsibility a reality—is predicated on the existence of a competitive political system where constituents have a genuine choice, *i.e.,* where the representatives are periodically confronted with the real possibility of removal from office. The sanction of removal inherent in a competitive party system serves to focus respresentatives' attention on their district rather than the state as the crucial point of reference. Representatives from competitive areas are more likely to be district-oriented than representatives from one-party areas, while representatives from one-party areas are more likely to be state-oriented than those from competitive areas.

An initial, though crude, test of this hypothesis is possible by examining the distribution of areal role orientations in the four states. Tennessee representatives might be expected to be less district-oriented than representatives in the other states, in view of the predominant one-party character of Tennessee politics. As Table II indicates, the data support this hypothesis. Though the percentage differences are small and statistically not significant, except in the California-Tennessee contrast, only 21 per cent of the Tennessee representatives are district-oriented as against 35 per cent in California, 27 per cent in New Jersey, and 28 per cent in Ohio. But the most noticeable aspect of Table II is the fact that Tennessee representatives in significantly greater proportion failed to express themselves spontaneously in this connection. Why this is so can, at this point, be only a matter of speculation. Tennessee representatives may take whatever areal foci they have so much for granted that they feel no need to mention them, or they may simply be less articulate than representatives elsewhere. Finally, while there is a somewhat sharper differentiation between district and state role orientations in California than in New Jersey and Ohio (where the combined category figures more prominently), relatively few representatives in all states mentioned the state alone as the focus of their areal orientation.

Table II. ***Distribution of Areal Role Orientations in Four States***

Areal Role Orientation	Calif. (N =113)	N.J. (N =79)	Ohio (N =162)	Tenn. (N =120)	Total (N =474)
District	35%	27%	28%	21%	27%
District-and-State	14	28	25	8	19
State	20	14	16	9	15
No mention	31	31	31	62	39
Total	100%	100%	100%	100%	100%

A more severe test of the hypothesis is possible by relating areal role orientations to the political character of representatives' home districts. Because party competition as an independent variable has no room for operation in predominantly one-party Tennessee,[18] Table III presents the combined data for California, New Jersey and Ohio alone.[19] As Table III shows, 53 per cent of the representatives from competitive districts were district-oriented, while only 33 per cent of those from one-party districts were so classified. On the other hand, one-party district representatives held in significantly greater proportion a state orientation than those from competitive districts.[20] The data support the hypothesis that areal orientation varies with the political character of the district in which representatives are elected.[21]

Table III. ***Political Character of Electoral Districts and Areal Role Orientations in Three States****

Areal Role Orientation	Political Character of District: *Competitive (N=72)*	*Semi-competitive (N=77)*	*One-party (N=96)*
District	53%	48%	33%
District-and-State	28	34	33
State	19	18	34
Total	100%	100%	100%

*California, New Jersey and Ohio. "Non-respondents" on the areal dimension have been omitted.

VI

The analytical distinction between the foci and the style of representation is helpful in dissecting the representative's role. Actual behavior is not a function of discrete role orientations, however, but of a system of such orientations. It is the network of interpenetrating roles which gives pattern and coherence to the representational process. It is essential, therefore, to relate areal and stylistic role orientations to each other in terms of significant hypotheses about conditions of their co-variation in the representational system.

It has been suggested earlier that, analytically, stylistic role orientations are neutral. What correlation may be found empirically, therefore, should depend on some crucial attribute in the independent variable—in this connection the areal role orientation. It may be suggested that this crucial attribute is the condition of effective political responsibility. In so far as they differ, district-oriented representatives are ultimately responsible to their constituents, while state-oriented representatives are not responsible to an equivalent statewide constituency. The state-oriented representative cannot point to a state-wide clientele from which he could possibly receive a mandate.[22] Hence the hypothesis may be advanced that state-oriented representatives are more likely to be Trustees than district-oriented representatives, whereas the latter are more likely to be Delegates than the former. As Table IV demonstrates, this is in fact the case. While 84 per cent of the state-oriented representatives are Trustees, only 37 per cent of the district-oriented and 55 per cent of the district-and-state-oriented representatives are so. And while 36 per cent of the district-oriented representatives are Delegates, only 8 per cent of the district-and-state-oriented and none of the state-oriented hold a mandatory view of their representational role.

Moreover, Table IV supports some corollary hypotheses. In the first place, because a representative is district-oriented, he need not be a Delegate any more frequently than a Trustee. This simply means that though a representative may clearly have his district at his focus of attention, he may nevertheless act on behalf of the district, in his own conception, as a free agent. Such a representative will say that he knows and un-

Table IV. ***Areal-Focal and Representational Role Orientations in Four States****

Representational Role Orientation	District-oriented (N = 89)	State-District-oriented (N = 64)	State-oriented (N = 44)
Trustee	37%	55%	84%
Delegate	36	8	—
Politico	27	37	16
Total	100%	100%	100%

*χ^2 for the entire array = 37.759; d.f. = 4; $p < .001$.

derstands what the district needs and wants, and he rejects the notion that anybody in the district can tell him what to do. As Table IV shows, among the district-oriented representatives, almost equal proportions, 37 per cent and 36 per cent respectively, are Trustees and Delegates. On the other hand, state-oriented representatives are more likely to be Trustees than anything else. This hypothesis is based on the assumption that the state-oriented representatives do not and cannot recognize a state-wide areal clientele which could give them instructions. As Table IV indicates, none of the state-oriented representatives is a Delegate, and only 16 per cent are Politicos.

Finally, if the representative's areal focus is both his district and the state, one should expect that he will take the role of Politico more frequently than either the district- or the state-oriented representative. For, because he stresses both foci, he is likely to be subject to cross-pressures: as a district-oriented representative he will take the role of Delegate at least as frequently as that of Trustee; as a state-oriented representative he will take the role of Trustee more frequently than any other. We should expect, therefore, that this representative will not only be a Politico more frequently than the other two areal-orientational types, but also that he will take the Trustee role more frequently than the Delegate role. Both hypotheses find support in the data reported in Table IV. While the differences are small, 37 per cent of the district-and-state-oriented representatives are Politicos, while only 16 per cent and 27 per cent of the other two groups admit to this representational style. Moreover, a majority are also Trustees, while only 8 per cent are Delegates—evidence of the differential effect of areal role orientations on the particular stylistic roles which seem most appropriate.

This analysis supports the notion that the areal-focal and stylistic dimensions of representation give rise to role orientations which, though analytically distinct, constitute a role system, and that this system gives the process of representation both its structure and its function.

Notes:

1. For a convenient and comprehensive summary of definitions, see John A. Fairlie, "The Nature of Political Representation," *American Political Science Review,* Vol. 34 (April–June, 1940), pp. 236–48; 456–66.

2. An effort at conceptual clarification is made by Alfred De Grazia, *Public and Republic—Political Representation in America* (New York, 1951).

3. Herman Finer, *The Theory and Practice of Modern Government* (New York, rev. ed., 1949), p. 219.

4. In his "Speech to the Electors of Bristol" (1774), *Works,* Vol. II, p. 12.

5. *Cf.* Samuel H. Beer, "The Representation of Interests in British Government," *American Political Science Review,* Vol. 51 (September 1957), p. 613, who points out how little general legislation was proposed or enacted in those days.

6. For the conception of "bounded rationality" as well as the notion that roles constitute some of the premises of decision-making behavior, we are indebted to Herbert A. Simon's writings, notably *Models of Man* (New York, 1957). Our own formulations of the concept of role are developed

in John C. Wahlke and Heinz Eulau, *Legislative Behavior: A Reader in Theory and Research* (Glencoe, 1959).

7. For a perspicacious discussion of ambiguities in representation, see Harold F. Gosnell, *Democracy—The Threshold of Freedom* (New York, 1948), pp. 124–42.

8. Most theories of functional or proportional representation are motivated or supported by tacit and untested assumptions about the relationship of legislators' behavior to the process by which they are selected. This is merely a special case of the general democratic assumption that political responsibility is the mechanism *par excellence* for bringing legislators' actions in line with the expectations of the represented.

9. See, for instance, Julius Turner, *Party and Constituency: Pressures on Congress* (Baltimore, 1951); or Duncan MacRae, Jr., *Dimensions of Congressional Voting* (Berkeley, 1958).

10. See, for instance, Donald R. Matthews, *The Social Background of Political Decision-Makers* (Garden City, 1954); or Charles H. Hyneman, "Who Makes Our Laws?" *Political Science Quarterly,* Vol. 55 (December, 1940), pp. 556–81.

11. See Heinz Eulau, "The Ecological Basis of Party Systems: The Case of Ohio," *Midwest Journal of Political Science,* Vol. 1 (August, 1957), pp. 125–35.

12. The samples for the four legislatures are 91 per cent in Tennessee, 94 per cent in California and Ohio, and 100 per cent in New Jersey. The four states composing the total sample represent different regions of the country, different ratios of metropolitan and non-metropolitan population, and different degrees of party competition. The interviews, using fixed schedules, uniform in all four states and including both open-ended, focussed-type questions as well as closed, or fixed-answer type questions, averaged about two hours.

13. The reduction in the number of respondents from the total samples is, of course, due to the open-endedness of the question. Hence not all respondents could be used in the construction of the role types as they emerged from representatives' own definitions, and in the analysis.

14. In constructing stylistic and areal-focal role orientation types, the responses to the question were coded in terms of (a) characterization of job; (b) objectives of job; and (c) criteria of decision. Each total answer was broken up into individual statements and coded in terms of manifest content rather than latent meanings, though meaning was taken into consideration in locating manifest statements. Role orientation types were constructed by combining relevant manifest statements which seemed to make for a major orientational dimension. In general, data concerning criteria of decision yielded the stylistic orientation, and data concerning the objectives of the job yielded the areal orientation.

15. *Constitutional Government and Democracy* (Boston, rev. ed., 1950), p. 297.

16. In the years before the second World War, public opinion polls several times sampled expectations in this regard. Relevant poll questions were: (1) Do you believe that a Congressman should vote on any question as the majority of his constituents desire or vote according to his own judgment? (2) Should members of Congress vote according to their own best judgment or according to the way the people in their district feel?

(3) In cases when a Congressman's opinion is different from that of the majority of the people in his district, do you think he should usually vote according to his own best judgment, or according to the way the majority of his district feels? In three of four polls, 61, 63 and 66 per cent, respectively, of the respondents said the Congressman should vote the way people feel. In the fourth poll, only 37 per cent gave this answer. See Hadley Cantril, ed., *Public Opinion, 1935–1946* (Princeton, 1951), p. 133.

17. As the Trustee orientation includes responses stressing traditional moral values, it might be assumed that these virtues—such as following one's conscience or what one feels to be "right"—are more valued in rural Tennessee than in the three more urbanized states. But inspection of the frequency with which this attitude appears in Tennessee as against the other states does not reveal significantly different distributions of relevant responses: California—18%; New Jersey—8%; Ohio—28%; and Tennessee—23%.

18. Of the 46 Tennessee respondents who mentioned an areal orientation, only four came from competitive and five from semi-competitive districts.

19. Competition in district was severally defined in the four states on the basis of past election returns. Space limitations prevent us from specifying the criteria here. They may be obtained from the authors.

20. $x^2 = 9.238$ for the entire array, where d.f. $= 4$, $p \geq .05$. If the middle categories are omitted and only competitive and one-party districts are compared with respect to state and district orientation alone, $x^2 = 7.12$; d.f. $= 1$; $p < .01$.

21. However, this finding may be spurious. It might be less a function of the political character of the district than of its ecological character. Competitive districts are, more often than not, located in metropolitan areas, while one-party districts are more frequent in non-metropolitan areas. It seemed advisable, therefore, to control the districts' political character by this ecological character. For this purpose, the districts were divided on the basis of the 1950 Census specifications. The hypothesis concerning the relationship between political character of district and areal orientation was clearly maintained in both metropolitan and non-metropolitan districts. However, while the pattern proved similar in both ecological categories, a greater proportion of district-and-state-oriented representatives appeared in the non-metropolitan than in the metropolitan areas, suggesting a pull toward greater dichotomization of areal orientations in the metropolitan environment. In view of the intimate connection in industrialized states between metropolitan and state-wide problems, this result is not surprising. It seems that the state is more salient as a focus of attention for representatives from metropolitan districts (no matter what their political character) than from non-metropolitan districts.

22. He might, of course, receive instructions from a state-wide clientele such as a pressure group or political party, but these constitute other dimensions of his attention foci.

2 *Public Attitudes Toward the Representational Roles of Legislators and Judges**

by Carl D. McMurray and Malcolm B. Parsons

The major theoretical significance of this study is its bearing on the question of how public opinion in a democratic society is articulated with public policy decisions. Attitudes of the public and of governmental decision-makers on particular issues are frequently explored. In this study it is assumed that the representational role expectations and perceptions of those who are governed as well as those who govern are of basic importance. Attitudes of legislators toward their representational roles have been subjected to recent empirical study and logical analysis,[1] but little has been reported on public attitudes toward these roles and the related representational roles of judges.[2] This study records the findings of an investigation designed to describe public attitudes toward representational roles of legislators and judges at three different levels of American government—federal, state and local—and relates them to varying degrees of political participation,

Reprinted from *Midwest Journal of Political Science,* 9, 2 (May, 1965), 167–185, by permission of the authors and the Wayne State University Press.

*This investigation was supported by the Department of Government, the Institute of Governmental Research, the Institute for Social Research, and the Research Council of The Florida State University. All computer operations were performed at the Computing Center, The Florida State University, on an IBM 709 computer financed in part by a National Science Foundation Grant—NSF-G17467.

party affiliation, and differences in occupation, level of family income and formal education of the attitude holders. As an essential feature of the method, a factor analytic-scale procedure was used to identify underlying patterns of response in the basic survey data.

From Burke, there has developed a normative question as to whether a representative ought to serve local or broader interests, and in making that decision whether he ought to be governed by his constituency's will, as its *instructed delegate,* or his own judgment, as its *trustee*. Recent studies reveal that the legislators actually perceive their roles differently in relation to different issues and sets of interests, and they often oscillate from instructed delegate to trustee in acting out a third role that has been called *politico*.[3] Professors Miller and Stokes report from a survey of sample constituencies of members of the U. S. House of Representatives "that no single tradition of representation fully accords with the realities of American legislative politics. The American system *is* a mixture. . . ."[4]

In the study cited above, Eulau reported that in 1957, representatives in four state legislatures had the following average representational role orientations: trustee, 63 percent; delegate, 14 percent; politico, 23 percent.[5] These findings supported his proposition that "people may pay lip service to the notion that a representative should *not* use his independent judgment, but in fact they are unable, or do not care, to give him instructions as may once have been possible when the tasks of government were comparatively simpler." He went on to say that "the role orientation of Trustee may be a functional necessity, and one should expect it to be held by state legislators more frequently than that of Politico, and the latter more frequently than that of Delegate."[6]

It is the purpose of this study to inquire whether public attitudes are consonant with legislators' attitudes toward representational roles. The only reported data about such public attitudes are from four public opinion polls conducted 1938–1940, which measured support for the instructed delegate *vs.* trustee roles of Congressmen. As reported by Hadley Cantril, the first survey in 1938 showed 37.4 percent favoring the delegate role, and the three subsequent surveys, 1939–1940, yielded 61, 66, and 63 percent for the delegate role.[7] This study raises the kinds of questions asked in these pre-war surveys and considered in the Eulau investigation. It proceeds on the assumption that public attitudes toward representational roles may be more complex and may manifest greater ambiguity than the early findings indicated. The questions were posed in such a way as to allow not only the either-or choices of the Cantril polls, but ambivalent and less absolute choices as well. In this respect the questions offered a degree of ambiguity in response not unlike that confronting the citizen when he makes choices in his own political behavior. Finally, the data are analyzed through procedures that allow for the identification and delineation of individual attitudes or variations in attitude patterns among groups.

The Survey Data

Four sets of questions designed to measure respondents' attitudes toward the representational roles of legislators and judges at the federal, state and local levels of government were included as part of a more general statistical and attitude survey among a random sample (207 respondents) of the white population in Florida's Cape Kennedy area during the Spring of 1962.[8] The questions were stated in unequivocal terms to elicit clearcut expressed attitudes toward (1) the instructed delegate and trustee theories of legislative representation and (2) political immunity and public accountability of judges.

Respondents were given three options on each question—Favor, Oppose and Undecided—and each question was asked with regard to legislators or judges at the federal, state and local (city and county) levels of government. The questions and the percent of respondents indicating each option are listed below:

These preliminary tabulations provide simple, trichotomous description of attitude variations among respondents to the four questions. From this description some elementary conclusions can be drawn: (1) 72 percent of the respondents favored the delegate theory for state legislators—considerably more than in the last three pre-war opinion polls—thus apparently intensifying the divergence of public attitudes toward representational roles and Eulau's findings as to the role orientation of state legislators; (2) there is more popular support for the instructed delegate theory of legislative representation than for the trustee theory, but there is no one-to-one negative correlation between these attitudes since some respondents, apparently unaware of or unconcerned about the paradox, indicate that legislators should *always* act as instructed delegates *and always act as trustees;* (3) likewise we can infer, but from this tabulation cannot prove, that some respondents were unwilling to support either the absolute representational theory expressed in Question 1 or the one expressed in Question 2, and consistently opposed both; (4) the answers to Question 1

Question 1—"*An elected legislator should find out what his district wants and* always *vote accordingly.*"

	(a) Congressmen	(b) State Legislators	(c) City Councilmen
Favor	69.1%	72.0%	75.9%
Oppose	28.5	26.6	21.7
Undecided	2.4	1.4	2.4
	100.0	100.0	100.0

Question 2—"*An elected legislator should decide what he thinks is best, and* always *vote accordingly, even if it is not what his district wants.*"

	(a) Congressmen	(b) State Legislators	(c) City Councilmen
Favor	45.9%	42.5%	40.6%
Oppose	52.7	55.1	57.0
Undecided	1.4	2.4	2.4
	100.0	100.0	100.0

Question 3—"*Judges should be free from political pressure to insure that their decisions are impartial.*"

	(a) Federal Judges	(b) State Judges	(c) City or County Judges
Favor	98.5%	98.5%	97.6%
Oppose	.5	.5	1.4
Undecided	1.0	1.0	1.0
	100.0	100.0	100.0

Question 4—"*In a democracy judges should be accountable to the people for their official actions.*"

	(a) Federal Judges	(b) State Judges	(c) City or County Judges
Favor	65.2%	65.7%	66.2%
Oppose	32.4	32.4	31.9
Undecided	2.4	1.9	1.9
	100.0	100.0	100.0

and 2 also reveal a slight tendency to assign different representational roles to legislators at different levels of government, i.e., legislators at higher jurisdictional levels are expected progressively to be somewhat less influenced by the wishes of their constituents; (5) there is nearly complete agreement that judges at all governmental levels should be guaranteed political immunity; and (6) yet, there is substantial majority support for public accountability for judges.[9]

Factor Analytic-Scale Procedures

Data from these simple tabulations tell us nothing about individual attitudes or variations in attitude patterns among groups of individuals. In order to obtain such information across the four questions, answers to the three parts of each were assigned numerical values: Favor = + 1, Oppose = − 1 and Undecided = 0. A factor analytic and a scale procedure which incorporated these values were used (1) to identify linear relationships between response patterns to the various questions, plus the party affiliation of the respondents with Democrat = + 1, Republican = − 1 and Independent = 0; (2) to rate individual respondents on scales susceptible of analysis as measures of quantitative differences in attitudes toward theories of representation; and (3) to provide multidimensional descriptions of respondents' attitudes toward legislators' and judges' representational roles which could be related to questions regarding respondents' occupation, family income, formal education and degree of political participation.

Two separate computer programs were used for the factor analytic and scale operations. The initial program used individual responses as input data in constructing a matrix of factor coefficients that indicated linear relationships between patterns of responses to question components;[10] and the second program, through a three-step procedure, constructed for each factor a scale depicting in quantitative terms relationships between individual attitudes. In order of performances, the three steps of the scale procedure were: (1) under each factor, coefficients of the rotated matrix were assigned to the corresponding survey question as estimates of the question's relative worth in measuring the content of an attitude dimension; (2) a factor score equal to the sum of the products of his survey responses times the question weights were computed for each respondent; and (3) the respondents were arrayed along separate scales for each factor by the value of their factor scores, from highest to lowest.[11]

Although raw factor scores provide convenient means for identifying the relative position of an individual along a dimension, variation in the size of scores from factor to factor may limit their value for any study designed to compare patterns of distribution across several scales. To solve this problem we used the following procedure for connecting raw factor scores to a more compact and uniform scale:

1. For each of the original scales the raw factor score with the largest absolute value was divided into the quantity 10.
2. All factor scores on the original scale were multiplied by the quotient obtained in this computation, and the products were designated as Converted Factor Scores (CFS).
3. The CFS were arrayed along a (+ 10) – (– 10) scale which was divided into eight segments. Each of these segments was assigned to scale value ranging from + 4 to – 4:

10.0	7.5	5.0	2.5	0	–2.5	–5.0	–7.5	–10.0
+4	+3	+2	+1		–1	–2	–3	–4

4. Each respondent was assigned a scale score based on the value of his CFS.
   Examples:
   a. Respondent *A* had a CFS of 5.43 for the original Factor 1 scale. His new scale score became +3.
   b. Respondent *B* had a CFS of –9.83 for the original Factor 1 scale. His new scale score became –4.
   c. Respondent *C* had a CFS of 7.5 which fell on the value dividing two segments of the conversion scale. His new scale score became that of the segment nearer the median CFS for the survey population.

Conflict and Consensus: Patterns of Attitude Distribution

When the factor analytic and scale operations were performed on the survey data, the relationship between responses on any part of one question to other parts of the same question, or responses to other questions and party affiliation, was judged to be a function of the value of the factor coefficients in Table I. The four factors identified there show linear relationships to exist between the parts of each of the four questions as they deal with federal, state and local officials, but there is no showing of such relationship between the responses on any part of one question and any part of the other three. Further, there is no evidence of a linear relationship between respondents' answers on the basic questions and their party affiliation.[12] Each factor is thus viewed as a dimension descriptive of attitudes toward one, and only one, of the representational theories implicit in the four questions.

The factors and the attitude dimensions we associate with them appear as follows: *Factor 1,* attitude toward the instructed delegate theory of representation; *Factor 2,* attitude toward the trustee theory of representation; *Factor 3,* attitude on the question of political immunity for judges; and *Factor 4,* attitude toward the idea of public accountability for judges.

Table I. ***Rotated Matrix of Factor Coefficients Derived from Respondent's Answers on Questions Regarding Representational Roles of Legislators and Judges, Plus Party Identification***

Items	Factors			
	I	*II*	*III*	*IV*
Question 1 (a)	0.85059	0.19328	0.03026	0.01520
" 1 (b)	0.91673	0.14573	0.01481	0.03835
" 1 (c)	0.86590	0.16463	0.03278	0.00961
Question 2 (a)	0.20613	0.90158	0.05537	0.01186
" 2 (b)	0.15472	0.95689	0.04170	0.02797
" 2 (c)	0.13545	0.94257	0.02893	0.01685
Question 3 (a)	0.04532	0.05695	0.91948	0.01528
" 3 (b)	0.03352	0.03554	0.95075	0.02788
" 3 (c)	0.08233	0.02532	0.68871	0.05255
Question 4 (a)	0.00839	0.01203	0.01070	0.91940
" 4 (b)	0.03748	0.00525	0.02617	0.97510
" 4 (c)	0.01352	0.00514	0.02917	0.96628
Party identification	0.02132	0.03831	0.04509	0.03707

An individual respondent's relative location along these dimensions is determined by the quantity of an attitude he possesses, as this quantity is indicated by his factor scores (or Converted Factor Scores). For example, a respondent who supported the instructed delegate theory at the federal level but not at the state and local levels will be located on the scale for that dimension at a position between that occupied by respondents who consistently supported the theory at all levels of government and that occupied by those who as consistently opposed it.

Following Key,[13] we identified patterns of conflict and consensus in the distribution of attitude variations toward the proper representational roles of legislators and judges. Charts 1–4 furnish pictures of these patterns along the four dimensions from the factor analysis.

Although the patterns of disagreement depicted on Charts 1, 2 and 4 have somewhat different shapes, there are in each case a substantial number of respondents (i.e., 25 percent, or more) who express attitudes in opposition to a majority's view of the proper role of legislators or judges. Consequently, we have designated these as *conflict* dimensions, and they obviously describe attitude differences especially suited for additional analysis.

Chart 3, on the other hand, describes a segment of an attitude dimension along which substantial agreement is the dominant feature of the response. The support for political immunity of judges illustrated by this chart can surely be labeled *consensus* within the term's customary meaning of general agreement or concord.[14] It should be noted that most of the 130 persons who supported the idea that at all levels of government judges should be accountable to the people for their official actions (see Chart 4), also supported the proposition that judges should be free from political pressure to insure that their decisions are impartial. Apparently, a majority of the respondents believe public accountability of the judiciary to be compatible with freedom from political pressure. Generalization of this attitude would indicate the presence of latent majority support for the merits of the modified judicial selection systems, "ABA plan," etc., designed to accommodate the principles of political immunity and public accountability.

Attitude Groups and Their Characteristics

The remainder of this study is devoted to an analysis of the *conflict* patterns of distribution. By eliminating three persons who were consistently undecided or had no opinion, the remaining respondents were divided into eight groups with different patterns of dominant attitude characteristics across the three conflict dimensions represented in Charts 1, 2 and 4. The dominant attitude characteristic of each individual along each dimension was determined by the sign of his CFS (Converted Factor Score). Table II lists these eight groups, the percentage of respondents in each group, and the dominant attitude characteristic shared by group members on each of the four questions. Presentation of the data in this form serves the dual purposes of providing a clearer picture of the structure of public attitudes toward the representational roles of judges and legislators than was evident in our preliminary tabulation and, yet, keeping the respondents grouped in classes of manageable proportions for further analysis.

Table II. ***Dominant Characteristics of Attitude Groups Toward Representational Roles of Legislators and Judges***

		Legislators		Judges	
Group Number	Sample Population (%)*	*Instructed Delegate*	*Trustee*	*Political Immunity*	*Public Accountability*
1	33	Favor	Oppose	Favor	Favor
2	14	Favor	Oppose	Favor	Oppose
3	18	Favor	Favor	Favor	Favor
4	11	Oppose	Favor	Favor	Favor
5	8	Favor	Favor	Favor	Oppose
6	7	Oppose	Favor	Favor	Oppose
7	4	Oppose	Oppose	Favor	Oppose
8	5	Oppose	Oppose	Favor	Favor

*Percentage based on 204 respondents included in these eight attitude groups.

When the attitudes toward legislative and judicial roles shown on Table II are viewed separately, there are four distinct attitude groups with respect to legislative roles, and two with respect to the judiciary. Of the latter two, one group, including one-third of the respondents, is formed from the combined memberships of Groups 2, 5, 6 and 7, and it embraces those who consistently favor an independent judiciary by voting for political immunity and rejecting the idea that judges should be accountable for their official actions to the public. The remaining two-thirds of the sample population, persons in Groups 1, 3, 4 and 8, form a second group favoring political immunity *and* public accountability for judges.

Charts 1-4. ***Distribution of Attitudes Toward Representative Roles of Legislators and Judges.***

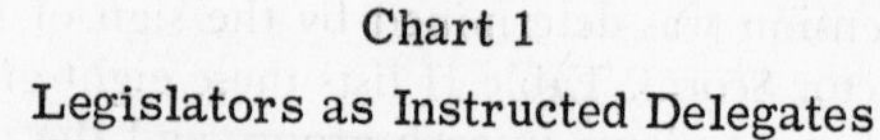

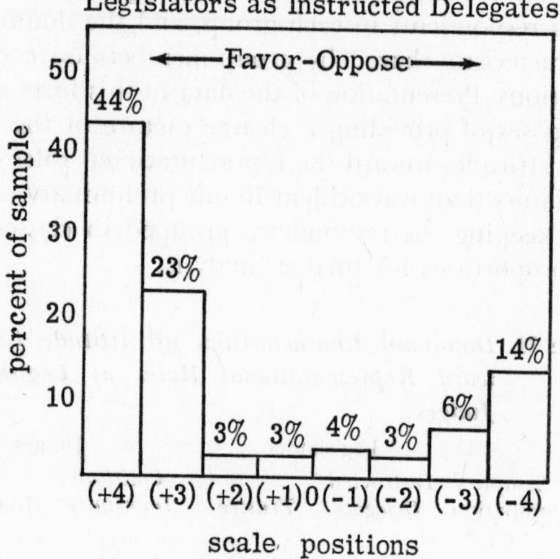

Chart 2

Legislators as Trustees

Favor-Oppose

percent of sample

50
40
30
20
10

18% 22% 2% 2% 2% 2% 8% 44%

(+4) (+3) (+2) (+1) 0 (-1) (-2) (-3) (-4)

scale positions

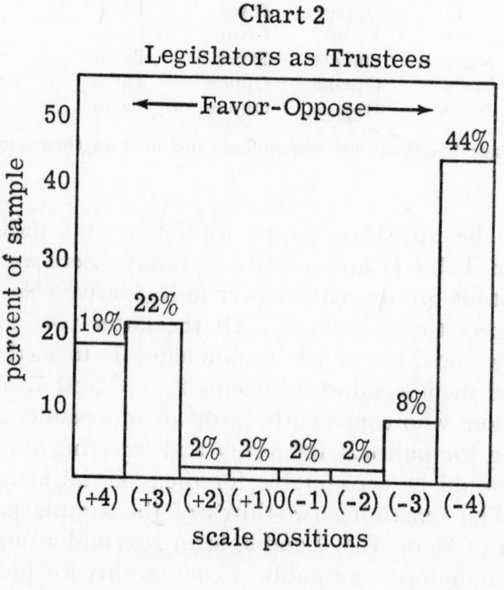

Charts 1-4. ***Distribution of Attitudes Toward Representative Roles of Legislators and Judges.***

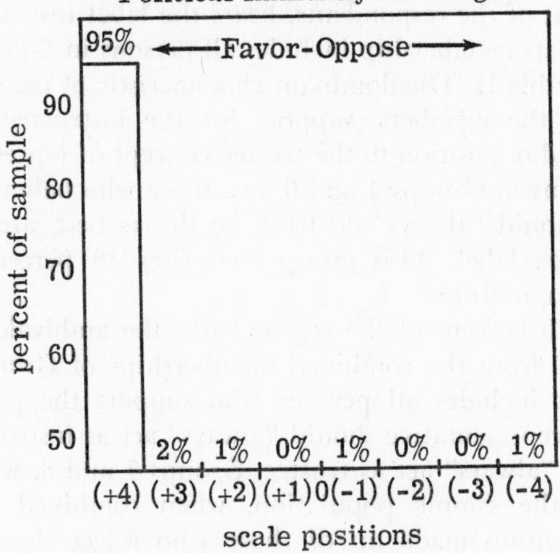

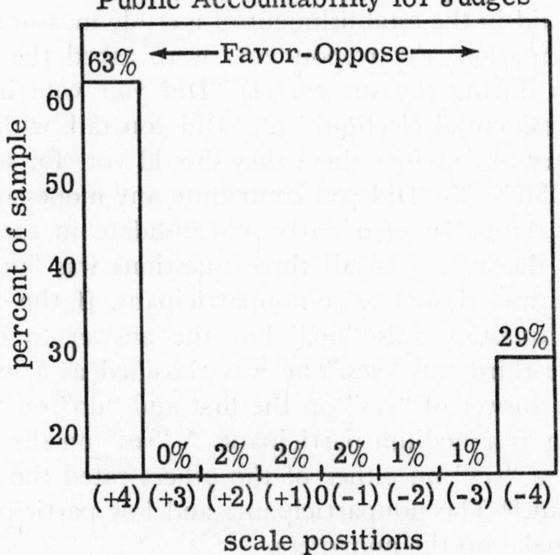

The four groups with distinctly different attitudes toward legislators are hereafter assigned "labels" associated with their dominant attitude characteristic: instructed delegate, trustee, ambivalent and politico. The largest of the four groups, with 47 percent of the respondents, bears the label instructed delegate, and its membership includes all persons in Groups 1 and 2 from Table II. The dominant characteristic of the combined group is the members' support for the instructed delegate theory and opposition to the trustee concept of representation. All persons in Groups 4 and 6, i.e., those who believe the legislator should "always" do what he thinks best, are assigned the trustee label. This group comprises 18 percent of the sample population.

With 26 percent of the respondents, the ambivalent group is formed from the combined memberships of Groups 3 and 5, and it includes all persons who support the proposition that the representative should "always" act as instructed delegate and "always" act as trustee. Groups 7 and 8, with 9 percent of the sample population, when combined form the politico group made up of those who reject the idea that legislators should "always" be either instructed delegates or trustees.[15] Tables III–VI summarize educational, family income, occupational and political participation characteristics of members of the four legislator-attitude groups.

The political participation index requires some explanation. To aid in the establishment of a crude measure of political participation, the respondents were asked the following questions during the survey: (1) "Did you vote in the last (1960) presidential election?" (2) "Did you talk with any people and try to convince them they should vote for some party or candidate?" (3) "Did you contribute any money or work to help the campaign of a party or candidate in the last election?" If the answer to all three questions was "no," the respondent was classed as a nonparticipant. If the answer to the first question was "no," but the answer to either the second or third was "yes," he was classified as a low participant. An answer of "yes" on the first and "no" on the others rated him as a medium participant. A "yes" on the first question and a "yes" on either of the others rated the title high participant.[16] The nonparticipants and low participants combine to make up the nonvoters.

Attitude Group Profiles

Members of the instructed delegate group, largest of the four categories, present a pattern of dispersion across the educational, occupational, income and political participation variables that is closest to the proportional distributions for the entire sample population. This heterogeneity is the distinguishing feature of that group. The second largest group, the ambivalent, differs markedly from all others in the high proportion of housewives, 40 percent, in its membership and the low proportion of persons in skilled and semiskilled occupations. Nearly two-thirds of the ambivalents have family incomes below $5,000, in contrast with slightly more than 50 percent below $5,000 for the sample population. The same group has a disproportionate share of persons with just grade school education. Any generalization from this finding, however, encounters a sizable hurdle in the fact that the three respondents with M.A. degrees and the two with Ph.D.'s are ambivalents. This group has the added distinction of having the largest proportion of nonvoters, 43 percent, as compared with 35 percent for the total population.

Of the trustee group, nearly one-half are in the professional and managerial occupational category, more than twice the frequency of persons in the instructed delegate and ambivalent groups. The trustee group has the largest proportion of persons in clerical and sales occupations, 11 percent more than the proportion for the sample population, and the lowest proportion of housewives. More than two-thirds of the persons in this group report family income of $5,000 or over. Also, it has only 3 percent, one-fifth the percentage for the total sample, of its members at the grade school educational level; and its 47 percent at the college level is 13 percent above the population average and is the largest concentration at that level among the legislator-attitude groups. In political participation, the proportion of nonparticipants among the members of the trustee group is substantially lower, and the proportion of high participants is substantially higher, than the sample averages.

The smallest attitude group, the politico, is second only to the trustee category in proportion of persons in professional and managerial occupations. In fact, this group is occupationally the most homogeneous with 68 percent of its members in the "skilled and semiskilled" or "professional and managerial" classes. Given this pattern of occupational homogeneity, we are not surprised to discover that some 47 percent of the politicos claim family incomes in the $5,000–6,999 bracket and that all persons in this group have at least a high school education. Also, it has the lowest proportion of political nonparticipants, 5 percent (actually one person), and the highest proportion of high participants, 58 percent—the next most active group being the trustees with 40 percent high participants.

Attitudes and the Independent Variables

From Tables III–VI it is apparent that there are sharp contrasts among the four legislator-attitude groups with respect to level of political participation and to the three demographic variables, education, family income, and occupation; and, the full extent of these contrasts cannot be known from the group profiles. Table III represents the relationship between formal education and attitudes toward the representational roles of legislators. Half the sample population are at the high school educational level, one-third at the college level, and the remainder at the grade school level. Uniformly, one-half the respondents in the grade school and high school categories support the instructed delegate role, with only a slightly smaller proportion, 43 percent, of the college educated supporting that role. There are more significant variations in educational levels of supporters of the other roles. Nearly one-half of the grade school category are ambivalent, as against one-fourth the high school and one-fifth the college educated respondents. While 17 percent of the high school and 25 percent of the college people support the trustee role, only 3 percent of the grade school people support it. All support for the politico comes from the high school and college educated. Thus, the highest proportion of ambivalence and the least proportion of support for the trustee and politico is found among the 15 percent of the sample population with the lowest level of formal educational attainment. About the high school and college educated, we can note (1) ambivalence is lower than among the grade school people, (2) the college edu-

Table III. *Number and Percent of Respondents at Different Educational Levels in the Legislator-Attitude Groups*

Education	No. of Respondents	Legislator-Attitude Groups: *Instructed Delegate*	*Trustee*	*Ambivalent*	*Politico*	*Total Percent*
Grade school	30	50%	3%	47%		100%
High school	105	49%	17%	23%	11%	100%
College	69	43%	25%	22%	10%	100%
Total	204					

Table IV. *Number and Percent of Respondents at Different Annual Family Income Levels in the Legislator-Attitude Groups*

Annual Family Inc.	No. of Respondents	Legislator-Attitude Groups: *Instructed Delegate*	*Trustee*	*Ambivalent*	*Politico*	*Total Percent*
Under $3,000	13	31%	15%	46%	8%	100%
$3,000-$4,999	96	52%	10%	29%	8%	99%
$5,000-$6,999	77	45%	25%	18%	12%	100%
$7,000 and Over	18	39%	28%	28%	5%	100%
Total	204					

Table V. *Number and Percent of Respondents of Different Occupations in the Legislator-Attitude Groups*

Occupation	No. of Respondents	Legislator-Attitude Groups: *Instructed Delegate*	*Trustee*	*Ambivalent*	*Politico*	*Total Percent*
Professional-Managerial	57	37%	30%	21%	12%	100%
Clerical-Sales	29	48%	31%	17%	3%	99%
Housewife	53	47%	6%	40%	7%	100%
Skilled-Semiskilled	42	57%	14%	14%	14%	99%
Unskilled	12	67%	8%	25%		100%
Unemployed-Retired	11	36%		55%	9%	100%
Total	204					

cated are more likely to accept the trustee role than the high school educated, and (3) there is little difference between these two groups in their support for the politico.

Table IV reports the relationship between annual family income and attitude toward the representational roles of legislators. Of the sample population, 85 percent (n = 173) are concentrated in the $3,000–6,999 annual family income range. Nearly 9 percent are above and slightly more than 6 percent are below that range. The largest proportion of the lowest income category is ambivalent, while the largest proportions for the other three income categories support the instructed delegate. There are, however, significant differences in the combined levels of support for the trustee and politico coming from persons with incomes below $5,000 and from persons with incomes above that amount. The largest portion of support for these two roles comes from members of the $5,000–6,999 range, 37 percent for either the trustee or politico; the next highest from persons in the $7,000 and over category, 32 percent; and lowest proportional support from the under $3000 bracket, 23 percent, and the $3,000–4,999 bracket, 18 percent. Family income differences, thus, do not present the same pattern of linear relationship we note between educational levels and attitudes toward representational roles. Where we can see a direct correspondence between increase in education and decrease in support of the instructed delegate and between increase in education and increase in support of the trustee, we see no direct correspondence between increase in family income and decrease (or increase) of support for any of the roles.

Table V depicts the relationship between occupation and attitudes toward representational roles of legislators. About 30 percent of the respondents are in professional or managerial occupations, 25 percent housewives, 20 percent skilled or semiskilled, 14 percent clerical or sales workers, 6 percent unskilled, and 5 percent unemployed or retired. The professional-managerial and clerical-sales occupations are parallel in that they provide the highest proportions of support for the trustee role. In fact, the level of support, approximately 30 percent, for that role is twice the proportional support, 14 percent, from the skilled-semiskilled category which has the next largest proportion of support for the trustee. Thus, the broadest range of support for the trustee comes from those occupational groupings with jobs that involve continuous interpersonal contact.

For the remaining occupational categories, housewives are almost equally divided between the ambivalent and instructed delegate groups, with only 13 percent of them supporting either the trustee or politico. The unemployed and retired show a pattern of attitudes similar to that of the housewives, but with a greater tendency to be ambivalent. Skilled-semiskilled and unskilled workers are the major sources of support for the instructed delegate, but they differ sharply in their support of the politico—the skilled and semiskilled offer the largest proportion of support for the politico while the unskilled offer no support for it. Since many of the skilled-semiskilled and unskilled workers are union members, we suggest that the similarities and differences in their attitudes may be explained as follows: (1) Their attitude toward the instructed delegate may be a product of their exposure to the common union demand that legislators give attention to the specific demands of labor groups, and (2) there is a tendency for skilled-semiskilled workers to reflect the appreciation for the politico role that we would expect to occur as the result of the higher educational attainments usually required for their jobs.

Table VI represents the relationship between political participation and attitudes toward the representational roles of legislators. The forty-three nonparticipants were notably different in most respects from the high participants. Nearly 60 percent of the nonparticipants supported the delegate role, as against 35 percent of the high participants. When comparisons are made in terms of voters and nonvoters, we see (1) there are more ambivalents among the nonvoters, (2) there is three times as much support for the politico among the voters, and (3) there is greater support for the trustee among voters. The most significant findings from Table VI, however, are the parallel relationships between low participants and high participants and between nonparticipants and medium participants. Remember that both the low participants and high participants were active in political campaigns, and the only distinction between them is the fact that the latter individuals voted in the last election. Since these two categories provide the only campaign activists, plus the lowest levels of support for the instructed delegate and the highest levels of support for the trustee and politico, we hypothesize that degree of involvement in political campaign activities is a better index of attitudes toward legislators' representational roles than the act of voting. Moving from this hypothesis back to our data, we conclude that persons who participate in campaign activities are more tolerant of the trustee and politico than persons who do not participate in these activities.

Table VI. ***Number and Percent of Respondents at Different Levels of Political Participation in Legislator-Attitude Groups***

Political Participation	No. of Respondents	Legislator-Attitude Groups: *Instructed Delegate*	*Trustee*	*Ambivalent*	*Politico*	*Total Percent*
Non-Participation	43	58%	9%	30%	2%	99%
Low Participation	28	39%	18%	36%	7%	100%
* (Total Non-voters)	(71)	(51%)	(13%)	(32%)	(4%)	(100%)
Medium Participation	68	54%	16%	22%	7%	99%
High Participation	65	35%	25%	23%	17%	100%
† (Total voters)	(133)	(45%)	(20%)	(23%)	(12%)	(100%)
Total	204					

*Non-participants and low-participants combined are the non-voters.
†Medium-participants and high-participants combined are the voters.

No tables are shown with similar breakdown of the two judiciary-attitude groups because we could find between those persons who consistently support an independent judiciary and those who gave ambivalent responses on the questions dealing with judges no significant distinctions in terms of the demographic characteristics or political participation index. In part, this lack of distinguishing features between the two groups may be traceable to (1) the fact that only on the parts of Question 4 is there any basic conflict in attitudes toward the judiciary and (2), perhaps more important, the concept "public accountability," as it is expressed in Question 4, may have had for the respondents meanings which we had not anticipated. In the light of our experience, we believe this question could have been stated in simpler terms specifying such methods for invoking accountability as elections, recall, and referenda.[17]

Conclusions

Eulau advanced the theory of a functionally related system of representational role foci and styles in which the trustee style may have become a functional necessity. The disparity between the trustee role orientations of nearly two-thirds of his state legislators and the opposite preference for the delegate role of nearly two-thirds of the public, as evidenced in Cantril's earlier public opinion polls, was explained in the view that people "pay lip service" preference for the delegate role style even though they are unable, or do not wish, to instruct their representatives.[18] The findings of this study suggest two modifications of these conclusions. First, the division of public opinion is neither as simple nor as heavily in favor of the delegate role as the last three Cantril polls seemed to show. When given the opportunity to react in different ways to the delegate and trustee roles, support from the public for the delegate amounts to only 47 percent, with the remaining 53 percent distributed 26 percent ambivalent, 18 percent trustee, and 9 percent politico. Since we expose a structure of public attitudes that is both more complex and more easily articulated with the role orientations of the legislators, we suggest there is as much public *tolerance* of the functionally necessary trustee role as for the less realistic delegate role.

Second, it should be recognized that the elected representative's role style includes his posture in the electoral campaign arena as well as in the legislative arena. The functional necessities of a legislator's representational role style in relation to his fellow legislators and his various policy constituencies are not always the same as the functional necessities of his electoral role style when he approaches the voters of his district during periodic election campaigns. If functional necessities in the first decision-making arena call for the trustee role, or some oscillation between it and the delegate role in the politico style, necessities in the electoral decision-making arena may require an ability to measure the expectations of different groups and assume the appropriate role style. On the other hand, the small number of persons in the politico group clearly suggests that the legislator is well-advised to assume in public the instructed delegate or trustee role, rather than try to explain to his constituents that the "bare facts" of life in the modern legislature compel him to oscillate between the two roles.

Notes:

1. See especially Heinz Eulau, John Wahlke, William Buchanan and LeRoy Ferguson, "The Role of the Representative: Some Empirical Observations on the Theory of Edmund Burke," *American Political Science Review,* Vol. 53 (September, 1959), pp. 742–56; Charles O. Jones, "Representation in Congress: The Case of the House Agricultural Committee," *American Political Science Review,* Vol. 55 (June, 1961), pp. 358–67; and Warren E. Miller and Donald E. Stokes, "Constituency Influence in Congress," *American Political Science Review,* Vol. 57 (March, 1963), pp. 45–56.

2. Hadley Cantril, ed., *Public Opinion, 1935–1946* (Princeton, 1951), p. 133, as cited by Eulau, *et. al., op. cit.,* p. 751. Miller and Stokes, *op. cit.,* explore the relationship between public attitudes and legislators' representational roles in sample constituencies of the U. S. House of Representatives. We were unable to find any study bearing directly on public attitudes toward representational roles of judges.

3. Eulau, *et al., op. cit.,* pp. 750 ff. and Jones, *op. cit,* p. 358.

4. *Op. cit.,* p. 56.

5. Heinz Eulau, *et al., op. cit.,* p. 751.

6. *Ibid.*

7. Hadley Cantril, *op. cit.,* Eulau, *et al.,* refer to these surveys in footnote 16, p. 751, *op. cit.*

8. The area centers around the fastest growing county in the United States, Brevard. The sample was drawn by Charles M. Grigg, Director, Institute of Social Reseach, The Florida State University.

9. It is noteworthy that on the factual question whether federal judges are appointed or elected 88 percent of those interviewed correctly said "appointed," 8 percent incorrectly said "elected" and 4 percent acknowledged they did not know.

10. For a more detailed account of the factor analytic technique employed, see Carl D. McMurray, "A Factor Method for Roll Call Vote Studies," *American Behavioral Scientist,* Vol. 6 (April, 1963), pp. 26–27. The factor analytic program employed the varimax rotation procedure developed by Henry F. Kaiser and was a straightforward application of one of a series of computer programs prepared by the Division of Biostatics, Department of Preventive Medicine and Public Health at UCLA. It may be found in most computer libraries under the title BIMD-17—"Factor Analysis and Rotate for Monitor and Non Monitor Operations." The program was prepared for use on the IBM 709/7090. The factor analysis was performed under the conditions of Case 1 in this program: "Where the number of factors to be rotated is equal to the number of eigenvalues of the correlation matrix (with ones in the diagonal) which are greater than unity."

11. The mathematical formula used to compute factor scores in the scaling program is

$$S_{ik} = \sum_{i}^{j} V_{ij} F_{jk}$$

where
V_{ij} = response of individual i on question j = −1, +1, 0
F_{jk} = coefficient of factor F_n for question j
S_{ik} = score for each individual for each factor

12. The reader must keep in mind that we are dealing with a mathematically defined "linearity" in the factor analytic procedure, and not "unidimensionality." Whether those variables having high factor loadings on a single factor are related "unidimensionally" within the definition of Guttman scaling, cannot be known from the factor analysis. Indeed, it cannot be assumed that there is an absence of "unidimensionality," once again within the definition of Guttman scaling, between variables with high loadings (approaching $\pm$ 1.0) and variables with low loadings (approaching 0.0) on the same factor. A simple statement of the principal characteristics of linear and nonlinear relationships appears in Charles Wrigley, "The University Computing Center," in *Computer Applications in the Behavioral Sciences* (Englewood Cliffs, 1962), edited by Harold Borko, pp. 160–61. A mathematical statement of a linear model is found in Harry Harmon, *Modern Factor Analysis* (Chicago, 1960), pp. 12–13.

13. V. O. Key, Jr., *Public Opinion and American Democracy* (New York, 1961), especially pp. 27–53 on consensus, and pp. 54–76 on conflict. Key also argues that on many questions there is a fundamentally different kind of distribution involving large numbers who have and large numbers who do not have opinions. These he calls patterns of concentration (concentrated opinion), pp. 77–93. In our survey, there was no significant portion of the public that held "no opinion," as the number of undecided, or those with no opinion, at no time exceeded 2.4 per cent of the respondents on any question. See the preliminary distribution above under "The Survey Data."

14. Cf. Key, *op. cit.*, p. 28: "In its most uncomplicated form 'consensus' means an overwhelming public agreement upon a question of public policy."

15. We had anticipated that more than four percent of our sample population would fall into the "politico" (Group 7) pattern of response. Underlying this assumption was the belief that a high level of political awareness by a respondent would produce a pattern of response that rejected both (1) the idea that the legislator should "always" be either instructed delegate or trustee, and (2) the inconsistency apparent in keeping judges immune from political pressure and accountable to the public for their official actions. In short, within the alternatives provided, the politico pattern seemed to be the most "reasonable" combination of attitudes. If our assumption about the relationship between political awareness and the rejection of ambivalent and "black and white" attitudes toward representational theories is correct, the number of persons in the sample with a high level of political awareness is small.

16. This measure of political participation is similar to the one developed in recent years by the Survey Research Center, University of Michigan.

17. For example, several respondents volunteered the information that they believed judges to be accountable to the people for their official action through impeachment proceedings.

18. Eulau, *et al.*, *op. cit.*, p. 751.

3 *The Role Concept in Legislatures: A Probability Model and a Note on Cognitive Structure* by Wayne L. Francis

Clarification and definition of the term "role" goes back at least as far as Ralph Linton's 1936 work, *The Study of Man.*[1] Linton's early formulations of the concepts "role" and "status" have proved useful analytical tools for a large number of social scientists. Recently John Wahlke has elaborated the appealing qualities of the concept "role" for the study of legislatures. He is impressed by the ease with which "role" can accommodate institutional, functional, and behavioral interests in political science.[2]

A concept which accommodates a wide variety of interests, however, can also have its deficiencies. George Homans points up the difficulty in applying the concept "role" to actual research when he argues: "We do not directly observe *status* and *role.* What we do observe are activities, interactions, norms, and controls. Status and role are names we give to a complex of many different kinds of observations."[3] How can "role" be meaningful without an understanding of the classes of observations which fall under it? If the classes of observations are fully understood, why should "role" have any greater deductive quality or theoretical import than any other general term (e.g., influence, or the symbol "X") which requires the same classes of observations?

Reprinted from *The Journal of Politics,* 27 (August, 1965), 567–585, by permission of the author and the publisher.

The difficulty is amply illustrated in the study of legislatures. In a 1954 article, Ralph Huitt wrote of shifting and conflicting roles played by the *same* senators. Senators changed their roles in response to the immediate environment. Huitt relied upon his knowledge of actual behavior and his insight into what roles such behavior might indicate. He found consistent role-playing (for example, Senator Robert A. Taft in the role of national party leader) more the exception than the rule.[4] Huitt's findings are both discouraging and informative. They are discouraging because they emphasize the disordering notion of inconsistent role-playing. They are informative because they exhibit the consequences of moving swiftly from a "second-order" abstraction, "Role," to reality.

The four-state study of Wahlke, Eulau, Buchanan, and Ferguson could be interpreted as an analytical modification of Huitt's earlier work. In fairness to Huitt, it must be said that he was primarily interested in providing a coherent description of one segment of legislative behavior and less interested in carrying on a debate over conceptual efficacy. The authors of the four-state study, however, devoted considerable effort to the development of a scheme of long-run theoretical payoff. They were careful to make explicit a variety of ways in which "role" can be applied to the study of legislatures.[5] Rather than reiterate their entire thesis, let it suffice to say that the most marked departure from Huitt's work was their great emphasis upon the "normative aspect" of "role."

The key to the change is best understood by applying Homans' insight. The authors of the four-state study focused upon a different "class of observations." Instead of observing specific legislative events, they observed interview responses. They were more interested in norms, expectations of behavior, or predispositions to behavior. Huitt was more interested in role-playing, role enactment, or "role behavior."

The easiest criticism of either study is that it neglected what the other emphasized. Presently I will attempt to demonstrate that the four-state study suggests a suitable way of treating the complex role-playing made all too evident by Huitt's writings on Congress. A more bothersome feature of the four-state study is its failure to show very clearly how one might make a transition from normative findings to legislative events. The problem is a familiar one. Many political scientists have developed data on political attitudes, but few have achieved a convincing technique for predicting behavior on the basis of attitude measurement. Applications of the role concept do not avoid this critical research problem, nor do they *necessarily* contribute to its solution.

One may well argue that the role concept confuses the issue. The concept asks for a redefinition of focus, resulting in a greater concentration upon information, attitudes, and behavior particularly relevant to the legislature as an institution. The shift appears desirable but the verbiage is distracting. The researcher is obligated to devise a *role name* for every set of observations which appears to have an institutional or functional type bearing upon legislative outcomes. Perhaps the *names* are heuristics, but heuristics for whom? The onslaught of jargon can continue indefinitely. Role "theory" and its concomitant terminology do not suggest how cognitive dispositions might be tested against behavior in the legislative framework. For example, Legislator L_1 is identified through interviewing as one who adheres to the representational role of "trustee," the pressure group role of "facilitator," and the areal role of "state oriented."[6] What is his expected behavior in relation to Bill X? To say that L_1 will play these roles in relation to Bill X is unnecessarily abstract. The contribution of the above categories rests in their derivation and not in the language or "theory" by which they are communicated. The expected behavior of L_1 must be estimated from the primitive and intrinsic meaning of the interview responses. *Role-thinking* will not help here.

A Probability Model

There are three typologies presented in *The Legislative System* which are of interest in this section: 1) the trustee, politico, delegate typology; 2) the facilitator, neutral, resister typology; 3) the state oriented, district-state oriented, district oriented typology. A legislator can be classified into one of three groups in each typology on the basis of interview responses. However, it does not make sense to call a legislator a trustee-delegate, a facilitator-neutral, or a state-district-state type. It does not make sense because each typology is arranged along a dimension. A dimension can be represented by a straight line. The straight line is divided into three sections. A legislator is placed at some point along the straight line. A legislator may be *typed* by providing a label for the section into which he falls. He does not fall at two or three points along the straight line.

The process of grouping just described is typical of procedures in attitude scaling research. Once the dimensional idea is accepted, inconsistent behavior is placed in proper perspective. A Congressman who is slightly favorable toward giving aid to neutral countries does not necessarily behave inconsistently when he opposes a particular foreign aid measure which is designed to help neutral countries. He has a limited commitment to this type of foreign aid. Similarly, a legislator who is classified as a facilitator, but behaves like a resister in a particular set of interactions, is not engaging in inconsistent behavior. His orientation to the role of facilitator is limited. The similarity is best illustrated in the facilitator, neutral, resister typology. Wahlke employs a Likert-type scale to divide legislators along a continuum or dimension of friendliness toward pressure groups.[7] The transition is a significant advance over earlier applications of "role." "Inconsistent role-playing" is set aside in favor of viewing a legislator as a truly multi-dimensional person whose behavior is determined by the relevance of different roles to a particular situation and the degree to which he is oriented to those roles.

DERIVATION OF PROBABILITY PARAMETERS

The role typologies discussed above imply attitude dimensions. Attitude dimensions, if clarified, imply particular kinds of behavior. Complete certainty, however, is seldom achieved; therefore, attitude studies allow us to make probability statements about the behavior they hope to describe. *If* probability statements are the most appropriate form of knowledge, then probability questions are the most appropriate form of inquiry. There are three sets of probability questions which are fundamental to this inquiry:

1. a) What is the probability that legislator L_1 will accept instructions?
   b) What is the probability that legislator L_1 will not accept instructions?

2. a) What is the probability that legislator L_1 will consult pressure group leaders?
   b) What is the probability that legislator L_1 will consult persons other than pressure group leaders?
3. a) What is the probability that legislator L_1 will consult on the state-level?
   b) What is the probability that legislator L_1 will consult on the district-level?

Each set of questions is based upon an attitude dimension. Each attitude dimension corresponds roughly to a typology presented in *The Legislative System* (see Table I). The attitude dimensions are not assumed to be synonymous with the respective typologies. They are loosely derived from the typologies.[8]

Table I. *Probability Representation of Parameters*

Source	Probabilities				
	Accepts Instructions				*Rejects Instructions*
Delegate	1.00	.75	.50	.25	0
Politico					
Trustee	0	.25	.50	.75	1.00
	Favorable to Pressure Group Leaders				*Unfavorable to Pressure Group Leaders*
Facilitator	1.00	.75	.50	.25	0
Neutral					
Resister	0	.25	.50	.75	1.00
	Favors State				*Favors District*
State oriented	1.00	.75	.50	.25	0
District-state oriented					
District oriented	0	.25	.50	.75	1.00

The features of reality borrowed for the model are attitudinal dispositions. The attitudes of legislators, it is assumed, will serve as rough guides to their official decision-making. For an attitude dimension to be useful, it must imply a particular kind of behavior. Behavior in the model is inferred from three sets of propositions:

1. a) Legislators who feel they ought to accept instructions from other people during the course of legislative

business are more likely to accept instructions than are other legislators.

b) Legislators who feel they ought to make decisions on the basis of personal philosophy, personal research, etc., are less likely to accept instructions.

2. a) Legislators who feel friendly toward pressure groups are more likely to interact with their leaders than are other legislators.

   b) Legislators who feel unfriendly toward pressure groups are more likely to choose other leaders on a given interaction.

3. a) Legislators who feel they ought to represent their district before the state are more likely to interact with people on the district level.

   b) Legislators who feel they ought to represent the state before their district are more likely to interact with people on the state level.

Each set of propositions envisions a "choice situation" which occurs frequently in the real world.

A "choice situation" in the cases to be considered represents a potential binary choice. Behavior will follow one of two paths, X or Not-X. The legislator does not need to be conscious of the alternatives. Each choice situation is represented in the following manner:

1. Will accept instructions $= P(A)$
   Will not accept instructions $= P(A')$, where $P(A') = 1 - P(A)$
2. Will consult pressure group leader $= P(B)$
   Will consult other leader $= P(B')$, where $P(B') = 1 - P(B)$
3. Will consult on state level $= P(C)$
   Will consult on district level $= P(C')$, where $P(C') = 1 - P(C)$

ASSUMPTIONS

The legislative conditions under which the probabilities can be applied have not been established. The limiting conditions of the model are expressed by the solid lines in Chart 1. The broken lines indicate other conditions under which behavior occurs and should suggest how the model might be

Chart 1. *Scope of Model.*

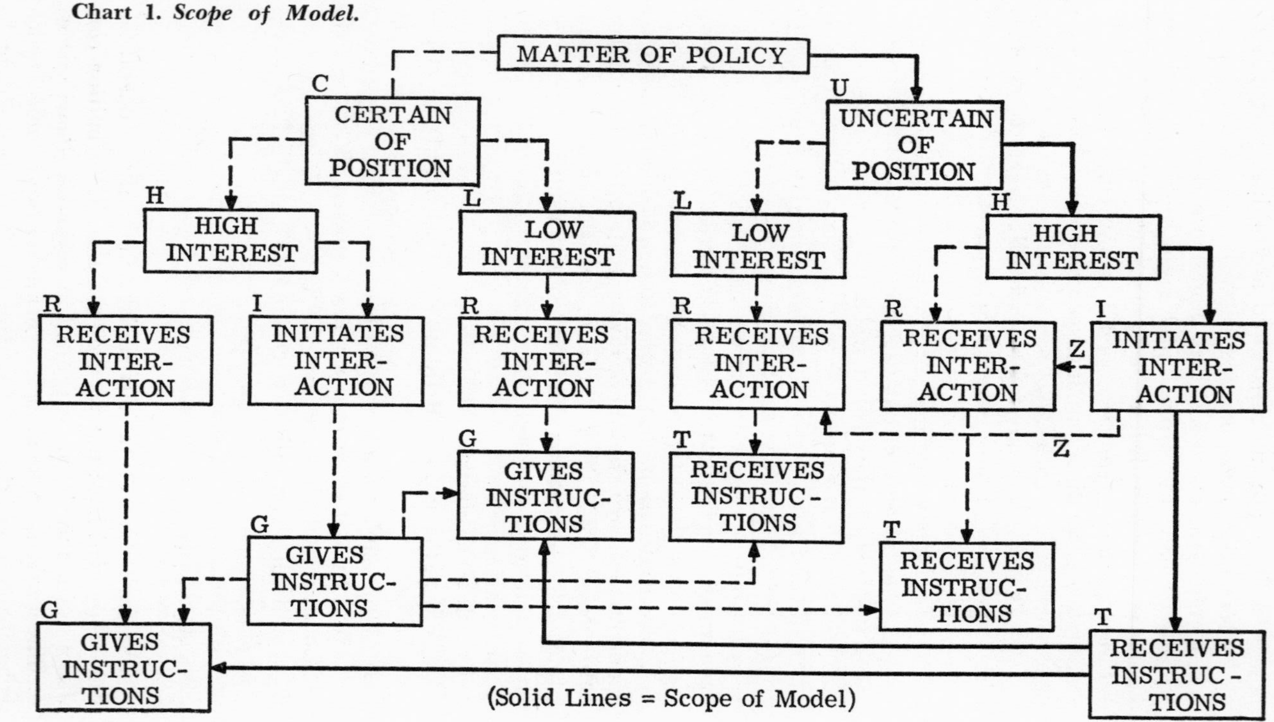

(Solid Lines = Scope of Model)

expanded. The probabilities apply to legislators when they are uncertain of their position toward a specific matter of policy and when they have sufficient interest in the matter. More accurately, the probabilities apply to behavior which occurs under the conditions of uncertainty and high interest, but not all such behavior. At the second level, only interaction which the legislator initiates and in which he receives instructions as a consequence is of concern. Within this framework the model serves as a predictive device. It predicts with whom a legislator interacts and whether he accepts or rejects instructions.[9]

There are many logically possible paths excluded from the model. They include CHRG, CHIG, CLRG, ULRT, HRT, and Z (Chart 1). First, when a legislator is *certain* of his position toward a matter of policy (C), complex considerations of influence and goal achievement arise. Because these conditions shape his behavior, the attitude parameters of the model will probably be poor indicators of the interaction he initiates. Second, when a legislator does not initiate the interaction over a matter of policy, but receives it instead (R), the attitude dimensions of the model would seem to have less bearing upon the nature of the interaction, especially in state legislatures where pre-arranged appointments are usually unnecessary. Third, interactions involving no instructions (Z) exclude a parameter of the model, and as a consequence are ignored in this treatment.

The above exclusions from the model are somewhat arbitrary, as might be implied by the very term "model." However, a sub-purpose of this paper was to obtain as much purity as possible in describing the way legislator dispositions related to legislative events. When a legislator is *uncertain* of his position and has *high interest* in a matter of policy, he initiates interaction over it with one main goal in mind—to remove his uncertainty, establish his position, or make a decision, whichever phrase seems most descriptive. When he achieves his goal, he will stop interacting under the conditions of the model.

Finally, it should be mentioned that the model is not limited to legislators. Ultimately legislators are asked to decide upon legislation, so an examination of their behavior does seem preeminent. The model, accordingly, begins with legislators, and then follows their interactions to all legislative participants.

In the model there are three sets of mutually exclusive events. If A occurs, A′ cannot occur, and vice versa. The same relationship exists betwen B and B′, and C and C′ for any specific event. In addition the occurrence of A or A′ is assumed to be independent of the occurrence of B or B′, and they in turn are independent of the occurrence of C or C′. For example, the probability that a legislator will accept instructions during a given interaction is not altered by the fact that he is more likely to consult on the district level than on the state level. Finally, all events in the model are tri-factor events. They can be described by A or A′, B or B′, and C or C′.

LEGISLATIVE PROFILES

Recall that all initial probabilities are one of three values, and that the values assigned to any one legislator will depend upon his location on three scales. The scales are derived from interview responses which indicate a legislator's: 1) willingness to accept instructions; 2) willingness to consult pressure group leaders; and 3) propensity to consult on the district level, or state level. Each legislator is said to have a probability description (sometimes called "loading") after the form presented in Table II.

Table II. ***Example of a Probability Description for a Single Legislator***

	Instructions		Consult		Consult	
Prob.	*Accept* P (A)	*Reject* P (A′)	*Pre-Grp* P (B)	*Other* P (B′)	*State* P (C)	*District* P (C′)
.75	x				x	
.50			x	x		
.25		x				x

With reference to a particular interaction of a single legislator, a large series of probability questions may be entertained and answered. Illustrative are the following statements which employ the probability description in Table II:

P(A and B and C) = P(A) • P(B) • P(C) = .28
Probability that legislator will accept instructions (P(A)) from a state-level (P(C)) pressure group leader (P(B)).
P(A′ and B) = P(A′) • P (B) = .125
Probability that legislator will reject instructions (P(A′)) from a pressure group leader (P(B)).
P(A′ or B) = P(A′) + P(B) – P(A′ and B) = .625
Probability that legislator will reject instructions (P(A′)) or consult a pressure group leader (P(B)).

The format for a single legislator may be generalized to apply to an entire legislative body. Instead of placing an "x" in the cells as in the case of a single legislator, a frequency would represent the number of legislators a particular cell describes. Then the frequency for each cell would in turn be converted to a percentage of the total number of legislator included in the study. A probability description results, as illustrated in Table III.

Table III. ***Example of a Probability Description for a Legislature (expressed in percentages)***

Prob.	P (A)	P (A′)	P (B)	P (B′)	P (C)	P (C′)
.75	6	81	23	40	24	55
.50	13	13	37	37	21	21
.25	81	6	40	23	55	24
Profile	.31	.69	.46	.54	.42	.58

The summary profile of the legislature is calculated by a simple weighting process (for example, (.75 x 6) + (.50 x 13) + (.25 x 81) all divided by 100 = .31). Within the uncertainty and interaction conditions of the model (Chart I), the profile probabilities serve as estimations of the character of a randomly selected interaction which is the first in a series of related interactions. All of the questions asked of a single legislator can now be applied to an entire legislative body.

Summary profiles are attractive because they aspire to a comparative level of analysis. State legislatures can be compared with ease once the difficult task of collecting the data is completed. A more enlightening and less superficial approach, however, would consider sub-group profiles in each legislature. Party affiliation, legislative experience, formal position, and district characteristics are accessible indicators which should make room for an ample supply of hypotheses.

PROBABILITY ARGUMENTS

Case I. The values comprising individual profiles can be accumulated into group or legislative profiles, but in neither case does the model do more than describe the probabilities relating to a single event. It does not relate first-instance events to the character of events which might follow. A first-instance event can be described as similar to drawing one card from a standard deck of playing cards. If the card is replaced and another is drawn after shuffling the deck, the two events will have no effect upon one another. They are independent, or first-instance events. The probability of drawing a spade at least once will be:

$$P(A \text{ or } B) = (1/4 + 1/4 - (1/4 \cdot 1/4) = .437$$

That this probability argument is least appropriate for social phenomena should become evident in the ensuing discussion.

Case II. In a second case the cards are not replaced after they are drawn, but are withheld until some goal is satisfied. A series of events will take place. The nature of each successive event is subject to a probability which is in turn conditioned by all preceding events. As long as sufficient knowledge of the universe is available (fifty-two cards, thirteen spades), conditional probabilities may be determined and the calculus may proceed. The probability of drawing a spade at least once in two draws will be:

$$P(A \text{ or } B) = (1/4 + 13/51) - (1/4 \cdot 13/51) = .441$$

The type of social interaction which interests social scientists may be better described by conditional probabilities. In other words, significant human events are conditioned by the nature of previous events. The appropriateness of conditional probabilities, however, must not be overestimated. Interaction and *series* of interactions are made meaningful through probability analysis other than that required by conditional assumptions.

Case III. In a third case let us assume that there is an infinite number of playing cards from which one can draw, and that the values are distributed in the same proportion as in a standard deck. Under the assumption of infinity the draw of a card will have no effect upon probabilities relating to subsequent draws, even though the card is withheld. In fulfilling a specified goal (e.g., to draw a spade), the probabilities will not change from one draw to the next. Conditional probabilities are inapplicable. The probability calculus employed in Case III is identical to the calculus employed for Case I.

Although reality offers few convincing examples of infinity, large numbers are a part of almost any field of empirical inquiry. An assumption of infinity proves to be useful when it yields the degree of accuracy necessary for a particular purpose. If in the above case there were actually 10 million playing cards, the probability of drawing a spade on the first attempt is about .25. For most betting purposes .25 would be a sufficient approximation for a staggering number of draws, even though all cards are withheld and the goal of drawing a spade remains unsatisfied. The population of any of the fifty states is large enough to apply the infinity assumption to a sampling technique. The probability of sampling a female will remain about the same over a large number of cases if a random technique is employed.

A less obvious root of the infinity assumption is found in the argument that an individual's basic attitudes change quite gradually. An individual will form his *fundamental* dispositions on the basis of a great number of experiences. A few additional experiences will not markedly alter his dispositions or attitudes. If the assumption is correct, attitude measurement techniques can be applied with confidence in the durability of results. As subjects are positioned on a scale, the positions serve as rough approximations for a suitable length of time unless a concerted effort to change the true positions is made.

The model assumes that probability *profiles* are constructed from attitude data. From one first-instance event to the next first-instance event, the probabilities will remain about the same. The propensity of a legislator to accept instructions, for example, will not change quickly, nor will his propensity to consult on the local level.

Mixed Events. Whenever multi-factor events are entertained, some combination of Case I, Case II, and Case III may be most appropriate. Each factor may have its own empirical or theoretical basis. In the model, tri-factor events are represented by a combination of Cases II and III.

INSTRUCTION-SEEKING BEHAVIOR: A CASE III APPLICATION

When a legislator is uncertain about a fairly important matter of policy, he will, if interested, seek out instructions. He can accept or not-accept instructions which are offered by any given individual. No event in the model will be interpreted as having an effect upon a legislator's general propensity to accept instructions. A legislator who is disinclined toward accepting instructions will continue to be such for every interaction described by the model.

The probability that a legislator will accept instructions during one event, or interaction, will be .75, .50, or .25. Let .75 be defined as Type I, .50 as Type II, and .25 as Type III. The probability that each type of legislator will accept instructions during the course of *two* interactions will be:

$$\text{Type I.} \quad (\tfrac{3}{4} + \tfrac{3}{4}) - (\tfrac{3}{4} \cdot \tfrac{3}{4}) = .94$$
$$\text{Type II.} \quad (\tfrac{1}{2} + \tfrac{1}{2}) - (\tfrac{1}{2} \cdot \tfrac{1}{2}) = .75$$
$$\text{Type III.} \quad (\tfrac{1}{4} + \tfrac{1}{4}) - (\tfrac{1}{4} \cdot \tfrac{1}{4}) = .44$$

Assume that in a particular series of interactions 94 per cent confidence that a legislator accepted instructions is desired. If he were a Type I legislator, only two interactions would be necessary, as illustrated above. If he were Type II, at least *four* consultations would be required. If he were Type III, *ten* interactions or consultations would be sufficient. Recall that in the model all people consulted offer instructions, and that the legislator in question must initiate the interaction.

The above calculations dictate that a Type I legislator (derived from "delegate") will normally arrive at a position through fewer consultations than would be necessary for Type II or Type III legislators. He will arrive at a position through fewer consultations because he is more likely to accept instructions from those he consults. Also, if degree of interest and the number of decisions a legislator wants to make are held constant, Type III legislators (derived from "trustee") will interact with more people than will Type I and II legislators. These deductions may seem insignificant in themselves, but they provide concrete ways of testing the model; that is, both the content and frequency of interaction are explicit, observable phenomena which provide means of moving between the model and reality.

In brief, factor A of the model (the value of P(A) or P(A′)) for any given value rests upon a Case III probability argument. The dependence of the general propensity to accept instructions upon each event is so slight that for all practical purposes it may be ignored. Conditional probabilities are inappropriate.

TEST OF CONSISTENCY

An interesting correspondence between research results and the model will be entertained before proceeding to factors B and C of the tri-factor model. The 1957 data of the four-state study, *The Legislative System,* provide a base from which portions of the model may be tested. A second and necessary set of data unfolds from a 1963 questionnaire survey of state legislators. By looking at the results of each study for California, New Jersey, Ohio, and Tennessee, central features of the model may be scrutinized.[10]

The logic of the consistency test begins by determining the positive half of the probability profiles for each state legislature (as illustrated in Table III). The states are rearranged so that on each of the three parameters the state with the highest value appears first (Table IV). The value of P(A) is the probability that a legislator will accept instructions on a particular interaction. The value of P(B) is the probability

Table IV. ***Rank Order Profile Values of Four State Legislatures on Three Parameters***

State	P (A)	State	P (B)	State	P (C)
Calif.	.412	Ohio	.552	Ohio	.455
Ohio	.398	Calif.	.545	N. J.	.452
N. J.	.390	N. J.	.535	Calif.	.445
Tenn.	.312	Tenn.	.438	Tenn.	.422

that a legislator will interact with a pressure group leader rather than any other leader. The value of P(C) is the probability that he will interact with someone on the state level rather than the local level.

In the questionnaire legislators were asked to recall a fairly important legislative proposal toward which they were initially uncertain. They were to name the proposal and then indicate the types of people they had contacted while trying to arrive at a decision. The alternatives provided in the questionnaire included: (1) Governor, (2) Lt. Governor, (3) Chamber Officer, (4) Legislator specialist in the area, (5) Administrator specialist in the area, (6) Interest group representatives (state-wide), (7) Community leaders from my district, (8) Legislator friend from my district or adjacent district, and (9) Other———.

The questionnaire, if properly interpreted, satisfies two conditions of the model. The condition of *uncertainty* is introduced by the question, and the fact that the respondent recalls a proposal and considers it "fairly important" is pretty good evidence that he had a reasonable degree of *interest* in it (See Chart I). It was not determined whether the respondents initiated or received the interactions which transpired.

For consistency the 1963 data should reveal that:

1. The higher the value of P(A) for a state legislature, the lower will be the mean number of alternatives selected, as deduced from a Case III argument.
2. The higher the value of P(B) for a state legislature, the more frequently will its members select the sixth alternative (interest group representatives).
3. The higher the value of P(C) for a state legislature, the more frequently will its members choose alternatives on the state level (1–6) over alternatives on the local level (7–8).

Ideally, the questionnaire should rank the states in the same order as in Table IV. The probability that such a correspondence would occur by chance is $1/24 \cdot 1/24 \cdot 1/24$, or .00007, assuming that each parameter is independent of the others. As might be expected, perfect correspondence was not achieved; however, the correspondence was close enough to statistically accept the hypothesis that the two rankings are derived from common elements $(1/3 \cdot 1/3 \cdot 1/24) = .005$, which is less than .01, meaning that the correspondence could occur by chance less than once out of a hundred.[11] The relationship may be illustrated as follows:

P (A)	P (B)	P (C)
Calif. – N. J.	Ohio – Calif.	Ohio – Ohio
Ohio – Calif.	Calif. – N. J.	N. J. – N. J.
N. J. – Ohio	N. J. – Ohio	Calif. – Calif.
Tenn. – Tenn.	Tenn. – Tenn.	Tenn. – Tenn.

In the first set only New Jersey is out of order, and in the second only Ohio. The third set contains no discrepancy.

These results not only relate the two research efforts, but more important for this paper, they support the arguments of the model. Let me summarize what has occurred. The data originally collected by Wahlke, Eulau, Buchanan, and Ferguson were organized into a number of typologies. Three typologies were selected for this presentation. It was then explained how these typologies might imply attitude dimensions. Each of the three attitude dimensions served as a parameter in a probability model. The probability model served as the vehicle for translating attitudes into behavior.

The model is then limited by a number of assumptions; that is, it translates only when certain conditions exist, or become approximated. The conditions were approximated in a 1963 questionnaire. Legislators were asked to recall with whom they interacted in regard to a specific issue about which they were uncertain. In this case legislators were recalling behavior rather than stating their attitudes. The results are consistent with the arguments of the model. When individual responses are totaled and standardized for each state, the states acquire relative positions similar to those developed through 1957 attitudinal-type data. Important is the fact that the model rises above what appear to be minor discrepancies between the assumptions of the model and the data collection and organization techniques. In spite of such discrepancies, the relationship between attitudinal position (role types) and behavioral indices (recollections) is established.

To extend the model beyond its present static nature, further information is needed. Factor A, the propensity to accept instructions, is treated as a constant and can be applied immediately to a causal chain or *series* of interactions (as such a series is determined to exist through factors B and C). A series of interactions begins when a legislator seeks instructions over a particular matter of policy. His communication with the first person who offers instructions is considered the first interaction. The series ends when he no longer consults over the particular matter of policy. The likelihood that he will consult pressure group leaders and people on the state or district level (P(B), P(C), and P(C′)) can vary from interaction to interaction within the series. A way of estimating the variance without complete information may be understood through the representation of cognitive structure.

A Note on Cognitive Structure[12]

The representation of cognitive structure inserts one more link to the chain which began with role typologies and ends with actual behavior or legislative events. The transition from role typologies to attitude dimensions, and attitude dimensions to probability statements, is further modified by knowledge of cognitive structure. In the model, knowledge of cognitive structure is necessary when one explores a *series* of interactions rather than a single, first-instance event.

When the conditions of the model apply, a legislator will initiate interactions after some describable pattern. The pattern will resemble the way in which people, events, and ideas are organized in his own mind, called *cognitive structure.* Environmental disturbances of the natural pattern occur, but not so frequently so as to render the simulation of cognitive structure a useless or minor endeavor. In fact, most simulations of the human mind thrive upon the relationships between environment and cognitive processes. Advanced simulations incorporate self-adapting mechanisms which are sensitive to specified changes in the environment.[13] The less ambitious purpose of this section is to set forth some basic patterns of cognitive structure which are, to a large extent, suggested to me by the probability model.

Let S(l) through S(n) represent the categories legislators employ to make sense out of the issues which come before the legislature. The categories may be *business, labor, taxation, agriculture,* and *education,* or they may be *private, public, fiscal, non-fiscal,* etc. The specific categories are not important here. A legislator will use discretion in consulting his colleagues, friends, and acquaintances for advice. When an education issue, for example, presents an enigma to the legislator, he will contact those people whose knowledge and opinions he considers worthy. They might or might not be the same people he would consult on a tax issue. There is no necessary correspondence between the content of S(1) and the content of S(2); that is, the people a legislator would consult in the area of education (S(1)) may be unrelated to his list of consultants in the taxation area (S(2)). For this reason, probability statements of the form P(B) = .75 (probability that a legislator will consult a pressure group leader about a matter of policy) are meaningful. The matter of policy is unknown, and therefore its cognitive referents are also unknown. If both were known, P(B) = 1, or 0, assuming availability of all who are referenced.

Chart 2. *Representations of Cognitive Structure.*

S(1)	S(2)	S(3)	S(4)	S(5)	S(6)	S(7)
I(1)	B	C	B	C	C′	B′
I(2)	I(2)	I(2)	C	B	I(25)	C′
I(3)	I(6)	I(4)	I(9)	I(2)	I(26)	I(25)
I(4)	I(7)	I(3)	I(1)	I(20)	I(8)	I(18)
I(5)	B′	C′	I(11)	I(5)	C	I(28)
I(6)	I(3)	I(6)	C′	I(21)	I(27)	C
	I(4)	I(8)	I(6)	B′	I(15)	I(29)
			I(12)	I(10)	I(5)	I(30)
			B′	I(8)		I(27)
			C	C′		B
			I(4)	B		C′
			I(15)	I(33)		I(34)
			C′	I(14)		I(33)
			I(18)	B′		I(12)
				I(24)		C
				I(32)		I(35)
						I(11)

The content of S(1), S(2), . . . S(n) may take several forms, as illustrated in Chart 2. In the chart, B is a list of pressure group participants, B′ is a list of non-pressure-group participants, C is a list of state-level participants, and C′ is a list of district-level participants. The lists B, B′, C, and C′ may also be sub-lists. I(1) through I(n) are elements of lists and sub-lists, and in this case identify people.

The content of S(1) is in random form; that is, factors B and C of the model are not relevant. S(2) is structured by B and B′, and S(3) by C and C′. S(4), S(5), and S(7) contain more complex structures. If S(1) through S(7) contained the total structure for a single legislator, there would be a tendency for him to consult state-level pressure group leaders (B and C), assuming, of course, that the issues are spread evenly over the seven major categories.

The scheme presented in Chart 2 helps clarify a number of theoretical matters which are of substantial discomfort to political scientists. These matters, which go beyond the applications of this paper, may be described in the following question-answer session:

Q. 1. Why does a legislator exhibit contradictory behavior even when he appears to be acting purely from his own cognition? An attitude test may show that a legislator feels he ought to represent his state's interests before those of his district; yet, he is seen consulting district officials on matters about which he is uncertain.

A. 1. The people a legislator consults will depend upon the nature of the matter over which he is uncertain. An attitude test is an index to his general propensity and would need to be applied to a large number of cases to be verified. Chart 2 lists seven categories (S(1) through C(7)). If a legislator perceives a matter of uncertainty in category S(3), he will consult a list of state-level participants first, whereas in S(6) he would consult district-level participants first.

Q. 2. Why is it, however, that a legislator can register pro-state, pro-pressure group on an attitude test, yet voluntarily consult non-pressure-group district-level people for a considerable proportion of the time?

A. 2. Most of the issues about which he is uncertain happen to get defined within the context of S (7), an area which is atypical.

Q. 3. Why do attitudes remain fairly stable over a period of time, even though a legislator has punishing experiences as a result of his attitudes?

A. 3. Looking at Chart 2, the rejection of one individual

(I(n)) of one list (S(n)) barely alters the structure. Furthermore, the rejection of I(9), for example, within the context of S(4) does not empty the list of state-level pressure group participants within that context. I(1) and I(11) remain.

The answers to the three questions could be approximated without any knowledge of Chart 2 and similar contrivances. However, such approximations are likely to be elusive and vague if not altogether mystifying. The advantage of the above scheme is that it is totally explicit and at the same time accommodates previous knowledge of attitudes and behavior. The task of mapping cognitive structure is made practical by the expanded memory (storage) capacity of the more recently developed computers.

Turning to the model, the scheme also provides a basis for estimating what takes place when a legislator does not accept instructions from the first person he consults. Unless specifically redirected during the first interaction, he will move down the list from the first element, taking each element in order. When the elements of S(4)-B-C are exhausted, he will continue with the elements of S(4)-B-C′. When he accepts instructions, he will stop searching the list. If he is generally unwilling to accept instructions he will consult many people, and many types of people as evidenced by the 1963 questionnaire survey. A final advantage is that the scheme is researchable, both in a hypothetical-type interview situation and in a direct observational fashion. The present scheme is purposely oversimplified. It would be helpful to know, for example, the number elements typical of a sublist in order to have a basis for assigning conditional probabilities to large aggregates of data.

Notes:

1. Ralph Linton, *The Study of Man* (New York, 1936).
2. John C. Wahlke, Heinz Eulau, William Buchanan, and LeRoy Ferguson, *The Legislative System* (New York, 1962), Chapter I, esp. pp. 9–14.
3. George C. Homans, *The Human Group* (New York, 1950), p. 12.
4. Ralph K. Huitt, "The Congressional Committee: A Case Study," *American Political Science Review,* Vol. 48 (1954), pp. 340–365.
5. John C. Wahlke, *et al., op. cit.*
6. *Ibid.*, Appendix I.
7. *Ibid.*

8. My interpretation of "delegate" as one who is inclined to accept instructions from anyone, not just constituents, is perhaps contrary to popular usage; however it is very close to the interpretation provided by *The Legislative System* on page 467, Appendix I.

9. A convenient way to interpret the scheme in Chart 1 is to envision two legislators satisfying one condition at each level, although not necessarily the same condition. If interaction between them over the matter of policy is possible or likely, the chart will describe how it occurs.

10. The data serving as a basis for Table IV were taken from Heinz Eulau, *et al.*, "The Role of the Representative: Some Empirical Observations on the Theory of Edmund Burke," *American Political Science Review,* Vol. 53 (1959), pp. 753–754. Also see Wahlke, *et al., op. cit.*, p. 327.

The questionnaire, supported by a New York Legislative Internship grant, was sent to 32 legislators in each of fifty states. The sample was random in each state. Naturally only a small portion of the questionnaire is used in this section. There were 22 returns from Tennessee, 19 from Ohio, 15 from California, and 13 from New Jersey. For this exploratory part of the study, there were 21 usable responses from Tennessee, 15 from Ohio, 13 from California, and 10 from New Jersey.

11. In this particular application it is easier to employ basic probabilities than any given statistical technique. Both Kendall's tau statistic and the Spearman rank order correlation coefficients' co-existing values of "p" (see, for example, Table XIII of Appendix in Allen L. Edwards, *Statistical Methods for the Behavioral Sciences,* 1960) are derived from the same probabilities and assumptions as are employed in this section. The calculations above begin by knowing that there are 4! or 24 possible orders in a ranking of four elements (states), therefore, the probability that the same order will be achieved in two separate rankings is 1/24, or .0417.

12. The writer wishes to express his debt to the Simulation of Cognitive Processes Institute (sponsored by Social Science Research Council and RAND Corporation during the summer of 1963) for stimulating the concluding ideas of this paper.

13. Most notable are the computer simulations. See for example Allen Newell, J. C. Shaw, and H. A. Simon, "Chess-playing programs and the Problem of Complexity," *IBM Journal of Res. and Dev.*, Vol. 2, pp. 320–335. For a more general discussion see Rufus P. Browning, "Computer Programs as Theories of Political Processes," *Journal of Politics,* Vol. 24 (1962), pp. 562–582.

B. *The Vertical Dimension—Groups*

4 *The Functions of Informal Groups in Legislative Institutions* by Alan Fiellin

Social scientists have long recognized the value of the two approaches combined in the analysis reported in this paper —namely, functional analysis and the study of informal groups. Political scientists, however, have been slow to apply them *systematically* in their investigations of political institutions and behavior. Neither has as yet achieved a permanent place in the methodology of our discipline. For this latter reason, it will be worthwhile to examine briefly the meaning of these concepts before presenting the substantive analysis.

The relationship of political scientists to functional analysis is roughly that of M. Jourdain to prose; not fully conscious of his methodology, the analyst fails to use it systematically and thus fails to take full advantage of its potential. A quick review of the literature of political science would reveal many references to the functions of political behavior patterns and institutions, but self-conscious systematic uses of the concept and approach would be hard to find. Moreover, owing to our traditional emphasis upon legal-constitutional and prescriptive

Reprinted from *The Journal of Politics,* 24 (February, 1962), 72–91, by permission of the author and the publisher.

analysis, many investigations have been limited to either the constitutionally prescribed functions[1] or functional prescriptions based upon the authors' values. Though both of these may be legitimate enterprises, they do not fully exploit functional analysis and without supplementation may lead to incomplete understanding and therefore superficial evaluation.[2]

Functional analysis is one way of viewing, understanding, or explaining behavior within a system. The observer asks what consequences a given behavior pattern has for the systems of which it is a part. For example, what are the functions and dysfunctions of boss-controlled political machines for the social, economic, and governmental systems of which they are a part,[3] or of seniority and the committee system for the legislative system, party system, and inclusive political system? The conclusions of such an analysis provide an understanding of the item as a functional unit of the institutions for which it is relevant.

Systematic functional analysis of social behavior requires more than the usual precision in the use of the term "function" and also requires that some distinctions between kinds of functions be made. The definition to be used here is that of Merton. "Functions are those observed consequences which make for the adaptation or adjustment of a given system."[4] As adapted to the present study, consequences make for the adaptation or adjustment of a given system when they (1) constitute positive and necessary contributions to the existence of the system, or (2) merely contribute to the achievement of participants' goals. Criterion 1 raises the issue and problems of the functional prerequisites of the systems considered. By supplementing this with the less demanding criterion 2, the problems involved in determining whether or not a particular function is vitally necessary are avoided. As the purpose of the analysis is to explain the existence of legislative informal groups, it seems justified to call attention to a variety of consequences without limiting attention to only those without which the various systems could not survive. Consequences which merely contribute to goal attainment are thus included not primarily for the purpose of avoiding problems but, more importantly, to permit a more complete explanation of informal groups.

The concept "dysfunction" is then used to refer to those

consequences "which lessen the adaptation or adjustment of the system."[5] Merton points out that our analytical framework must also take into account the possibility of non-functional consequences—those which are irrelevant to the adaptation or adjustment of the system. It should be noted that a given behavior pattern may have all three kinds of consequences.

In addition to the above, there is the equally important distinction between manifest and latent functions. "Manifest functions are those objective consequences contributing to the adjustment or adaptation of the system which are intended and recognized by participants in the system; latent functions, correlatively, being those which are neither intended nor recognized."[6] The principal importance of this distinction is that it brings the frequently overlooked latent functions to the attention of the observer. Perceptive explorations of the latent functions of behavior patterns, because they go beyond the frequently common knowledge of manifest functions, are likely to result in new insights. A few examples will most adequately demonstrate this point—Veblen's analysis of conspicuous consumption,[7] the catharsis and legitimizing functions of congressional committee hearings, the social mobility function of political machines.

The framework to be used here thus consists of three categories—behavior patterns to which consequences are imputed, the general and specific consequences of those patterns, and units or systems for which the behavior has consequences. The behavior patterns to be analyzed are those of individuals in informal legislative groups. The general consequences will be described using the classifications developed above—manifest, latent; functional, dysfunctional, non-functional. Only where the distinction seems to be of theoretical importance and there are sufficient data, will functions be classified as manifest or latent. Specific consequences are the ways in which the pattern promotes adaptation and adjustment—for example, the communication channels of informal groups facilitate negotiation and coalition formation. The several systems for which the behavior analyzed in this case study has consequences will be specified in the following section which outlines the kinds and sources of data used for the functional analysis.[8]

New York Democrats and Informal Group Behavior

The analysis presented in the following pages is based upon part of a larger study of one informal group in the House of Representatives.[9] All the members of the group are New York Democratic Representatives. The existence of an informal group within the delegation was not, however, inferred from the common membership of the Representatives in a state delegation.[10] Interview data on the interactions of the members were used to determine the existence and boundaries of a genuine interaction group. Thus the approximate correspondence of delegation and group boundaries was not assumed in the research design.[11]

Interviews in conjunction with participant-observation provided the data on the behavior patterns of the members.[12] These behavior patterns are of two types—(1) those interactions (communication and organization for example) which are group behavior patterns, and (2) individual behavior patterns common to all members which are not, however, group behavior.

The empirical basis for both the analysis and the hypotheses which are developed (the latter are outlined in the conclusion) was supplemented with information on informal group activities found in the literature. Though not rich in systematic analyses of informal groups, books and articles by both political scientists and congressmen do contain many scattered references to their activities and functions.[13]

Despite the use of supplementary information, the limitations of a case study have not been entirely avoided. We know that the members of Congress form a variety of kinds of groups. These groups find their roots in a variety of common experiences—party membership, state and regional representation, religion, committee membership, similarity of views on the issues of the day, friendship, and so forth. Some are cohesive, some not. Some are relatively permanent, others ad hoc and temporary. In some, leadership roles are differentiated and clearly defined, while in others leadership is quite informal, perhaps shifting from one member to another. Some groups have only a few members, others are quite large. A classification scheme which could be used for distinguishing the functions different kinds of groups perform may eventually be developed. In the present exploratory study, no such attempt is made. Thus the extent to which the findings are appropriately generalized from this one group to all others is problematic.[14]

For purposes of this analysis an informal group is defined as an identifiable, self-conscious, relatively stable unit of interacting members whose relationships are not officially prescribed by statutes and rules. The justification for approaching the study of Congress with this conceptual tool rests upon the assumption that such units exist and have important consequences for the nature of the legislative process. That the use of the approach will prove valuable seems likely in the light of the success researchers in other fields of social and political science have had with this approach[15] and our knowledge that Congress is a relatively unstructured legislative institution.[16] David Truman has indicated the reasons for using this approach in studying Congress.

> Such a body is not properly conceived as a collection of individual men, unorganized and without internal cohesion. Nor is it any better accounted for exclusively in terms of the formal, legal structure of the legislature. *A legislative body has its own group life, sometimes as a unit, perhaps more often as a collection of subgroups or cliques.* It has its own operating structure, which may approximate or differ sharply from the formal organization of the chamber.[17]

The following is an initial attempt to be reasonably systematic in analyzing the consequences of informal groups in the House of Representatives. Some limitations of the analysis, as previously explained, stem from primary reliance on data from a single case study. In addition, no attempt has been made to test rigorously hypotheses stating the functions of such groups. Rather the analysis is used for the purpose of generating hypotheses which may prove to be useful for future research.

In each of the following sections, one pattern of behavior is identified and explained and then the consequences of the pattern for relevant systems are suggested. The relevant systems for this analysis are (1) the members of the New York Democratic group, (2) the leadership of the group, (3) other members and groups in the House of Representatives, (4) the House itself as a legislative institution, (5) the electoral Democratic Party leaders of New York City and State, (6) New

York City as the collective constituency represented by the group.

Communication

From what is known about the behavior and functions of informal structures in other kinds of large scale organizations,[18] it is not surprising that the communication activities of the New York Democrats are functional for several units within the House. In fact, because of the absence of an effective hierarchical structure in the House, probably the most important functions of informal groups and relationships result from their use as communication networks.

The New York Democratic Congressmen. The communications network of the group performs three services for the individual members. It provides them with (1) "trustworthy" information on bills and legislative politics; (2) cues for making voting decisions;[19] and (3) adaptive norms, perceptions and rationalizations. All of these, since they are shared within the group, are socially supported. Providing social support for members' attitudes and behavior may thus be a latent function of informal groups.

It is a truism that legislators need information and advice. They must be informed on both the technical and political aspects of legislation in order to make those decisions which may determine their political futures.[20] Members of the House of Representatives, of course, receive information from many sources—committee hearings and reports, floor debate, personal staff, the Legislative Reference Service, interest groups, mass media, and so forth. In fact this profusion of information from so many sources probably complicates the problem of decision-making rather than facilitating its solution.[21] It is for this reason that communication within informal groups may be particularly valuable to the individual member. Information, advice, and voting cues come from trusted sources —those with similar or identical interests and views. Several interview respondents attested to the value of such information and suggested the reasons for its special quality.

> I can take the advice of other members of the group on what to do and how to vote because they not only have expert opin-

ions, their districts are essentially similar to mine. They have the same kinds of problems and the same basic viewpoint.[22]

In the particular case of the New York Democrats and other informal legislative groups based on the similar constituencies of the members, the reliability of information and advice is built-in. The constituencies of the members are essentially similar and the electoral party organizations and interest groups upon which they rely are either the same or have similar views and expectations.[23] Most important of all, perhaps, is that the member in taking cues from the New York group cannot get into electoral difficulties as a result of deviation. There is security in numbers. If the member honors this maxim and follows the advice of his informal group colleagues, he cannot be singled out for an "incorrect" decision.[24]

A division of labor, corresponding to the committee structure of the House, develops in some group and provides benefits for the individual. By virtue of his informal ties, the New York Democrat, for example, has ready access to committees of which he is not a member. Individual members may, and do, use group connections to check on the status and prospects of legislation in committees other than their own.[25] In the absence of personal ties with members of most House Committees, the task of quickly getting trustworthy information on the work of many committees would be most difficult.[26] The New York Democrat may save many hours of legwork, reading, and anxious deliberation by holding a brief conversation with a likeminded colleague who knows the material and has previously sifted through it.

Members on first entering the House have much to learn. They must learn to make sense of this new world and understand their place in it—in short, become socialized in a new institution and role. By providing the new member with a social and political home away from home, by offering him viable conceptions of the national legislative process and his role in it, the group performs important functions for the individual. Since the "regular" New York Democrat is automatically a member of the group by virtue of his election, some of his difficult initial role problems are solved by his acceptance of the group and its "folkways."[27]

This function may be of greater than normal importance

for the New York Democratic Representative because of his membership in what is pejoratively referred to as the "Tuesday to Thursday Club," i.e., the "deviant" practice of too often restricting one's stay in Washington to these three days of the week.[28] Because of his membership in the group, however, this deviant behavior and the accompanying rationalization are socially sanctioned and supported.[29]

Though the group's provision and support of role conceptions and norms is in general an important function in a loosely structured situation,[30] that some conceptions in this case are deviant may be dysfunctional for the individual. This is true to the extent that these particular deviations reduce the members' influence.[31]

Other informal groups and the House as a legislative institution. The communication which occurs through the channels of informal groups is functional not only for the individual members, but also for the institution and its component groups as well. It would be nearly impossible for the members of Congress to perform their legislative functions in the absence of such communication channels.[32] Committees, political parties, and floor debate solve only part of the communication problem of Congress. Informal groups supplement and fill in the remaining gaps. The following example of the operation of informal groups suggests that the functions of communication within and between such groups may lie especially in the area of forming coalitions, negotiating compromises, and developing legislative strategy.

An informal group of "Democratic Young Turks" was established during the 85th Congress.[33] The stated purpose of the group was to enhance the strength of Western and Northern Democratic "liberals" in Democratic Party and House politics. *Congressional Quarterly* expressed the view that the chief spokesman, Eugene McCarthy, was opposed to any formal organization as ". . . it might be construed as a direct challenge to Rayburn's leadership." The report goes on to state that nevertheless ". . . communication among the 80 signers of the program is effective even without a formal organization."[34] The relationship between this group and the New York Democrats, 14 of whom joined the "Young Turks," is instructive in demonstrating how a pre-existing informal group facilitated this communication.

Though much communication among the members took place in informal conversations on the floor of the Chamber and in the cloakrooms and dining rooms, the communication channels of informal groups were also used to disseminate messages quickly and effectively to all members. For example, Congressman Multer, the Democratic whip for New York State and a leader of the informal group, became an unofficial "whip" of the "Young Turks." In this way, liaison was established between the two informal House groups. The New York Democratic group "tied" its members to the outside legislative world while at the same time facilitating communication from outside groups to its members. Many messages were transmitted through these channels. At least in some of the "Young Turks'" meetings and conversations to plan program and strategy, one New York Democrat "represented" the entire group.

Though in this particular example the communication channels may have become more regularized than is customary, it does illustrate the kind of function which may be served by such groups. Until the business and politics of Congress becomes more completely structured by other kinds of organizations, one may expect informal groups to arise and facilitate a variety of essential kinds of communication.

New York party and public officials. It was expected by the author that group channels would be used by both party and public officials in New York City and State to communicate their views on legislation. Available data, which may be incomplete, suggest that this is not the case. On the contrary, interview data indicate that the few messages members receive in which public officials state their views on pending legislation are sent directly to the individual members rather than being channeled through group leaders.

Group Meetings

It is not uncommon for members of informal legislative groups to meet together regularly—frequently for lunch or dinner. In the extent to which business is formally conducted and group decisions reached during these meetings, there is probably considerable variation from group to group. The following procedure is that normally followed by the New

York Democratic delegation. That it is not an entirely unique case is evident from the descriptions of other group meetings found in the literature.[35]

Congressman Multer, the Assistant Whip for the New York Democrats, acts as the coordinator of these monthly meetings —setting the time and place and calling the members together. The manifest function of these meetings for the leaders is to discuss legislation and crystallize the position of the delegation. When a measure is scheduled for consideration in the House, Congressman Multer requests a summary of the bill and the pros and cons from that member of the delegation serving on the committee. At the next meeting of the group, Multer presents this information together with his and the committee member's recommendations for group action. The measure is then discussed and an attempt is made to arrive at a group decision.

In arriving at group decisions, the delegation follows rules similar to those of the party caucus. When there is disagreement within the group, the members of the majority, through persuasion, attempt to bring about unanimity. "Members in the minority are told what the New York City interest is, they are informed of the party position as expressed in the platform, and the interests of their constituencies are analyzed."[36] But if individuals persist in their dissent because of contrary campaign pledges or the dictates of conscience, then, in the words of one member, "we don't try to stop them."

Bailey and Samuel, in discussing the meetings of the Ohio Republicans, present additional evidence of the informational function of regular group meetings.

> For the members themselves, the weekly luncheons usually provided some information of value; at least one of the fourteen Ohio Republicans was bound to be a member of the committee handling the current legislation. Finally, for the Republican leadership, it was helpful to get the fourteen Ohio Republicans around the same table. After the meetings, Representative J. Harry McGregor of the 17th District who served as the Ohio whip could estimate with fair accuracy how his fellow members would vote.[37]

Thus the manifest functions of these meetings for members and leaders are (1) dissemination of information, (2) exchange of views on pending legislation, and (3) at least for the New York Democrats, determination of the group's position.

An important latent function of these meetings results from the social, convivial nature of the occasion. It is well known that for many groups such affairs have the effects of developing *esprit de corps* and of reinforcing group identity. These in turn contribute to unity of action which is necessary for the realization of group goals. From very meagre information on the New York Democrats' dinner meetings, it seems probable that they also have this latent emotional function in addition to their manifest functions of information, discussion, and decision.

Bloc Voting

In contributing to the achievement of goals in the House, bloc voting is functional for the group members and leaders, the electoral party leaders, and the collective constituency, New York City. Its special contribution to goal attainment consists in providing the group with a measure of influence out of proportion to the number of its members.

Leaders especially are aware of the positive consequences of bloc behavior, whereas some of the rank-and-file seem to be totally unaware of any purpose served by the group's cohesive voting. These variations in awareness of the benefits of group cohesion can be explained in part by the greater involvement of leaders in the House politics and their greater concern for the strategic problems of acquiring influence and achieving goals. As representatives of the group in negotiations concerning legislation, committee assignments, and so forth, the leaders of the delegation are made aware of the potential contribution of group unity to the achievement of desired ends.[38]

Votes are one medium of exchange in political bargaining; the ability to "deliver" a large bloc of votes may contribute mightily in bringing negotiations to a successful conclusion.[39]

Two minor incidents which were brought to the attention of the author suggest specific ways bloc voting might be used to advantage in House politics. On one occasion, reportedly, it was suggested to the members of the delegation that all vote in the Democratic caucus in favor of the appointment of a *non*-New York Democrat to a committee vacancy. It was argued that unanimity on the part of the delegation on this vote would enhance its future bargaining position for favorable committee assignments for its own members.

The other example comes from the administrative assistant of a House Democrat. With great admiration, he spoke of the "smooth" operation of the New York Democrats. He had observed his "boss" rounding up votes for a bill in which the latter was interested. In doing so, the Representative contacted, among others, only one New York Democrat. He confidently relied upon this single contact as sufficient for obtaining the full support of the New York Democrats (17 votes); he was not disappointed by the final results.

Truman also describes an example which illustrates the advantages of bloc behavior.

> An excellent illustration of logrolling. . . . occurred in connection with appropriations in 1950 for unemployment relief and farm parity payments. During that session the Farm Bureau's supporters in Congress had been in opposition to representatives from some of the Eastern cities on these two measures and on others. Neither had sufficient reliable votes on these bills to assure it a majority in the House. Under the leadership of Mayor LaGuardia of New York and President O'Neal of the Farm Bureau, an arrangement was made during the voting on parity payments in the House of Representatives. The votes of a number of urban congressmen on that measure were exchanged for those of certain representatives from farm areas on general relief appropriations.[40]

Such arrangements may of course be worked out in the absence of an appropriate informal group structure. Nevertheless, there is no doubt that such a structure facilitates the formation of coalitions, and that willingness to play the game increases the influence of stable groups. In contrast, individual members outside of the bloc structure will only in the case of very close votes have the necessary influence to enter into negotiations with sufficient leverage to expect a reasonably favorable *quid pro quo*.

These examples suggest how bloc behavior might be used by the leaders for their own success as well as the promotion of the interests of rank-and-file members, the group, the constituencies and interest groups.[41] They also provide additional evidence of the function of groups in facilitating legislative negotiations.

To appreciate fully the contribution of bloc voting to a member's legislative life and career it must be seen within the context of his total situation in the legislature. New York Democrats who come to Congress rarely achieve great individual influence. For a variety of reasons, their approach to Congress typically limits the likelihood of their joining the "inner circle." Their membership in the "Tuesday to Thursday Club," short tenure as congressmen, and a tendency to limit personal contacts to other New York Democrats combine to make it less than likely that individual members will be accepted by their colleagues as "congressmen's congressmen." Since we expect our representatives to acquire influence in order to further constituency interests (ample evidence from interviews indicates that New York Democrats define this as a central role expectation), the individual New York Democrat without the group as a channel of participation and influence might have some difficulty in meeting his role expectations. From this perspective, bloc voting and the resulting collective influence can be viewed as a substitute for individual influence. The members' obligations (manifest function) to promote and defend the common interest of their constituencies (New York City) is thus fulfilled. Success in this should be functional also for the electoral party's goal of winning elections.

Collective action may also provide, probably latently, a defense and protection for the individual in his relationship with lobbyists. For much the same reason that the British backbencher is relatively free of pressures from outside groups, the rank-and-file New York Democrat may be less besieged by them than is usual for members of the House.

The psychological, cue-giving function of informal group membership as it relates to the re-election problems of members was previously mentioned in discussing the communication functions of the group. It is pertinent to refer again to this function because of its direct connection with bloc voting. Voorhis in his insightful autobiography poignantly calls attention to the psychological and electoral problems of members, which may be partially solved by informal group memberships.

> Everyone desires the inner warmth that comes from the knowledge that he has friends who can be counted upon. The members of the organized groups desire this. So do the congressmen. It is, again, a formula for re-election.
>
> • • •
>
> Thus I have been able to understand why members sought a kind of political "home" in the bosom of some strong group, whose interests they would always protect and who could then be depended upon to go all out for the candidate for re-election whenever the need arose.[42]

In order fully to appreciate the importance of Voorhis' point for an understanding of the New York Democrat's group behavior in Congress, it is necessary to be aware of the ties between the congressional delegation and the electoral parties. Faithful membership in the delegation group is one way for the member to remain in good standing with party officials regarding his activities in Washington. In situations where party support is normally a *sine qua non* of re-election (and it probably is for most New York Democratic Congressmen) "belonging" is likely to be a high priority objective.

The "Tuesday to Thursday Club"

A practice which has both manifest functions and latent dysfunctions for the individual is his membership in the "Tuesday to Thursday Club"—that is, spending only three or four days in Washington while the House is in session. It is likely that the commuting involved is not welcomed by all members. Evidence from interviews suggests that party leaders and constituents partly because of established tradition *expect* their congressmen to maintain close contact with them by making frequent trips home. Both for re-election and for "promotion" to higher political office, their time should be divided between Washington and New York. Thus the practice has manifest functions for the individual's political career.

Many members also take advantage of the economic opportunities by maintaining their previously established law practices and businesses. In this way, they supplement their incomes and maintain non-political careers to which they may return in the event of electoral defeat or political retirement.

Though functional for the member's New York political

career, it seems probable that "Tuesday to Thursday Club" membership is dysfunctional for his congressional career. Frequent absence from "the Hill" earns the member a reputation as a parttime congressman. For many House colleagues, particularly those that count, this is a violation of the norm requiring that each member carry his share of the work load and spend nearly full-time in Washington while the House is in session. Some individuals (perhaps Congressman Celler, for example) may substantially overcome this handicap after long service and gain considerable influence both formally and informally. For most members, however, the deviation results in some reduction in prestige and influence with House colleagues.

Conclusion

The foregoing analysis of the functional meaning of some standardized behavior patterns of the members of one informal group in the House of Representatives suggests hypotheses for further research. Only those which may prove fruitful for the understanding of the functions of informal groups in general (as opposed to those whose meaning is limited to the particular characteristics of the New York Democrats) will be reformulated. Again the reader must be warned that these are suggested hypotheses, not firmly established propositions.

1. Informal groups arise in unstructured legislative situations.[43]
2. These groups perform manifest and latent functions (dysfunctions) for the members and the institutions.
3. Informal groups are the principal "socializing" agencies in such legislatures.
   a. Members learn role expectations and institutional norms within informal groups.
4. Informal groups may function to provide support for behavior adjudged to be deviant in the light of institutional norms.
5. Decisions of legislators depend, in part, on their informal group memberships.
6. Conscious bloc behavior is characteristic of informal groups under conditions of "sufficient" integration of the members and similarity of interests between them.

a. This bloc behavior is, by definition, manifestly related to political strategy and goal attainment.

7. Latent functions for the individuals and the group leadership result from the division of labor within these groups, e.g., access to a variety of committees in order to secure information and exercise influence.
8. Legislative functional requisites[44] are among the consequences of informal groups in legislatures.
   a. One function performed by informal groups is the exchange of political and technical information.
   b. Informal groups structure otherwise hopelessly confused legislative situations.
      b. 1. The politics of otherwise unstructured legislatures occur, for the most part, within and between these groups and through their channels, e.g., negotiation, compromise, and the formation of coalitions.
      b. 2. "Generalized support" will be characteristic of the relationship between these groups.[45]

Applying this orientation to the House of Representatives, it is hypothesised that House politics is not unintelligibly complex, consisting only of the individual behavior of each of 435 isolated members. Rather, it is much more simply structured through a network of informal groups and relationships. This network provides channels for information exchange, political negotiation, and the formation of compromises—probably impossible tasks for 435 atomized units.[46] Just as this structure makes House politics understandable for the participants, so it is through this perspective that the observer may understand them. It is by locating and "mapping" such groups and their intra- and inter-relationships that the observer may simplify the task of understanding what seem to be hopelessly confused political institutions and processes.[47]

Notes:

1. For a discussion of the limitations of traditional frameworks see Gabriel Almond's introductory chapter, "A Functional Approach to Comparative Politics," in Gabriel Almond and James S. Coleman, *The Politics of the Developing Areas* (Princeton: Princeton University Press, 1960), especially pp. 3–4.

2. A single example will clarify this point. The report of the Committee on Political Parties of the American Political Science Association, *Toward a More Responsible Two-Party System,* concentrates almost exclusively on the dysfunctions of United States parties and the functions which the authors feel they should perform (not actually do). A complete functional analysis in providing a more thorough understanding of the parties, would provide an appropriate basis for an evaluation of the net contribution of our parties to the political system and democracy.

3. See the systematic analysis of Robert K. Merton in *Social Theory and Social Structure* (Glencoe: The Free Press, 1957), pp. 71–82.

4. Merton, *op. cit.,* p. 51.

5. *Ibid.*

6. *Ibid.*

7. *Ibid.,* p. 69.

8. For more extensive discussions of functional analysis and some inherent problems see Merton, *op. cit.,* Chap. 1; Ernest Nagel, *Logic Without Metaphysics* (Glencoe: The Free Press, 1956), Chap. 10; Carl G. Hempel, "The Logic of Functional Analysis," in *Symposium on Sociological Theory,* ed. Llewellyn Gross (Evanston: Row, Peterson and Co., 1959); Marion J. Levy, Jr., *The Structure of Society* (Princeton: Princeton University Press, 1952).

9. Alan Fiellin, "The Behavior of a Legislative Group in the House of Representatives: A Case Study of New York Democrats" (Unpublished Ph.D. dissertation, Department of Government, New York University, 1960). The author wishes to express his special thanks to Professor Joseph Tanenhaus of New York University for his helpful supervision of this project.

10. Cf. David Truman, *The Congressional Party: A Case Study* (New York: John Wiley and Sons, 1959), Chap. 7.

11. A brief statement of the procedure followed and the results obtained will clarify this point. The members of the New York Democratic delegation in the 85th Congress were selected as the *initial* respondents for the interviews. It was thought likely that these respondents' frequent reference to Representatives outside the delegation would lead to the identification of an informal group consisting of both delegation and non-delegation members. This proved not to be the case. The seventeen members of the delegation constituted a rather uncohesive group; thirteen of these seventeen constituted the highly cohesive, relatively closed group of interactors. Each of these thirteen represented a district within New York City as did three of the others. Congressman Leo O'Brien of Albany was the only member of the delegation not from New York City.

12. The collection of data was made possible by a Congressional Fellowship for which the author wants to thank the American Political Science Association and the donors to the program.

13. See especially the following: Stephen K. Bailey and Howard D. Samuel, *Congress at Work* (New York: Henry Holt and Co., 1952); David Truman, *The Governmental Process* (New York: Knopf, 1951) and *The Congressional Party* (New York: John Wiley and Sons, 1959); Jerry Voorhis, *Confessions of a Congressman* (Garden City: Doubleday and Company, 1947).

The literature does contain at least two systematic studies of interpersonal relations in state legislatures. See Garland Routt, "Interpersonal Relationships and the Legislative Process," *Annals,* CXCV (January, 1938), pp. 129–36; Samuel Patterson, "Patterns of Interpersonal Relations in a State Legislative Group," POQ, XXIII (Spring, 1959), pp. 101–09.

14. For the complete analysis of the internal structure of the New York Democratic group see Fiellin, *op. cit.,* Chap. 3.

15. In the related fields of public administration and industrial management, the importance of informal groups as both facilitating and disturbing factors seems to be generally accepted. See Fritz J. Roethlisberger and William J. Dickson, *Management and the Worker* (Cambridge: Harvard University Press, 1939); Herbert A. Simon, *Administrative Behavior: A Study of Decision-Making Processes in Administrative Organization* (New York: Macmillan Co., 1947), pp. 147–49 and *passim;* Marshall E. and Gladys O. Dimock, *Public Administration* (New York: Rinehart and Co., 1953), pp. 104–06 and works cited therein. In the field of voting behavior see Bernard Berelson, Paul F. Lazarsfeld, and William N. McPhee, *Voting: A Study of Opinion Formation in a Presidential Campaign* (Chicago: University of Chicago Press, 1954), Chap. 6. For a thorough review of the literature in sociology and social-psychology as well as the report of an empirical study of opinion formation see Elihu Katz and Paul F. Lazarsfeld, *Personal Influence: The Part Played by People in the Flow of Mass Communications* (Glencoe: The Free Press, 1955).

16. The meaning of "unstructured" as used here is made more explicit in footnote 43, below.

17. *The Governmental Process,* p. 343, emphasis added. Truman goes on to point out that this informal structure will have important consequences for the access of interest groups.

18. Literature cited in footnote 15.

19. For the data and statistical verification of this point see Fiellin, *op. cit.,* Chap. 5. Truman's study of state delegations and congressional committees is also relevant. *The Congressional Party,* Chap. 7. Duncan MacRae, on the basis of the results of scale analysis, also infers that face-to-face relationships affect roll call vote decisions. "Roll call votes are taken in sequence, sometimes with a considerable interval of time between them. That social controls have ample time to operate accounts, in part, for the higher degree of consistency in scaling obtainable with roll calls than with questionnaire data. One result of these social controls may be that those individuals who change position on the continuum do so in groups on the basis of face-to-face association." "Some Underlying Variables in Legislative Roll Call Votes," *Public Opinion Quarterly,* XVIII, no. 2 (Summer, 1954), p. 194. On patterns of advice giving and taking in the U. S. Senate see Donald Matthews, *U. S. Senators and Their World* (Chapel Hill: University of North Carolina Press, 1960), pp. 251–54.

20. See David Truman, *The Governmental Process,* pp. 334–35; Roland Young, *The American Congress* (New York: Harper and Bros., 1958), pp. 78–79.

21. "Literally tons of information are available to Congress to keep it informed about what is happening in its own bailiwick and elsewhere in

the government. The trouble is that the data are not in a form that can be used easily. Members are supposed to keep up with the executive agencies by reading their annual reports. The latter are voluminous, and those who compile them tell Congress and the people to a considerable extent, only what they want known. But with the pressure of work already imposing a physical strain on many legislators, very few have time to read the reports." Estes Kefauver and Jack Levine, *A Twentieth-Century Congress* (New York: Duell, Sloan and Pearce, 1947), p. 203.

22. Reconstructed from interview responses.

23. For some groups of legislators, establishing "sameness" of party organization and "similarity" of constituencies and relevant interest groups would present some difficult problems of definition and require the use of precise indices. Refined measurement seemed unnecessary for this case study since all but one of the members of the delegation in the 85th Congress were from New York City. Though New York City congressional districts do vary in socio-economic composition, the variations are relatively minor. For occupational distributions within congressional districts see Duncan MacRae, Jr., *Dimensions of Congressional Voting* (Berkeley: University of California Press, 1958), Appendix B. All members of the group were, of course, within the jurisdiction of the same state party organization. The several county organizations involved, though independent and sometimes in conflict over local affairs, do frequently work together in city-wide affairs of concern to all and do seem to hold a common view of congressional politics. Certainly New York Democrats in the House tend strongly to identify themselves with the larger collective constituency, New York City.

24. Cf. Bailey and Samuel, *op. cit.* "In general, however, [Congressman Smith] was not inclined to compile a voting record that contrasted too sharply with the records of the other six members of the Mississippi delegation in the House," p. 131. "Often his decision followed hasty conferences with other members of the Mississippi delegation in the cloakroom outside of the Chamber," p. 132. On state delegation unity see also Bailey and Samuel, pp. 120–121; Voorhis, *op. cit.,* Chap. 7; Senator Tom Connally as told to Alfred Steinberg, *My Name is Tom Connally* (New York: Thomas Y. Crowell Co., 1954), p. 89.

25. It is also quite possible that this access to other committees is used to secure action on members' own bills. Thus, access to committees may be used to exert influence as well as secure information.

26. In the 86th Congress, 2nd Session, there were New York Democrats on all House committees with the following exceptions: Armed Forces, Government Operations, House Administration, Un-American Activities, and Veterans Affairs. U. S. Congress, *Congressional Directory,* 85th Congress, 2nd Session, 1958, pp. 241–47.

27. Evidence of this function can also be found in the literature. "The other members [of the Ohio Republican delegation], all of whom were veterans, had been helpful in showing him [Congressman Ayres] the ropes of Congressional procedure." Bailey and Samuel, *op. cit.,* p. 121. "Through our Young Turks meetings [an informal House group], through my committee meetings, through contacts on the floor and elsewhere I was learning about Congress and about congressmen as they actually are—not

as they are reported to be by the columnists or the humorists of the country." Voorhis, *op. cit.*, p. 31.

28. See discussion below and Donald Matthews, *op. cit.*, pp. 94–95.

29. For a complete discussion of this behavior and the reasons for it see Fiellin, *op. cit.*, pp. 24, 26 ff., 52 f., 147 ff., 163 ff.

30. On the role problems of legislators and politicians see Edward A. Shils, "The Legislator and His Environment," *University of Chicago Law Review,* XVIII (1950–1951), pp. 571–84; William C. Mitchell, "Occupational Role Strains: The American Elective Public Official," *Administrative Science Quarterly,* III (September, 1958), pp. 210–28.

31. See discussion below, pp. 100–1.

32. In other legislatures which are highly organized by parties or other agencies, communication through informal groups may be less important.

33. Eighty members of the House who had signed a manifesto were members. Information is from informal interviews and *Congressional Quarterly Weekly Report,* XV (February 22, 1957), pp. 224–25.

34. *Ibid.*, p. 225.

35. For information on the meetings of other legislative groups see Voorhis, *op. cit.*, pp. 30–31; Kefauver and Levine, *op. cit.*, pp. 89–90; Bailey and Samuel, *op. cit.*, pp. 108–09, 120–21, 125.

36. Paraphrased interview response.

37. Bailey and Samuel, *op. cit.*, p. 121.

38. Group leadership and its roles are discussed in Fiellin, *op. cit.*, pp. 58 ff.

39. Connally in his autobiography calls attention to the function of clannishness within the Texas delegation. "Although we Texans were a smaller House group than the members from New York, Pennsylvania, Illinois, or Ohio, as a rule the eighteen of us exerted a degree of influence far out of proportion to our numbers. For we generally voted together on a bill and this unity helped make up for the fact that we held no committee Chairmanships and that none of us was important except John Garner, then only fifth ranking man on the Ways and Means Committee." Connally, *op. cit.*, pp. 89–90.

40. *The Governmental Process,* p. 368.

41. Truman's point regarding interest groups' relations with legislators is pertinent to the above analysis. "A group [interest group] is handicapped if its only connections are with a maverick or a newcomer. It is not enough for the legislator to be a member, in some sense, of the interest group or even to be in a position of formal power. He must 'belong' within the legislature as well." *The Governmental Process,* p. 345. Influence in legislative negotiations depends upon one's ability to "tie in" to appropriate informal networks at some point.

42. Voorhis, *op. cit.*, p. 37.

43. This hypothesis asserts nothing about structured legislative situations. These terms, "structured" and "unstructured," will need to be more precisely defined. In the loose usage here, the distinction is being made between situations such as that of the British House of Commons, where much if not most of what transpires is determined by party and cabinet, and that of Congress, where no such all-important agencies exist. In the latter case, individuals are "forced" to be free, their behavior not having

been "pre-determined" to the same extent, and they must "improvise" mechanisms to perform functions which party and cabinet perform in the British example.

44. Using Merton's explanation of this concept, "it is assumed that there are certain *functions* which are indispensable in the sense that, unless they are performed, the society (or group or individual) [in this application it is the legislature] will not persist." Merton, *op. cit.*, p. 33.

45. This hypothesis has a theoretical basis in Talcott Parsons' formulations on the American political system. See his " 'Voting' and the Equilibrium of the American Political System," in *American Voting Behavior,* eds. Eugene Burdick and Arthur Brodbeck (Glencoe: The Free Press, 1959), pp. 89–90. Professor Parsons suggests that generalized support of leadership on the part of the electorate (a relationship in which *specific* policy commitments are absent) is necessary for "the political integration of a complex social system." The hypothesis stated above suggests that in the absence of *vertical* generalized support in the House (probably characteristic of the British House of Commons) one would expect *horizontal* generalized support (between groups and individuals) to develop. In other words, "logrolling" in which there is a specific and *explicit quid pro quo* will be relatively rare.

46. Katz and Lazarsfeld point out that in a variety of areas of social behavior, a simplified model of atomized individuals is inappropriate and misleading. *Op. cit.,* Introduction; Part I, chaps. 1–4. Many scholars are coming to realize that the same is true of Congress. In addition to the references cited throughout the paper, the works of Roland Young and Holbert Carroll contain references to the functions of informal relationships. Young writes, "In formulating policy Congress carries out its work through various types of units and alliances. Some of these units and alliances are recognized in the official rules; others are free-forming, as it were, operating within the legislative structure while not being a constituent part of the legal framework." *The American Congress* (New York: Harper and Bros., 1958), p. 47. Also see pp. 56, 157. Holbert N. Carroll, *The House of Representatives and Foreign Affairs* (Pittsburgh: The University of Pittsburgh Press, 1958), pp. 101, 237, 263.

47. Truman's warning should be kept in mind. "It is important not to assume that these interactions produce an integrated, hierarchical structure. They may, but the life of the legislative group as of others may as easily involve a loosely allied collection of cliques." . . . "Party government is a form of legislative group life, but it is not the only or the most common form in the United States." *The Governmental Process,* p. 346.

5 *The House Appropriations Committee as a Political System: The Problem of Integration**

by Richard F. Fenno, Jr.

Studies of Congress by political scientists have produced a time-tested consensus on the very considerable power and autonomy of Congressional committees. Because of these two related characteristics, it makes empirical and analytical sense to treat the Congressional committee as a discrete unit for analysis. This paper conceives of the committee as a political system (or, more accurately, as a political subsystem) faced with a number of basic problems which it must solve in order to achieve its goals and maintain itself. Generally speaking these functional problems pertain to the environmental and the internal relations of the committee. This study is concerned almost exclusively with the internal problems of the committee and particularly with the problem of self-integration.[1] It describes how one Congressional committee—The Committee on Appropriations of the House of Representa-

Reprinted from *American Political Science Review,* 56 (June, 1962), 310–324, by permission of the author and the publisher.

*The author wishes to acknowledge his indebtedness to the Committee on Political Behavior of the Social Science Research Council for the research grant which made possible this study, and the larger study of legislative behavior in the area of appropriations of which it is a part. This is a revised version of a paper read at the Annual Meeting of the American Political Science Association at St. Louis, September, 1961.

tives—has dealt with this problem in the period 1947–1961. Its purpose is to add to our understanding of appropriations politics in Congress and to suggest the usefulness of this type of analysis for studying the activities of any Congressional committee.

The necessity for integration in any social system arises from the differentiation among its various elements. Most importantly there is a differentiation among subgroups and among individual positions, together with the roles that flow therefrom.[2] A committee faces the problem, how shall these diverse elements be made to mesh together or function in support of one another? No political system (or subsystem) is perfectly integrated; yet no political system can survive without some minimum degree of integration among its differentiated parts. Committee integration is defined as the degree to which there is a working together or a meshing together or mutual support among its roles and subgroups. Conversely, it is also defined as the degree to which a committee is able to minimize conflict among its roles and its subgroups, by heading off or resolving the conflicts that arise.[3] A concomitant of integration is the existence of a fairly consistent set of norms, widely agreed upon and widely followed by the members. Another concomitant of integration is the existence of control mechanisms (*i.e.,* socialization and sanctioning mechanisms) capable of maintaining reasonable conformity to norms. In other words, the more highly integrated a committee, the smaller will be the gap between expected and actual behavior.

This study is concerned with integration both as a structural characteristic of, and as a functional problem for, the Appropriations Committee. First, certain basic characteristics of the Committee need description, to help explain the integration of its parts. Second comes a partial description of the degree to which and the ways in which the Committee achieves integration. No attempt is made to state this in quantitative terms, but the object is to examine the meshing together or the minimization of conflict among certain subgroups and among certain key roles. Also, important control mechanisms are described. The study concludes with some comments on the consequences of Committee integration for appropriations politics and on the usefulness of further Congressional committee analysis in terms of functional problems such as this one.

I

Five important characteristics of the Appropriations Committee which help explain Committee integration are (1) the existence of a well-articulated and deeply rooted consensus on Committee goals or tasks; (2) the nature of the Committee's subject matter; (3) the legislative orientation of its members; (4) the attractiveness of the Committee for its members; and (5) the stability of Committee membership.

Consensus. The Appropriations Committee sees its tasks as taking form within the broad guidelines set by its parent body, the House of Representatives. For it is the primary condition of the Committee's existence that it was created by the House for the purpose of assisting the House in the performance of House legislative tasks dealing with appropriations. Committee members agree that their fundamental duty is to serve the House in the manner and with the substantive results that the House prescribes. Given, however, the imprecision of House expectations and the permissiveness of House surveillance, the Committee must elaborate for itself a definition of tasks plus a supporting set of perceptions (of itself and of others) explicit enough to furnish day-to-day guidance.

The Committee's view begins with the preeminence of the House—often mistakenly attributed to the Constitution ("all bills for raising revenue," Art. I, sec. 7) but nevertheless firmly sanctioned by custom—in appropriations affairs.

It moves easily to the conviction that, as the efficient part of the House in this matter, the Constitution has endowed it with special obligations and special prerogatives. It ends in the view that the Committee on Appropriations, far from being merely one among many units in a complicated legislative-executive system, is *the* most important, most responsible unit in the whole appropriations process.[4] Hand in hand with the consensus on their primacy goes a consensus that all of their House-prescribed tasks can be fulfilled by superimposing upon them one, single, paramount task—*to guard the Federal Treasury*. Committee members state their goals in the essentially negative terms of guardianship—screening requests for money, checking against ill-advised expenditures, and protecting the taxpayer's dollar. In the language of the Committee's official history, the job of each member is, "constantly and courageously to protect the Federal Treasury against thousands of appeals and imperative demands for unnecessary, unwise, and excessive expenditures."[5]

To buttress its self-image as guardian of public funds the Committee elaborates a set of perceptions about other participants in the appropriations process to which most members hold most of the time. Each executive official, for example, is seen to be interested in the expansion of his own particular program. Each one asks, therefore, for more money than he really needs, in view of the total picture, to run an adequate program. This and other Committee perceptions—of the Budget Bureau, of the Senate, and of their fellow Representatives—help to shape and support the Committee members in their belief that most budget estimates can, should and must be reduced and that, since no one else can be relied upon, the House Committee must do the job. To the consensus on the main task of protecting the Treasury is added, therefore, a consensus on the instrumental task of *cutting whatever budget estimates are submitted.*

As an immediate goal, Committee members agree that they must strike a highly critical, aggressive posture toward budget requests, and that they should, on principle, reduce them. In the words of the Committee's veterans: "There has never been a budget submitted to the Congress that couldn't be cut." "There isn't a budget that can't be cut 10 per cent immediately." "I've been on the Committee for 17 years. No subcommittee of which I have been a member has ever reported out a bill without a cut in the budget. I'm proud of that record." The aim of budget-cutting is strongly internalized for the Committee member. "It's a tradition in the Appropriations Committee to cut." "You're grounded in it. . . . It's ingrained in you from the time you get on the Committee." For the purposes of a larger study, the appropriations case histories of 37 executive bureaus have been examined for a 12-year period, 1947–1959.[6] Of 443 separate bureau estimates, the Committee reduced 77.2 per cent (342) of them.

It is a mark of the intensity and self-consciousness of the Committee consensus on budget-cutting that it is couched in a distinctive vocabulary. The workaday lingo of the Committee member is replete with negative verbs, undesirable objects of attention, and effective instruments of action. Agency budgets are said to be filled with "fat," "padding," "grease," "pork," "oleaginous substance," "water," "oil," "cushions," "avoirdupois," "waste tissue," and "soft spots." The action verbs most commonly used are "cut," "carve," "slice," "prune," "whittle," "squeeze," "wring," "trim," "lop off," "chop," "slash," "pare," "shave," "fry," and "whack." The tools of the trade are appropriately referred to as "knife," "blade," "meat axe," "scalpel," "meat cleaver," "hatchet," "shears," "wringer," and "fine-tooth comb." Members are hailed by their fellows as being "pretty sharp with the knife." Agencies may "have the meat axe thrown at them." Executives are urged to put their agencies "on a fat boy's diet." Budgets are praised when they are "cut to the bone." And members agree that "You can always get a little more fat out of a piece of pork if you fry it a little longer and a little harder."

To the major task of protecting the Treasury and the instrumental task of cutting budget estimates, each Committee member adds, usually by way of exception, a third task—*serving the constituency to which he owes his election.* This creates no problem for him when, as is sometimes the case, he can serve his district best by cutting the budget requests of a federal agency whose program is in conflict with the demands of his constituency.[6a] Normally, however, members find that their most common role-conflict is between a Committee-oriented budget-reducing role and a constituency-oriented budget-increasing role. Committee ideology resolves the conflict by assigning top, long-run priority to the budget-cutting task and making of the constituency service a permissible, short-run exception. No member is expected to commit electoral suicide; but no member is expected to allow his district's desire for federal funds to dominate his Committee behavior.

Subject matter. Appropriations Committee integration is facilitated by the subject matter with which the group deals. The Committee makes decisions on the same controversial issues as do the committees handling substantive legislation. But a money decision—however vitally it affects national policy—is, or at least seems to be, less directly a policy decision. Since they deal immediately with dollars and cents, it is easy for the members to hold to the idea that they are not dealing with programmatic questions, that theirs is a "business" rather than a "policy" committee. The subject matter, furthermore, keeps Committee members relatively free agents, which promotes intra-Committee maneuvering and, hence, conflict avoidance. Members do not commit themselves to their constituents in terms of precise money amounts, and no dollar sum is sacred—it can always be adjusted without conceding that a principle has been breached. By contrast, members of committees dealing directly with controversial issues are often pressured into taking concrete stands on these issues; consequently, they may come to their committee work with fixed and hardened attitudes. This leads to unavoidable, head-on intra-committee conflict and renders integrative mechanisms relatively ineffective.

The fact of an annual appropriations process means the Committee members repeat the same operations with respect to the same subject matters year after year—and frequently more than once in a given year. Substantive and procedural repetition promotes familiarity with key problems and provides ample opportunity to test and confirm the most satisfactory methods of dealing with them. And the absolute necessity that appropriations bills do ultimately pass gives urgency to the search for such methods. Furthermore, the House rule that no member of the Committee can serve on another standing committee is a deterrent against a fragmentation of Committee member activity which could be a source of difficulty in holding the group together. If a committee has developed (as this one has) a number of norms designed to foster integration, repeated and concentrated exposure to them increases the likelihood that they will be understood, accepted and followed.

Legislative orientation. The recruitment of members for the Appropriations Committee produces a group of individuals with an orientation especially conducive to Committee integration. Those who make the selection pay special attention to the characteristics which Masters has described as those of the "responsible legislator"—approval of and conformity to the norms of the legislative process and of the House of Representatives.[7]

Key selectors speak of wanting, for the Appropriations Committee, "the kind of man you can deal with" or "a fellow who is well-balanced and won't go off half-cocked on things." A Northern liberal Democrat felt that he had been chosen over eight competitors because, "I had made a lot of friends and was known as a nice guy"—especially, he noted, among Southern Congressmen. Another Democrat explained, "I got the blessing of the Speaker and the leadership. It's personal friendships. I had done a lot of things for them in the past, and when I went to them and asked them, they gave it to me." A Republican chosen for the Committee in his first term recalled,

> The Chairman [Rep. Taber] I guess did some checking around in my area. After all, I was new and he didn't know me. People told me that they were called to see if I was—well, unstable or apt to go off on tangents . . . to see whether or not I had any preconceived notions about things and would not be flexible—whether I would oppose things even though it was obvious.

A key criterion in each of the cases mentioned was a demonstrable record of, or an assumed predisposition toward, legislative give-and-take.

The 106 Appropriations Committee members serving between 1947 and 1961 spent an average of 3.6 years on other House committees before coming to the Committee. Only 17 of the 106 were selected as first term Congressmen. A House apprenticeship (which Appropriations maintains more successfully than all committees save Ways and Means and Rules[8]) provides the time in which legislative reputations can be established by the member and an assessment of that reputation in terms of Appropriations Committee requirements can be made. Moreover, the mere fact that a member survives for a couple of terms is some indication of an electoral situation conducive to his "responsible" legislative behavior. The optimum bet for the Committee is a member from a sufficiently safe district to permit him freedom of maneuver inside the House without fear of reprisal at the polls.[9] The degree of responsiveness to House norms which the Committee selectors value may be the product of a safe district as well as an individual temperament.

Attractiveness. A fourth factor is the extraordinarily high degree of attractiveness which the Committee holds for its members—as measured by the low rate of departure from it. Committee members do not leave it for service on other committees. To the contrary, they are attracted to it from nearly every other committee.[10] Of the 106 members in the 1947–1961 period, only two men left the Committee voluntarily; and neither of them initiated the move.[11] Committee attractiveness is a measure of its capacity to satisfy individual member needs—for power, prestige, recognition, respect, self-esteem, friendship, etc. Such satisfaction in turn increases the likelihood that members will behave in such a way as to hold the group together.

The most frequently mentioned source of Committee attractiveness is its power—based on its control of financial resources. "Where the money is, that's where the power is," sums up the feeling of the members. They prize their ability to reward or punish so many other participants in the political process—executive officials, fellow Congressmen, constituents and other clientele groups. In the eyes of its own members, the Committee is either the most powerful in the House or it is on a par with Ways and Means or, less frequently, on a par with Ways and Means and Rules. The second important ingredient in member satisfaction is the government-wide scope of Committee activity. The ordinary Congressman may feel that he has too little knowledge of and too little control over his environment. Membership on this Committee compensates for this feeling of helplessness by the wider contacts, the greater amount of information, and the sense of being "in the middle of things" which are consequent, if not to subcommittee activity, at least to the full Committee's overview of the federal government.

Thirdly, Committee attractiveness is heightened by the group's recognizable and distinctive political style—one that is, moreover, highly valued in American political culture. The style is that of *hard work;* and the Committee's self-image is that of "the hardest working Committee in Congress." His willingness to work is the Committee member's badge of identification, and it is proudly worn. It colors his perceptions of others and their perceptions of him.[11a] It is a cherished axiom of all members that, "This Committee is no place for a man who doesn't work. They have to be hard working. It's a way of life. It isn't just a job; it's a way of life."

The mere existence of some identifiable and valued style or "way of life" is a cohesive force for a group. But the particular style of hard work is one which increases group morale and group identification twice over. Hard work means a long, dull, and tedious application to detail, via the technique of "dig, dig, dig, day after day behind closed doors"—

in an estimated 460 subcommittee and full committee meetings a year. And virtually all of these meetings are in executive session. By adopting the style of hard work the Committee discourages highly individualized forms of legislative behavior, which could be disruptive within the Committee. It rewards its members with power, but it is power based rather on work inside the Committee than on the political glamour of activities carried on in the limelight of the mass media. Prolonged daily work together encourages sentiments of mutual regard, sympathy and solidarity. This *esprit* is, in turn, functional for integration on the Committee. A Republican leader summed up,

> I think it's more closely knit than any other committee. Yet it's the biggest committee, and you'd think it would be the reverse. I know on my subcommittee, you sit together day after day. You get better acquainted. You have sympathy when other fellows go off to play golf. There's a lot of *esprit de corps* in the Committee.

The strong attraction which members have for the Committee increases the influence which the Committee and its norms exercise on all of them. It increases the susceptibility of the newcomer to Committee socialization and of the veteran to Committee sanctions applicable against deviant behavior.[12]

Membership stability. Members of the Appropriations Committee are strongly attracted to it; they also have, which bears out their selection as "responsible legislators," a strong attraction for a career in the House of Representatives. The 50 members on the Committee in 1961 had served an average of 13.1 years in the House. These twin attractions produce a noteworthy stability of Committee membership. In the period from the 80th to the 87th Congress, 35.7 per cent of the Committee's membership remained constant. That is to say, 15 of the 42 members on the Committee in March, 1947, were still on the Committee in March, 1961.[13] The 50 members of the Committee in 1961 averaged 9.3 years of prior service on that Committee. In no single year during the last fourteen has the Committee had to absorb an influx of new members totalling more than one-quarter of its membership. At all times, in other words, at least three-fourths of the members have had previous Committee experience. This extraordinary stability of personnel extends into the staff as well. As of June 1961, its

15 professionals had served an average of 10.7 years with the Committee.[14]

The opportunity exists, therefore, for the development of a stable leadership group, a set of traditional norms for the regulation of internal Committee behavior, and informal techniques of personal accommodation. Time is provided in which new members can learn and internalize Committee norms before they attain high seniority rankings. The Committee does not suffer from the potentially disruptive consequences of rapid changeovers in its leadership group, nor of sudden impositions of new sets of norms governing internal Committee behavior.

II

If one considers the main activity of a political system to be decision-making, the acid test of its internal integration is its capacity to make collective decisions without flying apart in the process. Analysis of Committee integration should focus directly, therefore, upon its subgroups and the roles of its members. Two kinds of subgroups are of central importance—subcommittees and majority or minority party groups. The roles which are most relevant derive from: (1) positions which each member holds by virtue of his subgroup attachments, *e.g.,* as subcommittee member, majority (or minority) party member; (2) positions which relate to full Committee membership, *e.g.,* Committee member, and the seniority rankings of veteran, man of moderate experience, and newcomer;[15] (3) positions which relate to both subgroup and full Committee membership, *e.g.,* Chairman of the Committee, ranking minority member of the Committee, subcommittee chairman, ranking subcommittee member. Clusters of norms state the expectations about the subgroup and role behavior. The description which follows treats the ways in which these norms and their associated behaviors mesh and clash. It treats, also, the internal control mechanisms by which behavior is brought into reasonable conformity with expectations.

Subgroup integration. The day-to-day work of the Committee is carried on in its subcommittees each of which is given jurisdiction over a number of related governmental units. The number of subcommittees is determined by the

Committee Chairman, and has varied recently from a low of 9 in 1949 to a high of 15 in 1959. The present total of 14 reflects, as always, a set of strategic and personal judgments by the Chairman balanced against the limitations placed on him by Committee tradition and member wishes. The Chairman also determines subcommittee jurisdiction, appoints subcommittee chairmen and selects the majority party members of each group. The ranking minority member of the Committee exercises similar control over subcommittee assignments on his side of the aisle.

Each subcommittee holds hearings on the budget estimates of the agencies assigned to it, meets in executive session to decide what figures and what language to recommend to the full Committee (to "mark up" the bill), defends its recommendations before the full Committee, writes the Committee's report to the House, dominates the debate on the floor, and bargains for the House in conference committee. Within its jurisdiction, each subcommittee functions independently of the others and guards its autonomy jealously. The Chairman and ranking minority member of the full Committee have, as we shall see, certain opportunities to oversee and dip into the operations of all subcommittees. But their intervention is expected to be minimal. Moreover, they themselves operate importantly within the subcommittee framework by sitting as chairman or ranking minority member of the subcommittee in which they are most interested. Each subcommittee, under the guidance of its chairman, transacts its business in considerable isolation from every other one. One subcommittee chairman exclaimed,

> Why, you'd be branded an impostor if you went into one of those other subcommittee meetings. The only time I go is by appointment, by arrangement with the chairman at a special time. I'm as much a stranger in another subcommittee as I would be in the legislative Committee on Post Office and Civil Service. Each one does its work apart from all others.

All members of all subcommittees are expected to behave in similar fashion in the role of subcommittee member. Three main norms define this role; to the extent that they are observed, they promote harmony and reduce conflict among subcommittees.[16] Subcommittee autonomy gives to the House norm of *specialization* an intensified application on the Appropriations Committee. Each member is expected to play the role of specialist in the activities of one subcommittee. He will sit on from one to four subcommittees, but normally will specialize in the work, or a portion of the work, of only one. Except for the Chairman, ranking minority member and their confidants, a Committee member's time, energy, contacts and experience are devoted to his subcommittees. Specialization is, therefore, among the earliest and most compelling of the Committee norms to which a newcomer is exposed. Within the Committee, respect, deference and power are earned through subcommittee activity and hence to a degree, through specialization. Specialization is valued further because it is well suited to the task of guarding the Treasury. Only by specializing, Committee members believe, can they unearth the volume of factual information necessary for the intelligent screening of budget requests. Since "the facts" are acquired only through industry an effective specialist will, perforce, adopt and promote the Committee's style of hard work.

Committee-wide acceptance of specialization is an integrative force in decision-making because it helps support a second norm—*reciprocity*. The stage at which a subcommittee makes its recommendations is a potential point of internal friction. Conflict among subcommittees (or between one subcommittee and the rest of the Committee) is minimized by the deference traditionally accorded to the recommendation of the subcommittee which has specialized in the area, has worked hard, and has "the facts." "It's a matter of 'You respect my work and I'll respect yours.'" "It's frowned upon if you offer an amendment in the full Committee if you aren't on the subcommittee. It's considered presumptuous to pose as an expert if you aren't on the subcommittee." Though records of full Committee decisions are not available, members agree that subcommittee recommendations are "very rarely changed," "almost always approved," "changed one time in fifty," "very seldom changed," etc.

No subcommittee is likely to keep the deference of the full Committee for long unless its recommendations have widespread support among its own members. To this end, a third norm—*subcommittee unity*—is expected to be observed by subcommittee members. Unity means a willingness to support (or not to oppose) the recommendations of one's own subcommittee. Reciprocity and unity are closely dependent upon one another. Reciprocity is difficult to maintain when subcommittees themselves are badly divided; and unity has little appeal unless reciprocity will subsequently be observed. The norm of reciprocity functions to minimize inter-subcommittee conflict. The norm of unity functions to minimize intra-subcommittee conflict. Both are deemed essential to subcommittee influence.

One payoff for the original selection of "responsible legislators" is their special willingness to compromise in pursuit of subcommittee unity. The impulse to this end is registered most strongly at the time when the sub-committee meets in executive session to mark up the bill. Two ranking minority members explained this aspect of markup procedure in their subcommittees:

> If there's agreement, we go right along. If there's a lot of controversy we put the item aside and go on. Then, after a day or two, we may have a list of ten controversial items. We give and take and pound them down till we get agreement.

> We have a unanimous agreement on everything. If a fellow enters an objection and we can't talk him out of it—and sometimes we can get him to go along—that's it. We put it in there.

Once the bargain is struck, the subcommittee is expected to "stick together."

It is, of course, easier to achieve unity among the five, seven, or nine members of a subcommittee than among the fifty members of the full Committee. But members are expected wherever possible to observe the norm of unity in the full Committee as well. That is, they should not only defer to the recommendations of the subcommittee involved, but they should support (or not oppose) that recommendation when it reaches the floor in the form of a Committee decision. On the floor, Committee members believe, their power and prestige depend largely on the degree to which the norms of reciprocity and unity continue to be observed. Members warn each other that if they go to the floor in disarray they will be "rolled," "jumped," or "run over" by the membership. It is a cardinal maxim among Committee members that "You can't turn an appropriations bill loose on the floor." Two senior subcommittee chairmen explain,

> We iron out our differences in Committee. We argue it out and usually have a meeting of the minds, a composite view of the Committee. . . . If we went on the floor in wide disagreement, they would say, "If you can't agree after listening to the testimony and discussing it, how can we understand it? We'll just vote on the basis of who we like the best."

> I tell them (the full Committee) we should have a united front. If there are any objections or changes, we ought to hear it now, and not wash our dirty linen out on the floor. If we don't have a bill that we can all agree on and support, we ought not to report it out. To do that is like throwing a piece of meat to a bunch of hungry animals.

One of the most functional Committee practices supporting the norm of unity is the tradition against minority reports in the subcommittee and in the full Committee. It is symptomatic of Committee integration that custom should proscribe the use of the most formal and irrevocable symbol of congressional committee disunity—the minority report. A few have been written—but only 9 out of a possible 141 during the 11 years, 1947–1957. That is to say, 95 per cent of all original appropriations bills in this period were reported out without dissent. The technique of "reserving" is the Committee member's equivalent for the registering of dissent. In subcommittee or Committee, when a member reserves, he goes on record informally by informing his colleagues that he reserves the right to disagree on a specified item later on in the proceedings. He may seek a change or support a change in that particular item in full Committee or on the floor. But he does not publicize his dissent. The subcommittee or the full Committee can then make an unopposed recommendation. The individual retains some freedom of maneuver without firm commitment. Often a member reserves on an appropriations item but takes no further action. A member explained how the procedure operates in subcommittee,

> If there's something I feel too strongly about, and just can't go along, I'll say, "Mr. Chairman, we can have a unanimous report, but I reserve the right to bring this up in full Committee. I feel duty bound to make a play for it and see if I can't sell it to the other members." But if I don't say anything, or don't reserve this right, and then I bring it up in full Committee,

> they'll say, "Who are you trying to embarrass? You're a member of the team, aren't you? That's not the way to get along."

Disagreement cannot, of course, be eliminated from the Committee. But the Committee has accepted a method for ventilating it which produces a minimum of internal disruption. And members believe that the greater their internal unity, the greater the likelihood that their recommendations will pass the House.

The degree to which the role of the subcommittee member can be so played and subcommittee conflict thereby minimized depends upon the minimization of conflict between the majority and minority party subgroups. Nothing would be more disruptive to the Committee's work than bitter and extended partisan controversy. It is, therefore, important to Appropriations Committee integration that a fourth norm—*minimal partisanship*—should be observed by members of both party contingents. Nearly every respondent emphasized, with approval, that "very little" or "not much" partisanship prevailed on the Committee. One subcommittee chairman stated flatly, "My job is to keep down partisanship." A ranking minority member said, "You might think that we Republicans would defend the Administration and the budget, but we don't." Majority and minority party ratios are constant and do not change (*i.e.,* in 1958) to reflect changes in the strength of the controlling party. The Committee operates with a completely non-partisan professional staff, which does not change in tune with shifts in party control. Requests for studies by the Committee's investigating staff must be made by the Chairman and ranking minority member of the full Committee and by the Chairman and ranking minority member of the subcommittee involved. Subcommittees can produce recommendations without dissent and the full Committee can adopt reports without dissent precisely because party conflict is (during the period 1947–1961) the exception rather than the rule.

The Committee is in no sense immune from the temperature of party conflict, but it does have a relatively high specific heat. Intense party strife or a strongly taken presidential position will get reflected in subcommittee and in Committee recommendations. Sharp divisions in party policy were carried, with disruptive impact, into some areas of Committee activity during the 80th Congress and subsequently, by way of reaction, into the 81st Congress.[17] During the Eisenhower years, extraordinary presidential pleas, especially concerning foreign aid, were given special heed by the Republican members of the Committee.[18] Partisanship is normally generated from the environment and not from within the Committee's party groups. Partisanship is, therefore, likely to be least evident in subcommittee activity, stronger in the full Committee, and most potent at the floor stage. Studies which have focused on roll-call analysis have stressed the influence of party in legislative decision-making.[19] In the appropriations process, at any rate, the floor stage probably represents party influence at its maximum. Our examination, by interview, of decision-making at the subcommittee and full Committee level would stress the influence of Committee-oriented norms—the strength of which tends to vary inversely with that of party bonds. In the secrecy and intimacy of the subcommittee and full Committee hearing rooms, the member finds it easy to compromise on questions of more or less, to take money from one program and give it to another and, in general, to avoid yes-or-no type party stands. These decisions, taken in response to the integrative norms of the Committee are the most important ones in the entire appropriations process.

Role integration. The roles of subcommittee member and party member are common to all.

Other more specific decision-making positions are allocated among the members. Different positions produce different roles, and in an integrated system, these too must fit together. Integration, in other words, must be achieved through the complementarity or reciprocity of roles as well as through a similarity of roles. This may mean a pattern in which expectations are so different that there is very little contact between individuals; or it may mean a pattern in which contacts require the working out of an involved system of exchange of obligations and rewards.[20] In either case, the desired result is the minimization of conflict among prominent Committee roles. Two crucial instances of role reciprocity on the Committee involve the seniority positions of old-timer and newcomer and the leadership positions of Chairman and ranking minority member, on both the full Committee and on each subcommittee.

The differentiation between senior and junior members is the broadest definition of who shall and who shall not actively participate in Committee decisions. Of a junior member, it will be said, "Oh, he doesn't count—what I mean is, he hasn't been on the Committee long enough." He is not expected to and ordinarily does not have much influence. His role is that of apprentice. He is expected to learn the business and the norms of the Committee by applying himself to its work. He is expected to acquiesce in an arrangement which gives most influence (except in affairs involving him locally) to the veterans of the group. Newcomers will be advised to "follow the chairman until you get your bearings. For the first two years, follow the chairman. He knows." "Work hard, keep quiet and attend the Committee sessions. We don't want to listen to some new person coming in here." And newcomers perceive their role in identical terms: "You have to sit in the back seat and edge up little by little." "You just go to subcommittee meetings and assimilate the routine. The new members are made to feel welcome, but you have a lot of rope-learning to do before you carry much weight."

At every stage of Committee work, this differentiation prevails. There is remarkable agreement on the radically different sets of expectations involved. During the hearings, the view of the elders is that, "Newcomers . . . don't know what the score is and they don't have enough information to ask intelligent questions." A newcomer described his behavior in typically similar terms: "I attended all the hearings and studied and collected information that I can use next year. I'm just marking time now." During the crucial subcommittee markup, the newcomer will have little opportunity to speak —save in locally important matters. A subcommittee chairman stated the norm from his viewpoint this way: "When we get a compromise, nobody's going to break that up. If someone tries, we sit on him fast. We don't want young people who throw bricks or slow things down." And a newcomer reciprocated, describing his markup conduct: "I'm not provocative. I'm in there for information. They're the experts in the field. I go along." In full Committee, on the floor, and in conference committee, the Committee's senior members take the lead and the junior members are expected to follow. The apprentice role is common to all new members of the House. But it is wrong to assume that each Committee will give it the same emphasis. Some pay it scant heed.[21] The Appropriations Committee makes it a cornerstone of its internal structure.

Among the Committee's veterans, the key roles are those of Committee Chairman and ranking minority member, and their counterparts in every subcommittee. It is a measure of Committee integration and the low degree of partisanship that considerable reciprocity obtains between these roles. Their partisan status nevertheless sets limits to the degree of possible integration. The Chairman is given certain authority which he and only he can exercise. But save in times of extreme party controversy, the expectation is that consultation and cooperation between the chairman-ranking minority member shall lubricate the Committee's entire work. For example, by Committee tradition, its Chairman and ranking minority member are both *ex officio* voting members of each subcommittee and of every conference committee. The two of them thus have joint access at every stage of the internal process. A subcommittee chairman, too, is expected to discuss matters of scheduling and agenda with his opposite minority number. He is expected to work with him during the markup session and to give him (and, normally, only him) an opportunity to read and comment on the subcommittee report.[22] A ranking minority member described his subcommittee markup procedure approvingly:

> Frequently the chairman has a figure which he states. Sometimes he will have no figure, and he'll turn to me and say, "——, what do you think?" Maybe I'll have a figure. It's very flexible. Everyone has a chance to say what he thinks, and we'll move it around. Sometimes it takes a long time. . . . He's a rabid partisan on the floor, but he is a very fair man in the subcommittee.

Where influence is shared, an important exchange of rewards occurs. The chairman gains support for his leadership and the ranking minority member gains intra-Committee power. The Committee as a whole insures against the possibility of drastic change in its internal structure by giving to its key minority members a stake in its operation. Chairmen and ranking minority members will, in the course of time, exchange positions; and it is expected that such a switch will produce no form of retribution nor any drastic change in the functioning of the Committee. Reciprocity of roles, in this case, promotes continued integration. A ranking minority member testified to one successful arrangement when he took the floor in the 83d Congress to say:

> The gentleman and I have been see-sawing back and forth on this committee for some time. He was chairman in the 80th Congress. I had the privilege of serving as chairman in the 81st and 82nd Congresses. Now he is back in the saddle. I can say that he has never failed to give me his utmost cooperation, and I have tried to give him the same cooperation during his service as chairman of this Committee. We seldom disagree, but we have found out that we can disagree without being disagreeable. Consequently, we have unusual harmony on this committee.[23]

Reciprocity between chairmen and ranking minority members on the Appropriations Committee is to some incalculable degree a function of the stability of membership which allows a pair of particular individuals to work out the kind of personal accommodation described above. The close working relationship of Clarence Cannon and John Taber, whose service on the Committee totals 68 years and who have been changing places as Chairman and ranking minority member for 19 years, highlights and sustains a pattern of majority-minority reciprocity throughout the group.

Internal control mechanisms. The expectations which apply to subcommittee, to party, to veterans and to newcomers, to chairmen and to ranking minority members prescribe highly integrative behaviors. We have concentrated on these expectations, and have both illustrated and assumed the close correlation between expected and actual behavior. This does not mean that all the norms of the Committee have been canvassed. Nor does it mean that deviation from the integrative norms does not occur. It does. From what can be gathered, however, from piecing together a study of the public record on appropriations from 1947 to 1961 with interview materials, the Committee has been markedly successful in maintaining a stable internal structure over time. As might be expected, therefore, changes and threats of change have been generated more from the environment—when outsiders consider the Committee as unresponsive—than from inside the subsystem itself. One source of internal stability, and an added reason for assuming a correlation between expected and actual behavior, is the existence of what appear to be reasonably effective internal control mechanisms. Two of these are the socialization processes applied to newcomers and the sanctioning mechanisms applicable to all Committee members.

Socialization is in part a training in perception. Before members of a group can be expected to behave in accordance with its norms, they must learn to see and interpret the world around them with reasonable similarity. The socialization of the Committee newcomer during his term or two of apprenticeship serves to bring his perceptions and his attitudes sufficiently into line with those of the other members to serve as a basis for Committee integration. The Committee, as we have seen, is chosen from Congressmen whose political flexibility connotes an aptitude for learning new lessons of power. Furthermore, the high degree of satisfaction of its members with the group increases their susceptibility to its processes of learning and training.

For example, one half of the Committee's Democrats are Northerners and Westerners from urban constituencies, whose voting records are just as "liberal" on behalf of domestic social welfare programs as non-Committee Democrats from like constituencies. They come to the Committee favorably disposed toward the high level of federal spending necessary to support such programs, and with no sense of urgency about the Committee's tasks of guarding the Treasury or reducing budget estimates. Given the criteria governing their selection, however, they come without rigid preconceptions and with a built-in responsiveness to the socialization processes of any legislative group of which they are members. It is crucial to Committee integration that they learn to temper their potentially disruptive welfare-state ideology with a conservative's concern for saving money. They must change their perceptions and attitudes sufficiently to view the Committee's tasks in nearly the same terms as their more conservative Southern Democratic and Republican colleagues. What their elders perceive as reality (*i.e.,* the disposition of executives to ask for more money than is necessary) they, too, must see as reality. A subcommittee chairman explained:

> When you have sat on the Committee, you see that these bureaus are always asking for more money—always up, never

> down. They want to build up their organization. You reach the point—I have—where it sickens you, where you rebel against it. Year after year, they want more money. They say, "Only $50,000 this year"; but you know the pattern. Next year they'll be back for $100,000, then $200,000. The younger members haven't been on the Committee long enough, haven't had the experience to know this.

The younger men, in this case the younger liberals, do learn from their Committee experience. Within one or two terms, they are differentiating between themselves and the "wildeyed spenders" or the "free spenders" in the House. "Some of these guys would spend you through the roof," exclaimed one liberal of moderate seniority. Repeated exposure to Committee work and to fellow members has altered their perceptions and their attitudes in money matters. Half a dozen Northern Democrats of low or moderate seniority agreed with one of their number who said: "Yes, it's true. I can see it myself. I suppose I came here a flaming liberal; but as the years go by I get more conservative. You just hate like hell to spend all this money. . . . You come to the point where you say, 'By God, this is enough jobs.'" These men will remain more inclined toward spending than their Committee colleagues, but their perceptions and hence their attitudes have been brought close enough to the others to support a consensus on tasks. They are responsive to appeals on budget-cutting grounds that would not have registered earlier and which remain meaningless to liberals outside the Committee. In cases, therefore, where Committee selection does not and cannot initially produce individuals with a predisposition toward protecting the Treasury, the same result is achieved by socialization.

Socialization is a training in behavior as well as in perception. For the newcomer, conformity to norms in specific situations is insured through the appropriate application, by the Committee veterans, of rewards and punishments. For the Committee member who serves his apprenticeship creditably, the passage of time holds the promise that he will inherit a position of influence. He may, as an incentive, be given some small reward early in his Committee career. One man, in his second year, had been assigned the task of specializing in one particular program. However narrow the scope of his specialization, it had placed him on the road to influence within the Committee. He explained with evident pleasure:

> The first year, you let things go by. You can't participate. But you learn by watching the others operate. The next year, you know what you're interested in and when to step in. . . . For instance, I've become an expert on the —— program. The chairman said to me, "This is something you ought to get interested in." I did; and now I'm the expert on the Committee. Whatever I say on that, the other members listen to me and do what I want.

At some later date, provided he continues to observe Committee norms, he will be granted additional influence, perhaps through a prominent floor role. A model Committee man of moderate seniority who had just attained to this stage of accomplishment, and who had suffered through several political campaigns back home fending off charges that he was a do-nothing Congressman, spoke about the rewards he was beginning to reap.

> When you perform well on the floor when you bring out a bill, and Members know that you know the bill, you develop prestige with other Members of Congress. They come over and ask you what you think, because they know you've studied it. You begin to get a reputation beyond your subcommittee. And you get inner satisfaction, too. You don't feel that you're down here doing nothing.

The first taste of influence which comes to men on this Committee is compensation for the frustrations of apprenticeship. Committee integration in general, and the meshing of roles between elders and newcomers in particular, rests on the fact that conformity to role expectations over time does guarantee to the young positive rewards—the very kind of rewards of power, prestige, and personal satisfaction which led most of them to seek Committee membership in the first place.

The important function of apprenticeship is that it provides the necessary time during which socialization can go forward. And teaching proceeds with the aid of punishments as well as rewards. Should a new member inadvertently or deliberately run afoul of Committee norms during his apprenticeship, he will find himself confronted with negative sanctions ranging in subtlety from "jaundiced eyes" to a changed subcommittee assignment. Several members, for example, recalled their earliest encounter with the norm of unity and the tradition against minority reports. One remembered his attempt to file a minority report. "The Chairman was pretty upset about it. It's just a tradition, I guess, not to have minority reports. I didn't know it was a tradition. When I said I was going to write a minority report, some eyebrows were raised. The Chairman said it just wasn't the thing to do. Nothing more was said about it. But it wasn't a very popular thing to do, I guess." He added that he had not filed one since.

Some younger members have congenital difficulty in observing the norms of the apprentice's role. In the 86th Congress, these types tended to come from the Republican minority. The minority newcomers (described by one of the men who selected them as "eight young, energetic, fighting conservatives") were a group of economy-minded individuals some of whom chafed against any barrier which kept them from immediate influence on Committee policy. Their reaction was quite different from that of the young Democrats, whose difficulty was in learning to become economy-minded, but who did not actively resent their lack of influence. One freshman, who felt that "The appropriations system is lousy, inadequate and old fashioned," recalled that he had spoken out in full Committee against the recommendations of a subcommittee of which he was not a member. Having failed, he continued to oppose the recommendation during floor debate. By speaking up, speaking in relation to the work of another subcommittee and by opposing a Committee recommendation, he had violated the particular norms of his apprentice role as well of the generally applicable norms of reciprocity and unity. He explained what he had learned, but remained only partially socialized:

> They want to wash their dirty linen in the Committee and they want no opposition afterward. They let me say my piece in Committee. . . . But I just couldn't keep quiet. I said some things on the floor, and I found out that's about all they would take. . . . If you don't get along with your Committee and have their support, you don't get anything accomplished around here. . . . I'm trying to be a loyal, cooperative member of the

> Committee. You hate to be a stinker; but I'm still picking at the little things because I can't work on the big things. There's nothing for the new men to do, so they have to find places to needle in order to take some part in it.

Another freshman, who had deliberately violated apprenticeship norms by trying to ask "as many questions as the chairman" during subcommittee hearings, reported a story of unremitting counteraction against his deviation:

> In the hearings, I have to wait sometimes nine or ten hours for a chance; and he hopes I'll get tired and stay home. I've had to wait till some pretty unreasonable hours. Once I've gotten the floor, though, I've been able to make a good case. Sometimes I've been the only person there. . . . He's all powerful. He's got all the power. He wouldn't think of taking me on a trip with him when he goes to hold hearings. Last year, he went to ——. He wouldn't give me a nudge there. And in the hearings, when I'm questioning a witness, he'll keep butting in so that my case won't appear to be too rosy.

Carried on over a period of two years, this behavior resulted in considerable personal friction between a Committee elder and the newcomer. Other members of his subcommittee pointedly gave him a great lack of support for his nonconformity. "They tried to slow him down and tone him down a little," not because he and his subcommittee chairman disagreed, but on the grounds that the Committee has developed accepted ways of disagreeing which minimize, rather than exacerbate, interpersonal friction.

One internal threat to Committee integration comes from new members who from untutored perceptions, from ignorance of norms, or from dissatisfaction with the apprentice role may not act in accordance with Committee expectations. The seriousness of this threat is minimized, however, by the fact that the deviant newcomer does not possess sufficient resources to affect adversely the operation of the system. Even if he does not respond immediately to the application of sanctions, he can be held in check and subjected to an extended and (given the frequency of interaction among members) intensive period of socialization. The success of Committee socialization is indicated by the fact that whereas wholesale criticism of Committee operations was frequently voiced among junior members, it had disappeared among the men of moderate experience. And what these middle seniority members now accept as the facts of Committee life, the veterans vigorously assert and defend as the essentials of a smoothly functioning system. Satisfaction with the Committee's internal structure increases with length of Committee service.

An important reason for changing member attitudes is that those who have attained leadership positions have learned, as newcomers characteristically have not, that their conformity to Committee norms is the ultimate source of the influence inside the group. Freshman members do not as readily perceive the degree to which interpersonal influence is rooted in obedience to group norms. They seem to convert their own sense of powerlessness into the view that the Committee's leaders possess, by virtue of their positions, arbitrary, absolute, and awesome power. Typically, they say: "If you're a subcommittee chairman, it's your Committee." "The Chairman runs the show. He gets what he wants. He decides what he wants and gets it through." Older members of the Committee, however, view the power of the leaders as a highly contingent and revocable grant, tendered by the Committee for so long and only so long as their leaders abide by Committee expectations. In commenting on internal influence, their typical reaction is: "Of course, the Committee wouldn't follow him if it didn't want to. He has a great deal of respect. He's an able man, a hard-working man." "He knows the bill backwards and forwards. He works hard, awfully hard and the members know it." Committee leaders have an imposing set of formal prerogatives. But they can capitalize on them only if they command the respect, confidence and deference of their colleagues.

It is basic to Committee integration that members who have the greatest power to change the system evidence the least disposition to do so. Despite their institutional conservatism, however, Committee elders do occasionally violate the norms applicable to them and hence represent a potential threat to successful integration. Excessive deviation from Committee expectations by some leaders will bring counter-measures by other leaders. Thus, for example, the Chairman and his subcommittee chairmen exercise reciprocal controls over one another's behavior. The Chairman has the authority to appoint the chairman and members of each subcommittee and fix its jurisdiction. "He runs the Committee. He has a lot of power," agrees one subcommittee chairman. "But it's all done on the basis of personal friendship. If he tries to get too big, the members can whack him down by majority vote."

In the 84th Congress, Chairman Cannon attempted an unusually broad reorganization of subcommittee jurisdictions. The subcommittee chairman most adversely affected rallied his senior colleagues against the Chairman's action—on the ground that it was an excessive violation of role expectations and threatening to subcommittee autonomy. Faced with the prospect of a negative Committee vote, the Chairman was forced to act in closer conformity to the expectations of the other leaders. As one participant described the episode,

> Mr. Cannon, for reasons of his own, tried to bust up one of the subcommittees. We didn't like that. . . . He was breaking up the whole Committee. A couple of weeks later, a few of the senior members got together and worked out a compromise. By that time, he had seen a few things, so we went to him and talked to him and worked it out.

On the subcommittees, too, it is the veterans of both parties who will levy sanctions against an offending chairman. It is they who speak of "cutting down to size" and "trimming the whiskers" of leaders who become "too cocky," "too stubborn" or who "do things wrong too often." Committee integration is underwritten by the fact that no member high or low is permanently immune from the operation of its sanctioning mechanisms.

III

Data concerning internal committee activity can be organized and presented in various ways. One way is to use key functional problems like integration as the focal points for descriptive analysis. On the basis of our analysis (and without, for the time being, having devised any precise measure of integration), we are led to the summary observation that the House Appropriations Committee appears to be a well integrated, if not an extremely well integrated, committee. The question arises as to whether anything can be gained from this study other than a description of one property of one political subsystem. If it is reasonable to assume that the internal life of a congressional committee affects all legislative activity involving that committee, and if it is reasonable to assume that the analysis of a committee's internal relationships will produce useful knowledge about legislative behavior, some broader implications for this study are indicated.

In the first place, the success of the House Appropriations Committee in solving the problem of integration probably does have important consequences for the appropriations process. Some of the possible relationships can be stated as hypotheses and tested; others can be suggested as possible guides to understanding. All of them require further research. Of primary interest is the relationship between integration and the power of the Committee. There is little doubt about the fact of Committee power. Of the 443 separate case histories of bureau appropriations examined, the House accepted Committee recommendations in 387, or 87.4 per cent of them; and in 159, or 33.6 per cent of the cases, the House Committee's original recommendations on money amounts were the exact ones enacted into law. The hypothesis that the greater the degree of Committee unity the greater the probability that its recommendations will be accepted is being tested as part of a larger study.[24] House Committee integration may be a key factor in producing House victories in conference committee. This relationship, too, might be tested. Integration appears to help provide the House conferees with a feeling of confidence and superiority which is one of their important advantages in the mix of psychological factors affecting conference deliberations.

Another suggested consequence of high integration is that party groups have a relatively small influence upon appropriations decisions. It suggests, too, that Committee-oriented behavior should be duly emphasized in any analysis of Congressional oversight of administrative activity by this Committee. Successful integration promotes the achievement of the Committee's goals, and doubtless helps account for the fairly consistent production of budget-cutting decisions. Another consequence will be found in the strategies adopted by people seeking favorable Committee decisions. For example, the characteristic lines of contact from executive officials to the Committee will run to the chairman and the ranking minority member (and to the professional staff man) of the single subcommittee handling their agency's appropriations. The ways in which the Committee achieves integration may even affect the success or failure of a bureau in getting its appropriations. Committee members, for instance, will react more favorably toward an administrator who conforms to their self-image of the hard-working master-of-detail than to one who does not—and Committee response to individual administrators bulks large in their determinations.

Finally, the internal integration of this Committee helps to explain the extraordinary stability, since 1920, of appropriations procedures—in the face of repeated proposals to change them through omnibus appropriations, legislative budgets, new budgetary forms, item veto, Treasury borrowing, etc. Integration is a stabilizing force, and the stability of the House Appropriations Committee has been a force for stabilization throughout the entire process. It was, for example, the disagreement between Cannon and Taber which led to the indecisiveness reflected in the short-lived experiment with a single appropriations bill.[25] One need only examine the conditions most likely to decrease Committee integration to ascertain some of the critical factors for producing changes in the appropriations process. A description of integration is also an excellent base-line from which to analyze changes in internal structure.

All of these are speculative propositions which call for further research. But they suggest, as a second implication, that committee integration does have important consequences for legislative activity and, hence, that it is a key variable in the study of legislative politics. It would seem, therefore, to be a fruitful focal point for the study of other Congressional committees.[26] Comparative committee analysis could usefully be devoted to (1) the factors which tend to increase or decrease integration; (2) the degree to which integration is achieved; and (3) the consequences of varying degrees of integration for committee behavior and influence. If analyses of committee integration are of any value, they should encourage the analysis and the classification of Congressional committees along functional lines. And they should lead to the discussion of interrelated problems of committee survival. Functional classification of committees (*i.e.,* well or poorly integrated) derived from a large number of descriptive analyses of several functional problems, may prove helpful in constructing more general propositions about the legislative process.

Notes:

1. On social systems, see George Homans, *The Human Group* (New York, 1950); Robert K. Merton, *Social Theory and Social Structure* (Glencoe, 1957); Talcott Parsons and Edward Shils, *Toward A General Theory of Action* (Cambridge, 1951), pp. 190–234. Most helpful with reference to the political system has been David Easton, "An Approach to the Analysis of Political Systems," *World Politics* (April, 1957), pp. 383–400.

2. On the idea of subgroups as used here, see Harry M. Johnson, *Sociology* (New York, 1960), ch. 3. On role, see specifically Theodore M. Newcomb, *Social Psychology* (New York, 1951), p. 280; see generally N. Gross, W. Mason and A. McEachern, *Explorations in Role Analysis: Studies of the School Superintendency Role* (New York, 1958). On differentiation and its relation to integration, see Scott Greer, *Social Organization* (New York, 1955).

3. The usage here follows most closely that of Robert Merton, *op. cit.*, pp. 26–29.

4. This and all other generalizations about member attitudes and perceptions depend heavily on extensive interviews with Committee members. Semi-structured interviews, averaging 45 minutes in length were held with 45 of the 50 Committee members during the 86th Congress. Certain key questions, all open-ended, were asked of all respondents. The schedule was kept very flexible, however, in order to permit particular topics to be explored with those individuals best equipped to discuss them. In a few cases, where respondents encouraged it, notes were taken during the interviews. In most cases notes were not taken, but were transcribed immediately after the interview. Where unattributed quotations occur in the text, therefore, they are as nearly verbatim as the author's power of immediate recall could make them. These techniques were all used so as to improve *rapport* between interviewer and respondent.

5. "History of the Committee on Appropriations," House Doc. 299, 77th Cong., 1st sess., 1941–1942, p. 11.

6. The bureaus being studied are all concerned with domestic policy and are situated in the Agriculture, Interior, Labor, Commerce, Treasury, Justice and Health, Education and Welfare Departments. For a similar pattern of Committee decisions in foreign affairs, see Holbert Carroll, *The House of Representatives and Foreign Affairs* (Pittsburgh, 1958), ch. 9.

6a. See, for example, Philip A. Foss, "The Grazing Fee Dilemma," Inter-University Case Program, No. 57 (University, Alabama, 1960).

7. Nicholas A. Masters, "House Committee Assignments," *American Political Science Review,* Vol. 55 (June, 1961), pp. 345–357.

8. In the period from 1947 through 1959 (80th to 86th Congress), 79 separate appointments were made to the Appropriations Committee, with 14 going to freshmen. The Committee filled, in other words, 17.7 per

cent of its vacancies with freshmen. The Rules Committee had 26 vacancies and selected no freshmen at all. The Ways and Means Committee had 36 vacancies and selected 2 freshmen (5.6 per cent). All other Committees had a higher percentage of freshmen appointments. Armed Services ranked fourth, with 45 vacancies and 12 freshmen appointed, for a percentage of 26.7. Foreign Affairs figures were 46 and 14, or 30.4 per cent; UnAmerican Activities figures were 22 and 7, or 31.8 percent. *Cf.* Masters, *op. cit.*

9. In the 1960 elections, 41 out of the current 50 members received more than 55.1 per cent of the vote in their districts. By a common definition, that is, only 9 of the 50 came from marginal districts.

10. The 106 members came to Appropriations from every committee except Ways and Means.

11. One was personally requested by the Speaker to move to Ways and Means. The other was chosen by a caucus of regional Congressmen to be his party's representative on the Rules Committee. Of the 21 members who were forced off the Committee for lack of seniority during a change in party control, or who were defeated for re-election and later returned, 20 sought to regain Committee membership at the earliest opportunity.

11a. A sidelight on this attitude is displayed in a current feud between the House and Senate Appropriations Committees over the meeting place for their conference committees. The House Committee is trying to break the century-old custom that conferences to resolve differences on money bills are always held on the Senate side of the Capitol. House Committee members "complain that they often have to trudge back to the House two or three times to answer roll calls during a conference. They say they go over in a body to work, while Senators flit in and out. . . . The House Appropriations Committee feels that it does all the hard work listening to witnesses for months on each bill, only to have the Senate Committee sit as a court of appeals and, with little more than a cursory glance, restore most of the funds cut." *Washington Post,* April 24, 1962, p. 1.

12. This proposition is spelled out at some length in J. Thibaut and H. Kelley, *The Social Psychology of Groups* (New York, 1959), p. 247, and in D. Cartwright and A. Zander, *Group Dynamics: Research and Theory* (Evanston, 1953), p. 420.

13. This figure is 9 per cent greater than the next most stable House Committee during this particular period. The top four, in order, were Appropriations (35.7%), Agriculture (26.7%), Armed Services (25%), Foreign Affairs (20.8%).

14. The Committee's permanent and well integrated professional staff (as distinguished from its temporary investigating staff) might be considered as part of the subsystem though it will not be treated in this paper.

15. "Newcomers" are defined as men who have served no more than two terms on the Committee. "Men of moderate experience" are those with 3–5 terms of service. "Veterans" are those who have 6 or more terms of Committee service.

16. A statement of expected behavior was taken to be a Committee norm when it was expressed by a substantial number of respondents (a dozen or so) who represented both parties, and varying degrees of ex-

perience. In nearly every case, moreover, no refutation of them was encountered, and ample confirmation of their existence can be found in the public record. Their articulation came most frequently from the veterans of the group.

17. See, for example, the internal conflict on the subcommittee dealing with the Labor Department. 93 *Cong. Record,* pp. 2465–2562 passim; 94 *Cong. Record,* pp. 7605–7607.

18. See, for example, the unusual minority report of Committee Republicans on the foreign aid appropriations bill in 1960. Their protest against Committee cuts in the budget estimates was the result of strenuous urging by the Eisenhower Administration. House Report No. 1798, *Mutual Security and Related Agency Appropriation Bill,* 1961, 86 Cong., 2d sess., 1960.

19. David Truman, *The Congressional Party* (New York, 1959); Julius Turner, *Party and Constituency: Pressures on Congress* (Baltimore, 1951).

20. The ideas of "reciprocity" and "complementarity," which are used interchangeably here, are discussed in Alvin Gouldner, "The Norm of Reciprocity," *American Sociological Review* (April, 1960). Most helpful in explaining the idea of a role system has been the work of J. Wahlke, H. Eulau, W. Buchanan, L. Ferguson. See their study, *The Legislative System* (New York, 1962), esp. Intro.

21. For example, the Committee on Education and Labor, see footnote 26.

22. See the exchange in 101 *Cong. Rec.,* pp. 3832, 3844, 3874.

23. 99 *Cong. Rec.,* p. 4933.

24. *Cf.* Dwaine Marvick, "Congressional Appropriations Politics," unpublished manuscript (Columbia, 1952).

25. See Dalmas Nelson, "The Omnibus Appropriations Act of 1950," *Journal of Politics* (May, 1953).

26. This view has been confirmed by the result of interviews conducted by the author with members of the House Committee on Education and Labor, together with an examination of that Committee's activity in one policy area. They indicate very significant contrasts between the internal structure of that Committee and the Appropriations Committee —contrasts which center around their comparative success in meeting the problem of integration. The House Committee on Education and Labor appears to be a poorly integrated committee. Its internal structure is characterized by a great deal of subgroup conflict, relatively little role reciprocity, and minimally effective internal control mechanisms. External concerns, like those of party, constituency and clientele groups, are probably more effective in determining its decisions than is likely to be the case in a well-integrated committee. An analysis of the internal life of the Committee on Education and Labor, drawn partly from interviews with 19 members of that group, will appear in a forthcoming study, *Federal Aid to Education and National Politics,* by Professor Frank Munger and the author, to be published by Syracuse University Press. See also Nicholas R. Masters, *op. cit.,* note 7 above, pp. 354-355, and Seymour Scher, "Congressional Committee Members as Independent Agency Overseers: A Case Study," *American Political Science Review,* Vol. 54 (December, 1960), pp. 911–920.

6 *Voting Blocs in Legislative Behavior: A Systematic Analysis** by John G. Grumm

I

Discovering and identifying voting blocs in the legislature is an interesting game for the amateur as well as the professional political analyst. Is there or is there not a "conservative coalition" in Congress? Is the "farm bloc" still effective in legislative politics? Who belongs to the "liberal bloc" in the Senate and how unified is it? Investigation of such questions as these can often lead to interesting findings that shed a good deal of light on the factors involved in legislative voting behavior.

It would appear obvious that bloc analysis should play an important role in the study of legislative behavior. The fact is, however, that it has not been well developed as a systematic research tool. Only a very few studies have shown a methodological concern with bloc analysis, and these have not been notably successful in resolving some fundamental difficulties of this approach.

Reprinted from *The Western Political Quarterly*, 18, 2 (June, 1965), 350–362, where it appeared under the title, "The Systematic Analysis of Blocs in the Study of Legislative Behavior," by permission of the author and the University of Utah, copyright owners.

*This study was assisted by a grant from the Social Science Research Council and the use of the facilities of the Governmental Research Center of the University of Kansas.

A comprehensive and systematic process for analyzing blocs should incorporate the following: (1) an objective means of defining the blocs in terms of their size, composition, and purpose; (2) a process for discovering the structure of the interrelationships within the blocs; (3) a basis for determining the cohesiveness of the bloc and its relationship to other blocs; (4) a means of determining the sorts of issues that engender a group response; and (5) a basis for analyzing the motivational factors involved in bloc behavior.

Although it might be employed for various purposes, the central concern of bloc analysis, as it is conceived here, is to account for or determine the causes of variances in legislative voting behavior. A systematic analysis that defines the major cohesive groupings emerging under various conditions could conceivably account, in this sense, for every vote by every legislator in a given session.

The major difficulty that has plagued most bloc analyses in the past has been the development of an objective process for defining the limits of a bloc and determining its membership. For example, we may wish to test for the existence and analyze the behavior of an "urban bloc" in the legislature. Whether we find one that behaves with any significant degree of cohesion depends upon where we draw the line between urban and rural, whether we include suburban within it, whether we exclude from it the representatives of the largest metropolitan areas, and other matters such as these. One might hit upon a basis for grouping that produced highly cohesive blocs; still he could never be sure that a different arrangement of the legislators might not have produced an even more solidly aligned configuration. The number of possible combinations of legislators is almost indefinite; so it is obviously not feasible to try them all.

Attempting to solve problems such as this, investigators have turned to various "clustering" processes that are independent of any prior definition of the groups or their composition and that rely solely on the voting patterns themselves to identify the most cohesive groupings. Several types of clustering processes have been devised, primarily for psychological research,[1] but the major techniques used in legislative behavior studies have been those of Stuart Rice[2] and Herman Beyle.[3]

Rice's method begins by calculating the percentage of

times that each legislator votes in agreement with each of the other legislators. The agreement percentages for all possible pairs of legislators are then listed in a table in order of their magnitude. Some "cut-off" point is then determined. Rice arbitrarily hit on 80 per cent as the limiting factor. The minimum size for a bloc is then determined. Rice suggested four members as a minimum, since it seemed unrealistic to think of a bloc as having only two or three members. Thus, a bloc is defined as a group of four or more members each of whom votes in agreement with each other member of the group 80 per cent or more of the time. The next steps, then, are to eliminate from consideration all pairs that have agreement scores of less than 80 per cent and, from those remaining, to eliminate all individuals who do not show 80 per cent agreement or more with at least three other individuals. The latter step may have to be iterated several times because, as individuals are eliminated, other individuals with whom they have been paired might fall below the criterion that they must have 80 percent agreement scores with at least three individuals among those who remain. Eventually, the legislators under consideration will probably be reduced to a number that will permit the analyst to examine all possible combinations capable of producing blocs of four or more with the required high cohesion of each member with each other member.

The most obvious defect of the Rice method is that it is only applicable to rather small bodies. Rice, himself, maintained that it was not practical, because of the excessive number of combinations possible, in bodies of more than 25 or 30.[4]

Beyle sought to improve on Rice by devising a method that could be used with bodies as large as those found in most state legislatures and also by establishing more objective criteria for identifying the bloc structure. In an attempt to inject some statistical refinement into his method, he devised an "index of significant cohesion of pairs" as a substitute for the simple percentage of agreement among pairs that Rice used. Beyle was interested, for reasons that were never quite clear, in examining agreements on the prevailing side of a vote separately from those on the non-prevailing side. He pointed out that the chances of two people agreeing on *either* side were one out of two, or even; but they were only half as great, or one out of four, for two people agreeing on a *given* side. He therefore defined "zero cohesion" as 25 per cent agreement or less, and referred to anything above this as "significant cohesion." All percentage figures that fell in the range from 25 to 100 were adjusted to fit into his range of zero to 100.[5]

Beyle's other contribution was to put the indices into a matrix in which all possible pairs of legislators were set forth with their respective indices and from which one could readily identify the most cohesive pair. Starting with this pair as a nucleus, he expanded by adding individuals whose cohesion scores were the highest with members of the original pair. Then others were added who had the highest scores with the newly added members and also with the original pair. In contrast to Rice, Beyle did not have a fixed cut-off point, but determined this empirically by noting where there were natural breaks in the data. Generally, he did not want to draw any hard and fast lines. After he had identified all the individuals who could conceivably belong to a cluster, he constructed a new matrix consisting only of these members. This matrix contained the most cohesive pair in the upper left-hand corner and shaded off to the least cohesive pair in the lower right. From it one could identify an "inner core," an "inner fringe," an "outer fringe," and so forth.

After this first cluster was defined, the highest index of cohesion among the remaining pairs was identified, and the same method was employed to construct a second cluster. If there were still some people left after this, the process would continue toward the definition of a third cluster. Usually, however, it would produce only two cohesive groups with some degree of overlapping by the least cohesive members of each group—plus a small number of unattached individuals who did not belong to either cluster and were not close enough to each other to form a cluster themselves.

A notable recent example of such an analysis is seen in David Truman's monumental study of the 81st Congress.[6] Essentially, Truman used Beyle's method with its matrices and its means of expansion starting from a single high-cohesion pair. Truman saw, however, that the statistical assumptions on which Beyle's index rested were unsound; so for his purposes he simply used raw agreement scores (the total number of votes on which the pair agreed) and avoided making any assumptions whatsoever about probabilities. Truman's results appear reasonable, and hence it appears that the Beyle method can be used satisfactorily without all of the complex statistical paraphernalia associated with his "index of significant cohesion of pairs."

Still, there are some things that are quite unsatisfactory about the method Truman used. Neither Truman's nor Beyle's method provides an exact guide for assigning members to a cluster or a means of determining the limits of a cluster. One cannot tell whether to give priority in constructing a cluster to the individual who has very high agreements scores with only a few members of the cluster nucleus or to the person having somewhat lower scores with a larger number of cluster members. At what point do the scores become too low to be considered a member of a cluster? Neither Rice, Beyle, or Truman provides satisfactory answers to these questions.

II

Fortunately, however, there are a number of clustering methods developed for use in other fields that can be adapted to legislative behavior research and that avoid the major defects of the methods outlined above. One of these that has been found to be the most useful by the present author is one devised by entomological researchers for the purposes of grouping species of insects into taxonomic systems.[7] The basic method has a wide application, and, in fact, it was originally developed for use with psychometric and sociometric data. Its use, therefore, in connection with legislators does not imply any invidious comparison to insects. This method is proposed here primarily because it is almost completely objective in its operation and employs a reasonable and objective criterion for defining cluster limits.

A crucial element in the clustering process is the measure of relatedness among members. Beyle was on the right track when he sought to give his index of cohesion a sound statistical base. His failure in this attempt should not obscure the necessity of adopting a measuring instrument based on statistical probabilities if one wishes to minimize the subjectivity in the process. An index of cohesion based on percentages is not amenable to tests of statistical significance. A number of measures are, however, and probably the best of these for clustering purposes is the phi coefficient. It is designed to measure the degree of correlation between two items (e.g., pairs of legislators) on a dichotomized variable (e.g., "yes" and "no" votes).[8] The probabilities associated with any value of phi may readily be determined since it is a function of chi-square.[9] In the same manner as a correlation coefficient, phi varies from -1 to $+1$. A negative value indicates opposition or disagreement among the two members, while a positive value indicates agreement. A zero coefficient suggests no relationship or a random relationship between the two.

Henceforth, in this paper the phi coefficient calculated for pairs of legislators on roll-call votes will be referred to as the "index of colligation" to distinguish it from the index of cohesion, agreement scores, etc.

Now to begin the actual clustering process. After indices of colligation are calculated for all possible pairs of legislators in the body under investigation, they are arrayed in a symmetrical matrix in which each legislator is represented by one column and one row. Therefore, if there is a total of k legislators, the size of the matrix is $k \times k$.[10] The next step is to scan the matrix and identify those cells containing an index that is both highest in the row in which it is contained and in its column. This "reciprocally highest coefficient" marks the formation of an initial cluster. For example, a given legislator, L_i, would cluster with a legislator, L_j, if L_i's highest index were with L_j and L_j's highest were with L_i. But if L_j's highest index were with legislator L_k, L_i would not be able to form an initial cluster with L_j (or with anyone at this point). Any matrix of this sort will contain at least one of these reciprocally highest coefficients, but it also might contain a great many of them.

The next step requires the computing of a new matrix in which the clusters or pairs of legislators are treated as individual variables. The next matrix is, of course, smaller. If on the preceding step eight legislators joined to form four clusters, the size of the new matrix would be $(k-4) \times (k-4)$. New indices must now be computed for each cluster against every other variable in the matrix (some of which might also be clusters). For this the Spearman sum of variables method is used.[11] If two variables (legislators), i and j, form a cluster, the combination coefficient of these two with k is computed as follows:

$$\varnothing_{ij.k} = \frac{\varnothing_{ik} + \varnothing_{jk}}{\sqrt{2 + 2\varnothing_{ij}}},$$

where $\varnothing_{ik}$ is the phi coefficient of variable i with k, etc. The combined coefficient of two clusters made up of i and j on the one hand and of k and l on the other is determined by the formula

$$\varnothing_{ij.kl} = \frac{\varnothing_{ik} + \varnothing_{il} + \varnothing_{jk} + \varnothing_{jl}}{2\sqrt{(1 + \varnothing_{ij})(1 + \varnothing_{kl})}}$$

The second matrix is treated in the same manner as the original matrix, and after the new clusters are identified a third and still smaller matrix is computed with the new clusters considered as single variables. It is therefore possible for a so-called variable in the third matrix to consist of a pair of pairs, a total of four of the original variables or legislators. This process can conceivably continue until the size of the last matrix is 2×2, at which point each of the two "variables" represents a large group of original variables that clustered together at various stages of the process.

Quite obviously, this whole process will require a tremendous number of mathematical calculations for even the smallest legislative bodies. It is, therefore, not practical to apply it to legislative behavior research without the assistance of an electronic computer. The method, however, is one that is readily handled by electronic computing equipment, and a program has been written for the IBM 650 digital computer that will perform all of the necessary operations.[12]

The definition of the cluster structure up to this point is entirely automatic and no subjective decisions are required of the analyst. The method assures that the successive units added to a cluster will be the ones that will maintain the highest average intercorrelation of cluster members. Except for ties,[13] at each stage of the process there is only one variable that meets this criterion. In other words, the process provides a unique solution to each cluster problem.

The clearest method of presenting the data from the output of the computer is shown in Chart 1. The code numbers of the legislators are arrayed across the top of the diagram. The degree of correlation at which two variables clustered (original phi coefficients or Spearman sum of variables) is determined by projecting onto the vertical axis the horizontal line connecting the two vertical stems. Generally, those variables joined at the higher end of the scale were clustered at an early stage in the clustering process, while those at the lower end were the last ones added to the clusters. Although the data on which this example is based are fictitious, the structure is fairly typical of those found in legislative bodies.

One may observe from Chart 1 that there are two major clusters. Within each it is possible to identify some highly cohesive pair (e.g., 3 and 21 in Cluster A, or 8 and 12 in Cluster B) and subclusters (e.g., 2, 6, 7, and 22 or 8, 12, 14, and 17). The horizontal line at the bottom results from continuing the process to its conclusion, which causes the two clusters to come together in the final 2×2 matrix. The level of the line therefore is indicative of the amount of agreement or conflict between the two clusters. The further it descends into the negative region, the greater the conflict between the two.

The process that reproduces this cluster structure is automatic, but we will usually wish to go beyond this, and therein lie some difficult problems of interpretation. Occasionally, one finds a rather clearly defined third cluster which only merges with one of the other two clusters at a relatively low level. The group at the far right in Chart 1 (i.e. 19, 18, and 23) might be considered in this category, though it is not very cohesive internally. Such instances raise the question of whether such a group should be considered a member of a larger cluster or a separate entity. A similar question is raised by the few individual members who are often tacked onto a cluster in the final stages of the process. For example, numbers 1 and 10 in Chart 1 merge with the rest of the group at a relatively low level and might equally be considered outsiders as members of the cluster. The basic question is, should we put asunder those elements that the cluster process has joined together but whose correlation is at a relatively low level?

Undoubtedly, some line does need to be drawn here. In each successive matrix of this process there will always be at least one mutually highest coefficient, and near the final stages these may become rather small, sometimes even slightly negative. Nevertheless, where a coefficient is mutually highest for both variables, they will be joined together. This is the reason that the process, as its final act, merges the last two variables, thus putting the whole legislative body back together again. It clearly should be stopped, analytically speaking, before it reaches this point.

Chart 1. ***Diagram of Cluster Patterns.***

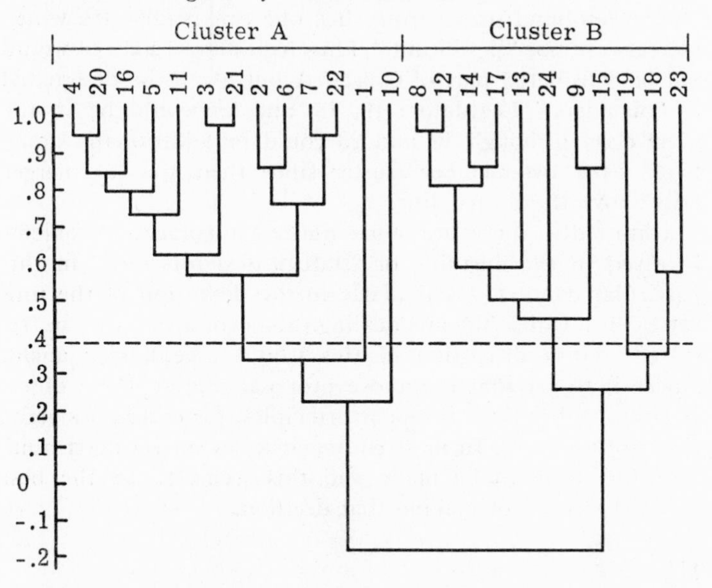

One solution to this might be to designate zero correlation as the stopping point. This might seem reasonable since any persons or groups joined above this level would show a positive amount of agreement among themselves. Such a limit, however, would almost always result in defining just two clusters, and in some cases they would be so loosely tied together that it would be unrealistic to regard them as voting blocs. Random or chance factors could often produce an indication of positive agreement where none actually existed.

It would probably be better therefore to establish as the cut-off point a level of correlation that was "significant" in the statistical sense. It is possible to do this since the basic index on which this process is based and the combined index are ones whose statistical distribution can be determined. One must merely decide then what probability level he would regard as significant and calculate the value of the index associated with his level. Any mergers between variables whose index was below this value would be rejected.

The procedure can easily be seen diagrammatically in Chart 1. Let us assume that the value of the index for our chosen level of significance is .400. A horizontal line can therefore be drawn corresponding to this value as represented on the left-hand scale. From this, one can readily see which mergers are not "significant." Thus legislators 1 and 10 would not be considered part of Cluster A but would be designated as "outsiders." Legislators 19, 18, and 23 would be in the same class, although 18 and 23 could be additionally designated as a two-member cluster since their line of merger falls above the dotted line.

Admittedly, there are some difficult theoretical problems involved in the meaning of "statistical significance" in this particular context—particularly in the definition of the universe with which we are dealing. Some of these can be resolved, but a discussion of this would take us far afield. Suffice it to say that the above proposal represents an objective means, based on accepted principles, for determining the limits of a cluster. In most cluster analyses such a determination will have to be made and this seems to be the best available means of making that decision.

III

To assess the practicality of this process in the analysis of actual legislative behavior and to see how well it met the requirements of systematic bloc analysis as presented in the beginning of this paper, it was applied to the voting records of some recent sessions of the Kansas legislature. This is a rather typical legislature; its two houses are of about average size; the legislative districts show about the average degree of malapportionment; and the two parties are represented in both House and Senate in a ratio that is not so far out of balance as to preclude party voting. Furthermore, voting data are abundantly available for any session of this legislature, since a recorded roll call is required on final passage of all bills, on concurrence with amendments by the other house, on conference committee reports, and on motions to override a veto.

The Kansas House of Representatives elects its 125 members every two years, while the Senate elects its 40 senators every four. The analysis here covers the 1959 session of the House and, since the membership was the same in both years, the 1957 and 1959 sessions of the Senate. In 1959 the parties were fairly closely balanced in the House, which had 69 Republicans and 56 Democrats; but the Senate that sat in the 1957 and 1959 sessions was predominantly Republican, with 32 Republican senators and only eight Democratic ones.[14]

The recorded roll calls reveal a striking degree of unanimity in both of these bodies during these sessions. In the Senate there were 603 roll calls on final passage in 1957 and 486 in 1959, a total of 1,089 for the two sessions. In the House there were 533 such roll calls in the 1959 session. The vast majority of these bills passed unanimously or nearly unanimously. For the purposes of our analysis, unanimous or nearly unanimous votes could add little or no information, and thus it was decided only to use those in which the minority on the vote represented 15 per cent or more of the total membership. By adopting this criterion, all but 57 of the Senate roll calls were excluded and all but 41 of those in the House were eliminated.[15]

In the Senate, twelve separate matrices were computed before the clustering process came to an end with all members clustered. The critical correlation value was set at +.26 ($p=.05$) and this had the effect of defining three major clusters and six isolates or outsiders. The largest of the clusters consisted of twenty members. This was labeled the "Republican" cluster (referred to as "R" cluster below) since it contained no Democratic members and all the Republican leaders of the Senate belonged to it. The next largest was a mixed cluster ("RD" cluster) consisting of five Republicans and three Democrats. The smallest was a four-member cluster and consisted of Democrats only ("D" cluster). The latter two clusters were merged by the process several stages before it was completed and at a relatively high, though not significant, level. These clusters were therefore closer to each other than either was to the first one. They signified, in a sense, the element of opposition (albeit, a divided one) to the dominant Republican power in the Senate. Of the six persons defined as outsiders, one was a Democrat—the assistant minority leader, incidentally—and five were Republicans.

A rough indication of the efficiency of this process is shown by comparing the cohesiveness of the groups produced by it with other designated groupings. A previous study indicated that the party grouping showed greater cohesiveness than any other tested.[16] The cohesiveness of the Senate parties and the three clusters was measured by computing the average index of colligation for all pairs in each of the groups.[17] These indices are as follows:

Republican Party	.125
R Cluster	.270
Democratic Party	.280
D Cluster	.317
RD Cluster	.273

Thus, the clustering process, by excluding mavericks from a group and admitting to membership only those closest to it, defines the most cohesive voting blocs.

The next phase in evaluating the process was to see what additional meaning could be attributed to the cluster groups and what inferences could be made regarding motivational factors involved in the behavior of the blocs. This started with the testing by means of analysis of variance of twenty-six hypothetically related variables pertaining to the senators and to their districts for significant relationships with the cluster grouping.[18]

As was to be expected, the association between the party affiliation variable and cluster membership was a significant one ($p=.01$). This was also true for party loyalty scores and percentage of registered Democrats in the senators' districts. The senators with the highest party loyalty scores were in the R and D clusters, while those in the RD cluster had the lowest scores. These were the only variables connected with the senators themselves that were significantly related to the cluster groupings.

The only variable associated with the senators' districts that proved significant ($p=.05$) was the percentage of population 65 years of age and over. However, coming very close to the .05 level of significance were the percentage population increase and median family income. The relationship was such that the R-cluster senators tended to represent districts with fewer old people, with higher incomes, and with population increases during the 1950's; while the RD-cluster and the D-cluster districts had more oldsters, less income, and decreasing populations. In these respects, the RD-cluster districts tended to be more extreme than the D-cluster ones. All three factors seemed to be closely related and therefore might be combined into a "growth-decline" index for the district. Thus we might characterize the R-cluster districts as growing economically and demographically, the RD-cluster districts as declining, and the D-cluster districts as rather stable though tending slightly toward the declining end of the scale.

It can be seen that senators of the same party tended to vote together when they came from districts typical of those represented by their party in the Senate. It is not possible from this analysis to determine to what extent party or district influences were responsible for the cohesion of these groups. It seems reasonable to assume, however, that both factors were involved and that they tended to reinforce one another. Further, the hypothesis is suggested that the bipartisan voting bloc, labeled the "RD cluster," owed its cohesion to a desire to protect the special interests of the "declining" districts. This would have to be tested, of course, by means other than those described here.

From an examination of the relationships between blocs, it was found that the RD cluster presented a more concerted and undivided opposition to the Republican majority than did the D cluster. This was not true for all of the bills examined, but it was true for most of them. Generally, H.E.W.-type measures and financial bills tended to mobilize the RD-cluster members in opposition to the "regular" Republican bloc.[19] On such votes, the D-cluster Democrats went along most often with the former, but they would occasionally divide, with some defecting to the Republican side.

The cluster analysis of the 1959 session of the House based on 41 roll calls produced a rather remarkable result and one quite different from that in the Senate. Two clusters were defined and they almost completely coincided with the two party groups. In fact, only one Democrat was found in the Republican cluster and no Republicans fell in the Democratic cluster. There were eight mavericks, four of them Republicans and four Democrats, but even these clustered with their respective party blocs when the process was carried slightly below the level of significance.

This suggests that party affiliation was much more important in the House than in the Senate during this session. Probably this is related to the fact that the parties were in closer balance in the House than in the Senate. This made it possible for the Democrats occasionally to defeat Republican-sponsored legislation if they remained united and had few abstentions.[20] Also, the Democrats had just enough members to sustain a veto by the Democratic Governor if they all voted together. The resulting unity of the Democratic party apparently forced the Republicans to make efforts to keep their own members in line if they hoped to enact a major portion of their program.

From this point in the analysis, it seemed that a close examination of the subcluster would be fruitful. The forty-eight-member Democratic cluster was analyzed first. It had two rather well-defined subclusters, one consisting of eighteen members (labeled "subcluster D_1") and the other of eight members ("subcluster D_2"). Most of the remaining twenty-two members joined the main cluster individually as the process continued and were therefore not considered to form separate subclusters themselves. A significant relationship was found to exist between the subcluster grouping and three of the independent variables: (1) the size of the representative's plurality in his last election, (2) his total number of active years in politics, and (3) his total number of years in the legislature.

The larger group, subcluster D_1, consisted primarily of freshman representatives plus the House minority leader and assistant minority leader. Thus, it appeared to be a group of two strong leaders and 16 more-or-less-willing followers. On the whole, the group stood the most solidly for what could be called the Democratic "party line" in the House. Because of this fact and the fact that it contained the party leadership, it might be considered the "nucleus" of the main cluster. The other subcluster, D_2, tended to be less solid in its support of the party line, although it generally voted with the rest of the party (otherwise it would not have been part of the main Democratic cluster).

Differences between the two subclusters regarding the three

significantly related variables seemed to add up to the fact that most of those in the first subcluster probably felt more insecure and unsure of themselves in their political and legislative roles than those in the small subcluster. The members of the first, excluding the two leaders, had been active in politics for an average of only 7.7 years as compared to 22.3 years for the members of the second. The majority of the first subcluster had not served previously in the Kansas legislature, while half of the second group had served at least two previous terms and the other half of the group had served one term. Finally, those in the first subcluster, excepting the two party leaders, had won their elections with an average of only 52.7 per cent of the two-party votes, while those in the second subcluster had received an average of landslide proportions—67.8 per cent. The cohesion of the first subcluster therefore seemed to have resulted from the need of the inexperienced legislator for guidance, plus the desire of these members to enhance their security by getting in the good graces of the party leadership. On the other hand, we could guess that those in subcluster D_2 were able to exercise more independence of party because they were more secure in their positions and had greater experience in and knowledge of the legislative process. The cohesion among the members of this second group could probably be attributed to friendships or close relationships developed through long association in the legislature and in the gatherings and councils of the Democratic party.

On the Republican side, the intra-cluster structure was not as well defined. A rather tightly knit subcluster of fifteen representatives was evident, while closely tied to it was another highly cohesive subcluster of thirteen members. These two, however, were considered to constitute a single subcluster of twenty-eight members since the Spearman sum of variables coefficient between the two was rather high (+.69). There were no significant differences between the two groups in terms of the 26 variables that were examined. After the formation of this twenty-eight-member subcluster, the rest of the members of the main cluster generally were added to it one at a time; hence, there was only this one definite subcluster (which could be regarded as the cluster "nucleus"), plus a large number of individuals whose relationships among themselves were not close enough to form a separate and distinct group within the main Republican cluster. There also were no significant differences between the single subcluster and the rest of the Republicans, although the individuals who were added to the cluster toward the end of the process tended generally to be from more urban districts than the members of the subcluster. Since ruralism is correlated with Republicanism in the Kansas House, it was thus not surprising that the more urban Republican representatives were only rather loosely attached to the bulk of the House Republicans. There was little evidence on the Republican side of voting differences between the more secure and less secure members, as was the case with the Democrats; although the behavior of the Republican cluster "nucleus" (which contained all the Republican leaders) bore some similarities to that of the Democratic "nucleus."

IV

This does not exhaust the kinds of analyses that might be made with these data and this process. Yet, we have probably proceeded far enough to demonstrate that the proposed process is consistent with the requirements of systematic bloc analysis as outlined in the beginning of this paper:

1. The clustering procedure provides a workable and objective means, based on probability standards, of defining the cohesive blocs within a legislative body. A unique solution that involves no subjective judgments is supplied for each cluster problem.
2. The process is carried out in such a way that the structure of the interrelationships within the blocs is readily revealed. Subclusters, cluster nuclei, and fringe members are easily identified.
3. The basic statistics used in the process (the index of colligation) can be used as a measure of cohesion within blocs, and the degree of conflict between blocs can be determined by a similar statistical device.
4. Once the blocs are defined by the clustering process, it is a relatively simple matter, by referring to the original voting data, to determine which issues are most likely to engender a bloc response.
5. By employing analysis of variance in conjunction with the clustering process, it is possible to make some inferences

regarding the motivational factors involved in bloc behavior.

In sum, the method meets the demands of rigorous analysis and seems to provide reasonable and meaningful results.

Notes:

1. For a summary of these see R. B. Cattell, "A Note on Correlation Clusters and Cluster Search Methods," *Psychometrika,* 9 (June 1944), 169–84.

2. Stuart A. Rice, "The Identification of Blocs in Small Political Bodies," *APSR,* 21 (August 1927), 619–27; reprinted in his *Quantitative Methods in Politics* (New York: Knopf, 1928), chap. 16.

3. Herman C. Beyle, *Identification and Analysis of Attribute-Cluster Blocs* (Chicago: U. of Chicago Press, 1931).

4. Rice, *op. cit.,* p. 627.

5. Beyle, *op. cit.,* pp. 29–32.

6. David B. Truman, *The Congressional Party: A Case Study* (New York: Wiley, 1959).

7. Robert Sokal and Charles Michener, "A Statistical Method for Evaluating Systematic Relationships," *University of Kansas Science Bulletin,* 38 (March 20, 1958), 1409–38.

8. For the purposes of computation the data should be arranged in a four-fold table in the following manner:

		Legislator X	
		+	-
Legislator Y	+	a	b
	-	c	d

Then these data are then entered into the phi coefficient formula as follows:

$$\O = \frac{ad - bc}{\sqrt{(a+d)\ (b+d)\ (a+b)\ (c+d)}}$$

9. The relationship may be expressed as follows:

$$\O = \sqrt{\frac{X^2}{n}}$$

Therefore the chi-square test may be performed by squaring the phi coefficient, multiplying by the total number of roll-call votes involved in its calculation, and entering a table of chi-square at one degree of freedom.

10. Since the upper right-hand triangle of the matrix is a mirror reflection of the lower left-hand triangle, and since the diagonal cells (which would presumably show the correlation of a variable with itself) are not used, it is only necessary to compute $\frac{k\ (k-1)}{2}$ correlation coefficients.

11. C. Spearman, "Correlation of Sums or Differences," *British Journal of Psychology*, 5 (March 1913), 417–26.

12. The author's program directs the computer to scan the rows and columns of the matrix for the reciprocally highest coefficients, cluster the proper variables, and compute a new matrix based on these clusters. It repeats the process until stopped manually or until all variables are clustered. The running time for a 40-member body is 15 to 20 minutes. Output data consist of the coefficients in each of the intermediate matrices, the code number of the variables that clustered in each matrix, and the coefficient for the clustering variables. Up to 115 variables can be handled at one time. A computer with a larger storage capacity than the IBM 650 could, of course, be programmed to deal with a larger number of variables. But this program may be used where the variables exceed 115 if the matrix is broken down into groups with overlapping membership and each group is run separately through the computer. Or if the variables only slightly exceed 115 (as in the case described below of the Kansas House of Representatives), preliminary clustering may be performed manually until a small enough intermediate matrix is produced.

13. The problem of ties is relatively insignificant if three-digit phi coefficients are used. In the case of a tie, the IBM program forms a cluster of the first pair encountered in scanning the matrix.

14. In the Senate two Republicans and in the House three Republicans were eliminated from the analysis because of their large number of absences.

15. Most of the bills that were passed unanimously or nearly unanimously were of a technical or otherwise noncontroversial nature. A few were politically important and controversial, which would suggest that some legislative decisions had been reached before the roll-call votes. Thus, an undetermined amount of information that might affect the clustering process is omitted from this analysis. The importance of this omission may not be very great, however, since it can be stated that the 98 votes represented in our analysis clearly included the bulk of the really significant legislation acted upon during these sessions.

16. Other groupings examined were based on characteristics of the legislative district and included urban and rural, eastern and western, and industrial and agricultural.

17. This is deemed by the author to be a more valid measure of group cohesion than the index of cohesion developed by Rice, since it actually measures the interrelationships among members over a series of votes and can be evaluated objectively by tests of statistical significance. Any positive value of the index is indicative of a cohesive grouping. Anything over .26 might be considered "significant."

18. The variables pertaining to the constituencies were the following: population increase or decline during the 1950–60 decade, per cent urban, per cent non-white, per cent over 65 years of age, per cent under 18 years, population fertility ratio, median family income, per cent Catholics, per cent engaged in manufacture, per cent owner-occupied dwellings, average size of farms, and an estimate of percentage of registered Democrats and Republicans. The variables pertaining to the candidate him-

self were as follows: number of years active in politics, years in the legislature, per cent that his vote in the last election bore to the number of registered voters in his party in the district, per cent that his plurality was of total vote in last general election, per cent that his plurality was of total vote in the last primary election, self-assessment party-loyalty score, party-loyalty score based on significant party votes, self-assessment liberal-conservative score, occupational status, years of schooling, religion (Protestant, Catholic, or Jew), population of his residential town, personal income, and party affiliation. The chi-square test, rather than analysis of variance, was used to test the relationship of the cluster grouping with religion and with party affiliation since these were attribute factors that could not be expressed quantitatively.

19. The vote that showed the greatest degree of conflict between the two groups dealt with a school district reorganization plan that would have used the disbursement of state aid as a means of forcing the small districts to combine. This was highly unpopular in the areas of declining population. A social welfare bill and an amendment to the property tax law also produced a significant degree of conflict between the R-cluster and the RD-cluster. Conflict was measured by computing a phi coefficient between the two groups for each of the roll-call votes. The value of phi corresponding to the .05 level of confidence was determined by converting chi-square at this level to phi.

20. A "constitutional" majority (63 votes) is required for passage of all legislation.

C. *The Horizontal Dimension—Strata*

7

Class and Party in Partisan and Non-Partisan Elections

by Robert H. Salisbury and Gordon Black

In a recent monograph, Professor Heinz Eulau begins his analysis by quoting two "evidently antagonistic formulations" of the theoretical underpinnings of voting behavior in the United States:[1]

1. "A person thinks, politically, as he is socially."
2. Crucial among the elements in the electoral decision are "traditional or habitual partisan attachments."

These rival conceptions of primacy among politically relevant variables are often summarized by the terms "class" and "party." As Eulau points out, "from Aristotle to Harold J. Laski, the relationship between class and party has been one of the 'grand problems,' so-called, of speculation about political systems. It has also remained one of the most neglected areas of systematic theory and of empirical analysis."[2] Data drawn from Survey Research Center surveys have recently been used to explore the relative importance and specify the interdependence of class and party in American voting.[3] Generally, they show party to be more immediately relevant to the voting decision than class, though class position clearly

Reprinted from *American Political Science Review,* 57 (September, 1963), 584–592, by permission of the authors and the publisher.

shapes and sets limits to possible party identification and party-related perspectives.

Difficult problems are involved in attempting to sort out and define the two postulated independent variables. The extent to which, in some sense, class determines party orientation is perhaps the most difficult. For example, even when it is found that a certain portion of the working class prefers the Republican party, it may still be that a generation or two earlier the families of this group were Republican on class grounds, and have perpetuated the identification through the socialization process. Campbell *et al.*, conclude that party identification has a "conserving influence," inhibiting or, at least, slowing down the political manifestation of changes in class position.[4] Their data strongly suggest that in any immediate situation class will be much less highly correlated with the vote than party preference. Campbell *et al.*, do not attempt to control for class in relating party identification to the vote, although they do explore the separate effect of class. Eulau deals with this problem at length, but his focus is rather different. He does not attempt to specify the relative weight of each independent variable in predicting the vote, but concentrates on exploring the interrelationships of the two variables.

The task of this paper is to specify as exactly as possible the relative weight of party and class in relation both to vote and to turnout in both partisan and non-partisan elections.[5] We have chosen one community, Des Moines, Iowa, and one period of time, 1951–61. By doing so we may observe on a contemporary basis, at least, the independent effect of each variable, recognizing that the long-term importance of class in shaping party identification may still be understated. The possibility that Des Moines constitutes a special case is also obvious, but this does not vitiate any hypothesis we may derive.

An analysis of this kind requires us to specify measures of party and of class which are independent of one another and which permit the statistical treatment involved in calculating partial correlation. Party identification presents relatively little difficulty. Since we are using precinct data, we simply take party registration by precinct as a measure of identification.[6] Class is more difficult. A variety of measures would be possible and might lead to somewhat varying results. We have chosen a measure which rates precincts on a five-point scale based upon type and quality of housing.[7] This measure had the great advantage of convenience since the data were easily available, but obvious objections of inadequacy may be leveled at this choice.

Generally, studies of the comparative virtues of indexes of class suggest that occupation is the most effective indicator of individual class-related life style.[8] Income tends to be less effective. These studies do suggest that housing quality and neighborhood type are also reasonably successful measures in predicting individual behavior. Since we are dealing with aggregate units—precincts—it is far easier to construct an index based on housing than to construct an occupation index. Other social area indexes, such as the Shevky-Bell index,[9] emphasize factors such as density and ethnicity which are relatively uniform in Des Moines and would provide less clear a basis for discrimination among precincts. Our index of class may not appear to facilitate exact comparisons with other communities. An appropriate ranking of precincts in New York City, for example, might have a good many more than five classes; a smaller town might have fewer. All that is really required to further comparative analysis, however, is that the system of ranking precincts establishes meaningful intervals using median rental values plus whatever qualitative dimensions are appropriate to that community. Correlations of such an index with the vote would produce findings that could be compared directly with ours. Our impressionistic knowledge of Des Moines persuades us that our index is meaningful for that community.

As Tables I and II indicate, the variance in our dependent variables that is unexplained by the combined independent variables is very small in the elections of candidates, and this also persuades us that we are using meaningful indexes. In the referenda election and with respect to turnout the unexplained variance is much greater, and we have not attempted to account for it.

One other difficulty with our index of class is that we have employed the same measure for the entire period, making no adjustments to take account of possible changes in the relative status of neighborhoods during the decade covered by our study. Thus if one neighborhood deteriorated relative to others during this interval, it would affect the validity of our findings. We found that party registration data in 1952 showed an intercorrelation with class of .77. A separately computed correlation using 1956 party registration data and the same measure of class showed an intercorrelation of .83. A portion of this change may have been accounted for by changes in relative class position of precincts, but we believe that the possible changes were small enough and the essential consistency of the two coefficients is high enough to warrant the use of the single class index for the entire period.

We are somewhat troubled as to what is meant by party identification once the class component is removed. Without trying to specify all the possible remaining dimensions of party, we shall content ourselves by calling this "traditional party identification," and we mean approximately what Key and Munger meant in their phrase quoted above. There are obviously strong elements of traditional attachment to the symbols and heroes associated with the party, probably acquired through family socialization, and possessing great potential for organizing the voter's cognitive and perceptual understanding of political events. As our data show, whatever may be involved in "traditional party identification," these elements shape voter responses not only in partisan election situations but also to a high degree in non-partisan situations.

One other limitation inherent in our data requires caution: the focus upon precincts, rather than individuals. The use of aggregate statistics poses an issue much debated in recent years.[10] Aggregate figures admittedly will tell us nothing directly about individual behavior. Nevertheless, they may be appropriate and certainly economical in studying certain relationships among variables, provided the units remain relatively small and as homogeneous as possible. By using precincts in a community well-known to us by long experience we believe we escape most of the strictures that have been leveled against the use of aggregate data.

Class and Party in Partisan Elections

Table I shows that the simple correlations between party registration and vote in partisan elections in Des Moines are uniformly high with one striking exception, the 1960 gubernatorial race. The slight negative correlation between Republican registrations and the vote for Republican candidate Erbe is apparently explained by the widespread perception of rural-urban differences reflected in Erbe's candidacy. Erbe was regarded as a rural Iowa candidate and his support fell off markedly among urban Republicans.

Table I. ***Partisan Elections, Des Moines, 1952–1960***

Candidate	Simple Correlation Party Registration and Vote	Partial Correlation *Party Registration and Vote*	*Class and Vote*	Multiple r
President, 1952	.88	.67	.55	.92
Governor, 1952	.91	.77	.39	.93
Senator, 1954	.90	.74	.39	.92
President, 1956	.94	.796	.455	.95
Governor, 1956	.95	.83	.38	.96
Senator, 1956	.95	.83	.45	.96
President, 1960	.86	.58	.33	.87
Governor, 1960	–.24	–.13	–.01	–.24
Senator, 1960	.93	.76	.33	.93

When we partial out the class component of party orientation we find both uniformities and variations of interest. In 1952 the vote for Eisenhower was on the surface almost as partisan a vote as that for Governor. When class is held constant by means of partial correlation, however, the picture changes. The part played by traditional party affiliation alone is less significant while the class variable is more significant than in other partisan races. We interpret this to mean that lower class Republicans were less enthusiastic for Eisenhower or middle class Democrats were more enthusiastic for him than customary. Presumably it was the latter. Interestingly, in 1956 Eisenhower received a "normal" traditional party vote and a "high-normal" class response. In 1960, the other deviant case, Mr. Nixon either lost Republican support, or gained Democratic support, beyond the usual limits and among voters who were rather evenly distributed across the class spectrum. On the latter and likelier supposition one might infer that the religious factor accounted for much of this result.

Despite these exceptions, it seems warranted to conclude that partisan candidates in Des Moines receive a predictable "party" vote of about .9, and this party vote is composed of a very substantial "traditional" party orientation (.7–.8) plus a smaller but significant class orientation (.33–.46) of middle class voters toward Republican candidates and of lower class voters toward Democratic candidates. Our data do not tell us how much each of these two possibilities contributes to this separate "class effect." Iowa is a "traditionally" Republican state, which might suggest that the major phenomenon operating here consists of lower class voters who register as Republicans for "traditional" reasons but vote for Democratic candidates. Des Moines, however, is fairly evenly divided in party support, and a closely competitive situation might be expected to reduce such "mis-identification." A longer time period and comparative data from other communities would be required to answer the question. No clear distinction appears among offices, although the deviant responses in the 1952 and 1960 Presidential races may suggest that such contests are more likely to depart from the "norm" than other partisan races.

Class and Party in Non-Partisan Elections

The analytical literature examining non-partisan electoral contests and comparing them with partisan elections is less extensive than the hortatory material. Some efforts have been made, however, to formulate systematically the possible consequences of non-partisanship, and some exploratory work has been done to test these hypotheses.[11] Perhaps the principal hypothesized effects of non-partisanship are that party electioneering activity will decline, as will voting in terms of party orientation; as a result, "local considerations," presumably unrelated to national party divisions will emerge as crucial;[12] and middle class Republicans will increase their influence in community affairs by voting in larger proportions than working class Democrats.[13] As Adrian has suggested, however, the effects of non-partisanship vary from city to city.[14] In Des Moines elections since the 1949 adoption of non-partisanship, party organizations have played little or no active role in the campaigns and candidates have not been perceived as Republican or Democratic. In some elections rival slates have competed with backing from sharply differentiated interest groups. In others the major groups have been relatively quiet. During the period we are examining it seems clear that there was no well defined political structure, partisan or otherwise, to the processes of recruitment and campaigning.[15] Thus our findings concerning voting patterns may be more indicative of durable perceptual and cognitive structures among the voters than if more sharply defined campaign contests were standard practice.

Table II. ***Non-Partisan Municipal Elections, Des Moines City Council, 1951–1961***

Candidates	Simple Correlation Party Registration and Vote	Partial Correlation *Party and Vote*	*Class and Vote*	Multiple Correlation r
1951, Holton	.82	.54	.44	.86
1953, Denny	.75	.47	.27	.77
Iles	.80	.51	.37	.80
Mills	.16	.20	–.13	.205
1955, Cleveland	.92	.77	.19	.92
1957, Carlson	.92	.77	.36	.93
Clarke	.82	.51	.34	.84
Grothe	–.87	–.65	–.23	–.87
Iles	–.85	–.59	–.31	–.87
Margulius	–.93	–.78	–.43	–.94
Myers	.92	.74	.30	.91
1959, Grothe	.89	.72	.17	.9
1961, Bradley	–.70	–.29	–.31	–.74
Harper	.88	.61	.41	.9
Iles	.88	.61	.38	.89

Table II presents our findings for six elections to the Des Moines city council. We have not listed results for all the candidates, but we have omitted none who showed striking deviations from the patterns observed in the reported data. With only one exception the simple correlation of party registration and vote for non-partisan candidates is very high, though the mean is not quite as high as for the partisan candidates listed in Table I.

A major difference between partisan and non-partisan situations appears, however, when one examines the partial correlations. Again, interesting variations emerge between candidates and between elections, and we shall discuss these in greater detail below. Taking all the elections together, however, we may say that traditional party affiliation makes a somewhat smaller contribution to the vote in non-partisan elections than in partisan elections and that the range of variation is greater. With respect to the independent effect of class, little difference appears between partisan and non-partisan races, the "normal" partial correlation ranging from about .3 to .44 in non-partisan elections, as compared with the .33–.45 range in partisan elections.

These findings clearly indicate that despite the non-partisan format of local elections in Des Moines, and despite a relative absence of overt electioneering by party organizations or partisan identification of candidates, cleavages are manifested in local campaigns which bear a close resemblance to partisan cleavages in the community. The larger variation in partial correlations of party and vote in non-partisan elections is significant however. What appears to happen is that when the intensity of the campaign controversy is low, the salience of variables associated with party affiliation is relatively low. This was notably the situation in 1951 and 1953, the first two elections held following the adoption of the city manager plan in 1949.[16] When the campaign is heated, and particularly when symbols like "pro-labor" and "anti-labor" are extensively used the importance of the party variable increases substantially.[17] This was the case in 1955, 1957 and 1959. In 1955 the elected candidates were widely perceived as representing organized labor although that campaign was not marked by intense oratory. Between 1955 and 1957, however, it was loudly argued that labor dominated the council and the manager as well. The controversy reached its climax in the 1957 election when two rival slates ran essentially pro and con a "labor control" platform. Turnout was very high in this election. In 1959 the voting patterns were similar, just as they had been in 1955, but the turnout declined. By 1961 the issue had subsided sufficiently so that broad spectrum support for candidates could begin to reappear.

Thus, paradoxically, when class themes are stressed in the campaign rhetoric, it is the non-class elements in party affiliation which respond. A tentative case might even be made, based upon 1955 and 1959, but not 1957, that with the heavy use of "labor" and "anti-labor" symbols, not only does party go up in importance but class goes down. We are not prepared to go quite this far. It is significant, however, that the issue of organized "labor control" of the city government evokes responses congruent with the "traditional" factors involved in party affiliation rather than with class position. This finding may be explained in part by the fact that Des Moines is not a major industrial center with a heavily unionized or militant labor force. Consequently, class consciousness in terms of labor and anti-labor is perhaps not highly developed. Instead the "labor power" issue is associated with national party symbols and appeal. Cognition of the issue is achieved through the structure of party identification and loyalty, and voting responses are therefore correlated with party registration. It may be, of course, that Des Moines is not atypical and that traditional party identification generally performs this function. It may also be that this variable is crucial with respect to other issues. Yet there are clearly issues and candidacies which are seen in terms neither of traditional party nor of class, as, for example, in the 1960 gubernatorial race. Some more comprehensive taxonomy of major types of relationships between issues and cognitive structures is called for.

A more consensual pattern may be observed in the elections of Mills in 1953 and Bradley in 1961. These two candidates, more than any others, received endorsements and active support from a wide range of interests. In Mills' election the group support resulted in a vote that most nearly approaches community consensus, at least in terms of our two variables. His traditional party support is slightly Republican while his class following, though not statistically of much significance, is very slightly in the opposite or lower class direction. Bradley's endorsements were not as comprehensive of the whole range of Des Moines groups. His vote, indeed, shows a simple correlation with party registration of .7. The partial correlations, however, show that Bradley's support was quite different from other, more clearly partisan, candidates. His vote is accounted for in almost equal parts by the two independent variables.

Candidates in 1951 received broad organized group support also, but that support was considerably more passive than in the case of Mills or Bradley. Overt conflict over issues was largely absent in both of the first two campaigns following the adoption of the city manager–non-partisan council system, and interest group participation was minimal. The result was a low turnout. Thus the hypothesis that class considerations will be more important relative to traditional party identification in non-partisan elections seems to hold true, if at all, only when group conflict and debate over issues are minimized; and it is, in some sense, a function of the size of the vote also. We shall examine this relationship further below. Unfortunately, our data are not extensive enough to permit further testing of this restated hypothesis, but the findings of Williams and Adrian, noted above, give it partial support.

The general significance of non-partisanship in local Des Moines elections may be summarized as follows:

1. Traditional party identification continues to play an important role or, at least, is associated with other variables that play an important role in affecting the vote in non-partisan elections.

2. In a non-partisan system, greater variations appear in the effect of traditional party identification on the vote. In a given case, the "party" dimension may be virtually eliminated, though this is unusual. Nevertheless, the style of campaign and specific alliance patterns may alter the impact of traditional party identification over quite a wide range—in our data from .2 to .78.

3. Non-partisanship has relatively little consistent impact on the salience of class considerations in voting for local candidates. We shall see below that class is related more strongly than party identification to *turnout* in local elections. With respect to the *direction* of the vote, however, class bears much the same relationship in non-partisan as in partisan elections, although there is a small increase in the range of the partial correlations (.17 to .44) in the non-partisan elections.

4. The principal effect of non-partisanship seems to be a loosening of the interconnections between traditional party identification and class. Whereas in partisan contests the relative weight of the two variables remained reasonably constant (especially if one excludes the 1952 and 1960 presidential contests), in the non-partisan elections the variations are substantial. In some instances party is high and class is low in significance; in other cases class is high and party declines; in still others both class and party variables fail to predict the vote. In a sense, this loosening of the structure of interrelationships between class and traditional party identification may be what is meant by "local considerations" to which non-partisanship is expected to give freer expression than a parti-

san format can do. If so, then our data suggest that non-partisanship leads to some of the hypothesized consequences.

Turnout

Williams and Adrian found that in the communities they studied which had at-large elections Republicans showed a significantly higher turnout than Democrats; and they concluded, with considerable qualification, that non-partisanship had some effect in increasing the relative strength of Republicans and decreasing the relative strength of Democrats.[18] Our findings support this hypothesis but add a further qualification. Table III summarizes the data. It is true that there is generally a higher simple correlation between party registration and turnout in municipal elections than in national elections, although the relatively high figure for the 1954 senatorial contest may imply that *any* off-year election, partisan or non-partisan, would show a similar correlation. The really striking thing about these data, however, is that with two exceptions the simple correlation is almost entirely accounted for by the class component of party affiliation.

Table III. ***Turnout, Des Moines, 1949–1961***

Election	Simple Correlation Party Registration and Turnout	Partial Correlation *Party and Turnout*	*Class and Turnout*	Multiple Correlation r
Charter Election, 1949	.36	.14	.3	.45
Municipal Election, 1951	.73	.41	.33	.76
National Election, 1952	.23	–.12	.35	.4
Municipal Election, 1953	.55	.04	.49	.68
Senatorial Election, 1954	.45	.08	.31	.53
Municipal Election, 1955	.42	.04	.29	.49
National Election, 1956	.18	.09	.24	.3
Municipal Election, 1957	.78	.39	.42	.82
Municipal Election, 1959	.64	.18	.39	.7
National Election, 1960	.15	–.1	.22	.26
Municipal Election, 1961	.6	.1	.41	.68

Of the two occasions when the "traditional" party variable did show a significant correlation, only 1957, we believe, gives direct support to the hypothesis that a non-partisan system will bring out a disproportionate Republican vote in the sense of traditional party identification. In 1951 the turnout was so low and the contest so spiritless that no real advantage can be said to have accrued to any group as a result of differentials in turnout. In 1953 this was even more true. In two of the hotly contested elections, 1955 and 1959, there was no significant connection between traditional party identification and turnout; and, of course, there was none in any of the national elections. Our data do not give us any clues concerning the possibility that Democratic adherents disproportionately fail to register. We can say, however, that—except in 1957—having registered, they are nearly as likely to vote as Republicans in both partisan and non-partisan contests, *insofar as "traditional" party factors are operative.*

The class component remains significantly related to turnout, however. This in turn means that lower income voters will vote less regularly than upper income residents. This relationship holds somewhat more strongly in municipal elections than in national elections, although the effect is apparent in both. We may conclude that non-partisanship gives some additional weight to class by means of differential turnout, and this in turn gives upper income groups relatively greater power in the local community. Again, however, the effect is accounted for in terms of class rather than traditional party identification.

Class and Party in Referenda

We have only a limited number of referenda issues with which to test the relative impact of class and party on the vote. Table IV summarizes these data. It will be seen that only in the case of the vote on the city manager plan was there a high correlation. In this case the class variable was especially prominent but the impact of traditional party orientation was also important. Both these findings are in accord with our expectation that local government reform would attract disproportionate support from Republicans *and* from upper status groups.

The findings on the bond tax are probably even less conclusive than the correlations suggest since the publicity and the vote on this measure were very scanty. The class variable appears to be significant but it is hard to tell how reliable the correlation is. The slightly negative correlation between class and approval of low rent housing, although not surprising, is not sufficiently strong to warrant any generalization.

Table IV. ***Referenda Votes, Des Moines, 1949–1960***

Issue	Simple Correlation Party Registration and Vote	Partial Correlation *Party and Vote*	Partial Correlation *Class and Vote*	Multiple Correlation r
City Manager Plan, 1949	.86	.62	.50	.90
Constitutional Convention, 1960	–.12	–.08	.02	–.12
Bond Tax, 1961	.51	.07	.31	.57
Low Rent Housing, 1961	.16	.20	–.14	.21

The data concerning the vote on calling a state constitutional convention is statistically insignificant, but that fact alone is interesting. This issue apparently combined a number of conflicting political dimensions. It had a large element of urban-rural conflict, with urban interests favoring a new constitution and rural interests opposed. It also involved a conservative-liberal division, however, with conservatives opposing and liberals favoring. Finally, there was some component of reformist spirit involved in the agitation for a convention. As a result, Des Moines Republicans were severely cross-pressured. As relatively conservative they opposed, while as residents of an under-represented city they supported a convention; on reformist grounds they were divided. Democrats favored the convention on the first two grounds and were unsure on the third. The insignificant correlations reveal the way in which these cross-pressures were resolved. Both party groups and all classes tended to divide in similar ways, favoring the convention by a margin of four to one.

We would anticipate that on most questions of municipal finance, and possibly on some other referenda matters, simple or partial correlational analysis of large cities—employing the two variables examined here—would typically produce insignificant results. We would anticipate a curvilinear relationship in which low income voters and middle-to-upper-middle income voters approved additional taxes or bond issues, while lower-middle-to-middle income groups opposed. In any event, our data suggest that voting patterns on referenda issues are generally quite unlike those for non-partisan local elections. Further analysis in other communities of the three types of voting situations—partisan, non-partisan, and referenda—are needed to permit more confident generalization.

Concluding Observations

A number of our findings call for additional analysis. One question that emerges more strongly than ever concerns the content of traditional party identification. Our findings show the importance of party identification in predicting the vote even when a class component is held constant. It is easy enough to say that this residual party variable is the product of socializing influences, primarily in the family, and we have no doubt that this mechanism is of crucial importance. Nevertheless, we need to know what the limiting conditions are in order to assess the likelihood of changes in the effect of party. We have shown that a non-partisan system has some effect, primarily to increase the range of impact of the traditional party variable. We have also found that heightened controversy, especially using "labor control" themes, increases the effect of party. These findings suggest that party identification, even when class is held constant, is linked with a significant element of socio-economic perspective of a quasi-class character.

We are dealing with a city, and this fact plus the absence of correlation between party and the vote for the rurally oriented Erbe in 1960 suggest that the urban-rural dimension is not present here as a component of party identification. The 1949 vote on the city manager plan suggests that there might be a reformist element involved, but this hypothesis is cast into question by the 1960 vote on the constitutional question.

It is possible, of course, that our measure of class taps only a portion of the class dimension, and that if we added measures of income and occupation we might further reduce the partial correlation between party and the vote and increase the predictive power of class. The inter-correlations among objective indexes of class, however, are generally reported to be high, and thus it is doubtful that additional measures of class would lower very much the reported correlations of party and the vote. A more likely prospect might be subjective class identification. It is possible that in Des Moines enough people identify with the middle or upper-middle class and the Republican party who, on "objective" grounds, are of lower or lower-middle class rank to account for the fact that party identification predicts the vote more fully that does class.

Although these possibilities cannot be rejected without further testing, we are inclined to think that traditional party identification is relatively independent of class and that this identification carries with it a mechanism for the perceptual and cognitive ordering of political events, even quasi-class events, whether occurring in a partisan or non-partisan electoral format. Some events, to be sure, are perceived in different terms, but with respect to candidates, at least, these are exceptional.

Campbell *et al.,* found a decline in class-related voting—status depolarization—in their analysis of national electoral behavior.[19] Our data do not reveal a clear tendency in this direction, although the 1960 results are lower in the correlations of class and voting than those of earlier years. Campbell, *et al.,* point out, however, that status depolarization is less likely to occur in an urban setting, so perhaps our data are not atypical for American cities.

One final dimension of our analysis that requires comment is that of time. Non-partisanship has been in effect in Des Moines for a little more than a decade. It is certainly possible that, given a longer period, local elections would be perceived and would evoke responses in less party-related terms; but there is no clear evidence of such a trend from our data.

We have attempted to determine the relative importance of class position and traditional party identification as variables affecting turnout and direction of the vote in both partisan and non-partisan elections. Although our findings are limited in time and space, they seem generally compatible with other studies.[20] But it will be important to determine the extent to which party and class are durable perceptual and cognitive mechanisms for organizing the political world, as well as the conditions under which other mechanisms—urban-rural identification, for example—are operative and the extent to which they reinforce or compete with traditional party identification and class.

Notes:

1. *Class and Party in the Eisenhower Years* (New York, 1962), p. 1. The first statement is drawn from Paul F. Lazarsfeld, Bernard Berelson, and Hazel Gaudet, *The People's Choice* (New York, 1948), p. 27; the second from V. O. Key, Jr. and Frank Munger, "Social Determinism and Electoral Decision: The Case of Indiana," in Eugene Burdick and Arthur J. Brodbeck, eds., *American Voting Behavior* (New York, 1959), pp. 281–2.

2. *Op. cit.,* p. 4.

3. See Angus Campbell, Phillip E. Converse, Warren E. Miller, and Donald E. Stokes, *The American Voter* (New York, 1960), esp. ch. 13.

4. *Ibid.,* pp. 364–8.

5. In Des Moines it is possible to register without declaring party affiliation, and about 13 percent of the electorate does so. There is very little variation, however, in the proportion of "no-party" registrants by precincts, and so we have excluded them in our calculations of party registration.

6. All correlations are Pearson product-moment correlations using percentages of voters registered Republican and neighborhood housing rating for each of 68 precincts as independent variables. The data are arranged so that positive correlations indicate positive relationships. Partial correlations greater than .3 are significant at the .01 level. Partial correlations greater than .23 are significant at the .05 level. Computer work was performed under a National Science Foundation grant to Washington University for unsponsored research.

We have chosen to report our data in terms of partial and multiple r's. An alternative method would utilize Beta scores which would indicate both the closeness of fit and the slopes of the regression lines, whereas the partial r's indicate only the former. The substance of our conclusions would not be altered by this method although the numerical values would. Partial r's are somewhat more familiar to social scientists and may provide more ready comparability.

7. Primarily because of its convenience for our purposes, we have used the neighborhood classification prepared by Howard J. Nelson, reported in *The Livelihood Structure of Des Moines, Iowa,* unpublished Ph.D. diss., University of Chicago, 1949, pp. 110–15 and map, figure 2. Nelson, in turn, followed the field classification procedures and categories developed by W. D. Jones, "Field Mapping of Residential Areas in Metropolitan Chicago," *Annals of the Association of American Geographers,* Vol. 21 (1931), pp. 207–14. Nelson utilizes five neighborhood categories and bases his classification of blocks on size of housing units, spacing, state of upkeep, need of major repairs or new facility, age, and median rental. In virtually every case, however, the assignment of a block to one category or another hinged upon the relative condition of housing in that block to other Des Moines housing. No absolute standard is involved.

8. See, particularly, Joseph A. Kahl and James A. Davis, "A Comparison of Indexes of Socio-Economic Status," *American Sociological Review,* Vol. 20 (1955), pp. 317–25.

9. It is premature, of course, to conclude that a Shevky-Bell index would not provide an adequate measure of class differentiation in Des Moines. It does appear, however, that as the index was designed for use in larger and more heterogeneous metropolitan areas, its ability to discriminate among rather narrowly differentiated class groupings would not be high. See Eshref Shevky and Wendell Bell, *Social Area Analysis* (Stanford, 1955).

10. For an excellent recent discussion of this problem, see Austin Ranney, "The Utility and Limitations of Aggregate Data in the Study of Electoral Behavior," in Ranney, ed., *Essays in the Behavioral Study of Politics* (Urbana, Ill., 1962), pp. 91–102.

11. See Eugene C. Lee, *The Politics of Nonpartisanship* (Berkeley and Los Angeles, 1960); Charles R. Adrian, "A Typology for Nonpartisan Elections," *Western Political Quarterly,* Vol. 12 (1959), pp. 449–58; Charles R. Adrian, "Some General Characteristics of Nonpartisan Elections," *American Political Science Review,* Vol. 46 (1952), pp. 766–76; Charles E. Gilbert, "Some Aspects of Nonpartisan Elections in Large Cities," *Midwest Journal of Political Science,* Vol. 6 (1962), pp. 345–62.

12. See, for example, the discussion in C. M. Kneier, *City Government in the United States,* rev. ed. (New York, 1947), pp. 497–508; Howard R. Penniman, *Sait's American Parties and Elections,* 4th ed. (New York, 1948), pp. 203–5. But *cf.* Adrian, "Some General Characteristics . . .," *loc. cit.,* pp. 773–4.

13. See, for example, Robert E. Lane, *Political Life* (Glencoe, Ill., 1959), pp. 269–71.

14. "A Typology . . .," *loc cit.* In Adrian's classification, Des Moines elections would appear to be Type III. *"Elections where slates of candidates are supported by various interest groups, but political party organizations have little or no part in campaigns, or are active only sporadically,"* p. 455, italics in original. Adrian notes that this is a very common type of non-partisan election. p. 456.

15. For a non-partisan city with highly structured local party organizations closely mirroring national party lines, see J. Leiper Freeman, "Local Party Systems: Theoretical Considerations and a Case Analysis," *American Journal of Sociology,* Vol. 44 (1958), pp. 282–9.

16. In the 1949 election on the adoption of the city manager system, 49.1 percent of the registered voters went to the polls. In subsequent municipal elections the turnouts were as follows: 34.3 percent in 1951; 20 percent in 1953; 39.3 percent in 1955; 45.7 percent in 1957; 39.3 percent in 1959; and 36.3 percent in 1961.

17. Oliver P. Williams and Charles R. Adrian found that in four Michigan communities with non-partisan elections, "the more assiduously issues in the non-partisan elections were pursued, the more the resulting vote conformed to the partisan pattern." "The Insulation of Local Politics under the Nonpartisan Ballot," *American Political Science Review,* Vol. 53 (1959), pp. 1052–63 at p. 1058. Our data suggest that not all issues have this effect in Des Moines, but the question of "labor power" certainly does.

18. *Ibid.,* pp. 1059–61.
19. *Op. cit.,* pp. 333–80. For evidence that depolarization may not actually have occurred in any consistent manner over time, see Robert R. Alford, "The Role of Social Class in American Voting Behavior," *Western Political Quarterly,* Vol. 16 (1963), pp. 180–95.
20. Especially, Williams and Adrian, *op. cit.*

8 *The Utilization of Political Resources: Variations on a Theme*

by Robert A. Dahl

Given the fact that most citizens are not engaged very much in politics, several conclusions are evident. First, in so far as participation is a valid measure of resource use, we must conclude that comparatively few citizens use their political resources at a high rate. Second, in so far as the use of political resources is a necessary condition for political influence, only citizens who use their political resources at a high rate are likely to be highly influential. It follows that the number of highly influential citizens must be a relatively small segment of the population.

What kinds of factors are likely to induce people to use their resources at a relatively high rate? [Earlier], four hypotheses were advanced to help account for variations in the amount of political resources different individuals actually used. It was hypothesized that one group of citizens is likely to use more resources than another if (1) their political resources are greater in amount, (2) their expectations of success are higher, (3) the payoff they expect from using their resources for non-political purposes is lower, or (4) the value they attach to the outcome of political decisions is higher. On the assumption that the rate at which a registered voter participates in politics

Reprinted from *Who Governs?*, by Robert A. Dahl (New Haven, Conn.: Yale University Press, 1961), pp. 282–301, by permission of the author and the publisher.

is a valid measure of the extent to which he uses his political resources, let us now examine these four hypotheses.

Variations in the Supply of Resources

Political participation does tend to increase with the amount of resources at one's disposal. For example, participation in local political decisions is:

> greater among citizens with high incomes than among citizens with low incomes;
>
> greater among citizens with high social standing than among citizens with low social standing;
>
> greater among citizens with considerable formal education than among citizens with little;
>
> greater among citizens with professional, business, and white-collar occupations than among citizens with working-class occupation; and greater among citizens from better residential areas than among citizens from poorer areas.[1]

For want of a better term, I shall refer to citizens who are relatively well off with respect to income, social standing, education, occupation, or residence as the Better-Off. To summarize: participation in local political decisions is higher among the Better-Off than among the less well off.

For three reasons, however, the matter is much more complex than this simple statement suggests. First, all the relationships mentioned above represent *statistical tendencies.* For example, it is true that the more income one has the more *likely* one is to participate in local political activity. Indeed with some kinds of participation the relation with income is quite striking. (Chart 1) But it is also true that 42 per cent of our sample of registered voters who reported incomes over $8,000 were relatively inactive; on the other hand, 17 per cent of those with incomes from $2,000 to $5,000 and 2 per cent of those with incomes from $5,000 to $8,000 were highly active participants in local decisions.

Second, because the number of Better-Off citizens is inevitably rather small, the *aggregate* activity of citizens with smaller resources is often impressively large. In our sample of

Chart 1. ***General participation in local political affairs* increases with income.***

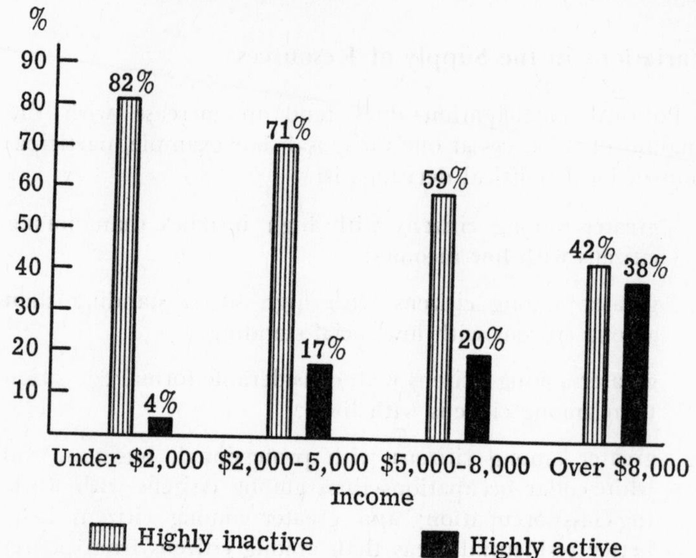

* Index of local action. Those with medium activity are not shown on the graph.

Chart 2. ***Although general participation in local political affairs varies with income, the Better-Off are a minority of all participants.***

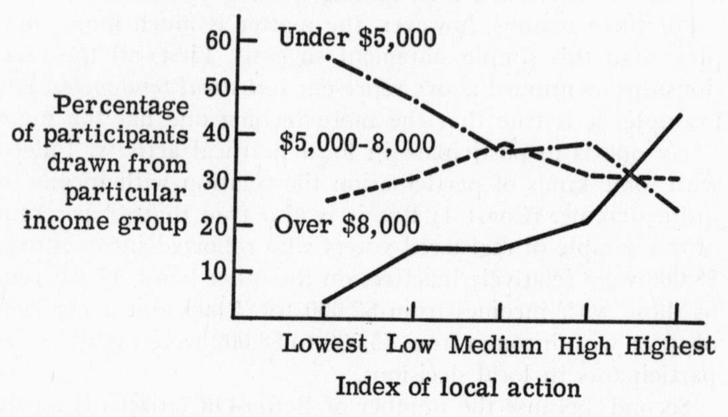

No information: 13% 6% 9% 7% 0%

N=525

registered voters, for every citizen who reported an income of over $8,000, more than five reported incomes less than that; in fact almost half the sample reported incomes less than $5,000. Consequently even though citizens with incomes in the lower brackets are much less likely to participate actively in local decisions than citizens with larger incomes, there are so many more in the first group that a smaller proportion of them can amount to an aggregate greater than the group of participants with larger incomes. For example, citizens with incomes less than $8,000 a year outnumbered those with greater incomes at *every* level of political participation from the lowest to the highest. In fact, as Chart 2 shows, citizens with incomes less than $5,000 outnumbered citizens with incomes over $8,000 at every level of activity except the highest; one-fourth of the people in the most active category and nearly two-fifths in the second most active group have incomes under $5,000.

In the third place, the extent to which the Better-Off citizens participate in local decisions varies a good deal, depending on the nature of the participation. They participate much more heavily in noncampaign than in campaign activities. Even at the highest levels of campaign participation, citizens with incomes under $5,000 greatly outnumber citizens with incomes over $8,000; moreover the proportions drawn from the less well off are not much lower among the most active participants than among the less active participants. (Chart 3, p. 180).

The greater readiness of the Better-Off to engage in *general* local action than campaign activities shows up in a variety of ways. Greater formal education, higher income, higher social position, better neighborhood, and a white-collar occupation are all associated less strongly with campaign participation than with general local action. If campaign activity is distinguished from exclusively noncampaign forms of political participation the differences are even more striking. Chart 4 shows that among the most active participants in noncampaign community activities the proportions of citizens who are Better-Off by four different criteria are all very much higher than among the less active. Chart 5 (p. 181), by contrast, shows that the participation of the Better-Off in campaign political activities is clearly much less pronounced.

Since the propensity among the Better-Off to engage more

Chart 3. *Campaign participation varies only moderately with income, and the less well off are the largest category at every level of campaign participation.*

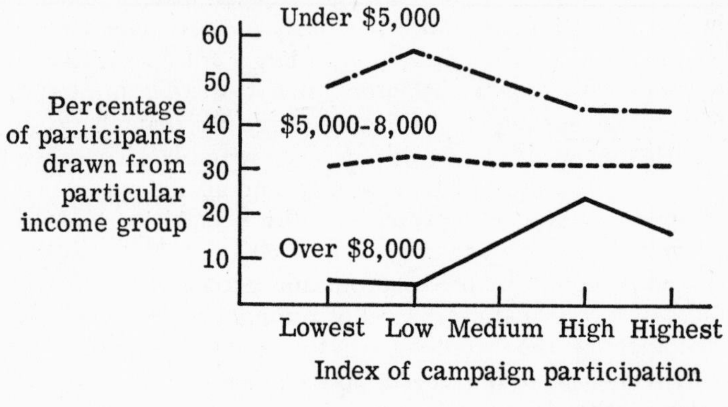

No information: 16% 4% 9% 3% 12%

N= 525

Chart 4. *The Better-Off participate heavily in noncampaign forms of political activity.*

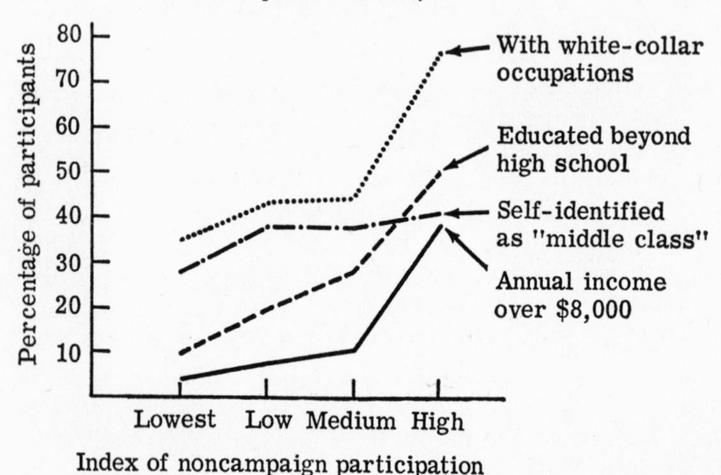

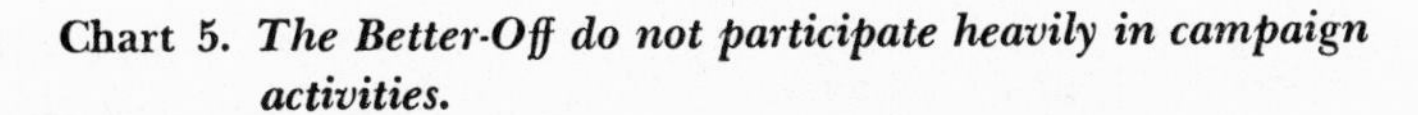

Chart 5. *The Better-Off do not participate heavily in campaign activities.*

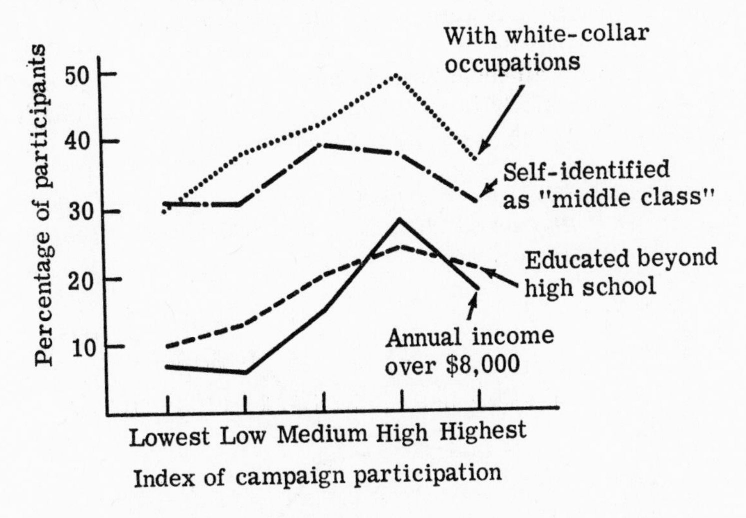

in noncampaign activities than in campaign activities evidently does not arise as a result of differences in access to resources among the Better-Off, other factors must be at work.

Variations in Political Confidence

I have suggested that an individual who is relatively confident of success in attempting to influence decisions is much more likely to make the attempt than one who fears failure. Confidence might vary with the specific political situation; if you happen to be a friend of the incumbent mayor and an enemy of his rival you might reasonably be more confident about succeeding now than if his rival wins the next election. However, confidence in capacity to influence government officials also seems to be a more general, pervasive, stable attitude in an individual. Some individuals bring into the political arena a durable optimism that survives occasional setbacks; others are incurably pessimistic. One of the striking characteristics of the activist in politics is his relatively high confidence that what he does *matters;* by contrast, the inactive citizen is more prone to doubt his effectiveness. A citizen who tends to feel that people like him have no say about what the local government does, or that the only way he can have a say is by voting, or that politics and government are too complicated for him to understand what is going on, or that local public officials don't care much what he thinks, is much less likely to participate in local political decisions than one who disagrees with all these propositions.[2] In short, the more one participates actively in local affairs the more confident one is likely to be in one's capacity to be effective. (Chart 6)

Chart 6. ***The more one participates in local political affairs, the more likely one is to have a high sense of political efficacy.***

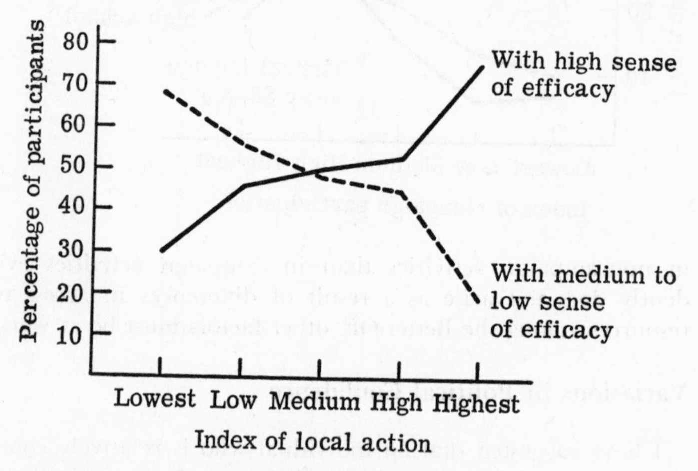

Participation and political confidence evidently reinforce one another. A citizen with a high sense of political efficacy is more likely to participate in politics than a citizen pessimistic about his chances of influencing local officials. Participation in turn reinforces confidence. Evidently as a citizen becomes more familiar with the operation of the political system and develops more ties with leaders, subleaders, and activists, he tends to asume that he can get the attention of officials for his views and demands. If he becomes a subleader, he is likely to have a very high sense of political efficacy. (Chart 7) Conversely, if one has little confidence in one's capacity to influence officials, one is less likely to participate and hence never acquires the skills, familiarity with the system, and associations that might build up confidence.

There is, however, a second and closely related factor associated with political confidence that might loosely be called the possession of "middle-class" attributes and resources: a college education, above-average income, a white-collar occupation, and the like. Level of education is particularly im-

Chart 7. *Subleaders have a very high sense of political efficacy.*

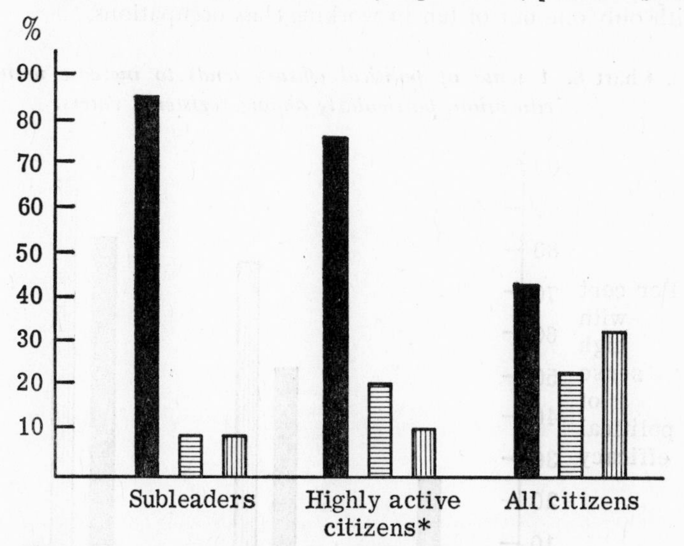

* Highest on index of local action. Those who did not answer are omitted from the graph.

portant. Among subleaders and registered voters alike political confidence is higher among citizens with a college education than among citizens with a high school education; the relation is much more apparent among registered voters than among subleaders. (Chart 8)

One might conjecture that the relationship between political confidence and "middle-class" attributes would disappear if one were to eliminate from consideration all those who are below a certain socioeconomic threshold and whose presence serves to pull down the averages for the working-class strata. However, this conjecture appears to be false. Table I includes only the registered voters in our sample who had at least a seventh grade education, over $2,000 income, and both parents born in the United States. Even among this group, twice as many persons with white-collar occupations of all sorts, from clerks to executives, were highly active as among persons with working-class occupations: one out of five registered voters with "middle-class" occupations was highly active compared with only one out of ten in working-class occupations.

Chart 8. ***A sense of political efficacy tends to increase with education, particularly among registered voters.***

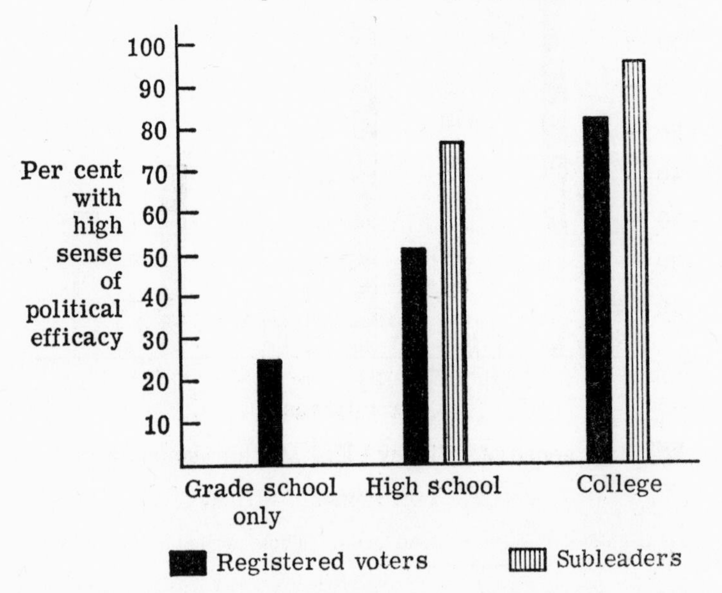

Moreover, twice as many from the middling strata had a high sense of political confidence as from the working strata; conversely, twice as many persons in the working strata had a low sense of their political efficacy as in the middling strata. In fact, among the middling strata, one-third were highly confident and only one-sixth had little confidence in their political efficacy; among the working strata, it was precisely the other way around—one-sixth were highly confident and one-third had little sense of confidence. (Table II)

The importance of confidence to political activity is indicated by the fact that the sharp differences between middling and working strata in the extent to which they participate in

Table I. ***Registered Voters with Middle-Class Resources Are More Likely to Be Politically Active than Skilled and Unskilled Laborers, Artisans, etc., Even if Groups Below the "Political Threshold" Are Eliminated***

Index of Political Action	Middle-Class Occupations %	Working-Class Occupations %
High	21	11
Medium	22	21
Low	57	68
Total	100	100
N	*162*	*152*

NOTE: Table includes only respondents who reported seven or more grades of formal education, over $2,000 income, and both parents born in the United States.

Table II. ***Registered Voters with Middle-Class Resources Are Also More Likely than Workers to Have a High Sense of Political Efficacy***

Sense of Political Efficacy	Middle-Class Occupations %	Working-Class Occupations %
High	33	18
Medium	51	50
Low	16	32
Total	100	100
N	*162*	*152*

NOTE: See Note, Table I.

local affairs very nearly disappear if one considers their level of political confidence. Among persons from the middling strata who have a high level of political confidence, one-third are highly active participants in local affairs; the same proportion holds among the working strata. Conversely, among middling strata with a low degree of political confidence, slightly over two-thirds participate little or not at all in local affairs; the same thing is true among the working strata. (Table III)

Because the Better-Off citizens with "middle-class" attributes and resources are also likely to participate more in political affairs, probably an important circularity develops that increases the influence of the Better-Off and decreases the influence of the working classes. In the way suggested earlier

Table III. ***Registered Voters with Similar Levels of Confidence Participate at About the Same Rate in Local Affairs Whether They Have White-Collar or Working-Class Resources***

Sense of Political Efficacy	Index of Local Action: *High* %	*Medium* %	*Low* %	*Total* %	*N*
HIGH					
Middle classes*	33	22	45	100	*54*
Working classes*	32	14	54	100	*28*
MEDIUM					
Middle classes	17	22	61	100	*83*
Working classes	5	19	76	100	*75*
LOW					
Middle classes	8	24	68	100	*25*
Working classes	6	29	65	100	*49*
Total					*314*

*Middle classes include executives, managers, professionals, administrative personnel, small businessmen, clerks, salesmen, technicians. Working classes include skilled manual employees, machine operators, semi-skilled and unskilled laborers.

NOTE: See Note, Table I.

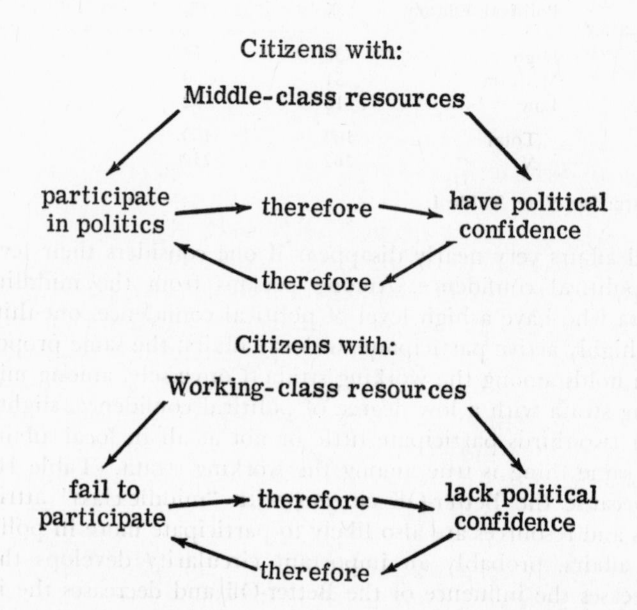

each characteristic reinforces the other. This process of reinforcement might be illustrated as shown on page 186.

Although this can hardly be the whole explanation, it helps to account for the fact that executives and professional people are more likely to attempt to influence city officials than clerks, salesmen, and manual laborers. (Table IV) The act of picking up a telephone and calling a public official in order to

Table IV. ***Professional Men and Executives Are More Likely to Attempt to Influence City Officials than Are Clerks, Salesmen, and Manual Laborers***

	Occupations			
	Professional and managerial %	*Clerical and sales* %	*Manual laborers* %	*Not ascertained* %
Attempt to influence politician or governmental official*	41	28	29	21
No attempt	59	72	71	79
Total	100	100	100	100
N	*99*	*65*	*153*	*29*

*"Have you ever contacted any local public official or politicians to let them know what you would like them to do on something you were interested in?"

NOTE: See Note, Table I.

make a request has many familiar analogues in the life of the business executive or professional man; it is hardly a strange or formidable activity. To the clerk or artisan, however, it is more unusual, though the easy availability of the alderman helps a great deal to make it less difficult.

Why is campaign participation so much less popular among the Better-Off citizens than other forms of participation? Evidently the circular process by which participation and confidence reinforce one another is attenuated by the plain facts of party life. Once the ex-plebes had taken over control of the parties and used them as instruments to appeal to the immigrants and their children, it became difficult for the Better-Off to succeed in party affairs, nominations, and elections; they became estranged from the men who governed the parties and alien to their problems and tactics. Today, two generations later, it is by no means unrealistic for the Better-Off citizen to be somewhat pessimistic about his chances of success in *party* politics and at the same time relatively confident about his capacity for influencing city officials in various other ways.

Variations in Alternative Opportunities

Citizens also vary in the rate at which they use their political resources because of differences in opportunities for achieving goals through means other than political action. In an affluent society dominated by goals that are typically sought through individual rather than collective action, citizens are confronted with a variety of opportunities for gaining their primary goals without ever resorting to political action at all. Essentially, this is why the level of citizen participation is so low.

Some citizens, however, have fewer alternatives to political action than others. Probably the most significant group in New Haven whose opportunities are sharply restricted by social and economic barriers are Negroes.

The Negroes are a relatively small though increasing minority in New Haven. In 1950 they were 6 per cent of the population. They comprised 9 per cent of our sample of registered voters. Although they are gradually dispersing, in 1950 they were concentrated in a few Negro ghettos; in fact, about 40 per cent of the Negro population was concentrated in only one of the city's thirty-three wards, the Nineteenth, where three out of four persons were Negroes.

Although discrimination is declining, in the private socioeconomic sphere of life New Haven Negroes still encounter far greater obstacles than the average white person. They find it difficult to move from Negro neighborhoods into white neighborhoods. Many private employers are reluctant to hire Negroes for white-collar jobs. In 1950, only four of the thirty-three wards had a smaller proportion of the labor force in white-collar jobs than the Nineteenth. Only three wards had a lower median income. These differences cannot be attributed solely to disparities in education, for in 1950 the median number of school years completed in the Nineteenth (8.8 years) was only slightly lower than for the whole city (9.1 years). Although nineteen wards were on the average better off in education, thirteen were worse off.

In contrast to the situation the Negro faces in the private socioeconomic sphere, in local politics and government the barriers are comparatively slight. There is no discrimination against Negroes who wish to vote; they have participated in elections for generations. Though they are a relatively small minority, both parties compete vigorously for their support. Partly because of their votes, Negroes are not discriminated against in city employment; they have only to meet the qualifications required of white applicants to become policemen, firemen, school teachers, clerks, stenographers. Negroes also share in city patronage, city contracts, and other favors. Because both parties nominate a Negro to run as alderman from the Nineteenth Ward, the Board of Aldermen always contains one Negro. Both parties nominate a Negro to one city-wide elective office. In 1954 Mayor Lee appointed a Negro as corporation counsel; in 1960 he appointed a Negro to the Board of Education.

In comparison with whites, therefore, Negroes find no greater obstacles to achieving their goals through political action but very much greater difficulties through activities in the private socioeconomic spheres. Consequently it is reasonable to expect that Negroes might employ their resources more in political action than the average white person does.

This hypothesis is strikingly confirmed by the evidence. For example, when we asked our sample of registered voters, "Assuming the pay is the same, would you prefer a job with the city government or with a private firm?" only 37 per cent of the white voters said they would prefer a city job, compared with 64 per cent of the Negroes. Thirty-eight per cent of the Negro voters said they would like to see a son enter politics, compared with 27 per cent among the whites.

What is even more impressive is the extent of Negro participation in politics. Although slightly less than one out of ten persons in our sample of registered voters was a Negro, nearly one out of four of the citizens who participated most in campaign and electoral activities was a Negro; in the next most active group one out of six was a Negro. With respect to local action generally, the percentages of Negroes in the two most active groups were 24 per cent and 16 per cent. Looking at the matter in another way, 44 per cent of the Negroes in our sample were among the two most active groups of participants in campaigns and elections compared with 20 per cent among whites (Chart 9); 38 per cent of the Negroes in our sample were among the two most active groups of participants in

Chart 9. *New Haven Negroes participate more than whites in campaigns and elections.*

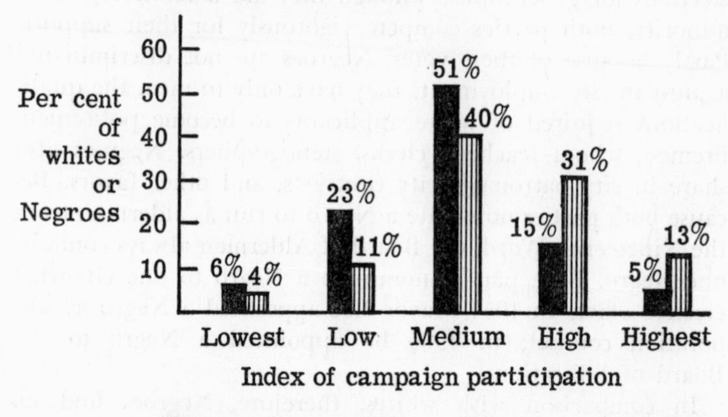

local affairs generally, compared with 17 per cent among the whites. (Chart 10)

The position of the Negro in New Haven helps us to explain why the Better-Off prefer to participate by means other than through political parties and campaigns. An important incentive for routine participation in party activities is the prospect of receiving favors from the city, particularly jobs, minor contracts for snow removal, printing, and the like. The large contractor who constructs buildings, streets, highways

Chart 10. *New Haven Negroes participate more than whites in local political affairs generally.*

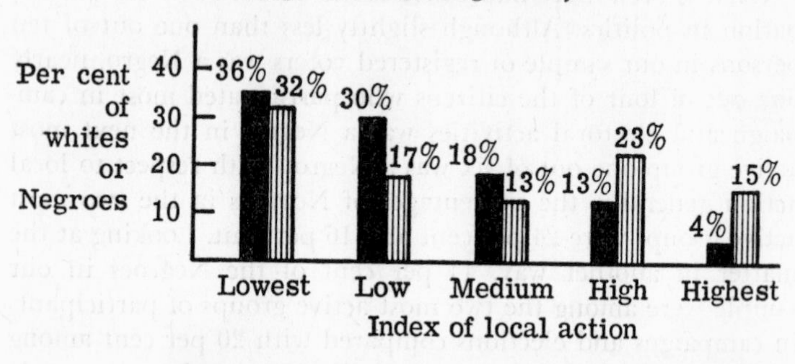

and other expensive projects is likely to participate more through financial contributions than party activity. It follows that the parties must recruit their rank-and-file workers in great part from groups in the community to whom the prospect of a city job or small contract for themselves, their families, or their neighbors is attractive. To the Better-Off, who have many other and better opportunities, a job with the city is likely to be much less attractive than it is to the less well off. Now it happens that in almost every major category of the city's registered voters, a majority would prefer to have a job with a private firm rather than with the city. But this preference is less marked among the rest of the population than it is among the Better-Off, who have attractive alternatives in the private sphere. If a citizen has only a grade school education, an income under $5,000 a year, or a relatively low social position, he is just as likely to prefer a job with the city as with a

Chart 11. ***The Better-Off a citizen is, the less likely he is to prefer a job with the city to a job with a private firm. The percentages in various categories who prefer a city job are:***

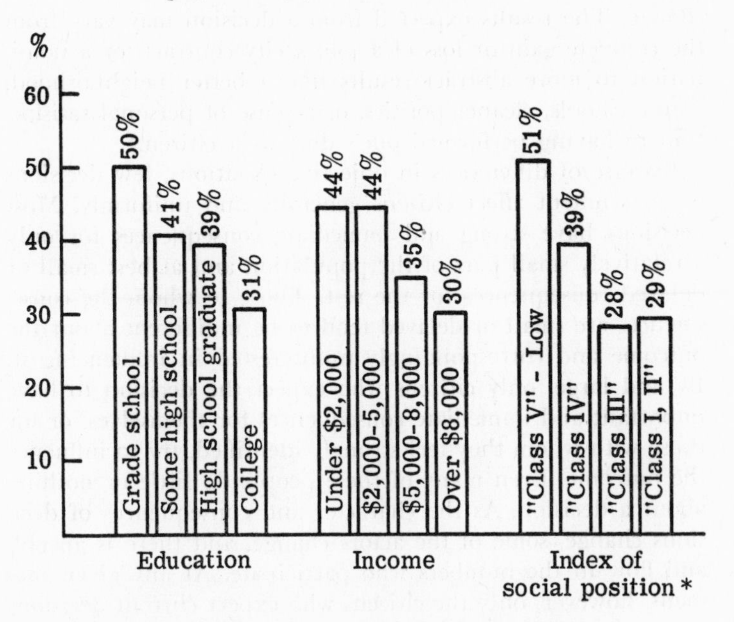

* A two-factor index based on residence and occupation.

private firm. But the higher a group is in its socioeconomic position, the smaller is the proportion which prefers city jobs. (Chart 11)

Variations in Rewards

As the preceding discussion suggests, citizens also vary in the value they attach to the outcome of a decision made by local officials. The bigger the reward they expect from a favorable decision, the more of their political resources they are likely to invest in trying to obtain the outcome they want.

The factors that affect one's evaluation of an outcome are numerous. As suggested earlier, citizens vary both in their objective situations and also, because of differences in information, predispositions, values, and identifications, in the subjective interpretations they give to events. The payoff from a decision may seem immediate to one person and remote to another; it may be specific or general, tangible or intangible. Almost always there is a set of citizens who feel that they benefit more from the existing situation, whatever it may be, than from any of the alternatives urged by those who favor a change. The results expected from a decision may vary from the concrete gain or loss of a job, a city contract, or a nomination to more abstract results like a better neighborhood, better schools, cleaner politics, or a sense of personal satisfaction in having performed one's duty as a citizen.[3]

Because of differences in objective situations, few decisions of government affect citizens generally and uniformly. Most decisions have strong and immediate consequences for only a relatively small part of the population and at best small or delayed consequences for the rest. Those to whom the consequences are small or delayed tend to be indifferent about the outcome and correspondingly uninterested in influencing it. By and large, only citizens who expect the decision to have important and immediate consequences for themselves, or for those with whom they feel strongly identified, try to influence the outcome. Even many of these people do little or nothing about a decision. As the character and consequences of decisions change, some of the actors change, and there is an ebb and flow in the numbers who participate. At any given moment, however, only the citizens who expect current decisions to have important and immediate consequences tend to be very active. And they are generally few in number.

However, a few citizens use their political resources steadily at such a high rate over such a broad range with such a comparatively high degree of skill that they might properly be called political professionals—even when they carefully cultivate the appearance of amateurism. To the professionals and the incipient professionals, the rewards from political activity are evidently very high indeed.

In a city like New Haven the number of highly rewarding positions, judged by the standards of the middling segments of the population, are few. The mayoralty is the key prize, and only one person in the city can be elected mayor. There are other prizes, but the number is not large. Hence at any given moment only a tiny number of people in the middling segments can have any hope of gaining rewards greater than those held out by careers in private occupations. For anyone who is not yet a member of one of the middling segments of the community, the chance of competing successfully for the chief offices is, as we have seen, dim. In sum, there are only a few large prizes; the only contestants with much chance of success are those from the middling layers who are prepared to invest their resources, including time, energy, and money, in the task of winning and holding the prize; and a full-time alternative career must be temporarily abandoned. Hence it is not too surprising that the number of professionals is small.

It is impossible to say with confidence why some citizens find participation in public life so highly rewarding that they are impelled along the path toward professionalism. Perhaps the most obvious requirement that one must have is an unusual toleration for creating and maintaining a great number and variety of personal relationships. This does not mean that the professional actually likes other people to any unusual degree or even that he has an unusual need to be liked by others. Indeed, a study by Rufus Browning indicates that among businessmen the "need for affiliation"—the desire to have the liking and approval of others—is lower among those who are active in politics than those who are inactive, and it is lower among leaders than among subleaders.[4] Browning's findings suggest the tantalizing hypothesis that the distinguishing characteristic of the professional is an inordinate capacity for multiplying human relationships without ever becoming deeply involved emotionally. Despite his appearance of friendliness and warmth, the professional may in fact carry a cool detachment that many citizens would find it impossibly wearisome to sustain.

Chart 12. ***The greater the participation in organizations, the greater the participation in politics.***

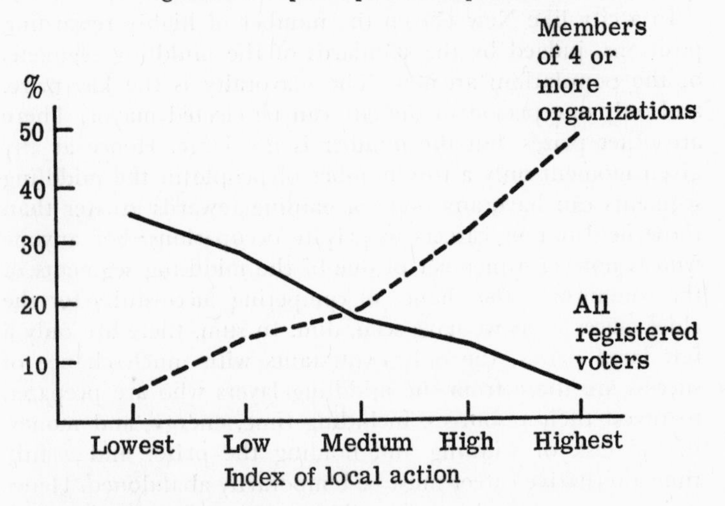

Number of registered voters: 525.

Number of registered voters who are members of four or more organizations: 89.

Whether or not this hypothesis is true, the capacity of the professional to sustain a variety of human relations is revealed in his unusual propensity for joining organizations of all sorts. The same predisposition is evident in our sample of registered voters: the more a voter participates in local political life, the more likely he is to participate in other forms of community organization, and conversely. (Chart 12) Now the propensity for joining organizations is partly a function of socioeconomic factors that are also associated with participation in political life; organizational memberships are higher among the Better-Off than among the worse off. However, one cannot explain the relation between political participation and other forms of participation merely by saying that *both* are functions of being better off, for the tendency of citizens who belong to numerous organizations to participate actively in political decisions holds up even when socioeconomic factors are held constant. For example, among citizens in our sample who were members of four or more organizations, the proportion of highly active citizens was just as great among those who had not completed high school as among those who had. (Table V) Moreover, the relationship held for both partisan and nonpartisan forms of participation.

Joining organizations and participating in politics reinforce one another. If a person participates in local political decisions, he widens his range of relationships in the community; moreover, if he is serious about politics he may deliberately join organizations in order to establish more contacts. Numerous memberships in organizations in turn establish contact with people involved in various ways in local affairs and increase the probability that he too may become involved.

Table V. ***Political Participation Among Citizens Who Belong to Four or More Organizations Does Not Rise with Increasing Education***

	Education	
Participation	*Less than 12th Grade* %	*12th Grade or More* %
High	47	46
Medium	43	37
Low	7	15
None	—	2
No answer	3	—
Total	100	100
N	*30*	*54*

The professional politician has to tolerate a profusion of human contacts that many citizens would find abrasive and exhausting. He must interact with great numbers of people, cultivate friendships with as many as possible, and convey the impression that he enjoys meeting them all. To work with the zest and energy necessary to his success, probably he must actually enjoy this very proliferation of human contacts. If a citizen does not enjoy the process of cultivating friendly though not always very deep relationships with a great variety of people, he is not likely to find political life highly rewarding. For a person who does, politics is by no means the only possible outlet, but it is a natural and obvious one.

Fluctuations in Participation

The differences among citizens discussed here—in political resources, political confidence, alternative opportunities, and rewards—help to account not only for the persistent tendencies among various segments of the population to use their resources at different rates but also for the fluctuations in participation, and presumably in the use of political resources, that occur over time.

There are important differences among participants with respect both to the *frequency* with which they participate and the *range* of issue-areas in which they participate. Some citizens participate frequently; others occasionally. Some citizens participate only in one issue-area; some in several. By combining these two characteristics—frequency and range of participation—we arrive at a convenient classification of participants into four types. These are shown in Table VI.

Table VI. ***Types of Civic Participation***

	Frequency	
Range	*Low*	*High*
One issue-area	a. Occasional, specialized participation	b. Frequent, specialized participation
Several issue-areas	c. Occasional, multiple participation	d. Frequent, multiple participation

Most citizens who participate at all are, as we have observed, occasional, specialized participants (*a* in Table VI). It may happen, however, that the consequences of policies under current discussion seem immediate and important to some of the occasional, specialized participants. Like the school teachers in 1945, or the citizens around Truman Street in 1953, they enormously step up their activity and become frequent though still specialized participants (*b*). If the decisions are moderately favorable, many specialized participants revert to their earlier level of infrequent participation. If the decisions are unfavorable, some of them may continue for a time, until either a more favorable compromise is arranged or they become discouraged. Occasionally, however, a few citizens discover that they enjoy their new activities. They have made a place for it in their lives, acquired new associates, new opportunities for conviviality, perhaps an office with prestige or obligations. These few now continue as frequent, specialized participants, some of them as subleaders—PTA officers, members of League of Women Voters' committees, ward leaders, perhaps even members of the Board of Education. As a result of exposure to new situations, now and again one of the frequent, specialized participants finds himself pulled into another issue-area; for example, his prominence in education makes him an obvious candidate for the Citizens Action Commission. Or perhaps he is elected to the Board of Aldermen, where he engages frequently in a great variety of decisions. In Table VI, he has traveled the route *a–b–d*. It is easy to see how he might move from *a* to *c* to *d*.

In addition to individual fluctuations there are changes in the level of political activity. Regularly recurring cycles of participation result from campaigns and elections. Political participation rises during a presidential campaign, reaches a peak on election day, and then drops rapidly into a long trough. Gubernatorial, congressional, and mayoralty elections create lower peaks followed by troughs. In New Haven, one of these elections occurs annually in November; hence there is an annual peak of activity on the Tuesday after the first Monday in November and an annual trough from election day to the start of the next campaign. Every four years a high peak is reached in presidential elections. Superimposed on these annual fluctuations are short-run cycles associated with meetings of the Board of Aldermen, Board of Finance, Board of Education, and the like. In addition, there are also erratic fluctuations associated with current decisions. Citizens to whom a decision is salient participate briefly and then for the most part return to their previous levels of activity.

Only a small group of citizens, the professionals, participate steadily throughout all the cyclical and erratic fluctuations. These are citizens to whom politics is a career, or at least an alternate career. They use their political resources at a high rate, acquire superior skills, and exert a very high degree of influence. These citizens, the professionals, are sources both of stability and instability in the political system.

Notes:

1. Based on the index of local action in the sample of 525 registered voters.

2. The "sense of political efficacy" is a widely used and well-tested scale consisting of these four items. In Chart 6 registered voters who disagreed with three or four of the statements were regarded as having a "high sense of efficacy." Those who agreed with two or more of the statements were treated as having a "medium to low sense of efficacy."

3. It is not unreasonable to suppose that a sense of civic duty might impel many citizens to action; the payoff would be their own sense of satisfaction in having performed their obligations as citizens. These considerations suggest that the most active participants in civic life might also have the strongest sense of civic duty. Unfortunately, the data from our study are inadequate for a good test of this hypothesis. While we cannot conclude that the hypothesis is false, it is clearly not confirmed by our data, and in fact such evidence as we have seems to run counter to it. However, given the nature of the evidence perhaps the best position one can take on the question is a combination of skepticism and open-mindedness.

4. Rufus Browning, "Businessmen in Politics" (Doctoral dissertation, Yale University, 1960).

Part II. The Cultural Context of Political Behavior

Political behavior is cultural behavior. Human behavior is cultural when two or more people hold common orientations toward each other and toward the world around them. These orientations may be cognitive, affective, or evaluative. Cognitive orientations include both knowledge and beliefs about the social and physical environment; they provide the maps that guide political action. Affective orientations find expression in the common signs, symbols, and rituals that aid people in identifying with each other; they are thus powerful elements in a society's cohesion and maintenance. Evaluative orientations supply the normative standards in terms of which social goals are specified and assessed, judgments are made about the means to attain them, and political action is taken. Because all three types of orientation are widely shared, they make for patterns of political behavior that are regular and uniform within a culture.

Culture does not "exist," of course, independently of behavior that can be observed. The more or less permanent patterns of action and orientation to action are abstracted from the behavior of people. Culture, then, is a "construct" which aids the analyst in attributing meaning to behavior. Similarly, the notion of a "political culture" is an analytic tool that directs attention to and aids in interpreting the peculiar patterns of behavior that are characteristic of political processes. These may differ from the patterns and orientations of the wider culture because of the specific functions that politics performs, but they are not independent of, or radically different from, the more general cultural patterns. It is probably more accurate, therefore, to speak of a "political subculture."

NOTE: At this point, the interested student is referred to Chapter Three of *The Behavioral Persuasion in Politics,* which elaborates this view of the cultural context of political behavior.

In any case, locating behavior in its cultural context enables the political scientist to recognize both inter-cultural and intra-cultural similarities and differences in political behavior.

One of the difficulties of cultural analysis in a single political system is the absence of a comparative frame of reference. For the significant factor in the environment of any culture is always the existence of another culture, and it is through inter-cultural comparison that the analyst is sensitized to the subtleties of cultural differentiation. One alternative, in the absence of a comparative framework, is the use of a theoretical model that permits one to look at political behavior in a cultural perspective. For instance, the pervasiveness of Americans' liking for games and other competitive contests suggests such a model. American devotion to "deals"—whether in a game of cards, in business, or in politics—seems to be a deeply rooted and much-cherished part of the culture. "Square Deal" or "Fair Deal" are probably more characteristic expressions of the spirit of American politics than "New Frontier" or "Great Society." Frank Kent, the journalist, once spoke of American politics as "the great game," but the metaphor has rarely been applied systematically. Systematic application requires the translation of the metaphor into a model.

The concept of "game" implies that there are rules that define the game and restrict the players' conduct. The rules prescribe how the game is to be played; they are normative orientations which must be widely shared in order to make it possible to play the game. But, as Paul A. Smith also suggests in "The Games of Community Politics," the game also provides the players with goals as well as with criteria of success and failure. The political game is only one of the games that are played in the local community, but knowledge of overlapping games may be informative about a community's structure of power and authority. The fact that the community as a whole shows little awareness of the political game makes it possible for the political players to live by certain rules that, although they are not unrelated to general standards of conduct, are peculiar to politics. In other words, politics appears to be a kind of semi-autonomous subculture, yet one, as Smith puts it, which "is neatly consistent with the profound constitutionalism associated with the American political culture." By formalizing the rules of the political game, Smith shows that the game has a logic of its own that can be "explained" theoretically, if one translates rather loose, metaphorical formulations into a more systematic model.

In the case of a legislature, by contrast with a community, the context within which the political game is played according to common rules is more sharply delineated, for the institutional setting makes for many formal rules that define the game. In recent years, behavioral studies of legislatures have shown the pervasiveness and functionality of numerous informal rules of the game that do, in fact, make the legislature a political subculture. Allan Kornberg's "The Rules of the Game in Legislative Politics: A Comparative Study," which largely deals with the Canadian House of Commons, not only replicates some American studies, but, in distinguishing between the rules that guide members within and outside of the legislative chamber, gives some indication of the relationship between the general political culture and the legislative subculture. In using members' perceptions of conflict situations as variables, moreover, Kornberg makes a significant contribution to our understanding of the functions that the rules of the game perform in the legislative process.

While in Smith's one-culture community study and Kornberg's comparative legislative study normative orientations are largely treated as dependent variables, in Sidney Verba's "Organizational Membership and Democratic Consensus" cultural differences in political attitudes serve as independent variables. Verba seeks to examine the "cross-pressure hypothesis" that the existence of multiple, overlapping group memberships tends to reduce political conflict and to contribute to democratic consensus. Though his data are not sufficient either to confirm or falsify the hypothesis, the attempt to test it in different cultural milieux is suggestive of the implications of cross-cultural analysis for political theory. As Verba shows, only in Italy do the data fit the counter-hypothesis: that social conflict is exacerbated in an environment where social and political contacts are cumulative rather than fragmented. On the other hand, in the United States the data do not show that cross-pressures tend to reduce the intensity of political conflict. In other words, though the analysis is not conclusive, it reveals that many of our theoretical notions about the functioning of the American political process need to be reconsidered in the light of cross-cultural comparisons.

The consequences for political behavior of a changing

cultural context are explored by Robert S. Friedman in "The Urban-Rural Conflict in a New Perspective." To examine the validity of the assertion that present trends in internal migration, communication, industrial locations, and other social changes tend to make the traditional differentiation between urban and rural cultural areas largely meaningless for political analysis, at least in the United States, Friedman's research design singled out situations in which interests that are traditionally associated with urban or rural areas are present in the opposite context. While the findings are restricted to one state, one issue of public policy and a limited sample, the study shows that, where cultural homogenization of the environment has taken place, such social factors as industrialization, population characteristics, and political interests prove to be more meaningful variables for the analysis of conflict in the political process than the degree to which geographic areas may be urban or rural.

Population groups constituted along ethnic and income lines serve as indicators of "sub-cultures" in James Q. Wilson and Edward C. Banfield's "Public-Regardingness as a Value Premise in Voting Behavior." With the aid of aggregate statistics, the authors seek to test the hypothesis that some voter groups with particular sub-cultures are more inclined than others to base their voting decisions concerning local issues on some conception of "the public interest." They suggest that "public-regardingness" as a value premise in voters' choices is largely a function of their participation in a sub-culture that can be defined in ethnic and income terms. In other words, each sub-cultural group has its own idea of what a citizen ought to sacrifice for the best interests of the community and of what these interests are made of. But while the high-income "class" appears to be a sub-cultural group with an ethic of public-regardingness, income alone does not have this effect. Rather, ethnic attributes, or cultural orientations, are empirically associated with public-regardingness. This value orientation seems to be characteristic of those ethnic groups—notably the Anglo-Saxon and the Jewish—that belong to the upper-income class more frequently than do Negroes, Italians, or Poles. While they are aware of the provisional nature of a definition of a sub-culture in ethnic and income terms, Wilson and Banfield point out that these are, at least at present, the most serviceable criteria for this type of analysis.

A. *Cultural Patterns and Orientations*

1 *The Games of Community Politics* by Paul A. Smith

Within recent years political research on the "community" level has risen markedly in both vigor and sophistication. Its language reflects this clearly. Questions of power rather than of "local government"; of economic, social, and psychological variables related to politics, rather than of legal structures; of urban-suburban rather than of small town or rural problems, have taken precedence. Thus, in important respects, recent developments in community research reflect the same trends found elsewhere in the discipline—a concern for more precise though comprehensive definitions of political phenomena, a sensitivity to interdisciplinary concepts and to systematic techniques of investigation, and an intensified search for general propositions and explicit theory.[1]

As usually happens in intellectual arenas experiencing an influx of new ideas and methods, sharp issues have arisen concerning what is to be studied and how. *Cognoscenti* know, for example, that one of the most clearly defined issues is whether to take a "reputational" or "decision" approach to community power.[2] By and large, users of reputational techniques have found monolithic structures of power, in contrast to the pluralism discovered by those who have focused on decision-mak-

Reprinted from *Midwest Journal of Political Science,* 9, 1 (February, 1965), 37–60, by permission of the author and the Wayne State University Press.

ing. That such conceptual (and methodological) differences are not to be taken lightly is emphasized by their effect upon comparative analysis. It is admitted on all sides that the development of effective theory about community politics hinges upon the accumulation of comparative data. Yet our acute disagreements over the validity of certain methods, and thus findings, have unquestionably restrained the construction of inductive generalizations, even though studies of numerous communities have now been completed.[3]

The foregoing suggests that a different conceptual framework, depending less upon inductive generalizations and avoiding, at least at first, the areas under dispute, might be worthwhile. In what follows I shall propose that community politics be viewed in terms of a rather thoroughgoing concept of games. I shall try to show that it is useful to begin with loose, commonly understood notions of what is involved, to incorporate empirical elements into these, and finally to move toward more formal models of game theory. Hopefully, this will be an operational way to explain a broad range of political outcomes while minimizing problems of translation.

I

Let us suppose that every community is a system of games.[4] Taking a modest-size midwest city as an example,[5] there are business games, labor games, education games, newspaper and radio games, and so on. Abstracting from our common understanding of the word, each game has rules, players, scores, and often audiences. Usually there also are particular skills and strategies associated with playing the game well, and even more specialized techniques for parts or positions of the game. Thus we can translate virtually any enduring pattern of social interaction involving conflicting interests into game terminology. Furthermore, the fact that an expanded universe of human activities is being so defined makes it clear that there is nothing necessarily trivial or merely entertaining about games. This becomes evident when we give more generalized meanings to the major components of this construct.

The rules provide limits to how a game may be played. They define those patterns of action that *are* the game.[6] Hence, they encompass physical limitations of the players, resource limitations of the environment, and normative restrictions enforced by both social mechanisms and internalized values and beliefs. They may apply to players differentially. Some may be relatively disadvantaged by the rules; and within a general game the rules may distinguish positions having unique limitations of their own.[7] This enables the analyst to achieve either greater specificity or generality, depending on his purposes.

Scores are the "payoffs" of the game. They determine to what extent a player is operating successfully and hence mark the value or utility of the game's outcome. Although games are competitive by definition,[8] it is apparent that this requires that certain outcomes be more desirable than others, and that some players will usually receive greater payoffs from the game than will others. Moreover, some games will embody more value and afford greater payoffs than other games.[9] It will also be noted that any *system* of games, with its necessary intersections, requires a certain "community," or common perception of relevant rules and payoffs.

Strategies are comprehensive plans for playing the game. They involve patterns of "moves" selected on the basis of what other players will do, and thus require interpersonal assessments of intent. This usually introduces considerable uncertainty into the game. Some strategies yield greater payoffs or higher scores than others, and some players are almost always more skillful than others in strategy selection.

Players are those persons (or coalitions) who have certain conflicting interests, actively follow the rules, and reap the payoffs. Though I have distinguished the audience from the players, the former also are rather deeply engaged in the game. In most games, however, it seems wise to maintain the distinction between the two activities of playing the game and of observing—even contributing to—it as part of the audience.

A game thus provides its players with goals, measures of success or failure, and guides to preferable conduct. It also differentiates between more or less successful players, between players and non-players, and between non-playing persons with varying degrees of knowledge about what is going on. Once identified, games provide comprehensive explanations for behavior, predictions of social value distributions, and a framework for the construction of "rational" theory.[10]

II

It is clear that individuals may and usually do play a number of games, though one (ordinarily their occupation) is much more engrossing than the others. Thus in terms of elementary set theory, we can say that certain games intersect. The amount of intersection, that is the number and scope of subsets, depends upon the overlap of players, rules, and payoffs. Some games form more subsets than others and there is more intersection among certain games than among others—just how much can be determined empirically by comparing the intersection of players, rules, and payoffs. The more two games intersect, the more they are functionally related.

We, of course, are interested in political games and their intersections with other games in the community. If we take as political games those having in common rules, players, payoffs, strategies, etc., devoted to authoritative allocations of values in the community,[11] the overlap of these games with others will tell us a lot about such things as the structure of power and authority. In order to bring empirical data to bear upon these constructs and to expedite analysis, I shall define the major political game in the city of Mayburg as involving the attainment and manipulation of formal offices of city government. The players of this game attend to the conscious allocation of values for the entire territorial community. They are not, of course, limited to office-holders alone. Those who recruit or influence officials may also be players, depending on their level of activity.

Let us make three major hypotheses: (1) The local (city) government game is residual. That is, it is played as a minor game after the demands of more important games are met. (2) There is no single subset of successful players; in other words, no overlapping group of players that may be called a power elite. (3) Participation and influence in local politics can be deduced from the rules and payoffs of the political game.

If the local political game is entered as a "secondary" activity, its payoffs should reflect this relative value position. What is the status of the political game relative to others? To supplement national survey data concerning the prestige of politics and governmental offices,[12] a representative public sample, government office-holders, and business leaders of Mayburg were asked to make preference rankings of political and other symbols.[13] Several of the relevant sets are presented in Table I.

Table I. *Preference Rankings of Selected Political Symbols*

Symbols	Mean Rankings by: Public Officials* (n = 18)	Business Leaders* (n = 37)	Public* (n = 227)
Business Leader	1	1	2
Church Leader	2	2	1
Political Leader	3	3	3
City Council	1.5	2.5	1
Chamber of Commerce	1.5	1	3
School Board	3	2.5	2
Politics	3	3	3
Business	1	1	1
Farming	2	2	2

*For each set of symbols, differences between ranks are significant at the .01 level. Calculations of significance are based on Kendall's S. See Maurice G. Kendall, *Rank Correlation Methods* (1955), pp. 49–53; and Florence R. Kluckhohn and Fred L. Strodtbeck, *Variations in Value Orientations* (1961), especially pp. 124–127, for a specific example of how these data were manipulated. I wish to thank Marie H. Martin for helping with the calculations.

See Note 13 for an explanation of the groups and the survey procedure.

Three things are plain from this table. First, the data confirm the generally modest status of political games in the eyes of both leaders and non-leaders in the community. Second, the prestige of the game varies rather consistently with the way it is labeled—the institutional "City Council," for example, fares better than either "Political Leader" or "Politics." While not surprising, this has an important implication, for what is often postulated as one of the more compelling payoffs of the political game—the value of the play itself—may run a serious risk of being disparaged. Third, different segments of the community place different valuations on certain games. We can see that public officials and businessmen have more favorable views of "Chamber of Commerce" and "Business Leader" than does the public as a whole.

Obviously, it would be difficult to establish a comprehensive prestige order of community games with this sort of ranking device (barring complete transitivity), or to connect verbal reactions (to symbols) with significant behavior patterns. More directly relevant, therefore, is our accumulated evidence that leading players of certain "high value" games, such as banking, industrial or business management, medicine, law, and so on, are not only reluctant to move into political games, but also treat them as lesser pastimes when they do play them. City Council membership since World War II shows this rather clearly, with top business executives, civic group leaders, and professional men, being notable for their absence.[14] Moreover, when respondents—both the public and the leaders themselves—were asked why these "top leaders" did not hold official governmental or party positions, their most frequent response was that, after all, such individuals *had more important things to do.*[15] Further evidence was found in a common career pattern, wherein a good number of these "top players" of other games had at one time held positions in local government, but had dropped this activity as the status and demands of their major game positions increased.

Of course, the possibility remains that the "real" political game is played outside the arena of formal government; that these top players of business, professional, etc., games do in fact play the game of authoritatively allocating community values, but do not make their moves in public. Nonetheless, insofar as such value allocations ordinarily require at least the legitimation of formal decisions at some point, this "real" activity must sooner or later affect these decisions. Here, our data, though less systematic, strongly suggest that the top players of other games play politics little more than they do the formal governmental games in the community. Total political participation scores of these top players vary enormously.[16] But their average, while not low, is not extremely high either, being distinctly below that of less successful players (of these other occupations) who, however, participate formally in the political game.

By no means should this be taken to mean that leading players of other games universally eschew politics.[17] But the *degree* to which these players also enter the political game will depend upon the relative payoffs of the respective games and their positions in them. Even though top businessmen, for example, might find payoffs of political games relatively unenticing, we have seen that just the opposite might be true for their fellow players lower down the payoff hierarchy. While the preceding supports our first hypothesis, in that the local political game appears to carry but modest payoffs and to attract players of "modest degree" from other games, the

Table II. *Differences in Rank of Persons Attributed Influence in Various Policy Areas***

Person	General Influence Rank (n=84)	Economic Influence Rank (n=77)	Education Influence Rank (n = 110)	Political Influence Rank (n = 40)	*(Total Sample n = 234)*
A	1	1	12	2	
B	2	3.5	22.5†	14	
C	3	5.5	22.5†	14	
D	4	24†	1	26.5†	
E	5	2	22.5†	19.5	
F	6	5.5	22.5†	26.5†	
G	7.5	24†	22.5†	1	
H	7.5	24†	22.5†	4.5	
I	9	9	22.5†	19.5	
J	10	7.5	22.5†	24.5	

*In each policy area there is a rank order of attributions. The rank correlation coefficient of the General and Economic rank orders is .52; for the General and Political, –.12; and for the General and Education, –.34. The rankings were carried out to more than twenty.

†These persons were not even ranked in this policy area. They are assigned tied-rankings below the bottom rank for purposes of illustration.

possibility remains that the political game has been too narrowly defined in terms of activity; that the players and even payoffs are different if community influence and reputation are taken into account. To examine this, we need to consider the community's identification of influentials and then the rules of the political game.

In Mayburg, the representative sample referred to earlier was asked to name those persons most influential *Generally* in the community, those most influential in the area of *Economic Development,* those in the area of *Education,* and those in the area of *Political Recruitment.* Named persons were then ranked according to the frequencies of their attributions in each policy area. Table II presents the results for the upper part of our list of attributed leaders. If we assume that these data accurately reflect the views of the community as to who has influence and where, it is clear that the sets of persons to whom are attributed General and Economic influence intersect to a greater degree than any of the others. Hence, in terms of community *reputation,* we may infer that successful players of business games are more likely to have reputations for overall community influence than persons who play education or political games. This is borne out by the intersection of the Economic Dominant and Attributed Influential sets.[18] Seven of the top ten and ten of the top twenty reputed to be General Influentials are also Economic Dominants. From the actual names involved in Table II, one thing is clear. In this community, the middle-level executive, the modest store owner, and the rising lawyer and real estate man, who actually play both games, are not attributed as much general public influence as their more advanced teammates.

All this brings us to the inevitable question, if the political game is neither played by or attributed to the top players of other games, why are its players drawn so predominantly from middle-level economic positions and not from other games as well? The answer must lie in the rules. While the determination of intersecting rules among different games is empirically manageable, I shall concentrate here upon the nature of political rules alone. To begin with, the rules of any game may not coincide with its formal prescriptions, something well known to students of bureaucracy and administration. In fact, most rules are defined and enforced by other players and to a lesser extent by the audience. For rules to be operational, the probable cost of breaking them must exceed the probable gain. This shows that in an important sense the payoffs or rewards of a game are a function of its rules and vice versa. It also implies that some rules are more important (i.e., more costly to break) than others.

Compared to other games, politics has a multiplicity and ambiguity of players and audiences, varying from a clearly identified professional elite of other players, on one hand, to *usually* unknowing and indifferent general observers on the other. All play a part in defining and enforcing the rules, thus giving rise to significant uncertainty about what rules actually apply in a given situation. Complex relationships link players with the audience and with players of other games.[19]

The variability of participation in political games is well documented. In Mayburg, a survey of adult citizens[20] one week before the municipal election (to be discussed later), which produced a record turnout and the replacement of a long-established regime with a dissident set of players, yielded the results shown in Table III.

Table III. ***Quality of Public Political Knowledge***

Identification of Political Leaders*			Knowledge of Election Issues†		Perception of Community Problems‡	
Low	0-1	33%	Don't know any	56%	Don't know	20%
	2-3	39%	Personalities	18%	Vague, unspecific	18%
	4-5	25%	Vague, unspecific	6%	1-2, specific	61%
High	6-7	3%	"Need change"	12%	More, specific	1%
		100%	1-2, specific	7%		100%
			More, specific	1%		
				100%		

n = 178

*Respondents were asked to identify by office and party a list of seven public and party officials in the community. Only office identification is used here.

†". . . What would you say are the main issues in this election?"

‡"What do you think is the main problem that this community faces today?"

On the whole, the community exhibited little awareness of political players or issues, and only a modest perception of community problems, which presumably form the grist for future political games. And without benefit of a "score card" identifying the players, citizens did even worse. This may be seen in Table IV, which presents the results of interviews with

Table IV. ***Proportion of Respondents Naming Influentials***

	In the Area of:			
Percentage of	*General Influence*	*Economic Development*	*Political Recruitment*	*Education*
Random Sample (n = 234)	36%	34%	26%	47%
Public Officials (n = 37)	78	70	57	62
Influentials (n = 36)	82	94	77	94

three different sets of respondents, all of whom were asked to name community influentials.[21] At their best (in the area of Education), fewer than half of the public sample named any influential at all. The situation was dismal in the Political area, where almost 75% named no one. In every group, respondents were apparently less knowledgeable about the identity of successful political players than about those of other games. It would seem that while its formal rules (constitutional and statutory) "open up" the political game to a wide variety of players, other limitations have a contrary effect. This suggests that operational community expectations about the playing of politics do little to encourage actual participation. We have already noted that the modest payoffs associated with the game serve to discourage intensive participation by successful players from "prestige" games. More than this, however, the prevailing uncertainty and lack of information about the game make it extremely costly to play for individuals on the other end of the social scale (i.e., the unskilled, low-educated, and poor). The situation of these persons is such that the costs of the game might become prohibitive—leading them to abstain altogether.[22] The obvious implication that the actual rules do not distribute advantages equally throughout the community cannot be pursued here. However, some evidence of what the community expects of players is presented in Table V on page 276.

These data point unmistakeably to rules of public conduct that political players break at their peril:

(1) Public decisions should be made carefully, avoiding haste and partiality. (The Prudence Rule)
(2) These decisions should be made in the open, in full view of the community. (The Visibility Rule)
(3) Before final decisions are made, public support should be sought and the opinions of the people given faithful attention. (The Responsiveness Rule)
(4) Politics should not be used as a vehicle for personal gain. (The Disinterest Rule)

From other evidence, four more may be added:

(5) Harsh debate and aggressive argumentation are unseemly in public life. Most issues should be settled in an orderly and essentially quiet fashion. (The Moderation Rule)
(6) Laws, especially as enunciated by courts and attorneys, are the touchstone of correct public behavior and are to be scrupulously observed. (The Legality Rule)
(7) No group (or coalition) should be permanently in power. (The Change Rule)
(8) Leaders should have an "interest" in the community,

best indicated by economic commitment, length of residence, and experience. (The Community-Stake Rule)

The first reaction of the political scientist to this set of rules for community politicos is that they have been cribbed from some high school civics book. Since the political game isn't "really" played this way, we have been duped! But in Mayburg accumulated evidence shows that most of the players most of the time *do* play the game according to these rules. Moreover, this should not be surprising in light of recent findings about political socialization in the United States.[23] It is neatly consistent with the profound constitutionalism associated with the American political culture.

Although fragmentary, the foregoing evidence of the payoffs, players, and rules of the local political game exhibits internal consistency. We have seen that the political game is accorded modest value,[24] that its players are not drawn from the highest positions in other games, and that its rules would not make the life of a "power elite" an easy one. (Nor do they encourage populist democracy!) A vital factor in the political game is the inordinate amount of uncertainty, arising from variations in who is playing, how intensely, and by what rules. This, plus the rules and payoffs that are understood, makes politics a risky game, especially for the top and bottom economic positions. Even though here displayed crudely and imperfectly, the game construct thus appears to offer both explicit guides to empirical evidence and coherent explanations for the observed events of local political life.

III

All of these considerations lead to what may be the most intriguing component of political games, that of strategy. It is here that we may move from a largely metaphorical treatment of the phenomena to more formal analytic game theory. In doing so, I shall follow what seems to me the unusually promising "theory of political coalitions" formulated by William Riker.[25] Essentially, Riker argues that there are "abstract considerations of strategy" in the growth of coalitions and that these can be identified and tested.

A good place to see if this is so in our local community is the city council, particularly since the last election left the

Table V. *Attributed Obligations of Community Leaders**

Top Quartile Mean Rank† by:	Public Sample (n = 211)	Influentials (n = 29)
Investigate all problems thoroughly before making a decision	1	1
Have a great interest in people	2	5.5
Keep the community fully informed about what is going on	3	4
Be willing to change your mind as new evidence is available	4	2
Listen carefully to all complaints	5	5.5
Actively seek able people to participate in community affairs	6	3
Take an active interest in state and national affairs	7	7
Cooperate with all organizations in the community	8	10.5
Bottom Quartile		
Defend past policy	27	27
Engage in public debates with those who oppose him	28	31
Take a neutral stand in any issue on which the community is evenly split	29	30
Try to settle community issues quietly, behind the scenes	30	27
Occasionally compromise with local pressure groups	31	29
Vigorously change the way things are done	32	32
Use influence to further personal ambitions	33	33
Make major changes without seeking public support	34	34

*Both a public sample and attributed influentials were asked to evaluate thirty-four statements about what community leaders should do. Only the *top* and *bottom quartiles* are included here. The statements were formulated inductively from responses to open-ended questions about "rules of the game" from previous interviews. Respondents associated each statement with one of the following: (1) Absolutely must. (2) Preferably should. (3) May or may not. (4) Preferably should not. (5) Absolutely must not. The respondent groups are the same as those used in Table IV, the smaller n's being due to the failure of some respondents to complete this question.

†For the items included, r′ = .92 between rank orders. For all thirty-four items, r′ =.94. Standard deviations calculated for all thirty-four items reveal that leaders were in significantly greater agreement about item rank than followers. The most obvious explanation for this is the higher level of interaction between leaders than between followers.

council in a situation inviting both conflict and coalition formation.[26] An incumbent coalition called the "Citizens" party, which had dominated Mayburg government for over a decade, was swept from office, leaving only one member on the six-man council. Surveys taken before and after the election indicated that the Citizens had been victims of the Change Rule (7), though the winning "Peoples" coalition preferred to believe that their victory resulted from the Visibility Rule (2). (See p. 214, above.) While Citizens leaders clearly valued the Moderation Rule (5) over the Visibility Rule,[27] our findings showed that Mayburg voters valued both rules at the same time, giving no measurable advantage to one or the other. The same may be said for the Citizens emphasis upon the Community-Stake Rule (8), compared to the Peoples stress upon the Responsiveness Rule (3).

There are two important points here. First, the rules of the game were apparently themselves a decisive issue in the election. In short, for the competing players (coalitions), the rules were a key payoff of the game, with the Peoples coalition proposing to play by somewhat different rules from the Citizens if they took over the game. Obviously, we have a case of conflicting rules. Each candidate for the council had to estimate the *probability* that one set of rules defined the game the audience (voters) wanted to have played more than the other. The Citizens failed to estimate the increasing probability that the Change Rule would dominate.[28]

Second, the probabilistic nature of the rules, the extraordinary complex rule permutations and combinations that affect these probabilities, and especially the existence of a rule such as Change (7), suggest a built-in source of political instability. This is somewhat different from, yet related to, the two inherent disequilibriating conditions in zero-sum games of politics seen by Riker.[29] Several specific ingredients of these are changes in "weight" of the coalitions, changes in the rules, and the tendency of leaders to make sidepayments too high—thus bringing about their own bankruptcy.

In the actual community situation before us, the disequilibriating election of 1961 more than anything else resulted from a change in rules, but not as Riker uses the term to relate rules to weights (increasing electorates, etc.).[30] Rather, the rules were used mainly as *direct* sidepayments, and hence were what Riker terms "payments of emotional satisfaction."[31] In this sense, Citizens leaders had been making sidepayments to their followers out of "working capital," using a currency which steadily depreciated in value until overtaken and passed by the value of other currency (rules).[32] Thus Peoples leaders found a sufficient market for their alternative sidepayments, with which they constructed a winning coalition.

Immediately following the 1961 election, the city council

was composed of two subsets of players: the winning Peoples coalition (P^2) with five members plus the mayor,[33] and the losing Citizens coalition (Q^2) with one member. The prospects of winning for strategically weak (Q^2) were apparently nil.[34]

On the basis of Riker's analysis of coalition-building strategy, however, and especially his "size principles,"[35] (P^2) would be expected to reduce its size by one or two members (depending on the role of the mayor) in order to become a more desirable minimum winning coalition. It should be added that at that stage of the game there was little uncertainty about either the weights or the values of the players—two factors that tend to produce oversized coalitions.

The expected is almost precisely what happened. Within two months after the new council took office, (P^2) had lost a two-player minority and divided into subsets (P^3) and (Q^3). At this point the following situation existed:[36]

$$I = \left\{ \begin{array}{c} \text{City council: a, b, c, d, e, f} \\ \text{Mayor: g} \end{array} \right\} n = 7$$

$$\text{Peoples Party: } \left\{ \begin{array}{l} a, b, c, d, e \\ g \end{array} \right\} \qquad \text{Citizens Party: } \{f\}$$

$$P^2 = \left\{ \begin{array}{l} a, b, c, d, e \\ g \end{array} \right\} \quad Q^2 = \{f\} \quad w(P^2) > m > w(Q^2)$$

$$P^3 = \left\{ \begin{array}{l} a, b, c \\ g \end{array} \right\} \quad Q^3 = \{d, e\} \quad R^3 = \{f\} \quad w(P^3) = m > w(Q^3) >$$

$$w(P^3 \cup Q^3) > w(P^3 \cup R^3) > m > w(Q^3 \cup R^3)$$

I = The universal set composed of the entire council.

P = A subset or partition of I. The superscripts indicate the number of subsets in I. P is always the largest subset, Q the second largest, etc.

w = The weight of a partition or coalition.

m = A minimum winning coalition, i.e., a majority, $m > \frac{1}{2} \sum_{i=1}^{n} w_i$.

$\cup$ = Union or "plus."

$\lessgtr$ = Inequalities: less than, greater than.

This left (P^3) at worst a "uniquely essential proto-coalition,"[37] meaning that it would always be in the winning coalition. Since larger payoffs could be distributed among fewer remaining members, the reduction in size was a rational move. While the evidence is inconclusive, it appears that (Q^3) resigned from (P^2) rather than was expelled. Hence the interesting question: Why did this minority choose to place itself in a hopeless position outside the winning coalition?[38] One explanation is simple irrationality. If this is so, the situation depicted above has little to offer, inasmuch as the winner is always assured. In the Mayburg city council game, however, some revealing strategies became evident as each subset of the council coped with emerging issues. A series of six of these issues is abstracted in Table VI[39] on page 220.

The most striking aspect of the winning coalitions on all but the first issue is the presence of *f* in each. This would not be surprising if the coalitions tended to be ($1P^3 \cup 1R^3$), a "uniquely preferable winning coalition."[40] But save for Issue F, they do not. The minority, *d, e,* which initially resigned from ($1P^2$) to become ($1Q^3$), continually attempted to coalesce with *f* in order to form a blocking coalition on the order of (assuming the mayor would not vote) $w(3P^3)=w(3Q^3 \cup 3R^3) < m$. That this strategy was basically successful is shown by the failure of ($1P^3$) to alone be the winning coalition following Issue A.

IV

What explains this success of ($1Q^3$) and ($1R^3$), the occurrence of unanimity, and especially ($1P^3$)'s failure to do better in view of Riker's advice that ($1P^3$) "minimize losses by accepting a minimal payoff in coalition with ($1R^3$) *or* ($1Q^3$)"? Although efforts to implement this rational strategy were frequently observed in ($1P^3$)'s attempts to form coalitions with (R^3) rather than (Q^3), only on Issue F did this succeed; and there it is significant that (P) had different members than it had for the previous issues. Otherwise, except for the isolation of its member *b* in ($2S^4$), ($1P^3$) avoided a universal coalition only on Issue A.[41]

The reasons why this strategic pattern occurred appear to be intimately related to the dimensions of the game and to the rules discussed earlier. These are illustrated by the strategies used on Issues D, E, and F. Issue D involved the efforts of the member *b* to be remunerated for certain services performed for the city. Subset ($1Q^3$) asserted that such payments would be illegal. In the face of this assertion, which was affirmed by the city attorney between stages (r–1) and (r), the

Table VI. ***City Council Coalition Formation on Selected Issues***

Time ⟶

Issue	Coalitions at stage: (r − 2)	(r − 1)	(r = Decision)
A1	$w(P^2) > m > w(Q^2)$ ⟶	$w(P^2) > m > w(Q^2)$ ⟶	$w(P^2) > m > w(Q^2)$
B1	$w(P^2) > m > w(Q^2)$ ⟶	$w(P^3) = m > w(Q^3) > w(R^3)$ ⟶	$w(P^3 \cup Q^3 \cup R^3) > m$
C2	$w(P^3) = m > w(Q^3) > w(R^3)$ ⟶	$w(P^3) = m > w(Q^3 \cup R^3)$ ⟶	$w(P^4 \cup Q^4 \cup R^4) > m > w(S^4)$
D2	$w(P^3) = m > w(Q^3 \cup R^3)$ ⟶	$w(P^3) = m > w(Q^3 \cup R^3)$ ⟶	$w(P^4 \cup Q^4 \cup R^4) > m > w(S^4)$
E3	$w(P^3 \cup R^3) = m > w(Q^3)$ ⟶	$w(P^3) = w(Q^3 \cup R^3) < m$ ⟶	$w(P^3 \cup Q^3 \cup R^3) > m$
F4	$w(P^2) = w(Q^2) < m$ ⟶	$m > w(P^3) > w(Q^3) > w(R^3)$ ⟶	$w(P^3 \cup R^3) = m > w(Q^3)$

[1]Where: $P^2 = \begin{Bmatrix} a, b, c, d, e \\ g \end{Bmatrix}$ $Q^2 = \{f\}$ $P^3 = \begin{Bmatrix} a, b, c \\ g \end{Bmatrix}$ $Q^3 = \{d, e\}$ $R^3 = \{f\}$

[2]Where: $P^4 = \begin{Bmatrix} a, c \\ g \end{Bmatrix}$ $Q^4 = \{d, e\}$ $R^4 = \{f\}$ $S^4 = \{b\}$

[3]Where: $P^3 = \{a, b, c\} < m$ $Q^3 = \{d, e\}$ $R^3 = \{f\}$ $n = 6$ (Mayor definitely not voting.)

[4]Where: $P^2 = \{c, d, f\}$ $Q^2 = \{a, b, e\}$ $P^3 = \{c, d, f\}$ $Q^3 = \{a, b\}$ $R^3 = \{e\}$

other members of ($1P^3$) expelled *b* (who became $2S^4$) and formed a coalition with ($2Q^4$) and ($2R^4$). As we shall see in a moment, the final condition on this issue represents the compelling value of the Legality Rule (6).

Issue E does likewise. This was a complicated situation in which a businessman petitioned the city to close an alley so that he might expand into the space. Interestingly enough, leaders of the Citizens party supported the businessman, and ($3P^3$) and ($3R^3$) found themselves initially in coalition. The position of ($3Q^3$) was supported by a legal opinion from the city attorney, following which the council unanimously denied the petition.[42]

If issues D and E cast doubt upon player rationality, Issue F's coalition formation appears to be a veritable model of rational strategy. But the issue involved more traditional and tangible payoffs than did the others. Residents of a particular section asked the city to bear the cost of solving a water drainage problem. ($4Q^2$), not members from this section, argued that the city as a whole should not underwrite the cost of this improvement. With the defection of sympathetic councilman *e* from ($4Q^2$) to form ($4R^3$), and the final coalition $w(4P^3 \cup 4R^3) = m$, we have Riker vindicated and rational behavior by every player in terms of an electoral payoff.

A major purpose of applying formal models of politics to actual political behavior is to discover and then to explain deviations from the models. In the case before us, it may be seen that at various times (moves) the Mayburg city council diverged from rational strategies of coalition formation. At the same time it needs to be emphasized that a leading deduction from Riker's coalition theory—that the largest "protocoalitions" or non-majority subsets are strategically weak—has been richly illustrated. Indeed, in the present instance, a *majority* subset turned out to win less for its members than did two strategically weak minorities!

I have suggested above that the actual rules and payoffs of the council game held at least part of the answer to why ($1Q^3$) left ($1P^2$) and ($1P^2$) was so inept. Observations and interviews showed that players *d* and *e*, ($1Q^3$), resigned from ($1P^2$), and then allied with ($1R^3$) to block ($1P^3$), principally because they were convinced that ($1P^3$) was breaking the rules (but see footnote 35, p. 228). Furthermore, for virtually all the players, the payoffs from not breaking such rules as Visibility

(2), Responsiveness (3), Disinterest (4), and especially Legality (6), and the *intrinsic* value of these rules themselves were considered greater than the more immediate payoffs at hand.[43] The sidepayments, for example, offered by ($1Q^3$) to both ($1R^3$) *and* potential defectors from ($1P^3$) were the values of Prudence (1), Visibility (2), Disinterest (4), and Legality (6). A corollary of the Moderation Rule (5), to the effect that public decision-making bodies should avoid petty disunity, also helped persuade ($1P^3$) to forego its strategic advantage and give in to the position of ($Q^3 \cup R^3$) on such issues as B and E.

Yet these rule-payoffs remain rather abstract feelings of emotional satisfaction, and the game itself breaks sharply away from the zero-sum condition, if it is limited to the city council arena. A sounder approach is to view the council game first as a subset of the community's greater political game—one that includes elections and a wider effective audience—and second as intersecting with various non-political games of the community. During the first six months or so of the game, only one or two councilmen showed explicit sensitivity to the electoral implications of their moves.[44] However, as the 1963 election drew closer, the electoral payoffs of rule-abiding play were definitely recognized by most of the players. (P^3)'s willingness to give up its strategic advantage in the final stage of decisions testifies to its fear of being labeled a rulebreaker. It also points to an important theoretic explanation for the apparent deviations from rationality that we have noticed.

I remarked earlier upon the high degree of uncertainty that characterizes the rules and thus the payoffs of the political game. This arises from the interests which play or affect the game. We have seen that city councilmen are highly sensitive to the rules of their game. But as the game expands (to include elections, for example, and hence additional players), the nature of these rules, and the probability of their enforcement through electoral consequences, becomes increasingly uncertain. The overriding appeal of the Legality Rule (6) arises from its effectiveness as a device for *uncertainty* absorption. Not only are its provisions usually precise and clear cut, but even when debatable, their meaning can be secured through the intervention and institutional status of the city attorney.[45]

But the concept of uncertainty, though useful, does not

extricate us from our difficulties with Riker's model. For the basic obstacle occurs with the intersection, mentioned above, of *other* games with that of the city council. This produces more than rule uncertainty; it multiplies as well the possible payoffs to a point where the zero-sum condition might or might not obtain.[46] Hence, the conceptual expansion of the council game to conform to the empirical evidence of its dimensions may solve some questions of rules and payoffs, but it is also likely to complicate enormously the calculations or strategy.[47]

Using the concept of games, I have tried to show how political analysis at the community level (and presumably elsewhere) can move from rather loose, metaphorical formulations to more formal analytic models. The difficulties encountered in the application of game theory to the luxuriant ingredients of community politics have been apparent and should not be minimized. Yet these difficulties need not foreclose attempts to overcome them. To look at politics as one kind of game, among many others, provides a comprehensive set of interrelated explanations for political life. At the moment, only a few of these can be developed and tested as hypotheses of analytic game theory; but those that can are probably worth a high price in labor and frustration. Serious efforts to abstract and formalize "real-life" situations may be destined either to miss "essential facts" of the empirical world, or to impair the elegance of some deductive structures—perhaps both. But they also may be effective ways of gradually achieving systematic theories of politics.

Notes:

1. These points are elaborated by Nelson W. Polsby, *Community Power and Political Theory* (1963). See, also, Robert E. Agger, *et. al., The Rulers and the Ruled* (1964).

2. Since it is not my purpose to review the development of community political research, or the controversies which have enlivened it in recent years, I shall merely cite some useful sources for those who might be interested: Peter Bachrach and Morton S. Baratz, "Two Faces of Power," *American Political Science Review,* 56 (December, 1962), pp. 947–952; Edward C. Banfield, *Political Influence* (1961); Robert A. Dahl, *Who Governs* (1961); Lawrence J. R. Herson, "In the Footsteps of Community Power," *American Political Science Review,* 55 (December, 1961), pp. 817–830; Floyd Hunter, *Community Power Structure* (1953); Morris Janowitz, ed., *Community Political Systems* (1960); Roscoe C. Martin,

et al., Decisions in Syracuse (1961); Nelson W. Polsby, "How to Study Community Power: The Pluralist Alternative," *Journal of Politics,* 22 (August, 1960), pp. 474–484; Peter H. Rossi, "Power and Community Structure," *Midwest Journal of Political Science,* 11 (1960), pp. 390–401; and Raymond E. Wolfinger, "Reputation and Reality in the Study of 'Community Power'," *American Sociological Review,* 25 (October, 1960), pp. 636–644.

3. A good example of this is the (reputational) research approach popularized by Floyd Hunter. It is systematic, uncomplicated, and easy to apply. Moreover, it has been standardized in the "Miller-Form" technique, which is so invitingly simple that comparative analysis leading to powerful generalizations might be expected to prosper. Yet it is safe to say that the latter has not occurred. See David A. Booth and Charles R. Adrian, "Simplifying the Discovery of Elites," *The American Behavioral Scientist,* V (October, 1961), pp. 14–16. Of those who criticize Hunter, the clearest may be Wolfinger, *op. cit.*

As an example, however, of what can be done to construct useful inductive generalizations from diverse cases, see the excellent monograph by James S. Coleman, *Community Conflict* (1957).

4. Many of the ideas found in this part of the analysis have been lifted directly from Norton E. Long's highly suggestive article, "The Local Community as an Ecology of Games," *The American Journal of Sociology,* 64 (November, 1958), pp. 251–261. I avoid Long's "natural ecology" references in order not to confuse my already highly metaphorical usage of games.

5. All of the primary data used in this paper are drawn from an Iowa city having just under 20,000 inhabitants and noted by pollsters for its "typical" characteristics. It is the site of several large manufacturing concerns, one employing about one-fifth of the wage-earners in the surrounding county. Vigorous labor, business, fraternal, and civic organizations are present, and the income, occupational, and educational profiles of the community closely approximate those of the state and the United States. Though city elections are formally non-partisan, well organized "citizen groups" support opposing tickets of candidates. Both major political parties are also in a healthy state of repair, with the Democrats gradually gaining in strength, until they are today an immediate threat to Republican superiority. (The county itself, up to the 1960 election, was one of the half-dozen or so in the nation that always voted for the winning Presidential candidate.) In short, this community embodies a wide range of historical, social, and political characterstics. We have chosen the pseudonym, Mayburg, for this city.

6. Actually, it may be argued that all a game is are rules, other terms being added mainly to clarify our analytical operations and enhance our translations from "real life." While there are substantial similarities, the game components defined here will not be identical to those of formal game theory.

7. Take the local politics game, for example. The players obviously are limited in their actions by a host of factors, ranging from their physical make-up to their constituencies. Some citizens have a better chance to get what they want than others. Some positions will be more difficult

of access than others, and positions will vary in their behavioral requirements (or duties). Some of these points will be developed later.

8. I am not ruling out cooperation among players. However, all games are marked by competition, if only with nature. Scarcity does not imply that a game must be "zero-sum" (that one side loses what the other side gains), but it does demand competition for the limited positive payoffs (utilities) which are the object of the game.

9. It is evident, I think, that this analytic framework comes very close to functional theory in sociology. There we find functional differentiation of human actions and social positions. This will be manifested in performances of distinct roles and ordinarily will generate unequal rewards arising from hierarchical functional evaluations. For several brief discussions of functional analysis see the articles by Harold Fallding, Wilbert E. Moore, and Melvin Tumin, *American Sociological Review,* 28 (February, 1963), pp. 5–28. Moore's remarks, pp. 13–18, make the similarity especially evident.

10. It should be added that games are intellectual constructs not to be reified. Community players obviously need not be expected to perceive their games as the researcher does. On the other hand, it has been claimed that men are "game-playing animals," and we were continually impressed by the apparent meaningfulness of game terminology to our respondents in the community being studied. This was particularly true for "the political game."

11. This definition is taken from David Easton, *The Political System* (1953). More accurately, *the* political game involves the authoritative allocation of values. Various subgames may be specified that perform this function in particular ways or with respect to particular values. For example, the Federal Trade Commission and the local city council are both subgames of the greater political game. However, I shall not maintain this distinction here and will treat subgames as games, thus usually speaking in the plural.

12. For a summary of national rankings of political and other occupations and a good discussion of the problems of analysis, see William C. Mitchell, "The Ambivalent Social Status of the American Politician," *Western Political Quarterly,* 12 (September, 1959), pp. 683–698.

13. The public sample used here and elsewhere was a carefully designed area probability sample, in which each household in the city had an equal chance of being selected. Public officials were those members of the city government holding offices of a substantial decision-making sort, i.e., mayor, councilmen, city clerk, city attorney, police-chief, and so on. Business leaders were those persons who had served on the Board of Directors of the Chamber of Commerce during the preceding decade *and* who remained active business owners or executives.

All respondents were presented with a list of three-symbol sets and for each set asked to "rank these names from one to three according to how *desirable* or *preferred* each name is to you."

14. Of the 29 different members of the City Council since the war, four were top business executives, ten were middle- or low-level executives in large business firms, eleven were modest or small-sized private owners, and one had been a successful labor leader. The four top men

all served at a time of "economic crisis" in the community, and even then two of them were below the top positions they hold now.

15. Perhaps the most amusing and palpable instance of this view occurred in a recent election. One of the candidates for a high city office, upon learning that his cement company would no longer be able to do business with the city if he were elected, made a vigorous effort to avoid election, and succeeded.

16. These were calculated from the respondent's party activity, his interaction with other persons holding public office or known to be politically active, and the amount and intensity of his political discussion. They depend primarily upon the degree to which he engaged in influencing decisions about public issues.

17. It might be pointed out that Norton Long comes to about the same conclusion for New York City as I do for Mayburg. In both places, public roles are generally unable to elicit the commitments of time and effort characteristic of top business positions, etc. Even in small communities, such as "Springdale," where there appears to be generalized, integrated leadership, there seems to occur what Schulze has called the "withdrawal of economic dominants from active direction of the political and civic life . . ." Robert O. Schulze, "The Role of Economic Dominants in Community Power Structure," *American Sociological Review,* 23 (February, 1958), p. 8; and see Arthur J. Vidich and Joseph Bensman, *Small Town in Mass Society* (1958), especially Ch. 10. But this does not obviate the intersection of business and political games. See *ibid.,* pp. 278 ff.

18. Economic dominance involves the ownership or control of great economic resources. The criteria of economic dominance, and especially the empirical data available to establish it, leave much to be desired. See Robert O. Schulze, *op. cit.,* pp. 3–9; and Dahl, *Who Governs,* pp. 67–68 and p. 332.

19. The case of a city councilman is illustrative. In this particular subgame, other players include other councilmen, government officers, party leaders, etc. But these players follow strategies involving the general public in order to maximize their winnings. In doing this, they must use players of other games, such as the newspaper game, and are in turn themselves used by players of such other games. Norton Long makes an important point of this functional interdependence of players in certain different games.

20. This is not the same population sample referred to earlier and described in Note 13. It was drawn about nine months earlier, using the same area probability methods—that is, it was a random sample of city households—but with a smaller sample n of 200. The interviews were also shorter and 178 were completed.

21. This Random Sample is the same one referred to in Note 13. The Public Officials, however, here represent all city officials, including members of the School Board, the Planning and Zoning Commission, and so on. Hence the set is larger than that used in Table I. The Influentials are those persons attributed influence by at least five respondents in the public sample and comprise roughly the top 40% of all those attributed influence in all areas.

22. See especially, Anthony Downs, *An Economic Theory of Democracy* (1957). A major reason for what in some ways might seem a surprising lack of enthusiasm for politics on the part of these low-status persons (in view of the comparatively high payoffs the political game could yield them) is their slender chance of success. This low probability, as we have seen, results from the rules, which favor players with higher (status) occupations, educations, incomes, and so forth.

23. David Easton and Robert D. Hess, "The Child's Political World," *Midwest Journal of Political Science,* 6 (August, 1962), pp. 229–246; and Fred I. Greenstein, "The Benovolent Leader: Children's Images of Political Authority," *American Political Science Review,* 54 (December, 1960), pp. 934–943.

24. There is one very important payoff I have mentioned only in passing. This is the value of the play iself, and—if successful play is assumed—of power itself. This is difficult to distinguish from other values of the game, but our empirical data provide scant indication that this was seen as a major payoff by the players of Mayburg. The rules, of course, proscribe many of the activities commonly associated with "playing politics," and this is a critical factor in lowering the payoffs of the game.

25. William H. Riker, *The Theory of Political Coalitions* (1962).

26. Mayburg municipal elections are formally non-partisan. But distinct "tickets" or parties have existed in the community for years. By the fall of 1961, one, the "Citizens Committee," had been continuously in power for about a dozen years—repeatedly beating off the (usually) poorly organized challenges of the "Peoples" party. Both "parties" have no discernible *formal* organization, but tickets are formed for every municipal election and most community leaders have little difficulty in identifying themselves with one or the other. The Citizens are definitely business and Republican oriented, while the Peoples are a varying collection of interest generally sympathetic to labor, small business, and the Democratic party—and opposed to the Citizens. Much to almost everyone's surprise, the Peoples ticket won five out of six council seats and the mayorship in the 1961 election.

27. Even today, two years later, and with another election imminent, every member of the original Peoples coalition stresses Rule 2, while Citizens leaders deride it as an irresponsible appeal to popular passion (Rule 5).

28. In one sense there was little they could do except to lower this probability by appealing to conflicting rules, such as the need for experience and continuity in leadership. However, they even ignored such obvious devices as offering new players (candidates) and payoffs (programs) in order to weaken the relevance of the Change Rule.

29. "(1) A change in the weight of two or more participants, and (2) willingness on the part of the winner to set high stakes." Riker, *op. cit.,* pp. 189 ff.

30. *Ibid.,* pp. 199–202. There also is strong evidence that Mayburg's Democratic organization, at the height of its powers following the 1960 Presidential election (which it lost), had much to do with increasing the turnout of Peoples voters.

31. *Ibid.*, pp. 113–114. I am not denying that these alternative sets of rules for the Mayburg game would have other payoff consequences (i.e., more favorable decisions for certain segments of the population). But empirical evidence showed little awareness among either leaders or followers as to what, if anything, these would be.

32. When the Citizens coalition was originally formed in 1947–1948, the payoffs or sidepayments to followers were substantive policies involving industrial development, and these were explicitly connected to Citizens rules. By 1960, however, this connection was no longer clearly perceived by followers of the coalition.

33. The mayor in this mayor-council form could vote only in cases of ties and then only on certain questions. At first members of the council had different (and unclear) understandings of this rule, which enormously complicated the game. After the definite establishment of coalitions (P^3), (Q^3), and (R^3), however, the mayor followed an operating rule of not voting, though legally he could have done so to break most ties.

34. While in what follows the reader doubtless will find the special symbolism rather formidable, describing the players and issues in ordinary narrative terms would, in my judgment, have added considerable length without commensurate clarity.

35. "In n-person, zero-sum games, where sidepayments are permitted, where players are rational, and where they have perfect information, only minimum winning coalitions occur." *Ibid.*, p. 32 ff. Riker's model demands the zero-sum condition.

36. Here and elsewhere I follow Riker's notations wherever possible. I am particularly indebted to Mr. J. Michael Young, for his very able help in applying Riker's model to a number of political situations.

37. "One which appears in all winning coalitions when no other proto-coalition is so favored." A proto-coalition is any subset of the universal set I (city council), when I is partitioned into three or more subsets such that no subset has the weight m in any stage preceding r. *Ibid.*, pp. 104–107. In our case, since (P^2) and (P^3) $\geqq$ m, these are not strictly proto-coalitions, and their failure to dominate as majority coalitions becomes even more noteworthy.

38. Whatever the explanation, it was not entirely clear to the players. Repeated efforts to learn why *d* and *e* left (P^2) produced various and unsubstantiated accusations of corruption or foul play. It should be noted that (Q^3 claimed that the majority of (P^2) had tried to operate behind their backs (Rule 2), while (P^3) suggested that personality needs and payoffs from the Citizens party (Rule 4) motivated *d* and *e* to leave.

Actually, the separation of (Q^3) from (P^2) closely approximates the "dynamics of controversy," wherein issues shift from the specific to the general, diversify, and turn from policy disagreements to personal antagonism, described by Coleman, *op. cit.*, pp. 9–14. Coleman's formulation, however, does not fit rational players and games of strategy very well.

39. The shifting membership of the proto-coalition sets creates problems of how this may be symbolized. Since the subscripts, 1–4, identify set composition, these numbers will be used in the form of prefixes for

similar identification in the text (e.g., $(4P^2) = (P^2)$ on issue F, $(2P^3) = (P^3)$ on issues C and D, etc.).

40. One such that "it has a greater value than any other one possible, given the particular partition . . . , and in which all the participating proto-coalitions can satisfy their initial expectations." Riker, pp. 129–130.

41. The reason why most of the final coalitions, and especially any universal coalition, are considered irrational is the "size principle" and ultimately the zero-sum condition. If winners get only what losers lose, and there are no losers, no one receives a positive payoff.

42. What made this event particularly instructive was the use by the Citizens (speaking through the businessman) of the *former* city attorney to argue the case for approval of the petition. It became almost painfully obvious that both he and $(3Q^3)$ were concentrating their efforts upon $(3R^3)$. Though this attorney's argument was highly legalistic, the opposing but stylistically similar argument of the incumbent city attorney was accepted as *authoritative* by *all* the players. The researcher at the scene felt, however, that petitioner's legal argument was in fact more compelling.

43. There was often an intimation that the rule-abiding payoffs would occur in the future. Yet none of the players was articulate about precisely what or when. The value of simply upholding the rules, even when this meant immediate felt costs, should not be underestimated in this community.

44. During the first year of observing this council in action, and repeatedly conducting informal interviews with its members, we were struck by their disinclination to assess the electoral effects of their actions. One member was frequently ridiculed for his supposed concern for his political future. At times this seemed to be an unconscious fulfillment of Rule (4).

45. In a very real sense, rather than a game composed only of subsets of councilmen, we had an additional set—that one having a weight that varied, but was not continuous, from 0 to 1! The problem is *who* is to be considered in the game. If the city attorney, why not the city engineer? Or why not the newspaper editor, whose stories had considerable impact on council play? This can only be answered by referring to the actual rules of the game.

46. For example, two members of the present council plan to retire to their private businesses following this session, and one has already done so. These and others have repeatedly expressed the view that their occupations are more important than their council positions.

47. Even assuming a zero-sum condition, Riker finds that the calculations (needed to analyze the relative position of proto-coalitions) for four- and especially five-set partitions become "tedious," and I would say oppressive. See *op. cit.,* especially pp. 130–146 and 279–292. Ordinarily, the number of partitions will increase with the expansion of a game.

2 *The Rules of the Game in Legislative Politics: A Comparative Study*

by Allan Kornberg

Although, as Aristotle observed, man is a social animal, in any group there exist certain norms of behavior which structure the interactions of the individual in that group so as to enable it to achieve its purposive goals and/or maintain its viability. Such norms may be formal ones which require certain types of behavior or they may be informal expectations, conventions or obligations. The latter no less than the former set forth the expectations that the group has for its members and define appropriate and inappropriate actions.

The formal rules which govern the functions of and procedures within legislative bodies have long been subjects of study of political scientists. It has been relatively recently, however, that the attention of the discipline has focused on the informal norms of legislative behavior. David Truman has pointed out the importance of these informal "rules of the game" for understanding legislative behavior:

> A legislative body has its own group life, sometimes . . . it has its own operating structure which may approximate or differ sharply from the formal organization of the Chamber. When a

Reprinted from *The Journal of Politics,* 26 (May, 1964), 358–380, where it appeared under the title, "The Rules of the Game in the Canadian House of Commons," by permission of the author and the publisher.

man first joins such a body, he enters a new group. Like others, it has its standards and conventions, its largely unwritten system of obligations and privileges. To these the neophyte must conform, at least in some measure, if he hopes to make effective use of his position.

• • •

Failure to learn the ways of the legislative group, to play ball with his colleagues is almost certain, especially in a large body like the U. S. House of Representatives, to handicap the proposals in which the freshman legislator is interested and to frustrate his ambitions for personal preferment.[1]

The only systematic empirical investigations of these informal behavioral norms have been those carried out by Donald R. Matthews in his study of the Senate,[2] and by John Wahlke and his colleagues in their study of American State legislators.[3]

Our intentions were to determine what the rules of the game are for the Canadian House of Commons,[4] to make some meaningful comparisons of these rules with those discovered by the Wahlke group in their study, and to ascertain whether independent variables such as experience, party affiliation and so forth affect both the legislators' awareness of rules of the game and sanctions and the types of rules and sanctions they articulated. In order to carry out the first two intentions, the legislators were asked the following question:[5]

> We have been told that every legislature has its unofficial rules of the game, certain things members do and certain things they must not do if they want the respect and cooperation of fellow members. What are some of these rules that a member must observe to hold the respect and cooperation of his fellow members?

Since it was assumed that the primary functions of group behavioral norms are to maintain the viability of the group and to enable it to achieve its goals,[6] it was felt that the rules of the game in the Canadian House of Commons would serve primarily three functions. These would be: (1) to expedite the flow of legislative business, (2) to channel and mitigate conflict, (3) to defend members against external criticism.

The first assumption is based on the knowledge that all democratic legislatures have had to handle an increasingly large volume of work in this century. As the positive functions of government, particularly national governments, have increased, the amount of legislation with which legislators have had to deal has increased correspondingly.[7] In Canada, every major piece of legislation introduced in Parliament is almost always commented on by the leaders and the relevant subject matter specialists of *each* of the *four* parties,[8] a practice which consumes large quantities of the time in the House of Commons. The problem is further aggravated by the custom of allowing freshmen members to make at least one fairly lengthy speech during the course of a legislative session. One result of these practices, taken together with an increased work load, has been the continuous lengthening of legislative sessions since World War II. It therefore seemed reasonable to assume that some of the informal rules would encourage members to help speed the legislative process.

A democratic legislature necessarily presupposes that formal decisions will be made only after the opposition has been given a hearing and had an opportunity not only to influence the policy proposals under discussion but also to present alternative proposals. Of necessity then, democratic legislative decision-making generates conflict. In the United States this conflict is in part mitigated by the loosely disciplined parties which permit the crossing of party lines and the development of inter-party alliances. Such an arrangement is precluded by the nature of the Canadian party system. It was assumed that if conflict, a "normal" product of the democratic decision-making process which presumably is intensified by Canada's disciplined parties, was allowed to remain unchecked, it would be capable of obstructing the attainment of legislative goals and perhaps destroying the system itself. It appeared therefore, that an important function of the rules of the game in the House of Commons would be to help soften and channel conflict.

Like legislators in most countries with free speech and a free press, the Canadian legislator is a vulnerable, and sometimes an extremely attractive target for the barbs of a discontented group, or a newspaper seeking a boost in circulation by headlining a tale of supposed legislative misdeeds.[9] It was assumed that such criticism would tend to promote legislative solidarity regardless of party, and establish norms designed to discourage behavior which might bring the system and its members under attack from outsiders.

The data showed that the rules of the game in the Canadian Parliament appear to perform these three functions and in addition that they *also* appear to reinforce formal House rules, to propagate the system of disciplined parties, to mitigate intra-party conflict, to encourage members to become subject-matter experts and to perform the necessary labor required from a member of Parliament.

Canadian Perceptions of Rules of the Game

Rules listed by respondents fall into general categories: those which apply to behavior in the House itself and those which apply to behavior outside the House Chambers but within Parliament itself or to behavior entirely outside of Parliament. The following are the rules given by the legislators themselves grouped under these two headings and further categorized according to the functions they seem to perform in the legislative system:

RULES IN THE HOUSE CHAMBER BY PRIMARY FUNCTIONS

A. *Rules to decrease conflict* N = 57 % = 35.2
   1. No personal attacks on a member, never bring personalities into debate
   2. Don't be overly or stupidly partisan
   3. Be generous in your praise of opponents at the proper time

B. *Rules to expedite legislative business* N = 16 % = 10.0
   1. Do not speak too often
   2. Do not speak too long
   3. Do not be a bore
   4. Do not speak without proper knowledge of the subject

C. *Rules which discourage conduct that would invite criticism* N = 18 % = 10.9
   1. Don't curse or use improper language
   2. Always be neatly dressed, shaved, properly attired
   3. Never enter the House inebriated

D. *Rules which encourage propagation of the party system* N = 23 % = 14.0
1. Maintain party solidarity
2. Don't break party ranks
3. Don't make a speech in the House you know will offend some of your party colleagues

E. *Rules which encourage expertise and performance of labors* N = 16 % = 10.4
1. Do your homework before you speak, know what you are talking about
2. Do your proper share of the work
3. Attend House sessions, do not be absent too often

F. *Rules which reinforce respect for formal rules* N = 7 % = 3.4
1. Know the proper rules of debate, observe the rules of debate
2. Extend the proper courtesies
3. Know the correct forms of address

RULES OUTSIDE OF THE CHAMBER BY PRIMARY FUNCTIONS

A. *Rules to decrease conflict* N = 35 % = 21.3
1. Do not be rude or arrogant with other members
2. Be friendly, courteous, respect other members in your relations outside the House
3. Do not bring your partisanship out of the House, do not be partisan at social affairs, mix with everybody

B. *Rules which discourage conduct that would invite criticism* N = 81 % = 48.9
1. Be discreet in your comments to the press
2. Do not pass on confidential information to the press
3. Be honorable, honest, trustworthy, never make another member look bad, do not get another member in trouble with your remarks to the press
4. Have good manners, behave yourself,

act the same way you would in any good social club

C. *Rules which encourage work* N = 10 % = 6.2
   1. Attend party caucus, do your share of assignments, pull your weight with your colleagues

D. *Rules which discourage intra-party conflict* N = 10 % = 6.2
   1. Do not be too pushy, overaggressive
   2. Do not try too hard to advance yourself over your party colleagues

Unlike the American State legislators studied by Wahlke and his colleagues, a considerable proportion of Canadian legislators seemed to perceive no rules. Fully 16.1% said they were not aware of any rules "in the House" and 17.4% were unaware of rules "outside of the House." If rules of the game are in part learned by experience the high percentage (38.7) of Freshman legislators may in part account for this large proportion of legislators who were "ignorant" of the rules. However, the data show that there are no appreciable differences among Freshman and other legislators in their awareness of the rules of the game. Another more cogent reason may have been a suspicion on the part of some of the respondents that the acknowledgment of such existing rules might be construed and reported unfavorably by the interviewer, that is, that such rules might be perceived as being underhanded, or operating to the advantage or disadvantage of some members. Hence they may have been reluctant to commit themselves.

Response typical of legislators who said they were unaware of such rules were:

> "What do you mean, rules of the game, what rules? I've been around here for a long time and if there are any rules I don't know of them."
>
> or "There are no rules, none that I've ever heard of."
>
> or "Well there may be but I'm not aware of any. I haven't really been here long enough to know. I suppose I'll learn."
>
> or "No, no rules except that you are honest in your dealings with people."
>
> or "No, there are no rules, but you should know the House rules."

Sanctions

Although a majority of the legislators were aware of the rules of the game, only a relatively small number were cognizant of existing sanctions to enforce the observance of the rules. In contrast to the American State legislators, all but 11% of whom mentioned specific sanctions available, *83.6% of the legislators were unaware of sanctions that could be applied in the House itself and 47.5% were unaware of any available sanctions outside the House.*

In response to the statement, "I imagine things would be made rather difficult for someone who didn't follow the rules?" typical responses were:

"No!"
or "I don't know of anything."
or "Not necessarily! It depends on whose toes you step on. You can be popular with the leaders and unpopular with the members or vice versa. If you're popular with the leaders, there isn't much that can be done to a guy!"
or "Maybe, but I haven't been here long enough to find out what."
or "Unfortunately, no!"
or "I don't think so! Anyone who ignores the rules is so egotistical or has such a thick skin, it's impossible to get through to him at all."
or "No. If you win big, if the party needs you, you can get away with anything. —— is the biggest boor in the world but he's tolerated!"

Legislators who replied to the statement in the affirmative were asked "Can you give me some examples of those things?"

The responses again could be classified into those sanctions applied in the House Chamber and those applied outside of the House.

There were two types of sanctions applied in the House, one by the members, the other by the Speaker. Examples of the first type of sanction were:

"Yes, there are. If you get up to speak, everyone suddenly starts to leave or if they stay they heckle, laugh, hoot at you. You get the idea."

or "Yes, people will whisper and talk when you try to speak in the House."
or "He'd lose status in the House. People will rise, walk out on him when he tries to speak. They wouldn't listen, they'd jeer."

Illustrative of the second type of sanction employed were:

"Mr. Speaker has a blind eye for such people. When he gets up to speak someone gets up with him and the Speaker recognizes the other person."
or "Oh sure, the Speaker will make sure he doesn't get the floor. Then when he goes to the Speaker, he will be told off!"
or "Such people are simply ignored by the Speaker."

There were four types of sanctions employed outside the House: (1) social ostracism, (2) sanctions from the offender's party, (3) sanctions from members outside the offender's party, and (4) sanctions from the constituency. The following are illustrative of these sanctions.

"Certainly. Fortunately, this type doesn't last very long. They're usually defeated. Here they simply ignore you socially. It's like anywhere else. Who's going to like you if you won't go along? You certainly aren't going to get much consideration from the party or the Ministers if you don't play ball."
or "I have watched people who have built up a pretty good political image by being a maverick. But then there comes a time when the House becomes adamant and you as a maverick get no consideration from your own party or the government. Oh, the Liberals and Conservatives have ways—no campaign funds, no patronage, keep him from the nomination. They're very adept at this."
or "You just don't invite the guy in for a drink. You don't have lunch with him, you ignore him. It's like any other social group."
or "Yes! He wouldn't have the respect of his colleagues for one thing. He'd feel it. For another he'd get no consideration from his colleagues. If he were a member of the Government he'd have real trouble getting through to certain key people."
or "He is socially kept out of it. He isn't invited to certain functions. He gets the cold shoulder. He's on the awkward squad!"

Table I. *Sanctions Employed in the Canadian House of Commons*

	N	%
Sanctions Applied in the House		
1. Sanctions from colleagues	19	11.7
2. Sanctions from the Speaker	7	4.7
Sanctions Applied Outside the House		
3. Social ostracism	53	31.7
4. Sanctions from the party	13	7.6
5. Sanctions from members	19	11.8
6. Sanctions from the constituency	2	1.3

The question arises as to why such a large percentage of the legislators either were unaware of, or stated emphatically that there were no sanctions in existence. It is suggested that there are three possible explanations for this phenomenon.

If we define a sanction as *an action which is deemed punitive or detrimental to the incumbent of the legislative position,* the key words are "deemed punitive or detrimental." In other words in order for the sanction to be effective, it must first be *perceived* by the legislator as being harmful or detrimental to him. Either through inexperience or individual personality differences, what one individual deems detrimental to him, for example social ostracism, may not be so perceived by another individual, who prefers to be left largely alone.

Another factor may be that the sanction system for enforcing adherence to the informal behavioral norms in the Canadian House of Commons may not be working effectively because of a lack of consensus about the Canadian legislator's role. That is, his party, the other legislators, and his constituents may not agree on the kinds of legislative behavior an M.P. should avoid. For example, one constituency may approve of behavior that draws the attention of the mass media to their representative because they may feel he is putting them "on the map." Another constituency, however, may feel that similar behavior on the part of their legislator should be punished by switching their support to another candidate. Similarly a member's rigid adherence to the demands of party leaders may be approved of by the members of one party, while similar actions elicit only scorn from the members of another party.

Yet another reason for failing to recognize the existence of a system of sanctions may stem from the desire of the legislator to project a favorable image of himself and the group to the interviewer. By acknowledging the existence of a system of sanctions he implicitly acknowledges that his "correct conduct" as a legislator is motivated more by an anticipation of possible punishment than by some intrinsic virtue. Similarly his loyalty to the system of which he is a part may preclude him from acknowledging the existence of what in reality are extra-legal measures, and which may therefore be perceived by the "outsider" (the interviewer) as being somewhat sinister or undemocratic.

The Bases of Rules and Sanctions

Wahlke and Ferguson suggest that legislators' occupations have a greater impact upon a legislator's ability to articulate rules than do either education or the demographic characteristics of the legislators' constituencies.[10] Furthermore, their data did not demonstrate that the length of a legislator's experience had any marked impact on his ability to articulate rules of the game. Since in this study not more than two of the responses were coded the analytic concern here is with legislators' ability to perceive rules and sanctions and the types of rules and sanctions they perceived, rather than with the *number* of rules that a respondent mentioned.

Our data support Wahlke's finding that the length of a legislator's service had little impact upon his ability to articulate rules (if the ability to perceive rules and sanctions is considered a criterion of articulative facility). It seemed reasonable to assume that the longer the legislator's period of service in the House, the more he would be aware of the rules, and the sanctions available to enforce the rules. However, the data show that although slightly more long-service legislators than Freshmen were aware of the rules, *one quarter of all legislators who had at least six years of experience were unaware of any sanctions available in the House to enforce adherence to the rules. In addition there was a higher proportion of legislators with seventeen years or more of service than there were Freshmen legislators who were unaware of any sanctions invoked outside the House Chamber.* Nor were there any really significant differences among them in the types of rules or sanctions that they perceived.

Other significant independent variables we should expect to find related to the legislators' awareness of rules and sanctions and the types of rules and sanctions to which they were sensitive are party affiliation, positions of leadership,[11] differences in education, and the legislators' positions on the conflict indices.[12]

Table II. ***Sensitivity to Rules and Sanctions by Experience***

	Perceived No Rules in the House	Perceived No Rules Out of the House	Perceived No Sanctions in the House	Perceived No Sanctions Out of the House
Freshmen	18.7%	17.4%	85.5%	54.5%
"Diefenbakers"*	12.2	21.3	82.7	53.5
6-10 years service	25.4	11.9	93.2	57.7
11-16 years service	13.3	0.0	76.7	53.3
17 plus years service	13.3	13.3	63.3	66.7

*By "Diefenbakers," we mean those legislators who were first elected in the narrow Conservative victory of 1957 at which time Mr. John Diefenbaker became Prime Minister, and then re-elected in the overwhelming Conservative sweep of 1958.

The assumptions underlying the selection of these variables were:

1. The New Democrats, being the most politically sophisticated group of legislators,[13] would be more aware of the rules and sanctions in existence. The corollary of this would also be true, that is, the Liberal and Social Credit groups, the least politically sophisticated would be the least aware of rules and sanctions.
2. The Conservatives, the Government party, would most often mention rules that tend to expedite legislative business.
3. The New Democrats, the most party-oriented of the legislators,[14] would mention rules that help propagate the party system.
4. Leaders would be more aware of rules and sanctions than those who were not leaders because of their greater political sophistication.[15]
5. Leaders would more often mention rules that mitigate intraparty conflict and that encourage legislators to work at their jobs.
6. Legislators in the high conflict categories on the constituency conflict index would be less aware of sanctions

available, since they would most likely perceive sanctions coming from their legislative districts.

7. Legislators with a college education, and who have been exposed to educational institutions outside of their own province would theoretically be more aware of rules and sanctions than either college educated legislators whose education had been confined to their own provinces or legislators who have less than a college education.[16]

Examination of the data confirmed some, but not all of these assumptions. With respect to party affiliation, for example (see Table III), the New Democrats *were* the party generally most aware of the existence of rules and sanctions. However, although the Social Credit members were least aware of rules in the Chamber and sanctions outside of it, the Conservatives, rather than the Liberals, were the party least sensitive to rules and sanctions. Also, contrary to our assumption, it was the New Democrats, rather than the Conservatives who had the highest proportion of members who mentioned rules that help expedite legislative business.

Similarly, it was the Conservative and Social Credit parties, rather than the New Democrats, who mentioned rules that help propagate the party system in the legislature. The Social Credit party were almost alone in mentioning rules that function to reinforce the formal rules of debate. In addition they had the highest percentage of legislators who perceived sanctions emanating from the Speaker.[17] It would appear, therefore, that although differences in party affiliation affect the legislators' sensitivity to both rules and sanctions and the type of rules and sanctions they are aware of, these differences do not always coincide with theoretical expectations.

This was also found to be the case when we tried to explain differences in awareness and sensitivity to certain types of rules and sanctions in terms of the occupancy of leadership positions. For example, the data[18] only partially support the assumption that leaders are more sensitive to rules and sanctions than those who are not leaders. Contrary to expectations, leaders did not mention rules that discouraged intra-party conflict or encouraged members to work at their jobs more often than non-leaders.

However, a substantially higher percentage of leaders

Table III. ***Relation Between Rules of the Game and Sanctions Available and Political Parties***

	S.C.	Conserv.	Liberal	N.D.P.
Rules in the House				
Not aware of rules	21.1%	18.0%	16.1%	0.0%
Rules that decrease conflict	21.1	28.6	40.9	61.5
Rules that expedite business	9.9	10.6	6.5	23.1
Rules that discourage criticism	4.3	5.9	17.4	15.4
Rules that propagate party system	22.5	22.7	4.8	0.0
Rules which encourage expertise and hard work	0.0	14.2	11.7	0.0
Rules which reinforce formal rules	21.1	0.0	2.6	0.0
Total	100.0	100.0	100.0	100.0
(Chi Square = 218.72 D.F. = 21 P < .005)				
Rules Outside the House				
Not aware of rules	8.5%	25.5%	13.5%	7.6%
Decrease conflict	18.3	20.7	22.6	23.1
Discourage criticism	60.5	41.3	49.1	69.3
Encourage work	8.5	4.7	8.7	0.0
Discourage intra-party conflict	4.2	7.8	6.1	0.0
Total	100.0	100.0	100.0	100.0
(Chi Square = 63.92 D.F. = 18 P < .005)				
Sanctions in the House				
Not aware of sanctions	77.5%	87.5%	84.4%	75.0%
Sanctions from members	12.7	11.0	11.3	16.7
Sanctions from Speaker	9.8	1.5	4.3	8.3
Total	100.0	100.0	100.0	100.0
(Chi Square = 14.14 D.F. = 6 P < .025)				
Sanctions Outside the House				
Not aware of sanctions	62.0%	48.6%	42.2%	46.2%
Social ostracism	4.2	31.0	39.6	38.5
Sanctions from party	21.1	6.3	6.4	0.0
Sanctions from members	12.7	14.1	8.3	15.3
Sanctions from constituency	0.0	0.0	3.5	0.0
Total	100.0	100.0	100.0	100.0
	(N=23)	(N=66)	(N=63)	(N=13)
(Chi Square = 66.18 D.F. = 12 P < .005)				

(48.7%) mentioned rules that tend to soften the conflict between the parties and leaders (40.5%) were also more sensitive to the possibility of social ostracism than were those not in leadership positions. Except for these differences, the occupancy of formal leadership positions did not appear to have an appreciable impact on this aspect of legislative behavior.

Perceptions of conflict appeared to be a more important determinant of the legislator's ability to perceive rules and sanctions. Generally, the more conflict he perceived with his

Table IV. ***Relation Between Rules of the Game and Sanctions and Legislators' Positions on District Conflict Index***

	No	Low	Moderate	High
Rules in House				
Not aware	10.6%	18.9%	17.2%	18.1%
Expedite business	11.8	9.1	11.0	8.0
Decrease conflict	34.2	34.2	35.1	37.6
Discourage criticism	9.9	11.0	17.3	5.1
Propagate party-system	9.9	12.8	11.0	23.2
Encourage work and expertise	14.3	12.2	8.4	5.8
Reinforce formal rules	9.3	1.8	0.0	2.2
Total	100.0	100.0	100.0	100.0
(Chi Square=76.45 D.F.=21 P<.005)				
Rules Outside House				
Not aware	13.7%	15.2%	18.6%	23.2%
Decrease conflict	13.7	20.1	21.4	31.9
Discourage criticism	54.7	53.7	49.0	36.2
Encourage work	11.7	4.3	5.5	2.9
Discourage intra-party conflict	6.2	6.7	5.5	5.8
Total	100.0	100.0	100.0	100.0
(Chi Square=60.39 D.F.=18 P<.005)				
Sanctions in House				
Not aware	86.0%	75.6%	86.9%	89.1%
From colleagues	11.5	13.4	13.1	8.7
From Speaker	2.5	11.0	0.0	2.2
Total	100.0	100.0	100.0	100.0
(Chi Square=30.37 D.F.=6 P<.005)				
Sanctions Outside House				
Not aware	55.9%	48.8%	37.2%	47.1%
Social ostracism	27.3	37.2	29.0	33.3
From party	8.1	6.7	9.7	5.8
From colleagues	8.7	7.3	18.6	13.8
From constituents	0.0	0.0	5.5	0.0
Total	100.0	100.0	100.0	100.0
	(N=48)	(N=45)	(N=35)	(N=37)
(Chi Square=46.05 D.F.=12 P<.005)				

district the more unaware he was of the rules (see Table IV). Such legislators were also less aware of sanctions outside the House than were those in the No Conflict category. One would expect that his constituency would be a salient factor for a legislator who perceived himself in conflict with it, and his

Table V. ***Relation Between Rules of the Game and Sanctions and Legislators' Positions on Party Conflict Index***

	No	Moderate	High
Rules in House			
Not aware	14.2%	19.6%	16.3%
Expedite business	9.5	9.2	14.0
Decrease conflict	35.5	30.4	44.2
Discourage criticism	10.9	14.0	3.5
Propagate party system	15.1	10.3	17.4
Encourage work	10.4	13.0	4.6
Reinforce formal rules	4.4	3.3	0.0
Total	100.0	100.0	100.0
(Chi Square=45.11 D.F.=14 P<.005)			
Rules Outside House			
Not aware	11.2	19.0	38.4
Decrease conflict	19.6	20.6	30.2
Discourage criticism	52.9	49.4	31.4
Encourage work	8.9	4.3	0.0
Discourage intra-party conflict	7.4	6.7	0.0
Total	100.0	100.0	100.0
(Chi Square=72.48 D.F.=12 P<.005)			
Sanctions in House			
Not aware	84.1	85.3	81.4
From colleagues	12.0	8.7	14.0
From Speaker	3.0	6.0	4.6
Total	100.0	100.0	100.0
(Chi Square=4.90 D.F.=4 P<.500)			
Sanctions Outside House			
Not aware	42.6	54.3	52.3
Social ostracism	22.7	31.5	24.4
From party	9.2	3.8	9.3
From colleagues	21.1	10.4	14.0
From constituents	2.4	0.0	0.0
Total	100.0	100.0	100.0
	(N=92)	(N=50)	(N=23)
(Chi Square=17.85 D.F. P<.025)			

tendency to be less aware of the rules may be related to the fact that "his mind is on his district." Assuming that this is the case one would also expect him to perceive sanctions emanating from his district. However, it was the legislator on the Moderate rather than on the High position of the Conflict index who tended to perceive the possibility of district sanctions.

Table VI. ***Relations Between Awareness of Rules and Sanctions and Legislators' Educational Backgrounds***

	College and Some Education Out of the Province	College in Province	No College and All Education in Province
Not aware of rules in House	6.2%	18.0%	23.5%
Not aware of rules out of House	10.2	21.1	19.4
Not aware of sanctions in House	89.8	75.5	91.6
Not aware of sanctions out of House	41.9	49.8	50.0

High conflict legislators were most sensitive to rules that decreased conflict and those which tended to maintain the party system. Conversely, *they were least aware of the rules which function to avoid criticism. Perhaps one reason they perceive themselves in conflict with their constituents is that they are more likely to behave in ways that evoke criticism from their constituents.*

A considerably higher percentage of legislators who were in conflict with their *parties* were unaware of the rules outside the House Chamber than those not in conflict (see Table V). These legislators were also less aware of the possibility of sanctions operating outside the Chamber.

As was the case with the legislators in conflict with their districts, those in conflict with their parties also were more sensitive to rules that decreased inter-party conflict both in and out of the House. They were also *less concerned with rules that encourage legislators to work and rules whose function is to encourage "good" behavior.* One can speculate *that their perceived differences with the party may be related in part at least to this seeming indifference to both work and good behavior.*

Another factor, the assumption that a university education and exposure to an environment which differs from the one in which a legislator is socialized would be manifested in an increased awareness of both the rules and sanctions was generally supported by the data (see Table VI). The "cosmopolitan" college graduates were more aware of the rules and sanctions in effect outside the House than were the other two categories of legislators. However their "provincial" colleagues who also attended institutions of higher learning were more aware of sanctions in effect within the House. Legislators who were not college men, aside from their lack of sensitivity to the rules and sanctions were not *markedly* different in the emphasis they placed on those rules and sanctions which they did articulate than were their better educated colleagues.[19]

Conclusions

A study of the informal behavioral norms and sanctions in operation in the Canadian House of Commons reveals that such rules appear to be functional both for the maximization of the goals of the system and for the maintenance of the viability of the system itself. Essentially the rules expedite the flow of legislation, encourage members to work hard and become somewhat expert in different areas, maintain the party system and the strength of the parties and foster respect for the formal rules of the House. Members are at the same time urged to keep their conflict and animosities within certain limits and to avoid behavior that may draw criticism to both them and the institution of Parliament. To enforce adherence to these norms, the members are made aware that deviations will provoke sanctions from other members, from colleagues in the party, from officials in the system, and even from constituents.

Some rules receive more emphasis than others. Inside the House, stress is placed on rules which mitigate personal conflict and channel it into conflict between the parties. In other words conflict is legitimized and made predictable so that the stability of the system is not threatened as it might be if conflict was personal, intermittent and unpredictable.[20]

The relatively little emphasis placed on rules that expedite the flow of legislation is surprising but probably stems from the fact that in the Canadian system the program of legislation before the House is almost entirely the responsibility of the Government. Hence, the essential responsibility for controlling both the type of legislation and the speed with which it is considered is probably also perceived as primarily a function of the government party.

Outside the House Chamber, the rules most often stressed were those which encouraged the type of conduct that does not invite criticism. Such rules apparently function in two ways to maintain the viability of the system. First, by making the legislators aware of the fact that they face the criticism and hostility of "outsiders," they (the rules) serve to promote the solidarity of the group against a perceived external threat. Second, by keeping outside criticism to a minimum, demands for changes in the system by those outside it are also kept to a minimum.

Although in articulating the rules outside the House, a smaller proportion of the legislators emphasized rules that mitigate conflict, such rules are still salient for the members. Since most of the social activities that legislators attend result chiefly from their official status as members of Parliament, they tend to interact almost as much outside, as in the House. Tensions built up in the House, which ordinarily would dissipate if legislators were not brought into continuous contact, tend to remain. Therefore, the rules require that all members are to be treated courteously, with deference and so forth. The rule requiring members not to bring their partisanship outside the House doors indicates that even "legitimate" party conflict must be restricted.

In contrast to the American Senate, relatively little attention is focused on the necessities of controlling intra-party conflict. This may arise from the fact that unlike the Senate, seniority is not a major determinant in the selection of leaders. Since members are encouraged to believe that individual ability and industry, meritorious service to the party, and not primarily seniority will result in the granting of preferred position, they are less likely to feel frustrated by the requirement of a long apprenticeship period. Consequently there is not here the same necessity for emphasizing the virtues of serving an apprenticeship, of not being overly-aggressive and of waiting one's turn, that there is in a system governed by the seniority rule.

Examination of the sanctions available to enforce compliance with the rules indicates that the sanctions were perceived as coming essentially from informal rather than formal sources. For example the most powerful and/or frequently employed sanction was the social ostracism of the offender by other members. The next most frequent sanction employed outside the House was both a formal one, in the sense that members of the opposition parties felt that they would receive little consideration from Ministers, and an informal one, in that they perceived the offender as not being able to secure understanding, help, or co-operation from the other members.

The only official sanctions that were mentioned were perceived as emanating either from the party, from the Speaker, and in a few instances, the constituency. One would assume that in a national legislature with disciplined parties, the initiative in enforcing the rules of the game would come from official sources rather than from individuals. This is not the case, it is suggested, because of the essentially extra-legal nature of the rules. Official sources can play only a limited part in securing their enforcement since the assumption by legal sources such as the Speaker, parliamentary disciplinary committees, or the heads of government departments, of too active a role in invoking sanctions might outrage the expectations of those outside the system, and endanger the system itself.

In attempting to assess the impact of different independent variables on both a legislator's awareness of rules and sanctions and the types of rules and sanctions of which he was aware, it was found that party affiliation, perceptions of conflict with party and constituency and to an extent, the length and type of education a legislator had enjoyed seemed fairly significant. On the other hand, leadership positions, occupation and length of experience in the Commons appeared relatively unimportant.

These findings suggest that the types of rules and sanctions that a legislator is sensitive to in any particular legislative system are primarily determined by what Professor Wahlke termed "circumstantial variables,"[21] that is, variables which are transitory and are relative to a particular point in time but which may be particularly salient to the legislators being studied. For example, the data show that the Social Credit and Conservative legislators were more sensitive than were the Liberals or New Democrats to rules which promote party solidarity and propagate the party system. This is particularly interesting since the members of the latter two parties were more party oriented. Why then should a considerably larger percentage of the former two parties emphasize rules that function to promote party solidarity?

It is suggested that circumstantial variables, that is, the Conservative's minority government position and the Social Credit Party's internal troubles made such rules particularly salient for them. The life of the minority Government which the Conservatives formed was continually threatened by the possibility that the opposition parties might unite against them on a vote of confidence or that dissatisfaction with the party would result in sufficient numbers of Conservatives abstaining on a vote to bring down the government. The minority position of the Conservatives may also account for their failure to articulate rules which function to expedite the flow of legislation through the House. We had expected this to be particularly important to the Conservatives since they formed the government and the latter is charged with the responsibility for introducing most of the legislation the House will consider.[22] However as a minority government their chances of being defeated by the opposition parties were directly related to the amount of legislation they introduced, since the more legislation they tried to push through the greater the probability that on a particular bill a coalition would form which would defeat them. Consequently rules which function to expedite the flow of legislation may have been the furthest thing from their minds at the time.

For the Conservatives, then, any informal rules which functioned to promote party unity or solidarity were particularly salient at that time while those which expedite legislation were not. This might not have been the case had the Conservatives been a majority rather than a minority Government party.

Rules that tend to promote party solidarity may have been even more important to the Social Credit group who were made up of a majority wing of twenty-six members from Quebec and a minority wing of four members from the far western provinces of Alberta and British Columbia. Even before the twenty-fifth parliament assembled it became evident that party leader Robert Thompson would have a difficult time controlling either the Quebec wing or their ebullient leader, Real Caouette. The latter frequently issued public statements which were diametrically opposed to the "official" party policy enunciated by Mr. Thompson. Subsequent votes of confidence during the parliamentary session indicated that there were serious internal divisions within the party.[23]

Similarly, the high percentage of members from both minority parties who mentioned rules that function to discourage public criticism may have been related to the widespread criticism of the Social Credit Deputy-Leader occasioned by some of his rather intemperate remarks to the press, and by the unwanted attention the New Democrats received as a result of remarks about the new African States by one of their veteran parliamentary members.[24]

Still another finding which leads us to feel that circumstantial variables are important determinants of the types of rules articulated is the fact that not one of the respondents in the two minor parties mentioned rules which encourage expertise and hard work while 14.2% of the Conservatives and 11.7% of the Liberals articulated such rules. Since the Conservatives formed the government and the Liberals were the only party with a real chance of displacing them, such rules were understandably important for respondents who perceive hard work and expertness in a field as a potential vehicle to a Cabinet post but less so for members of parties with virtually no chance of forming a government in the immediate future.

Finally, the emphasis placed by legislators in conflict with party and constituency on rules that function to mitigate conflict, the concern of Social Credit members with rules that reinforce formal rules and the higher percentage of their members who perceived sanctions emanating from the Speaker, reinforce the feeling that circumstantial variables which are salient to the legislator determine the type of rules and sanctions he articulates.

The findings from this study lend support for Wahlke and Ferguson's feeling that rules of the game exist in every legislature. Although there is a remarkable similarity in the types of rules articulated in the House of Commons, the American Senate, and the four State legislatures studied previously, there are also some differences, primarily the significantly higher proportion of Canadian legislators who are unaware of the rules and the sanctions available to enforce adherence to them.

Although only further studies can definitely establish why these differences should exist, we suggest that they may in part be related to the fact that the Canadian House of Commons is a parliamentary system modeled on the British.

In the American Senate and in the State legislatures studied by Professor Wahlke and his colleagues the individual legislator is much more of a "free agent" and has considerably more opportunity to influence the output of the legislative system than in the Canadian Parliament. In the latter system the individual is much more of a "bit player" and the party as a whole the actor who plays the leading roles. Since the individual American legislator has more "to do" in helping the system attain its primary goal—the making of authoritative decisions in the form of legislation—he may be more aware of the informal behavioral norms which are related to that purpose. Another factor *may* be the relative lack of political sophistication of Canadian Members of Parliament in comparison with their American counterparts. The considerably smaller proportion of public offices available to potential aspirants in Canada as compared to the United States coupled with the rise of multi-partyism since the thirties has manifested itself in the following situation: Four parties must recruit candidates in two hundred and sixty-five districts, in which frequently two or even three of them have little chance of winning. This forces them to frequently recruit "amateurs"[25] whose chief virtues may be that they have sufficient resources to help pay part of the campaign costs and/or be able to maintain two homes on the relatively modest salaries paid Members of Parliament.[26] The fact that the least amateur of our respondents, the members of the New Democratic party, were *all* aware of rules in the House while only one of them was not aware of rules outside the House offers some support for this assumption.

Much more difficult to explain is the lack of awareness of sanctions among Canadian legislators. A number of suggestions have been made as to why this should be the case, not the least important of which may be that an imperfect consensus exists there as to what constitutes a sanction. This is certainly an area which requires further empirical study.

Notes:

1. David Truman, *The Governmental Process* (New York: Alfred A. Knopf, 1960), pp. 343–345.

2. Donald R. Matthews, *U. S. Senators and Their World* (New York: Vintage Books, 1960). Matthews lists six categories of rules of the game recognized by Senators: Apprenticeship; Legislative Work; Specialization; Courtesy; Reciprocity; and Institutional Patriotism.

3. John Wahlke *et al.*, *The Legislative System: Explorations in Legislative Behavior* (New York: John Wiley & Sons, Inc., 1962). Wahlke and Ferguson have categorized the rules of the game according to the functions they perform. These are: Rules that promote group cohesion and solidarity; rules which promote predictability of legislative behavior; rules which channel and restrain conflict; rules which expedite legislative business; rules which serve primarily to give tactical advantages to individual members and desirable personal qualities cited as rules.

4. This report is part of a larger statistical study carried out by the author in 1962 at which time a weighted stratified sample of 165 Members of Parliament were interviewed.

5. This question was taken directly from the questionnaire employed by Wahlke and his colleagues in their study of State Legislators.

6. See Dorwin Cartwright and Alvin Zander, *Group Dynamics: Research and Theory* (Evanston: Row, Peterson and Company Inc., 1953) for a complete discussion of the functions of group norms.

7. For a discussion of the effects of the increase of the volume of legislation on the formal rules of Parliaments see Gilbert Campion, *Parliament: A Survey* (London: Allen and Unwin, 1952).

8. The four parties in Canada fall quite naturally along the traditional left-right political continuum: The New Democrats, the party of the far left had a house membership of nineteen; the Liberals, the party of the Left-Center had a membership of one hundred; the Progressive-Conservatives, the party of the Right-Center had a membership of one hundred and sixteen and formed the minority government for Canada's twenty-fifth Parliament; while the Social Credit, the party of the far Right had a membership of thirty.

9. For example during the months of November and December when these interviews were taken, Canadian Members of Parliament came under fire in the nation's press for their conduct and performance at the NATO meetings in Paris, for their conduct during a tour of some of the new African states and for excessive drinking and absenteeism.

10. Our own data (not shown) offer only partial support for this finding. Although, like Wahlke we found that differences in the demographic characteristics of the legislators' constituencies had little relation to their sensitivity to rules and sanctions, we found that differences in awareness of rules and sanctions that could be attributed to occupational differences were both insignificant and inconsistent. For example, although a higher percentage of legislators with blue collar occupations were unaware of rules outside the House than were legislators with professional or managerial occupations, the former were more sensitive than managerial types to rules in the House and more sensitive to sanctions both in and out of the House than either legislators with professional or business-managerial occupations.

11. All Cabinet Ministers, Parliamentary Secretaries, party and deputy party leaders, former Cabinet Ministers, Caucus chairmen and party Whips who fell within the sample were classified as party leaders. All others were classified as non-leaders regardless of any positions held in the party organization outside of Parliament.

12. To facilitate analysis, a number of indices were constructed which attempt to measure the effect of certain cultural and political variables

on the values, attitudes and behavior of Canadian Members of Parliament. The codes for all variables were 0, 1, 2. If a respondent did not fit the description of the variable he was coded "0," if the information had not been ascertained he was coded "1," and if he fit the description, he was coded "2." Since excessively high variance together with low correlations to other items was not a factor for any of the variables employed, no special weighting was required and a respondent's position on any index was arrived at simply by summing his coded responses. The Tau Gamma rank order correlation test indicated that all correlations among the variables for each index were high enough to be judged significant. The constituency conflict index was constructed of five variables and measures the extent to which a legislator perceives conflict between himself and his constituents on goals, expectations for the legislative position, and position on certain policy issues. The four categories of the index are No Conflict, Low Conflict, Moderate Conflict and High Conflict. The Party conflict index is made up of three variables and measures the degree to which the legislator perceives himself in conflict with his party on three policy issues. The categories of the index are No Conflict, Some Conflict, and High Conflict.

13. By political sophistication we mean that the legislators had been raised in highly politicized environments, that is, their families were active politically, politics was frequently discussed at home and so forth. In addition they had held elected public and party offices at various levels before becoming candidates for Parliament.

14. Party oriented legislators were those legislators who asserted: a) a party caucus decision was always binding; b) it is *always* necessary to vote with your party; c) one had to choose the party over the constituency in the event of conflict between the two. The Tau Gamma statistic indicated that there was a significant relationship among these variables.

15. Data not shown.

16. For a discussion on the relationship between education and democracy see Seymour M. Lipset, *Political Man* (New York: Anchor Books, 1963), pp. 39–42.

17. The concern of the Social Credit group with formal rules and sanctions from the Speaker may have been related to the fact that during the first session of the twenty-fifth Parliament, a number of Social Credit members clashed frequently and sharply with Mr. Speaker. The latter actually had one of these legislators temporarily expelled from the House, an event which occurs very infrequently in the Canadian House of Commons.

18. Data not shown.

19. Data not shown.

20. Wahlke and Ferguson found that the function of certain informal rules in the State Legislatures was to make legislators' behavior predictable. *Op. cit.,* p. 160.

21. Wahlke *et al., ibid.,* pp. 18–20.

22. *Supra,* p. 29.

23. As this was being written, Mr. Caouette formally disavowed the leadership of Mr. Thompson and with eleven other Social Credit members from Quebec formed a new party, Le Ralliement des Creditistes.

24. Mr. Harold Winch's statements to the press on his return to Canada

from a visit to Africa, in which he expressed alarm and concern over both the lack of democratic practices in the new African States and the racist attitudes of some African elites, received considerable attention in the national press. It was felt by some that Mr. Winch's statements were also tinged with "racism."

25. For example, 54.4% of our respondents had never held a public office before becoming a candidate for Parliament, 26.6% had never held an office in their party and 17.8% had never held either a public or a party office. In addition 34.5% were socialized in an environment almost devoid of any mention of politics and 54.8% said they did not seek the office but were recruited by the parties.

26. At the time these interviews were taken Canadian Members of Parliament were being paid an annual salary of ten thousand dollars. Since then the salary has been increased to eighteen thousand dollars.

3 *Organizational Membership and Democratic Consensus* by Sidney Verba

The role of private, non-governmental organizations in democratic government has been dealt with from a variety of points of view. Three of the most important are: pressure group politics, mass politics, and theories of cross-pressures. The concern of pressure group theorists has been largely with the problem of the allocation of goods and services in a society—with the classic question of who gets what, when and how. The concern of "mass politics" theorists has been with the role of such organizations as mediators between rulers and ruled. The "cross-pressures" focus involves the role of non-governmental organizations in structuring political competition, in particular in mitigating the intensity of such competition.[1] Non-governmental organizations, thus, have been dealt with in relation to three of the most important theoretical problems that arise in democratic politics: the problem of the allocation of values among competing groups; the problem of citizen participation in politics; and the problem of the structuring of patterns of conflict among competing groups. And these organizations may become especially important at a time when other institutions are operating less effectively in these areas. With the decline of ideology, the waning of parliamentary opposition, the inability of political parties to structure meaningful electoral issues, and the in-

Reprinted from *The Journal of Politics,* 27 (August, 1965), 467–497, by permission of the author and the publisher.

ability of parliaments to control major policy decisions (all characteristics of politics in many contemporary democracies), the locus of politics may move out of the political party-electoral system-parliamentary nexus into a realm where interest groups and other associations play a major role.

This paper will deal with the third theoretical problem discussed above—cross-pressures and the structuring of patterns of conflict within political systems. It will try to test some of the hypotheses about the effects of multiple group affiliation on the intensity of political conflict using data from a cross-national survey of attitudes toward politics.[2] That the data come from several different political systems—the United States, Britain, Germany, Italy and Mexico—is important. The multiple membership theories have been developed in an American context and applied to American politics. The cross-national validation of the hypotheses or the specification of the conditions under which the hypotheses hold or do not hold should do much to illuminate the theory. Furthermore, though the theory developed within the American context, there has been relatively little empirical work done to test it even within that context.[3] There is often a danger that useful suggestions—especially when they are as interesting and compelling as the multiple membership theories—will be taken as fully validated conclusions about politics. Though the data presented here will be far from adequate to support or refute the hypothesis that multiple group affiliation tends to mitigate political conflict, it should make some contribution to that task.

Multiple, overlapping memberships in organizations, according to cross-pressure theories, prevent the polarization of political conflict. This takes place in two ways. On the elite level, organizational leaders reduce the intensity of their claims on other social groups because of the diversity of membership in their organization. On the level of the organizational rank and file, so the argument goes, the individual shares membership—and consequently shares some goals as well as perhaps has personal contact—with people with whom he differs politically. And this exposure tends to lower the level of opposition to political opponents. William Kornhauser aptly characterizes the pluralist system of affiliation. "Cross-cutting solidarities . . . help prevent one line of social cleavage from becoming dominant, and they constrain associations to respect the various affiliations of their members lest they alienate them. . . . They may be contrasted with situations in which religious and class lines tend to closely correspond, as in France where anti-clericalism is largely a working-class phenomenon."[4] An overlapping pattern of organizational affiliation, it should be noted, is a way of *managing* the strains that arise from patterns of cleavage in a society, not a way of *eliminating* cleavage. The latter is not a meaningful possibility in a modern democratic state. To manage cleavage implies that the intensity of competition among political opponents remains low enough to make the alternation of power from one group to another acceptable to the competitors. This means that differences in policy preferences must be kept in bounds: they must be negotiable, and the differences must not be so severe as to make the accession to power of one's political opponents a matter of severe danger to one's own interests. Policy controversies have to be kept from escalating to controversies over total ways of life or among irreconcilable groups.

In this connection it is possible to distinguish two types of partisanship: one involves the positive commitment of an individual or group to a particular political party; on the individual level it involves identification with and willingness to support a party; while on the group level it involves the extent to which a particular social group supports the party that is closest to its interests. The other type of partisanship is more negative, and involves the extent to which supporters of one party are hostile to the opposition. The two types of partisanship are closely related, but the existence of the former does not necessarily imply the latter. And the two types of partisanship have different social consequences.[5] Indeed, a general problem in democratic politics is how to prevent a politicized electorate organized around the support of competing parties from becoming a deeply divided electorate organized into two hostile camps. Here voluntary associations may play an important role. There is evidence that organizational membership—in particular, union membership—is related to an increase in what we have called positive partisanship.[6] Multiple-membership theories would suggest that such affiliation would also be related to a reduction in negative partisanship. It is this latter relationship we shall explore in this paper.

Overlapping memberships should reduce conflict by changing the social level at which conflict is resolved. One can conceive of a political system made up of two closed camps with no overlapping of membership. The only channels of communication between the two camps would be at the highest level—say when the leaders of the two camps meet in the governing chambers—and all conflict would have to be resolved at this highest level. Politics comes to resemble negotiations between rival states; and war or a breakdown of negotiations is always possible. At the other extreme is the system with many cross-cutting solidarities. Conflict is resolved not on the highest but on the lowest level—within the mind of the individual as he tries to balance off his commitment to several sides at once. The result, if the works on cross-pressures are correct, is for the individual to take a less intense political stance and for partisanship in general to be less negative.

Conflict resolution at an intermediary level is also consistent with the cross-pressures approach. Ordinary organization members may not modify their political views if exposed to cross-cutting solidarities, but organizational leaders who are more sensitive to such matters may take less extreme positions because of their multiple clientele.

Thus a network of non-governmental organizations with overlapping memberships does not reduce the overall amount of conflict in a society; rather it takes it out of the realm of *political* conflict. Conflict is resolved within the individual or, on a somewhat higher level, within the organizations themselves. "The essential fact here is that most structurally important groupings in the society will contain considerable proportions of adherents of *both* parties. To an important degree, therefore, the structural ties that bind them together on non-political bases cut across their political allegiances. Hence the tendency to political cleavage will tend to be checked by a set of mechanisms that operate *below* the level of party division. . . ."[7]

Conflict reduction, according to the theories of multiple membership, depends on *overlapping* membership. Multiple membership in organizations might indeed have the opposite effect if memberships were cumulative rather than overlapping. The multiple-membership hypotheses assume a chain of relations something like this: 1) organizational membership, 2) exposure to or identification with others of opposing political views, 3) cross-pressures, 4) reduction in intensity of political competitiveness. The second step is crucial. If organizations were homogeneous in membership from the point of view of the major lines of social and political cleavage—e.g. drawing all members from one political party, one religion, one region, one social class—individuals would be placed in situations where their political views would be reinforced and levels of conflict would increase. In that case the chain of connection would be as follows: 1) organizational membership, 2) exposure to or identification with others of like background or political views, 3) reinforcement of views, 4) increase in intensity of political competitiveness. Overlapping membership should result in lower intensity of political commitment, indecision about political commitment, indecision about political choices, increased tolerance of political opponents, withdrawal from political conflict situations, and so forth. Cumulative memberships should result in increased political involvement, increased commitment to a particular point of view, increased hostility to political opponents, and so forth. Thus the social composition of organizations is a crucial variable as is their communication structure. The latter affects awareness of and interaction with others in the organization. Furthermore, it is not the number of organizations involved that is crucial but the number of psychologically meaningful affiliations. The role of membership in formal organizations is to increase the chance of being placed in either a psychologically meaningful cross-pressured situation or a situation of cumulative social contacts. But membership in even a single organization could have either of these opposing effects, depending upon whether the membership exposed the individual to others of similar or different social background and political inclination.

Most of the evidence on the effects of multiple memberships relates to what are considered above to be intervening variables.[8] Thus it has been shown that individuals who do experience some psychological cross-pressures—say prefer the candidate of one party and the policies of the other—are likely to be less interested in politics, to delay in making decisions, and to withdraw from the decision by not voting. Or individuals whose social affiliations are inconsistent—that is, the majority of those in one social group with which they are affiliated have political leanings different from the majority in some other group with which they are affiliated—are also likely to be somewhat less intensely politically committed.[9] Conversely, there is evidence that those who come from homogeneous and isolated political environments are more likely to be intense in their political commitment. Thus workers living in working class districts are more likely to be politically active than workers living in middle class districts (and vice versa for the middle class), and political radicalism is more often found among groups isolated from the rest of society—miners, lumberjacks, and other isolated professions.[10]

The role of formal organizations in this process has been less frequently directly studied. But this deserves direct consideration as well. Such organizations grow in importance with economic and social modernization, and the implications of this growth for democratic politics would be greatly illuminated by evidence on the relationship between formal associational membership and political conflict. This is especially the case since the mere growth in the number of affiliations would have opposite effects depending on whether the intervening process was one of overlapping memberships or of cumulative memberships. In this respect our ability to test some of these hypotheses with data from several nations is important. The hypotheses would be that in the United States, from whose politics the cross-pressures hypotheses have been derived, organizational membership would be related to a reduction of intergroup hostility. On the other hand, organizational affiliation in Italy should be of the cumulative kind and produce an increase in intergroup hostility. As Joseph LaPalombara has pointed out, "formal interest groups in Italy frequently organize *within* . . . sub-cultures; very few of them cut across sub-cultural lines, even when the logic of a common economic interest would appear to compel such unification. . . . Even within each of the sub-cultures, the groups are further fragmented. It is not uncommon, for example, to find Communist, Catholic, Socialist, Republican, and Neo-Fascist rough equivalents of the League of Women Voters."[11] The pattern of organizational composition that one would expect in the other three nations is somewhat more ambiguous. In Britain one might expect a pattern something like that in the United States but probably more homogeneous in class terms. In Germany one might expect a similar pattern. Though pre-Nazi organizational life was very much like the fragmented picture we have for Italy, the structure of organizational life has become less fragmented—as evidenced best by the non-partisan DGB, the German trade union organization.[12] The expectations in Mexico are even more ambiguous because of the lack of a firm structure of political competitiveness (due to the essentially one-party system). For this reason we shall concentrate largely on the comparison between the United States and Italy, the two countries where our expectations are clearest.

This paper will deal with individualistic hypotheses about conflict resolution—that is with those hypotheses about the impact of overlapping membership on systems of conflict that relate such memberships to the attitudes of the individual members of organizations. To confirm the individualistic hypotheses as to the effects of multiple organizational membership on political conflict, one would have to be able to demonstrate, at minimum, that such memberships expose individuals either to cross-pressures or reinforcement of their political beliefs; and that the cross-pressures of the heterogeneous environment result in a reduction in the intensity of political conflict among individuals while a homogeneous environment increases that intensity. Thus for the individual one would have to know whether or not he belongs to any organization, the social composition of the organization, whether the individual is in fact exposed to the presumed social pressures, and whether these exposures are related to differences in political attitudes. Even such information would allow us to confirm these hypotheses only on the individual level—that is, we could show that individuals modified their political views under such conditions, but would not be able to show that this resulted in a reduction of political tension for the system as a whole. Such a confirmation on the individual level would be useful nevertheless given the paucity of data to support the hypotheses so far.

But even the individual level confirmation of the multiple-membership hypotheses in the full sense spelled out above will not be possible with the data to be presented in this paper. The data were gathered in the course of a survey study of individual attitudes, a survey conducted for other purposes than the direct testing of these hypotheses. The data are therefore somewhat indirect. We do know the number of organizations to which an individual belongs. What we do not know, and what could not be ascertained in individual interviews, is the composition of these organizations, in particular the extent to which they involve either overlapping or cumulative memberships. This means that the crucial intervening variable remains unmeasured. But since we do have clear expectations as to these intervening organizational compositions in at least two of the nations, we can at least ask if the results in terms of political attitude change are what one would expect.

The Political Attitudes of Organization Members

There is much evidence that organizational membership is associated with political participation and involvement. The cross-national survey whose results are reported in *The Civic Culture* found that in all five nations studied, the associational member is more likely to be politically active, to be informed about politics, to be involved and care about political affairs, to believe himself to be a competent citizen, and to express support for democratic norms. Furthermore, the type of organization to which an individual belongs, the number to which he belongs, and the extent of his activity within the organization are all related to his political activity and involvement. Members of organizations that are somewhat involved in politics, members of more than one organization, and active members tend to be more politically involved. But more important, perhaps, is the finding that *any* membership —even if the individual is but a passive member of his organization, or the organization has no political content—is associated with higher levels of political activity and involvement.[13]

These data clearly suggest that voluntary organization membership plays an important role in the maintenance of a participatory political system. This is relevant to the problem of the relationship between organizational membership and political conflict. For one thing, the results cited above suggest that the measure of organizational membership is a powerful one; it does differentiate similarly among political actors in all five countries in terms of some important political attributes. Furthermore, since organizational members are likely to be heavily concentrated in the politically active strata, the relationship between organizational membership and attitudes toward political conflict takes on increased importance in terms of the overall level of political conflict in the society.

A relationship between organizational affiliation and the extent of political conflict in a nation would be hard to sustain if there were no variation in the frequency of such membership from nation to nation. As Table I indicates, however, there is substantial variation in the frequency of organizational membership and in the frequency of multiple membership. In the United States one-third of the total sample belongs to more than one organization, while 16 per cent in Britain, 12 per cent in Germany, 6 per cent in Italy and 2 per cent in Mexico are multiple members.[14]

As we have pointed out, where memberships overlap, the individual with multiple affiliations should have a greater tolerance of political opposition. One would expect that the intensity of political differences will be tempered and that even if the extent of *political* difference is held constant, common identification will reduce the general hostility to political opponents. On the other hand, where memberships cumulate, one would assume greater hostility to political opponents among organization members.

Thus, based on our assumptions as to the nature of the associational systems in the United States and Italy, we would expect that organizational membership is associated with a more tolerant and open view of political opponents in the United States and a more hostile view in Italy. A measure of hostility to political opponents might be a question asked of respondents as to whether or not they would approve of the marriage of a son or daughter to a supporter of the opposition political party.[15] This question deals essentially with the limits of politics—how far are political criteria allowed to penetrate into personal life. The individual who considers such criteria irrelevant is saying, as it were, that there are limits to politics, and that in certain circumstances other values are more important than political ones. On the other hand, the individual who would reject someone for admission to the primary group on the basis of political criteria takes a more hostile view of political opponents. The latter tendency is, thus, an indicator of the degree of fragmentation of a political system into closed and competing political groups. Evidence of such fragmentation was found most fre-

Table I. ***Respondents Who Belong to One or More Organization, by Nation (in per cent)***

Per Cent Who	U.S.	U.K.	Germany	Italy	Mexico
Belong to one organization	25	31	32	24	23
Belong to two organizations	14	10	9	5	2
Belong to three organizations	9	4	2	1	0
Belong to four or more organizations	9	2	1	—	—
Total per cent multiple members	32	16	12	6	2
Total per cent members	57 (970)*	47 (963)	44 (955)	30 (995)	5 (1007)
Per cent of members who are multiple members	55	34	27	20	8

*Numbers in parentheses refer to the bases upon which percentages are calculated.

quently in Italy, and with intermediate frequency in Germany and Mexico. On the other hand, the great frequency with which American and British respondents reported that partisan affiliation was an irrelevant criterion for admission to the primary group was taken to be an indicator of a less fragmented political system in which partisan disputes were "kept in their place" by not being considered proper criteria for more intimate social relationships.[16] But we are not interested here in the relative frequency with which such hostility to political opponents is expressed, but with the relationship between this and organizational affiliation. If cross-pressures mechanisms are at work, a "closed" attitude toward those of opposing political views would be *less* likely among those with many memberships. If reinforcement mechanisms are at work, a "closed" attitude would be *more* likely.

The data in Table II offer little evidence to support the hypotheses that cross-pressures mechanisms are at work. The expectation would be that in the United States at least and perhaps elsewhere those respondents who are members of more than one organization would be more likely than the members of one organization to say that partisan affiliation is irrelevant for admission to close personal relationships, and that the members of one organization would in turn be more likely to be "open" to political opponents than would those who are unaffiliated. But in the United States, Britain, and Germany frequency of organizational affiliation appears to be unrelated to one's views on the admission of a political opponent into the primary group. And this pattern appears on both educational levels.

There is some tendency for the relationship expected from a cross-pressure situation to appear in the Mexican data. Nonmembers are somewhat more likely than members, and members of one organization somewhat more likely than multiple members to express hostility toward political opponents. But the tendency is not very strong and appears only among Mexican respondents on the lower educational level; among those with secondary education or better there is a slight opposite tendency. And the few respondents with more than one membership makes the comparison between multiple members and single members not very reliable.

The only nation in which there is a definite relationship between group affiliation and inter-party hostility is Italy.

Table II. ***Organizational Membership and Attitude Toward Marriage of a Child to a Supporter of the Opposition Party (supporters of major parties only)***

Attitude Toward Marriage of Child to Supporter of Opposition Party	U.S.			U.K.			Germany			Italy			Mexico		
	Non-Mem.	*Sing. Mem.*	*Mult. Mem.*	*Non-Mem.*	*Sing. Mem.*	*Mult. Mem.*	*Non-Mem.*	*Sing. Mem.*	*Mult. Mem.*	*Non-Mem.*	*Sing. Mem.*	*Mult. Mem.*	*Non-Mem.*	*Sing. Mem.*	*Mult. Mem.*
Total															
Displeased	4%	3%	4%	7%	8%	7%	14%	17%	13%	43%	54%	64%	26%	22%	6%
Indifferent	93	91	95	91	90	91	73	68	76	39	35	32	60	68	84
Other	3	5	3	1	1	—	2	6	5	12	6	3	9	7	11
Don't know	—	1	—	—	—	1	10	9	1	5	4	—	4	4	—
Total number	299	196	267	375	223	136	314	192	63	296	124	31	405	167	17
Primary Education or Less															
Displeased	5%	4%	6%	8%	6%	6%	13%	15%	13%	41%	55%	[56]%	26%	20%	*
Indifferent	91	88	89	91	94	94	76	70	80	41	34	[44]	63	68	*
Other	4	6	4	—	—	—	1	7	4	12	8	—	9	9	*
Don't know	1	2	—	—	—	—	10	8	2	7	4	—	3	2	*
Total number	194	122	193	272	137	68	275	158	46	229	84	18	352	124	7
Secondary Education or Above															
Displeased	3%	1%	2%	4%	13%	9%	24%	23%	[13]%	48%	53%	[77]%	25%	28%	*
Indifferent	96	95	96	95	85	89	64	59	[67]	35	42	[15]	51	64	*
Other	1	3	2	1	2	0	9	3	[13]	15	3	[8]	12	2	*
Don't know	0	0	0	0	0	1	3	15	[7]	1	3	[0]	12	7	*
Total number	105	74	183	98	79	64	33	34	15	66	38	13	53	43	10

*Too few cases.

And here we find confirmation of the alternate hypothesis to the cross-pressures one. As we predicted for Italy, members of more than one organization are *more* likely to oppose entry into the primary group of a political opponent than are members of one organization, and members of one organization in turn express inter-party hostility more frequently than do respondents who report no organizational affiliation. Sixty-four per cent of the multiple members would be displeased if a son or daughter married the supporter of an opposition party, in contrast with 54 per cent of the single members, and 43 per cent of those with no organizational affiliation.

A quite similar pattern is apparent if we use as an index of inter-party hostility the type of terms the respondent chooses to describe political opponents. Respondents were asked to characterize the supporters of the various political parties.[17] For our purposes, we are interested in respondents who choose negative terms ("ignorant people," "selfish people," etc.) to describe the supporters of opposition parties. Table III reports the relationship between number of organizational memberships and the selection of negative terms to describe one's political opponents. The findings parallel those in Table II, and again offer little evidence that organizational affiliation is related to a reduction in the extent of partisan hostility. In the United States, Britain, Germany and Mexico there is little apparent relationship between frequency of organizational membership and the use of negative terms to describe one's political opponents.

Again, the only relationship between group membership and opinions of opposition party supporters is found in Italy. And again, the reinforcement hypothesis is confirmed, for it is precisely among those respondents with the greatest number of group affiliations that hostility toward the opposition party is most frequently expressed; and among the organizationally unaffiliated respondents that negative terms to describe one's political opponents are least frequently employed. It is, of course, not unexpected that such negative views or so frequent opposition to marriage with a political opponent is expressed in Italy. We are, after all, asking supporters of the Christian Democratic party how they feel about the Communists, and the Communists and Socialists (the interviewing took place in 1959, long before the "opening to the left") how they feel about the Christian Democrats. But what is of in-

Table III. ***Percentage of Respondents Who Choose Negative Terms to Characterize Supporters of the Opposition Party by Organizational Membership (supporters of major parties only)***

Nation	Total			Primary or Less			Secondary or Above		
	Non-Members	*Members of One Organization*	*Members of More than One Organization*	*Non-Members*	*Members of One Organization*	*Members of More than One Organization*	*Non-Members*	*Members of One Organization*	*Members of More than One Organization*
U.S.	12%* (299)†	14% (197)	13% (276)	15% (194)	17% (122)	21% (93)	6% (105)	8% (75)	9% (183)
U.K.	41 (377)	45 (222)	41 (134)	42 (277)	48 (134)	48 (67)	38 (96)	43 (81)	36 (64)
Germany	14 (314)	16 (192)	9 (63)	12 (275)	15 (158)	9 (46)	24 (33)	12 (34)	13 (15)
Italy	43 (296)	56 (124)	71 (31)	41 (229)	50 (84)	61 (18)	51 (66)	67 (39)	85 (13)
Mexico	20 (405)	20 (167)	6 (17)	20 (352)	25 (124)	‡	18 (53)	9 (43)	‡

*i.e. 12 per cent of non-members use negative terms to characterize the supporters of the opposition party.
†Number in parentheses refers to the base upon which percentage is calculated.
‡Too few cases.

terest here is not the absolute level of such hostility, but the fact that the organizational system reinforces this hostility. Here is an example then of a situation in which organizational membership (and we assume that the intervening process involves cumulative, not overlapping, memberships) acts to increase social tension and fragmentation.

Table IV. ***Percentage of Respondents Who Choose Negative Terms to Characterize Supporters of Opposition Party by Number of Organizational Affiliation (U.S., U.K., and Germany)***

No. of Organizations	U.S.		No. of Organizations	U.K.		Germany	
None	12%	(299)*	None	41%	(377)	14%	(314)
One	14	(197)	One	45	(222)	16	(192)
Two	15	(117)	Two	39	(86)	8	(49)
Three	14	(79)	Three or more	45	(49)	[14	(14)]
Four or more	9	(80)					

*Number in parentheses refers to base upon which percentage is calculated.

The Italian results are expected. It is more surprising that one does not find evidence for the conflict-reducing effects of an overlapping pattern of membership elsewhere; particularly in the United States and perhaps in Britain. Organizational membership has been shown to have an important relationship with other political attitudes and behaviors—those relevant to the degree of participation and involvement—and this makes the lack of pattern in connection with inter-party hostility even more surprising.

The situation is highlighted if we look more closely at the effect of the number of organizational affiliations on attitudes toward those who support political parties other than one's own. In Tables II and III we compared non-members and single members with multiple members. Table IV breaks down the multiple member groups more finely. Yet, even when we compare respondents who belong to three or four or more organizations with those who belong to one or no organization, we find that the degree of hostility toward supporters of the opposition party—as measured by the use of negative terms—does not decline. In the United States, those with most memberships (four or more) are somewhat less likely to choose hostile terms to describe political opponents than are those with fewer memberships, but there is little difference among those with one, two or three memberships—and those who belong to one, two or three groups are *more likely* to choose hostile terms than are those respondents who are non-members. And in Britain and Germany, the group of respondents with most memberships (three or more) are as likely or more likely than those with no memberships to choose hostile terms. And the situation is similar with regard to inter-party marriage. Unless we are to assume that the member of three, four, or more organizations in these countries is no more likely to mingle with those of opposing parties than is the man who belongs to no organization—a situation that is not impossible, though unlikely if the assumptions, at least about American organizations, are true—we must also call into question the assumption that such common memberships lead to a reduction in the intensity of political antagonism.

A similar measure of inter-party conflict reveals a similar pattern for the supporters of the various political parties in the nations studied. One way in which a sense of confidence in one's political opponents facilitates democratic politics is that it makes the losers in political contests more willing to turn the reins of government over to the winners. Table V reports the views of the supporters of the party in power in the five nations as to whether they believe that the accession to power of the leading opposition party would be likely to "seriously endanger the country's welfare;" as well as the views of the supporters of the leading opposition party as to whether the actions of the incumbent party might involve a similar danger.[18] The figures reported refer to the difference between the percentage saying that such serious danger "probably wouldn't" occur and the percentage saying it "probably would"—the higher the figure the more frequently the particular groups expressed confidence in their political opponents. If organization membership was acting to increase cross-pressures and to reduce interparty hostility, one would assume that expressions of serious concern over the activities of one's political opponents would decline as one moved from non-members, to members, to multiple members. Conversely, if the organizations were cumulative in impact, one would expect the opposite. In Italy, as expected, organization members are less likely to trust their political opponents. For the other nations, the data in Table V are far from unambiguous, but they do suggest that organizational membership is as likely to be associated with greater concern about the activities of one's political opponents as it is with less. In the United States, no clear pattern exists as to the views of Democrats about Republicans, while there is some evidence that Republicans who are members of more than one organization would be less fearful about a Democratic accession to power. In Britain one finds no pattern for Conservatives and a tendency for Labour Party supporters to be more fearful if they belong to organizations. In Germany, the supporters of both major parties appear somewhat less fearful of the opposition if they are organization members, though among the CDU supporters the tendency is far from clear. And in Mexico, organization members are somewhat more fearful of their political opponents.

The Organizational Leaders

The lack of confirmation of the overlapping membership hypotheses calls into question the extent to which cross-pressures mechanisms operate to reduce the intensity of political conflict on the level of the ordinary organization member. But this does not mean necessarily that the system of organizational affiliations plays no role in conflict reduction. As was pointed out earlier, even if conflict reduction does not take place on the lowest level—i.e., within the mind of the ordinary citizen—cross-pressures may operate and conflict resolution take place on the level of the organizational leaders.

There are a number of reasons why one would expect the impact of the organizational system on patterns of conflict to be greater on the level of the organizational leadership. The commitment of many members of voluntary associations to their association is often minimal, and such minimal commitment would serve to reduce the impact of membership on their political attitudes. On the other hand, leaders of organizations are in the center of communications networks and are more likely to be aware of and sensitive to the views of their memberships. Thus, though we do not find evidence to support the overlapping membership hypotheses on the level of the ordinary group member, perhaps we shall find it on the level of organizational leadership. And the pattern of intensification of conflict associated with organizational membership in Italy will perhaps be stronger on the level of the organizational leadership.

Table V. ***Index of Trust in Opposition* Party and Organization Membership (proportion of respondents saying the opposition party would probably not harm nation minus the proportion saying it would)***

Nation	Party	Non-Member		Single Mem.		Multiple Mem.	
U.S.	Republican view of Democrats	51%	(111)†	51%	(69)	62%	(127)
	Democrats view of Republicans	53	(186)	41	(128)	45	(148)
U.K.	Conservative view of Labour	—7	(175)	—11	(104)	—6	(79)
	Labour view of Conservatives	51	(200)	37	(119)	33	(57)
Germany	CDU view of SPD	16	(188)	10	(107)	31	(39)
	SPD view of CDU	25	(126)	22	(85)	[54	(24)]
Italy	DC view of PCI	—47	(227)	—63	(101)	—68	(25)
	PCI/PSI view of DC	—10	(67)		—22	(32)‡	
Mexico	PRI view of PAN	16	(356)	13	(145)	§	
	PAN view of PRI	8	(50)	—21	(22)	§	

*"Opposition" refers to the party the *respondent* opposes.
†Numbers in parentheses refer to base on which percentage is calculated.
‡"One" and "multi" combined because too few cases in either separately.
§Too few cases.

Table VI distinguishes between organizational members who have ever held a position as an officer in one of the organizations to which they belong and those who have not. In cases where overlapping membership mechanisms were operating, we would expect that officers of organizations would manifest less hostility to political opponents than would rank and file members, whereas they would manifest more hostility where cumulative membership mechanisms were at work. Similarly, the differences between members of one organization and members of more than one would be greater among those who hold some leadership position than among those who are more passive members.[19]

The data in Table VI do not support the hypothesis that overlapping membership mechanisms leading to a reduction in political hostility are operating on organizational elite levels in the United States. As the pattern of responses to the questions on inter-party marriage and on the characteristics of political opponents indicate, there is little difference between officers of organizations and rank and file members, or, indeed, between officers and non-members. And just as the members of a single organization are little different from the members of more than one organization, so the officers with a single affiliation are quite like the officers with multiple affiliations. If anything, there is some slight tendency for officers

Table VI. ***Leaders and Followers***

Percentage Opposed to Interparty Marriage (in per cent)

Nation	Non-Members	Officers		Ordinary Members	
		One Organization	*More than One Organization*	*One Organization*	*More than One Organization*
U. S.	4 (299)*	2 (44)	3 (182)	3 (149)	4 (92)
U. K.	7 (375)	18 (40)	10 (70)	6 (180)	5 (66)
Germany	14 (314)	18 (17)	16 (19)	17 (175)	11 (44)
Italy	43 (296)	65 (26)	[73 (11)]	51 (96)	58 (19)
Mexico	26 (405)	19 (95)†		31 (148)†	

Percentage Choosing Negative Terms to Characterize Opponents

Nation	Non-Members	Officers		Ordinary Members	
		One Organization	*More than One Organization*	*One Organization*	*More than One Organization*
U. S.	12 (299)	16 (45)	14 (182)	13 (149)	13 (92)
U. K.	41 (377)	46 (37)	35 (69)	45 (182)	47 (66)
Germany	14 (314)	18 (17)	10 (19)	14 (175)	9 (44)
Italy	43 (296)	77 (26)	[82 (11)]	51 (96)	63 (19)
Mexico	20 (405)	15 (95)†		22 (148)†	

*Number in parentheses refers to the base upon which the percentage is calculated.

†Single and multiple memberships combined in Mexico due to small number of Mexican multiple members.

to manifest somewhat greater hostility to opponents than do non-members or rank and file members—using the question of the terms used to describe opponents as the indicator of this. Thus there is no more support in the American data for the proposition that conflict reduction mechanisms are operating on the organizational elite level than there is for such a process on the rank and file level.

In the British data, there is some evidence on the elite level for the pattern one would associate with cross-pressures mechanisms. Though officers are not less hostile to political opponents than members—and, indeed, on the inter-marriage question they are somewhat more hostile—officers with multiple affiliations are less hostile than officers with a single affiliation, a difference that does not appear when we compare multiple and single members on the rank and file level. In Germany and Mexico, however, there is little difference between officers and rank and file members.

In Italy, on the other hand, there is confirmation of the hypothesis of the greater impact of a cumulative system of memberships on the organizational elite level than on the rank and file level. Officers of organizations are more hostile to their political opponents on both of the measures of such hostility, though the effect of the number of organizations is roughly the same for both officers and rank and file members.

In general, the pattern found for organizational elites is similar to that found for members in general. The cumulative membership hypotheses are confirmed in Italy. The overlapping membership hypotheses are not confirmed elsewhere. It is true that the measure of organizational elite status is a relatively weak one—the official positions held within the organization can be quite minor for someone to be considered an officer by our measure. It is possible that if one had a sample of top organization leaders the overlapping membership hypotheses would be confirmed. But the elite data presented in Table VI give little indication of such confirmation.

Type of Organization

In the data that has been presented so far we have been lumping together a wide range of organizations, and this might have something to do with the fact that the expected pattern does not emerge in the American data. Ideally we should be able to separate out those organizations with heterogeneous memberships from those with homogeneous memberships, but our data do not allow that. We can, however, separate out one type of affiliation that should be closely related to the heterogeneous-homogeneous distinction—union membership. We would assume that union membership would involve a more homogeneous environment than other organizations. But when we compare those who are union members, either as their only affiliation or in conjunction with some other affiliation, with respondents who are affiliated with other types of organizations, we find little systematic difference among these groups in terms of the particular dimensions with which we have been dealing. There is little regular relationship between union affiliation and the expression of inter-party hostility. More important, if we consider only those single and multiple members whose associational affiliation does not include union affiliation, we still find no evidence for the conflict reducing effects of organizational affiliation that we expected to find.[20] Similarly, if we separate out politically involved organizations from politically uninvolved ones (using the respondent's estimate as our measure) we find it makes no difference.

Communications Patterns

Much of the hypothesized connection between organizational membership and political attitudes involves the intervening effect of the communications patterns to which the individual is exposed within his organization. If shared membership is to affect one's political views, the views of fellow members must be communicated. Explicit political discussion may not be necessary; but at minimum the individual concerned has to receive some communication about the political characteristics of his fellow members as well as other relevant characteristics—their social characteristics, their religious views, and so forth—if his contact with them is to have any effect. Though we do not know the social composition of the various organizations, we do know something about the communications activities of those who are organizational members, and this may help us to explain the nature of the impact of these organizations.

Organizational members are more likely to report that they discuss politics than are non-members. Whether this is due to the opportunities presented by the social contacts that organizations afford, or to the interest in political matters that may be aroused in organizational participation, or just to the fact that those who are more interested in politics are also more likely to be joiners, is not relevant at this point. What these data indicate is that those who are in organizations are more likely to be exposed to discussion about political matters. But what kind? This is the crucial question for understanding the role of such organizations in relation to the conflict system within a nation.

Some indication of the effects of organizational membership on the nature of political communications can be seen if we consider the responses to another set of questions about political discussion. Respondents were asked about the number of people with whom they avoided political discussion. Did they avoid all political discussion, did they restrict political discussion to certain people, or did they feel free to discuss politics with anyone?[21] Thus respondents could give what might be called a "closed" response, that they discuss politics with no one; a "cautionary" response, that they discuss politics only with certain people; or an "open" response, that they feel free to discuss politics with anyone. What is of interest here is the way in which organization members differ from non-members in their reported freedom to discuss politics. One would assume that this freedom would be affected by both the homogeneity and the tolerance of the groups to which they belong. If an organization is politically homogeneous, one would assume that there would be little need for restrictions on political discussion. Not that everyone would discuss politics, but if one wanted to do so there would be no reason for caution since all members would agree. On the other hand, if the organization were heterogeneous in its political composition, the freedom to discuss politics might depend upon the degree of tolerance one found for disparate political views. And since even in the most tolerant societies, informal and formal pressures exist for conformity to group norms, one would assume that in heterogeneous organizations, some caution would be appropriate.

The responses of non-members and members as to their freedom to discuss politics are reported in Table VII. Some generalizations are possible from the table. In all nations (and on both educational levels) organizational members—and multiple members even more so—are not likely to be political isolates. They are least likely to say that they avoid all discussions. In all nations cautionary responses (i.e., that there are some or many people with whom they avoid discussion) increase as one moves from non-members to members to multiple members. But the most interesting response category in the table is that referring to those who report themselves completely open in political discussion; who say they feel free to discuss politics with anyone. Here the contrast between the United States and Britain on the one hand and Italy on the other is particularly striking. In the former two nations, members are not more likely than non-members to report that they feel free to discuss politics with anyone. If anything, they are slightly less likely to report such freedom. In these two nations organizational membership is associated with a sharp reduction of political isolation; but this isolation is replaced by a sense of caution in political discussion. In Italy, in contrast, organization members and especially multiple members are more likely to report that they feel free to discuss politics with anyone. The data would then support the hypothesis that organizations in Italy tend to be homogeneous in political composition.

In Mexico, the pattern is as in the United States and Britain in that the frequency of completely "open" responses does not change (if one ignores the multiple members who are few in number) while in Germany the pattern is between that of Italy and the United States and Britain.

Table VII also reports the percentages of respondents who said they feel free to discuss politics with anyone for the supporters of the leading political parties in the five nations. The results are suggestive in terms of our interest in homogeneous versus heterogeneous organizations. For the supporters of the two American and the two British parties, organizational membership is not associated with a greater sense of freedom in political communications. With the Italian Christian Democrats, the German Social Democrats, and (to a lesser extent) the CDU supporters, and the supporters of the Mexican PRI, organizational membership is associated with a greater sense of freedom of discussion and, inferentially, a more homogeneous political environment. The contrast between the CDU and the SPD is instructive, for though both exhibit a pattern of somewhat greater freedom to communicate among organization members, the more homogeneous SPD exhibits a somewhat greater degree of such freedom. The PRI data may not be comparable to that from the other nations due to the relative lack of competitiveness of the party

Table VII. ***Freedom to Discuss Politics and Organization Membership (by nation and education)***

Reported Freedom to Discuss Politics	U.S.			U.K.			Germany			Italy			Mexico		
	Non-Mem.	*Sing. Mem.*	*Mult. Mem.*	*Non-Mem.*	*Sing. Mem.*	*Mult. Mem.*	*Non-Mem.*	*Sing. Mem.*	*Mult. Mem.*	*Non-Mem.*	*Sing. Mem.*	*Mult. Mem.*	*Non-Mem.*	*Sing. Mem.*	*Mult. Mem.*
Total															
Open	31	25	27	30	28	27	19	29	28	20	23	36	19	20	8
Some restrictions	27	35	43	30	38	43	11	17	21	12	22	29	20	30	46
Many restrictions	17	19	21	18	19	23	18	26	36	15	21	14	20	27	33
Closed	24	21	9	15	11	4	42	21	14	38	28	16	23	14	8
Other, don't know	0	0	—	7	3	3	10	7	1	12	5	4	17	8	4
Total cases	414	242	314	509	294	160	536	308	111	201	239	55	765	220	22
Primary or Less															
Open	28	19	23	26	29	26	17	28	30	17	20	27	19	22	†
Some restrictions	24	32	39	30	32	37	11	15	17	9	18	23	18	24	†
Many restrictions	18	18	23	19	29	30	18	26	35	12	22	19	18	31	†
Closed	30	30	13	16	13	4	44	23	16	45	33	31	24	16	†
Other, don't know	0	0	—	8	4	3	10	7	1	17	7	0	21	8	†
Total cases	261	149	107	352	168	73	471	239	82	516	150	26	697	169	11
Secondary or Above															
Open	37	34	29	38	28	29	36	35	18	29	28	46	15	13	†
Some restrictions	34	40	44	30	47	48	16	23	30	19	28	32	33	47	†
Many restrictions	15	19	29	16	15	17	20	25	41	24	20	11	31	18	†
Closed	14	6	6	13	9	3	22	12	11	19	19	4	14	8	†
Other, don't know	—	—	—	4	2	2	5	4	0	8	3	7	6	13	†
Total cases	153	93	207	157	126	87	55	68	27	183	88	28	67	50	10

Reported Freedom to Discuss Politics	U.S.			U.K.			Germany			Italy			Mexico		
	Non-Mem.	*Sing. Mem.*	*Mult. Mem.*	*Non-Mem.*	*Sing. Mem.*	*Mult. Mem.*	*Non-Mem.*	*Sing. Mem.*	*Mult. Mem.*	*Non-Mem.*	*Sing. Mem.*	*Mult. Mem.*	*Non-Mem.*	*Sing. Mem.*	*Mult. Mem.*
Party in Power															
	(Republican)			*(Conservatives)*			*(CDU)*			*(DC)*			*(PRI)*		
Open	30	25	30	26	21	23	18	27	26	17	22	36	15	24	†
Some restrictions	29	42	42	33	41	42	11	21	33	14	24	32	23	32	†
Many restrictions	16	19	20	22	24	30	18	27	28	18	24	24	24	30	†
Closed	25	14	8	15	11	4	42	20	10	36	25	8	19	10	†
Other, don't know	—	—	—	4	1	1	11	6	3	15	6	—	18	7	†
Total cases	111	69	127	175	104	79	188	107	39	227	105	25	356	145	13
Party Out of Power															
	(Democrats)			*(Labour)*			*(SPD)*			*(PCI/PSI)*			*(PAN)*		
Open	32	25	28	31	30	30	24	32	[12]	36	31	*	27	28	†
Some restrictions	30	34	40	30	39	46	9	15	[25]	10	22	*	22	24	†
Many restrictions	18	19	24	16	17	17	29	26	[54]	13	12	*	16	24	†
Closed	20	21	8	14	9	3	29	18	[8]	31	31	*	21	21	†
Other, don't know	—	—	—	8	5	3	8	9	—	9	3	*	14	3	†
Total cases	186	128	148	200	119	57	126	85	[24]	67	32*	*	50	22	3

*"One" and "multi" combined because of too few cases in either separately.

†Too few cases.

system. Thus in a system in which the leading party receives the support of close to 90 per cent of the voters, supporters of that party are likely to find a homogeneous environment as they enter organizations.

In general, then, the data suggest that organizational membership in the United States and Britain (and to a lesser extent in Germany and Mexico) is related to a reduction of the isolation of the individual. Members are open to at least some political discussion. But they are not placed in an environment where indiscriminate political discussion is warranted. Rather they are placed in heterogeneous environments where they must use some caution in choosing with whom they discuss politics. On the other hand, in Italy, organizational members find themselves in a much more homogeneous and therefore permissive political atmosphere; one in which they can feel free to discuss politics with anyone. These data might help explain why our hypothesis was not confirmed in the United States and Britain, but the alternate hypothesis was confirmed in Italy. In the heterogeneous organization in which cross-pressures mechanisms operate there may be informal inhibitions to political discussion, and this may in turn dampen the effects of the increased contact. Where memberships are cumulative, on the other hand, such inhibition on communication may be less frequent.[22] In this sense, cumulative membership patterns may have a greater impact than overlapping ones.

Conclusion

Earlier in this paper two possible models of the relationship between organizational affiliation and political conflict were presented—the cumulative and the cross-pressures model. Our hypothesis was that the relationship between organizational membership and conflict in Italy would approximate the cumulative model; while that in the United States would approximate the cross-pressures model. In the other three nations we expected an intermediate pattern. The data presented for Italy fit our hypothesis. Both the data on attitudes toward political opponents and on communications patterns within organizations support the hypothesis that Italian organization members are exposed to cumulative social and political contacts and that these contacts reinforce the political views that were originally held, thus exacerbating political conflict in the society.

The data for the United States, however, do not support our hypothesis that organizational members become exposed to more heterogeneous political environments due to their organizational membership, and that the resulting cross-pressures lead to a reduction in the intensity of political opposition. When contrasted with the results as to the strong relationship between organizational membership and other attitudinal and behavioral measures, this failure to confirm the hypothesis is surprising.

There are a number of possible reasons why this expected pattern did not appear. Any one of the links in the chain of relationships that was posited earlier may be weak. In the first place organizational membership may not expose individuals to as varied a set of social contacts as assumed. After all, organizational members are not selected on a purely random basis. Though organizational membership may not be as stratified politically as our data suggest is the case in Italy, it is likely that memberships tend to cluster politically thereby eliminating much of the "expansive" character associated with such memberships. Secondly, even if membership in organizations results in contact with others of differing political views, the effects of such contact may be dampened by informal inhibitions on communications within these organizations. Our communications data suggest that this may be the case. Lastly, it is possible that organizational membership does lead to exposure to a more varied social group and that this does lead to cross-pressures, but that cross-pressures do not result in a reduction of hostility to political opponents. This is the least likely explanation, since there is substantial evidence to support this last link in our chain. Where cross-pressures have been observed—between attitudes, or between one's own views and those of one's friends—the results have been usually as predicted. Perhaps, then, the linkages between organizational affiliation and the development of cross-pressures situations are the weak ones in the argument.

These results, it may be repeated, cast doubt on the hypotheses about organizational affiliation and the reduction of political conflict only insofar as these hypotheses are about the effects of multiple memberships on the political attitudes of the individual member as individual. It may be that the effect of overlapping membership is greatest on the level of the organization itself. Top leaders may be more sensitive to multiple pressures and, *in their organizational roles,* may take less intensely partisan political positions. Thus conflict resolution will be moved to the level of the organizational elites, and the system of overlapping memberships will still play a major role in reducing the intensity of such conflict. Our data on organizational leaders do not support this point, but it may be that we were not dealing with a high enough level of leadership. Furthermore, we related organizational leadership to the personal political views of the leader. It is possible that these views would be unaffected by the nature of the organization led, but that the leaders when acting in their formal leadership roles may take less intense positions. This needs further research.

In terms of the more interesting set of hypotheses dealt with in this paper—about systems of overlapping memberships—the results reported here are negative. In a discipline with well established theoretical underpinnings, such findings are of course most exciting because they cause one to reconsider accepted theories. In a discipline such as political science where we have few generally accepted hypotheses and fewer tested ones, such negative findings are often the cause of disappointment. The bottom file drawers of political scientists are probably filled with such negative findings. But this is unfortunate, for the major reason for collecting empirical data is to test our hypotheses or notions about political reality.

The negative findings in this case are particularly interesting because of the widespread use of the overlapping membership theory and the paucity of empirical testing of it. The data are a bit too indirect to challenge this theory too strongly. The data do not support the hypotheses, but it would be going too far to say that they refute them. Yet in the absence of better data supporting the overlapping membership hypotheses, these data give one pause. And such a pause would be useful if it led to further, more direct attempts to test these hypotheses. If they are to be central to theories of functioning democracy, they deserve that testing.

Notes:

1. The classic works are, of course, Arthur F. Bentley, *The Process of Government* (1908) and David Truman, *The Governmental Process* (New

York: Knopf, 1959). Most relevant from the point of view of theoretical analysis and comparative politics are Gabriel A. Almond, "A Comparative Study of Interest Groups and the Political Process," *American Political Science Review,* LII (1958), pp. 270–82; Harry Eckstein, *Pressure Group Politics* (Stanford: Stanford University Press, 1960), Chapter 1; and Joseph LaPalombara, "The Utility and Limitations of Interest Group Theory in Non-American Field Situations," *Journal of Politics,* XXII (1960), pp. 29–49. There have been numerous recent critiques of the pressure group approach. The one that is most relevant to the concern of this paper is by William C. Mitchell. In an unpublished manuscript on *Some Recent Theories of American Politics* he stresses both the limitations of group theory as an allocational theory as well as the paucity of data that exists to support it. On the mass society approach, see William Kornhauser, *The Politics of Mass Society* (New York: The Free Press of Glencoe, 1959).

2. The data is based upon a cross-national survey conducted in five nations—the United States, Great Britain, Germany, Italy, and Mexico. Approximately 1,000 interviews were conducted in each country using a stratified, multi-stage probability sample. The interviews were conducted in early summer, 1959, with the exception of those in the United States which were in March, 1960. For a fuller discussion of the data and for some other results based upon this survey, see Gabriel A. Almond and Sidney Verba, *The Civic Culture: Political Attitudes and Democracy in Five Nations* (Princeton: The Princeton University Press, 1963). The samples are described in Appendix A.

3. See Mitchell, *op. cit.*

4. Kornhauser, *op. cit.,* pp. 80–1. See also Talcott Parsons, "'Voting' and the Equilibrium of the American Political System," in Eugene Burdick and Arthur J. Brodbeck, editors, *American Voting Behavior* (Glencoe, Ill.: The Fress Press, 1959), p. 102; and Bernard Berelson and Gary A. Steiner, *Human Behavior: An Inventory of Scientific Findings* (New York: Harcourt, Brace and World, 1964), p. 620.

5. On the different forms of partisanship and their different consequences, see Almond and Verba, *op. cit.,* pp. 288–95.

6. See, for instance, Bernard Berelson, Paul F. Lazarsfeld, and William N. McPhee, *Voting* (Chicago: University of Chicago Press, 1954), pp. 51–52; Angus Campbell, *et al., The American Voter* (New York: Wiley, 1960), pp. 379–80. Linz reports similar findings for Germany. See Juan J. Linz, *The Social Bases of West German Politics,* unpublished Ph.D. dissertation, Columbia University, 1959, Chapter 26.

7. Parsons, *op. cit.,* p. 102.

8. The work of the Survey Research Center at Michigan has concentrated on what is to us the intervening variable of attitudinal cross-pressures and their impact on political attitudes. As they put it, they "... proceed without inquiring into what has led to attitudinal cross-pressures. It is the effect, rather than the cause, of conflict that is of primary interest." Angus Campbell, *et al., op. cit.,* pp. 80–1.

9. See Paul F. Lazarsfeld, Bernard Berelson, and Hazel Gaudet, *The People's Choice* (New York: Duell, Sloan and Pearce, 1944), pp. 53 ff.; Bernard Berelson, Paul F. Lazarsfeld, and William N. McPhee, *op. cit.,*

pp. 128 ff.; Campbell, *et al., op. cit.,* pp. 87–8; V. O. Key, *Public Opinion and American Democracy* (New York: Knopf, 1961), p. 69; Martin Kriesberg, "Cross-Pressures and Attitudes: A Study of the Influence of Conflicting Propaganda on Opinions Regarding American-Soviet Relations," *Public Opinion Quarterly,* XII (Spring 1949), pp. 5–16. For a critique of many of these studies, see H. Daudt, *Floating Voters and the Floating Vote* (Leiden: Stenfert Kroese N.V., 1961).

10. See Kornhauser, *op. cit.,* Chapter 13; and Seymour M. Lipset, *Political Man* (Garden City: Doubleday, 1959), Chapter 4.

11. LaPalombara, *op. cit.,* p. 43. See also his *Interest Groups in Italian Politics* (Princeton: Princeton University Press, 1964).

12. See, for instance, Joseph Kaiser, *Die Repräsentation Organisierter Interessen* (Berlin: 1956); and Rupert Breitling, *Die Verbände in der Bundesrepublik* (Meisenheim am Glan, 1955).

13. See Almond and Verba, *op. cit.,* Chapter 11. Similar data is reported in Key, *op. cit.,* pp. 504–6 and Linz, *op. cit.,* Chapter 25.

14. The figures reported are for the response to a question "Are you a member of any organization now (trade or labor union, business organization, social group, professional or farm organization, cooperative, fraternal or veteran's group, athletic club, political, charitable, religious or civic organization) or any other organized groups?" The absolute amount of memberships reported varies somewhat from other studies of the subject, largely due to our inclusion of trade unions within the question. Membership in political or religious organizations did not include party or religious affiliation itself, but includes organizations that are politically related or church related. For a discussion of the distribution of these memberships within the nations studied and of the kinds of memberships these entail, see Almond and Verba, *op. cit.,* pp. 301–7 and p. 320.

One of the objections to the multiple membership theories that can be made is that the system on which the theory is originally based, the United States, is one in which the rate of organizational membership is not as high as folklore suggests. Everyone is not a member of some organization, and few are members of more than one. But the theory of multiple memberships does not require that every citizen be a member of more than one organization, but merely that a sufficient number are members to make an impact on politics. How many is a sufficient number is hard to define. But the comparative evidence suggests that though it is true that not every American is a member of some such organization, there is sufficient variation among nations in the frequency of such membership—with the frequency of such membership being quite a bit larger in the United States—that it is plausible to consider these differences as significant factors having effects on political systems.

15. The question read, "Suppose a son or daughter of yours were getting married. How would you feel if he or she married a supporter of the —— Party? Would you be pleased, would you be displeased, or would it make no difference?" The question was asked about all the major parties in each of the nations studied. See *ibid.,* pp. 132–60 for a discussion of this question and a report of the responses to it. The data that will be reported in Table II refer to the attitudes of the supporters of the major parties in each nation toward marriage of a

child to the supporter of the major opposition: in the United States, Republican attitudes toward marriage of a child to a Democrat; in Britain, Conservative attitudes toward Labour; in Germany, CDU attitudes toward SPD; in Mexico, PRI attitudes toward PAN; and vice versa in each case. In Italy three parties are involved. Table II reports the attitudes of Christian Democratic supporters toward the marriage of a child with a Communist supporter, and the attitudes of both supporters of the PCI and PSI toward marriage with a Christian Democrat. In Table II, education is controlled. The use of other socio-economic variables would make little difference in the results.

16. See *ibid.*, pp. 288–99 for a discussion of this subject.

17. The question read, "We're interested in what sorts of people support and vote for the different parties. If you had to generalize, which expressions on this list come closest to describing the kinds of people who vote for the —— Party?" The list contained the following items: People interested in national strength and welfare; selfish people, interested in their own welfare at the expense of others; intelligent people, religious people; betrayers of freedom and the country's welfare; ignorant and misguided people; Fascists, militarists; people interested in the welfare of humanity; atheists, godless people. The first two responses were recorded. Other answers, not on the list (in particular, the answer that "all sorts of people" support a particular party) were recorded as well. The question was asked about each of the major parties. The data in Table III refer to the same parties as in Table II. (See footnote 15.)

18. The questions read, "The —— Party now controls the national government. Do you think that its policies and activities would ever seriously endanger the country's welfare? Do you think this probably would happen, that it might happen, or that it probably wouldn't happen?" "Let me ask you about some other parties that might someday take control of the government. If the —— Party were to take control of the government, how likely is it that it would seriously endanger the country's welfare? Do you think that this would probably happen, that it might happen, or that it probably wouldn't happen?" The name of the party in control of the government in the respective nation was inserted in the first question, while the follow-up questions were asked about all of the leading opposition parties.

19. On Table VI, "ordinary members" are those respondents who report that they have never held a position as an officer in any of the organizations with which they are affiliated. Officers are those who have held such a position in at least one of the organizations with which they are affiliated. Thus, those listed as "Officers, more than one" are respondents who are members of more than one organization, but who may have been officers in either one of those organizations or in more than one.

20. One would have expected, furthermore, that unions would play a reinforcement role for the supporters of the left party and a cross-pressures role for the supporters of the right party. When one breaks down the sample this way, there are too few cases to make many reliable comparisons, but the comparisons that can be made offer little support for this. In Germany the hypothesis received partial support. Among CDU sup-

porters, union members are less hostile to the SPD than are the members of a non-union organization; while among SPD supporters there is no difference between union members and members of other kinds of organizations in their inter-party hostility. In Britain we find, contrary to expectations that Conservative supporters who are in unions express more hostility toward Labour Party supporters than do Conservatives who belong to some other kind of organization (as measured by the frequency with which they select negative descriptive terms to describe them), though on other measures of inter-party hostility there is no difference. And there is little pattern among Labour supporters. In the United States, there is little pattern. But, again, in most instances the number of cases is too few for more than tentative comparison.

21. The question read, "If you wanted to discuss political and governmental affairs, are there some people you definitely wouldn't turn to, that is people with whom you feel it better *not* to discuss such topics? About how many people would you say there are with whom you would *avoid* discussing politics?"

22. These inhibitions to communication may not be severe and the sanctions for engaging in political discussion with those of opposing views may not be great. It may be rather a tendency to avoid disharmonious interpersonal contact. When those who reported some limitation on their freedom to discuss politics were asked why they avoided such discussions, the most frequent answer in the United States, Britain and Germany was that such discussions can be unpleasant and can disturb interpersonal relations. (The percentages so answering being 35% in the United States, 43% in Britain, and 25% in Germany.) In Italy, this type of inhibition appeared less frequently; the most frequent reason for avoidance of political discussion being that the respondent feels too ignorant and the second most frequent that others are too biased. But 17% of the Italian respondents who avoid political discussion did say that it was because such discussions can be unpleasant and disturb personal relations. In Mexico, only 4% gave this latter response. The most frequent reason for avoiding political discussion in Mexico was that people are biased and dogmatic, and that, therefore, such discussions are useless.

B. *Cultural Change and Changing Values*

4 *The Urban-Rural Conflict in a New Perspective*

by Robert S. Friedman

"Urban-rural dichotomy," "urban-rural continuum," and "urban-rural conflict" are terms which have permeated the language of the social sciences for a generation. Accessibility of census data, persistence of nineteenth-century stereotypes of rural virtue and urban corruption, and a revolutionary shift in the population of the United States from countryside to city have all encouraged researchers to treat urban-rural differences as a critical variable in social processes.

The social and economic upheaval which drove rural dwellers from country to city continues unabated. However, instead of a unidirectional movement toward the city, present trends are multidirectional and involve far more than movement of people. In fact many of the aspects of urban and rural living which have seemed to distinguish the two types of areas may be losing their distinctive character. As a result it becomes imperative to re-examine the meaningfulness of urban and rural as independent categories in the study of politics. This paper represents an effort to spell out the usefulness of existing literature on urban-rural conflict toward

Reprinted from *The Western Political Quarterly*, 14, 2 (June, 1961), 481–495, where it appeared under the title, "The Urban-Rural Conflict Revisited," by permission of the author and the University of Utah, copyright owners.

this end and to describe the findings of an exploratory study designed to examine the continued significance of the urban-rural cleavage.

I

Use of the term "urban-rural conflict" seems to fall into two categories based on characteristics involving numbers of people, density of settlement, and heterogeneity of inhabitants and their group life. The first of these emphasizes spatial factors and relies primarily on legal and census distinctions. According to this usage everything physically within the legal limits of a municipal corporation or which meets other criteria of the Census Bureau definition of urban is treated as such. In some instances, however, the term "urban" is rejected in favor of "metropolitan."[1] Researchers using this more restricted term distinguish standard metropolitan areas from all other areas and categorize only the former as urban. In still other instances arbitrary definitions like "urban places with 25,000 inhabitants" are used as lines of demarcation. Irrespective of which of these is used, the assumption made by social scientists in using urban and rural distinctions of this kind is that the term, while not precise, provides a useful tool for distinguishing socio-economic group interests which tend to congregate in the two different types of environments. As a result, urban areas are more likely to house people associated with the interests of industrial as opposed to agricultural workers, interests concerned with the promotion of the fine arts as contrasted to hunting and fishing interests, etc. Similarly because of greater heterogeneity in race, creed, color, occupation, and other characteristics akin to these, a vastly different socio-political amalgam is thought to exist in urban areas than in rural.

The second category of urban-rural definition differentiation is a derivative of the first. Scholars who rely upon it start by acknowledging ecological differences and make use of these in terms of shared attitudes. Therefore, exponents of the fine arts and those who express tolerance of diverse ethnic and religious groups are regarded as urbanites or cosmopolitans regardless of where they reside. Those who worship the wide open spaces or extol agrarian virtue are regarded as ruralites or locals regardless of their residence.[2] In using this type of urban-rural categorization it is unnecessary to deal with the spatial location of those who share the attitudes.[3] Concern is with shared attitudes and describes ideological positions in somewhat the same way that a body of shared attitudes is described as liberal and conservative.

Although fruitful results might be obtained from investigations based on the shared attitude distinction, treatment of urban-rural differentiation in the literature of political science has been almost exclusively that of the spatial or physical category.[4] Inquiry has dealt with two primary areas—representation and voting behavior. Representation studies have generally started with the implicit or explicit value position of a representative system based on the "one man one vote" doctrine. The most carefully documented of these, Gordon Baker's *Rural Versus Urban Political Power,* outlines state and national representative institutions and the failure of the spatially urban population to obtain representation according to numbers.[5] Relying upon a series of case studies, he suggests the existence of a positive relationship between this "imbalance" and the success or failure of certain predominantly urban groups to accommodate their interests. In his conclusion he urges a number of reforms which would presumably restore the "balance" and again make the rules of the political contest "fair."

Regardless of the value position of authors of this type of study, the description of the conflict itself is usually somewhat less than exhaustive. Most authors are satisfied to describe formal representative schemes, assume discrimination against urban areas, and urge reform. Baker has most certainly not been guilty of this charge. He has been meticulous in his study in indicating that other approaches are available to urban interests when the legislative hurdle proves insurmountable. His description of the consequences of "imbalance," however, is restricted to only a few cases and these include so many uncontrolled variables in addition to urban versus rural that there is very serious doubt raised as to whether urban-rural makes an independent contribution in explaining the struggle for accommodation of interests.

For example, a classic case of "urban frustration" has been Chicago's fate at the hands of a hostile legislature in revenue matters. A recent reapportionment has taken place in the state of Illinois which would, in one house at least, meet the standards of advocates of "equal representation." Nevertheless, there is no evidence that any dramatic changes have resulted with respect to Chicago's revenue system.[6] The fact that reapportionment has not led to an adjustment of the financial dilemma of the city may be due in part to altered population patterns which have reduced the city's proportion of the state's population. Other factors which probably have played a role include partisan issues, both interparty and intraparty, Illinois' unique cumulative voting system, the nature of leadership at both city and state administrative levels, conflicts between competing economic interests, and perhaps city-county animosities so deep-seated that they make rapprochement difficult. All of these must be placed in proper perspective before the urban-rural conflict can be identified as a meaningful variable in politics. None of the representation studies have attempted this type of analysis.

Studies of voting behavior incorporating urban-rural conflicts as a variable have been of two kinds—electoral behavior and legislative roll calls. A variety of statistical techniques have been employed to test differences in urban and rural vote patterns.[7] Drawing upon an enormous body of empirical electoral behavior data, V. O. Key has concluded, "The cleavage between metropolitan residents and rural and small town dwellers has become a most significant foundation for dual systems of state politics."[8]

After detailed quantitative analysis of roll calls in four congressional sessions, Julius Turner concluded that there was sound basis for the assertion "that Congress was influenced by conflicting pressures from metropolitan and rural constituencies and that this pressure did not diminish with the passage of time."[9] He further concluded that the issues on which conflicting pressures were most often displayed were prohibition, immigration, farm legislation, and some issues involving foreign policy and governmental control.

In contrast to these findings studies of both electoral behavior and legislative roll calls in several highly urbanized states have tended to downgrade the significance of an urban-rural cleavage. A study of the extent of urban-rural cleavage in the operation of the Maryland county unit primary election system, for example, disclosed no discernible pattern.[10] In some primary contests the cleavage was found to be great but in others it was found to be nonexistent. Although explanation of the phenomenon was somewhat speculative a number of important ecological characteristics were noted which indicated that Maryland displayed greater uniformity between urban and rural areas than many other states. Among examples were the presence of a number of rural counties with high percentages of employment in manufacturing, and rural counties with high percentages of Catholic and Negro population. In addition, Baltimore was found to have fewer foreign born in relation to its total population than most cities of its size. The implication drawn from this was that rural areas in Maryland, *in toto,* seem to display socio-economic characteristics more like those of the state's metropolis than has been thought to have been the case in many other states.[11]

Maryland may be *sui generis.* However this is not an isolated situation. In studies of Illinois and Missouri roll-call voting, David Derge found only a minute number of instances in which conflict displayed a high level of metropolitan out-state cleavage.[12] One commentator has astutely observed that Derge's findings "should not be taken to mean that there is no difference in interests, values, or perspectives between people who live in large cities and those who live in smaller towns and on farms. What it does mean is that this broad differentiation does not often lead to sufficiently fundamental or pervasive conflict to account for the behavior of the legislature."[13]

The lesson to be drawn from studies such as these is that if present trends continue in migration, communications, industrial location, and like characteristics throughout the United States the urban-rural differentiation will lose meaning universally. In an article written in 1940 Arthur Schlesinger, Sr., offered an explanation of political conflict in nineteenth-century America based primarily on urban-rural conflict. In his conclusion, however, he pointed out that this conflict began to lose its significance as early as the 1890's.

> The last decade of the century beheld an ampler provision of rural educational facilities, a rapid extension of the good roads movement due to the bicycle craze, the penetration of the countryside by an increasing network of interurban trolley lines, the introduction of rural free delivery, and the spread of farm telephones. All these events helped to break down the ancient

> isolation and loneliness and lent a new attraction to country existence.
>
> Yet these mitigations seem small compared with the marvels which the present century has wrought. The automobile has shortened all distances, while the radio and the movie have brought urbanizing influences to nearly every rural home. At the same time the tractor and other labor saving devices have lightened the drudgery of the day's task.[14]

Corollary to this, Schlesinger pointed out that there have been numerous ruralizing forces at work on the urban dweller resulting from the growth of parks, playgrounds, suburbanization, and other similar phenomena.

II

In the two decades since Schlesinger's article appeared the tendency toward uniformity between urban America and rural America has continued unabated. The mass media have become even more accessible to rural citizenry. School districts have been consolidated and standardized sufficiently by state action so as to provide substantially the same public educational facilities. In addition urban dwellers of all ethnic and religious backgrounds continue to move further and further from the heart of the city and those associated with rural areas into the city. Perhaps equally important, industries long associated with the urban center have tended to decentralize and move into rural areas. There is every reason to believe that if these trends continue urban-rural differentiation will cease to be a measurable variable in American politics in the foreseeable future.

Stated differently, conflicts which superficially may be described as setting urban areas against rural areas are more satisfactorily explained in terms of conflict among social, economic, and cultural interests which have incidentally been associated with urban and rural areas, at least in the past. Present trends, in the United States, find these interests rearranging themselves in such a way that within the foreseeable future the ability to describe conflict in terms of urban-rural difference, even superficially, will disappear.

These assertions will be verified or rejected with the passage of time, but evidence of their validity may be obtained by isolating circumstances in which interests traditionally found in either urban or rural areas are already to be found in the opposite physical setting. In such instances, if those associated with such interests show a greater propensity to each other, regardless of physical setting, than they do with others in similar physical surroundings, then the physical setting is probably not a critical variable in political activity.

By way of example, if people living along the east and west coasts of the United States were generally more favorable in 1940 to "aiding the Allies," regardless of urbanization, and people in the midcontinent area were generally opposed, it would be probable that physical proximity to areas of hostility was the important consideration. It should, of course, be noted that a fairly high correlation might have been obtained along urban-rural lines as well because of the heavy urban concentrations in coastal areas.

Similarly in other political struggles the occupational pattern is likely the critical factor. For example, industrial workers are cooped up in factories throughout the long hot summer days. Extension of daylight hours through the technique of changing time zones or adoption of daylight savings time would enable them to enjoy additional leisure time in daylight hours. These changes, however, probably mean little to farmers. In fact they are likely to elicit hostility because of decreased early morning daylight. If conditions of work represent the critical variable instead of the urban versus rural setting then industrial workers and their representatives in rural areas should act more like urban industrial workers than like farmers. Similarly farmers maintaining residence in urbanized surroundings are still likely to act like other farmers on this issue.[15]

To test this a sample of the Tennessee legislature was interviewed.[16] In choosing members to be interviewed three constituency characteristics were taken into consideration, urbanness, sectionalism, and industrialization. Constituencies were divided into three categories of urbanness; those with cities in excess of 50,000, classified as urban, those with cities under 50,000 but over 15,000, classified as mixed, and those with no urban center with as many as 15,000 inhabitants, classified as rural.[17]

Sectionally districts were classified as East, Middle, and West, the traditional Grand Divisions in Tennessee politics.

This was deemed of special importance with respect to daylight savings time since East Tennessee is at the western extremity of the Eastern Time Zone and therefore unlikely to be included in any "fast time" controversy. Also because of the great east-west range of the state, the western portion of the state is far enough west that pressure for "fast time" is likely to be less intense than in the middle portion of the state.

To establish the third category, industrialization, manufacturing employment data were used, with districts in which manufacturing employment figures were above the state average referred to as manufacturing and others as nonmanufacturing.[18]

"Fast time" has been a recurring issue in Tennessee state politics since World War II. A brief résumé of events prior to 1959 is therefore desirable for the purpose of understanding the choice of questions put to the legislators. The dividing line of Eastern and Central Time crosses Tennessee roughly along the dividing line between East and Middle Tennessee.[19] Because of the relatively early nightfall in those areas of Middle Tennessee nearest the dividing line, sporadic efforts have been made there to adopt summer daylight time. Efforts have also been made to move the Eastern Time Zone west to include Nashville.

In 1947 Nashvillians expressed their support for DST by a narrow margin in a referendum. Two years later the legislature enacted a statute forbidding localities to alter time fixed by the Interstate Commerce Commission. The roll-call votes were 31–2 in the Senate and 86–6 with six absences and one abstension in the House. All but one of the negative votes came from Davidson County (Nashville) and Hamilton County (Chattanooga), the two urban areas at the time most directly affected by DST. Most of the absentees were members from the unaffected East Tennessee area. In 1953 a local option bill was defeated in the House by a similar vote. In spite of the proscription against governmentally imposed daylight time, some private establishments voluntarily pushed clocks ahead in Nashville and several other communities. In the meantime the ICC adjusted the Eastern Time Zone in 1956 to encompass Chattanooga and eliminate the DST issue there. The following year, the legislature outlawed all voluntary efforts to push clocks ahead by a near unanimous vote. The

Senate voted 25–2 with six absent and the House voted 68–1 with a surprising thirty absent. Two of the three "No" votes were cast by Davidson County (Nashville) members. Most of the absences were among Davidson, Knox (Knoxville), and Hamilton (Chattanooga) delegations. The inference drawn here is that East Tennessee urban members, unaffected by the legislation, deferred to urban members opposed to legislation affecting them. This was the background available in developing a questionnaire. Efforts to move the Eastern Time Zone continued during the period of the study, but no daylight time legislation was introduced in the 1959 session of the legislature at which time the membership was interviewed.

Four questions were directed at the legislators on the DST issue which afforded some basis for measurement:

(1) Do you happen to know the attitudes or opinions of your constituents on the daylight savings time issue? Are they (a) strongly for; (b) slightly for; (c) evenly divided or indifferent; (d) slightly against; (e) strongly against; (f) don't know.

(2) Would you mind telling us how you would feel about a bill permitting counties or cities to enact local daylight savings time measures?

(3) How would you feel about a bill providing for summer daylight savings time in the Middle Tennessee area?

(4) As you know the Interstate Commerce Commission has been requested to move the Eastern Time Zone west to include Nashville. What is your reaction to the request?

As perceived by legislators interviewed very few constituencies are genuinely favorable to daylight savings time, although a considerable number are either neutral or evenly divided. Only four of the thirty-seven legislators interviewed felt that their constituents favored daylight time. Three of these were from urban areas and one from a rural district. Thirteen other interviewees felt that their constituencies were either neutral or evenly divided, whereas fifteen considered their constituencies opposed and five failed to answer the question. The constituencies thought to be evenly divided were predominantly urban. Constituencies thought to be against daylight savings time were all either mixed or rural. There was clearly a different reaction in urban constituencies from the reaction in rural constituencies since all urban constituencies were either in the "for," "neutral-even division," or "no answer" categories whereas an overwhelming majority of the rural constituencies were to be found in the "against" category. This pattern asserted itself both on a statewide basis and in Middle Tennessee, the areas most directly affected by daylight savings time.

Manufacturing constituencies tended to be less opposed to daylight time than non-manufacturing, but the reaction was not as significantly different as the urban-rural reaction. In fact such differentiation as was discernible may be attributed to the fact that all of the urban districts are also classified as manufacturing. This is made even more evident when only rural districts are considered. Reaction of members from both rural-manufacturing and rural-non-manufacturing districts was uniform opposition. If anything, in fact the non-manufacturing districts were thought to be slightly less hostile than manufacturing districts.

Table I. ***Constituent Attitudes on Daylight Savings Time as Perceived by Legislative Representatives***

	Statewide				Middle Tennessee			
District Category*	*For*	*Neutral/ Even Division*	*Agst.*	*No Answer*	*For*	*Neutral/ Even Division*	*Agst.*	*No Answer*
Urban	3	8	0	3	2	5	0	0
Mixed	0	2	3	2	0	0	3	0
Rural	1	3	12	0	0	1	11	0
Total	4	13	15	5	2	6	14	0
Manufacturing	3	9	4	5	2	5	4	0
Non-manufacturing	1	4	11	0	0	1	10	0
Total	4	13	15	5	2	6	14	0
Rural manufacturing	0	1	4	0	0	0	4	0
Rural non-manufacturing	1	2	8	0	0	1	7	0
Total	1	3	12	0	0	1	11	0
Mixed manufacturing	0	0	0	2	0	0	0	0
Mixed non-manufacturing	0	2	3	0	0	0	3	0
Total	0	2	3	2	0	0	3	0

*Several possible combinations of district classification did not fit any district in the state.

If the constituency attitude question had been the sole inquiry made of the legislators the results would have tended to reaffirm the traditional notions regarding urban-rural conflict, but strikingly different responses were forthcoming on all three questions involving legislative voting behavior.

The first of these—local option legislation—is susceptible to some ambiguity since local option bills always give rise to potential confusion because of variations in practice from county to county. In this case particularly, several legislators expressed opposition because of the possible confusion which might result. But this much is clear; those willing to support a local option bill can not possibly be strong opponents of daylight time for the position of the staunch opponent is characterized by opposition to every effort to alter the status quo.

Table II. ***Legislative Attitudes Toward Local Option on DST***

District Category	Statewide			Middle Tennessee		
	For	*Against*	*Neutral-No Answer*	*For*	*Against*	*Neutral-No Answer*
Urban	5	8	1	2	5	0
Mixed	0	6	1	0	3	0
Rural	4	12	0	2	10	0
Total	9	26	2	4	18	0
Manufacturing	7	13	1	3	8	0
Non-manufacturing	2	13	1	1	10	0
Total	9	26	2	4	18	0
Rural manufacturing	2	3	0	1	3	0
Rural non-manufacturing	2	9	0	1	7	0
Total	4	12	0	2	10	0
Mixed manufacturing	0	1	1	0	0	0
Mixed non-manufacturing	0	5	0	0	3	0
Total	0	6	1	0	3	0

Opposition to local option was fairly general throughout the state, and rather overwhelming in Middle Tennessee, the area in which greatest confusion would most likely occur. In general, urban area legislators were less opposed to local option than rural members, and the latter, in turn, were less opposed than members from mixed districts. This pattern was the same in Middle Tennessee as elsewhere, except that the favorable proportions were smaller there in each category.

On the surface it appears that the local option responses coincided with responses on constituency attitudes. An examination of reaction on the basis of manufacturing, especially in rural areas, suggests that this is not so and that manufacturing employment may be a more significant factor in the responses. The proportion of manufacturing district members friendly to local option was substantially larger than was the case among non-manufacturing district members (7–13 as opposed to 2–13). This figure also showed slightly greater cleavage than, for example, that elicited from urban and rural members who split 5–8 as opposed to 4–12. Most striking is the division among rural members only. Legislators from rural-manufacturing constituencies divided two "for" and three "against." Those from non-manufacturing constituencies split two "for" and nine "against." The Middle Tennessee legislators, as stated before, were more hostile over-all than members from other parts of the state, but relationships on the basis of urban, mixed, and rural categories displayed less sharp cleavage than between manufacturing and non-manufacturing.

The third question put to the interviewees—How would you feel about a bill providing for summer daylight savings time in the Middle Tennessee area?—met the issue head on. Urban members divided evenly (five "for," five "against" and four "neutral or no answer"). Mixed and rural constituency members were generally opposed, dividing 1–3–3 in the case of mixed and 5–9–2 in the case of rural districts.

Reaction of manufacturing district members, however, was strikingly different from that of non-manufacturing district members. Nine were favorable, seven opposed, and five uncommitted, whereas non-manufacturing district members split 2–10–4. Despite the rather small sample the difference appears to be significant. The division among only rural districts on the basis of manufacturing is similarly significant. Three of the five rural-manufacturing district members expressed a positive reaction to daylight savings time in Middle Tennessee, while non-manufacturing district members divided 2–7–2.

The responses to this question among Middle Tennessee

members were roughly the same as those on a statewide basis, the chief difference being that all but one member from the area was willing to be committed on the issue while eight respondents from the remainder of the state pleaded neutrality or failed to answer the question at all.

Table III. ***Legislative Attitudes Toward DST for Middle Tennessee***

District Category	Statewide			Middle Tennessee		
	For	*Against*	*Neutral-No Answer*	*For*	*Against*	*Neutral-No Answer*
Urban	5	5	4	4	2	1
Mixed	1	3	3	0	3	0
Rural	5	9	2	4	8	0
Total	11	17	9	8	13	1
Manufacturing	9	7	5	6	4	1
Non-manufacturing	2	10	4	2	9	0
Total	11	17	9	8	13	1
Rural manufacturing	3	2	0	2	2	0
Rural non-manufacturing	2	7	2	2	6	0
Total	5	9	2	4	8	0
Mixed manufacturing	1	0	1	0	0	0
Mixed non-manufacturing	0	3	2	0	3	0
Total	1	3	3	0	3	0

Reaction to the last question—movement of the Eastern Standard Time Zone west to include Nashville—also emphasized the significance of industrialization, despite the fact that almost half of the interviewees refused to be committed on the issue.[20] As on all other questions, urban legislators were more favorably disposed toward fast time than rural or mixed. The difference on this issue, however, was less noticeable than on the other three questions, urban members dividing four in favor, two against, and eight neutral or no answer. Members from mixed districts split 2–3–2 and rural members split 4–4–8. Division between manufacturing districts and non-manufacturing districts was 8–3–10 as opposed to 2–6–8, a remarkably significant difference among those willing to commit themselves. Similarly rural manufacturing district members divided 2–1–2 whereas their non-manufacturing compatriots split 2–3–6.

Table IV. ***Legislative Attitude Toward EST Being Extended to Include Nashville***

District Category	Statewide			Middle Tennessee		
	For	*Against*	*Neutral-No Answer*	*For*	*Against*	*Neutral-No Answer*
Urban	4	2	8	4	2	1
Mixed	2	3	2	0	3	0
Rural	4	4	8	3	3	6
Total	10	9	18	7	8	7
Manufacturing	8	3	10	5	3	3
Non-manufacturing	2	6	8	2	5	4
Total	10	9	18	7	8	7
Rural manufacturing	2	1	2	1	1	2
Rural non-manufacturing	2	3	6	2	2	4
Total	4	4	8	3	3	6
Mixed manufacturing	2	0	0	0	0	0
Mixed non-manufacturing	0	3	2	0	3	0
Total	2	3	2	0	3	0

It should be pointed out, of course, that in Middle Tennessee there was a difference between urban and rural reaction, and a difference of slightly larger proportion between manufacturing and non-manufacturing district members, but that no difference was discerned among the rural interviewees, whether manufacturing or not. The most noteworthy point, and perhaps the most important point in emphasizing the significance of industrialization with respect to the fast time issue, was that all Middle Tennessee mixed districts were uniformly unfavorable on this question and on all of the others.

Despite the small group interviewed and the apparent contradiction in some cases between constituency and personal attitudes[21] a number of tentative conclusions seem warranted:

(1) Urban area legislators' attitudes in Tennessee and attitudes which they believe their constituents to hold are friend-

lier toward fast time than those of their rural or mixed area counterparts.

(2) Manufacturing district legislators' attitudes toward fast time are also significantly more friendly than those of non-manufacturing district legislators.

(3) In large measure it is the level of manufacturing which is the critical factor. Evidence for this is based on: (a) greater discrepancy in responses on three of the four questions raised between manufacturing and non-manufacturing districts than between urban and rural; (b) greater favor on three of the four questions on the part of rural-manufacturing members and constituencies than rural-non-manufacturing; and (c) uniform antipathy among non-manufacturing mixed district members and constituencies equalling the antipathy of rural non-manufacturing legislators and constituencies.

These findings are, of course, restricted to one state, one issue, and a limited sample of respondents; but they tend to bear out the proposition that phenomena such as industrialization, ethnic background of the population, racial makeup of the population, religion, political party associations, and numerous other interests are more meaningful variables for analysis of conflict in the processes of government than urbanness or ruralness.

III

Despite the rapid social and economic changes taking place in urban and rural areas throughout the United States and the scattering of interest groups once associated either with urban or rural areas it is probable that participants in the political process will regard urban-rural conflict as an important element in the outcome for some time to come. Observations of a number of Tennessee legislators interviewed on the fast time issue seem to bear this out. From the rural vantage point one Middle Tennessee lawyer's comments are most illuminating:

> Generally we get along with the city boys fine. Just once in awhile they act superior about what they know, or what they can do. Usually that comes out after they have had a drink or two, but occasionally it comes out in the legislature. When it does we let them know we don't like it.

> Something like that happened the other day, —— introduced a bill on behalf of the Shelby delegation to create some new judgeships in Memphis. It was a local bill, and the Shelby delegation was agreed on it, so they didn't expect any trouble in passing it. Well he made it clear in speaking about the bill that the big city lawyers agreed it was a desirable thing, so that was that. The chip on his shoulder showed through a little bit. We had already seen enough of that attitude this session. So a couple of us made a little motion with our hands to some of the country boys to keep down the vote. None of us voted. The bill fell thirty votes short of a constitutional majority, and you should have seen the surprised looks on their faces!
>
> That night a Memphis official who accompanies the Shelby delegation got me in a corner and said, "What do you guys think you are doing any how? What is it you want?"
>
> So I said, "What do you mean what was I doing? —— explained the bill, and I guess all the big city lawyers understood it, but it was pretty complex for me. I'm just a country lawyer you know. So I decided it would be better if I just didn't vote on a bill that I really couldn't understand." He just gave me a dirty look and walked away.
>
> Some of them think we're hicks, messing around with little accident cases while they deal with their big corporations. We don't like that attitude. Next day they changed their attitude a little bit, and we let the bill go through.[22]

Some examples of urban responses:

(1) The House Speaker votes with the country boys. It's an individual matter. Some country boys see both sides, some city representatives alienate other city representatives.

(2) Rural members will outvote you every time.

(3) Country people can win anything they want.

(4) Rural members have the balance of power. However, on only three or four votes has there been a clear-cut city-country vote in this legislature.

Further evidence of this was discerned in additional questions raised with the Tennessee legislators interviewed on the daylight savings time issue. The thirty-seven interviewees were asked the following:

(1) To what extent do you consider city against country to be a major issue in Tennessee politics:
   (a) The most important
   (b) Among the five most important

(c) Fairly important but not top five
(d) Relatively unimportant
(e) Insignificant

(2) What are the main issues about which they differ (not asked if "e" was the answer to the previous question).

(3) From the following list check those about which city and country members are most likely to disagree (not asked if "e" was the response in question one).
(a) Legislative redistricting
(b) Permitting the sale of liquor
(c) Right to work legislation
(d) Return to localities of state collected taxes
(e) Equalization of property assessments
(f) Investigation of subversive activities
(g) School desegregation
(h) Urban redevelopment and public housing
(i) State financial aid to education
(j) Farm subsidies
(k) Public power vs. private power

Twenty-six of the thirty-five respondents willing to answer the first of these questions perceived the presence of some degree of urban-rural conflict. As Table V shows, a clear majority of legislators from districts in each category of urbanness saw urban-rural conflict as an important determinant in Tennessee politics. Urban members more often visualized urban-rural cleavages as important than did rural members. They also scaled it higher in intensity. For example, four of the urban members considered it the most critical issue facing the state, but not one rural member characterized it in those terms. Seven other urban members thought it among the five most important issues. It is perhaps natural for the urban members, a distinct minority in the Tennessee legislature, to read greater intensity into the struggle than the mixed and rural members. But the fact remains that a majority of all of the interviewees regarded urban-rural conflicts as among the most important in Tennessee politics.

Despite the belief that urban-rural conflicts are important in Tennessee politics, legislators, when asked to describe specific issues in controversy, were somewhat hard pressed to find them. Only two were volunteered by a substantial number of members—redistricting was named by twenty-five individuals and fiscal policy involving the distribution formula for state funds for public education by twenty-four. It should be added that a number of big city newspapers available to all members were dramatizing these two issues. Aside from these, only nine other choices were volunteered.

Table V. ***Perception of Urban-Rural Conflict as a Determinant in Tennessee Politics***

District Category	*Most Important*	*Among Five Most Important*	*Fairly Important*	*Unimportant*	*Insignificant*	*Total Respondents*
Urban	4	7	1	0	1	14
Rural	0	8	2	4	1	16
Mixed	1	2	1	2	1	7

The list of issues in the third question in this series was given to respondents only after they had completed answering the two previous questions. The "prompting" device evoked a stronger tendency to identify issues in which urban-rural conflicts play a role than was evidenced in the replies to the previous question. Apart from the two areas of controversy already cited however, the sale of liquor was the only specific issue indicated as an area of urban-rural conflict by the vast majority of respondents to the latter question.

Table VI. ***Scale of Identification of Urban-Rural Conflict over Selected Issues (N–37)***

Subject	Yes	No
1. Redistricting	33	4
2. Return of state taxes	32	5
3. State aid to education	26	11
4. Liquor sale	23	14
5. Right to work	19	18
6. Equalization of assessments	11	26
7. Farm subsidies	10	27
8. Urban redevelopment	5	32
9. Public vs. private power	4	33
10. Subversive activities	3	34
11. Desegregation	3	34

It seems apparent, therefore, that despite a number of issues on which Tennessee legislators discern urban-rural conflict, conflict is visualized in rather general terms almost as if it was expected of the interviewee to detect conflict because people have always acted as if the stereotypes of "city slicker" and "country hick" were real.

Summary

Evidence elicited from an exploratory study of urban-rural conflict as perceived by a sample of Tennessee legislators leads to the conclusion that urbanness and ruralness are far less useful in explaining the political processes in the United States than more detailed interest groupings. This alone does not represent a startling revelation. What is important is that as readjustments in the social and economic structure of urban and rural areas continue to take place this will become more pronounced, perhaps to an extent that ultimately the terms urban and rural will cease to have any usefulness in differentiating political interests.

However, notions about urban-rural conflict have permeated the language of politics to such an extent that not only will terms like urban-rural conflict, urban-rural cleavage, and city slicker and country hick persist as part of the language, but by definition they will continue to be part of the process. They will remain important as part of the folklore, part of the technique of political struggle, and part of the ideology of the participants regardless of whether they represent competing forces in the process or not. Therefore, even if urbanness and ruralness cannot be described as important interests exerting their influence as such, so long as politicians act as if they are in some way significant, it is incumbent upon political scientists to probe the role that these phenomena do play in politics.

Notes:

1. See especially Leon Epstein, *Politics in Wisconsin* (Madison: University of Wisconsin Press, 1958), chap. 4; and Nicholas A. Masters and Deil S. Wright, "Trends and Variations in the Two Party Vote: The Case of Michigan," *American Political Science Review,* LII (December 1958), 1078.

2. See Robert K. Merton, "Patterns of Influence: A Study of Interpersonal Influence and of Communications Behavior in a Local Community," chap. 12, in Paul Lazarsfeld and Frank Stanton, *Communications Research* (New York: Harper, 1948–49).

3. Perhaps the most succinct discussion of the meaning of urbanism is to be found in Louis Wirth, "Urbanism as a Way of Life," *American Journal of Sociology,* XLIV (July 1938), 1. See also Heinz Eulau, "Some Reflections on Urban-Rural Differentiation" (an unpublished working paper), which contains a list of useful references from the literature of sociology.

4. Current research being conducted by William Buchanan, Heinz Eulau, LeRoy C. Ferguson, and John C. Wahlke on critical roles of American state legislators represents a notable departure from traditional studies by political scientists regarding urban-rural differentiation.

5. Gordon E. Baker, *Rural versus Urban Political Power* (Garden City: Doubleday, 1955). Perhaps the most comprehensive of these studies is Thomas Page, *Legislative Apportionment in Kansas* (Lawrence: University of Kansas Bureau of Government Research, 1952). See also Thomas S. Barclay, "The Reapportionment Struggle in California in 1948," *Western Political Quarterly,* IV (June 1951), 313; Dean E. McHenry, "Urban v. Rural in California," *National Municipal Review,* XXXV (July 1946), 350; David O. Walter, "Reapportionment and Urban Representation," *Annals of the American Academy of Political & Social Science,* 196 (January 1938), 11; and "Legislative Reapportionment," *Law and Contemporary Problems,* Spring 1952.

6. A thoughtful treatment of Chicago's fiscal wars with the state of Illinois is found in Gilbert Y. Steiner, "Notes on the Formation of State-Municipal Fiscal Policy: Chicago and New York," *Political Science Quarterly,* LXX (September 1955), 387.

7. See, for example, the pioneer study of Stuart A. Rice, *Farmers and Workers in American Politics* (New York: Columbia University Press, 1924). See also V. O. Key, Jr., *American State Politics: An Introduction* (New York: Knopf, 1956), pp. 229 ff.; Samuel Lubell, *The Future of American Politics* (New York: Harper, 1951), chap. 2; Julius Turner, *Party and Constituency: Pressure on Congress* (Baltimore: Johns Hopkins Press, 1951), chap. 4. Among the voting studies tending to discount urban-rural cleavages in particular circumstances are David R. Derge, "Metropolitan and Outstate Alignments in Illinois and Missouri Legislative Delegations," *American Political Science Review,* LII (December 1958), 1051, and "Urban-Rural Conflict: The Case in Illinois" in John C. Wahlke and Heinz Eulau (eds.), *Legislative Behavior* (Glencoe: Free Press, 1959), p. 218; Robert S. Friedman, *The Maryland County Unit System and Urban-Rural Politics* (College Park: University of Maryland Bureau of Governmental Research, 1958); and Robert H. Salisbury, Jr., "Rural-Urban Factionalism in Missouri Politics" (a paper read at a meeting of the conference of the Midwest Political Science Association).

8. Key, *op. cit.,* pp. 229–30.

9. Turner, *op. cit.,* p. 74.

10. Friedman, *op. cit.,* p. 19.

11. *Ibid.,* p. 23.

12. Derge, *op. cit.,* p. 1057.

13. Robert H. Salisbury, "Missouri Politics and State Political Systems," in *Missouri Political Science Association: Research Papers 1958* (Columbia: Bureau of Governmental Research, University of Missouri, 1959), No. 2, p. 16.

14. Arthur M. Schlesinger, "The City in American History," *Mississippi Valley Historical Review,* XXVII (June 1940), 43.

15. See Howard W. Beers, "Rural-Urban Differences: Some Evidence from Public Opinion Polls," *Rural Sociology,* XVIII (March 1953), 1.

16. Legislators were chosen because of their accessibility, their reflection of widely held attitudes on public questions, and their direct relationship to controversies which might involve urban-rural conflict. Time necessitated using only a sample of the membership. The legislative session in the state in which the project was conducted is only 75 days and members are often inaccessible.

The author wishes to acknowledge the invaluable assistance of Paul Alexander, Jack Edwards, Norman Moore, and Bradley Reardon who helped in the formulation of the study, conducted the interviews, and aided in the analysis of the data. Several of the tables which follow are in large part derived from their efforts.

17. The category called "mixed" was included so that the "extremes" on the spatially urban-rural continuum could be more easily measured.

18. Altogether, a sample of representatives from forty-two constituencies in both houses of the legislature was chosen for interrogation, with an overloading of Middle Tennessee districts. Several possible combinations of the three categories did not exist. These included: (1) East Tennessee-mixed-nonmanufacturing; (2) Middle Tennessee-mixed-manufacturing; (3) West Tennessee-mixed-manufacturing; and (4) West Tennessee-rural-manufacturing. Interviews were conducted during February and March 1959 in Nashville. In some cases interviews were conducted during legislative sessions. In others they were held in hotel rooms. Several members from Nashville were interviewed at their homes.

19. Politically Tennessee is divided into three "Grand Divisions," East, Middle, and West, divided roughly by the Tennessee River. Each of the three sections has its own separate political traditions. As a result this is often regarded as a significant factor in Tennessee politics. See William Goodman, *Inherited Domain: Political Parties in Tennessee* (Knoxville: University of Tennessee Bureau of Public Administration, 1954).

20. Perhaps this was in deference to the Interstate Commerce Commission which was examining a petition requesting movement of the time zone at the time the interviews were being conducted.

21. A number of interviewees stated that their constituents were opposed to daylight time, but they expressed a personal willingness to support daylight time.

22. This interview was conducted and paraphrased by Jack Edwards, Vanderbilt University.

5 *Public-Regardingness as a Value Premise in Voting Behavior**

by James Q. Wilson and Edward C. Banfield

Our concern here is with the nature of the individual's attachment to the body politic and, more particularly, with the value premises underlying the choices made by certain classes of voters. Our hypothesis is that some classes of voters (provisionally defined as "subcultures" constituted on ethnic and income lines) are more disposed than others to rest their choices on some conception of "the public interest" or the "welfare of the community." To say the same thing in another way, the voting behavior of some classes tends to be more public-regarding and less private- (self- or family-) regarding than that of others. To test this hypothesis it is necessary to examine voting behavior in situations where one can say that a certain vote could not have been private-regarding. Local bond and other expenditure referenda present such situations: it is sometimes possible to say that a vote in favor of a particular

Reprinted from *American Political Science Review,* 58 (December, 1964), 876–887, by permission of the authors and the publisher.

*This is a preliminary report of a study supported by the Joint Center for Urban Studies of M.I.T. and Harvard University and the Rockefeller Foundation. The writers wish to acknowledge assistance from Martha Derthick and Mark K. Adams and comments from James Beshers, Anthony Downs, Werner Hirsch, Hendrik Houthakker, H. Douglas Price, and Arthur Stinchcombe. This paper was originally presented at the Second Conference On Urban Public Expenditures, New York University, February 21–22, 1964.

expenditure proposal is incompatible with a certain voter's self-interest narrowly conceived. If the voter nevertheless casts such a vote and if there is evidence that his vote was not in some sense irrational or accidental, then it must be presumed that his action was based on some conception of "the public interest."

Our first step, accordingly, is to show how much of the behavior in question can, and cannot, be explained on grounds of self-interest alone, narrowly conceived. If all of the data were consistent with the hypothesis that the voter acts as if he were trying to maximize his family income, the inquiry would end right there. In fact, it turns out that many of the data cannot be explained in this way. The question arises, therefore, whether the unexplained residue is purposive or "accidental." We suggest that for the most part it is purposive, and that the voters' purposes arise from their conceptions of "the public interest."

I

We start, then, from the simple—and admittedly implausible—hypothesis that the voter tries to maximize his family income or (the same thing) self-interest narrowly conceived. We assume that the voter estimates in dollars both the benefits that will accrue to him and his family if the proposed public expenditure is made and the amount of the tax that will fall on him in consequence of the expenditure; if the estimated benefit is more than the estimated cost, he votes for the expenditure; if it is less, he votes against it. We assume that all proposed expenditures will confer some benefits on all voters. The benefits conferred on a particular voter are "trivial," however, if the expenditure is for something that the particular voter (and his family) is not likely to use or enjoy. For example, improvement of sidewalks confers trivial benefits on those voters who are not likely to walk on them.

Insofar as behavior is consistent with these assumptions—*i.e.*, insofar as the voter seems to act rationally in pursuit of self-interest narrowly conceived—we consider that no further "explanation" is required. It may be that other, entirely different hypotheses would account for the behavior just as well or better. That possibility is not of concern to us here, however.

No doubt, our assumptions lack realism. No doubt, relatively few voters make a conscious calculation of costs and benefits. Very often the voter has no way of knowing whether a public expenditure proposal will benefit him or not. In only one state which we have examined (Florida) do ballots in municipal referenda specify precisely *which* streets are to be paved or *where* a bridge is to be built. Even if a facility is to serve the whole city (*e.g.,* a zoo, civic center, or county hospital), in most cities the ballot proposition is usually so indefinite that the voter cannot accurately judge either the nature or the amount of the benefits that he would derive from the expenditure. Similarly, it is often difficult or impossible for the voter to estimate even the approximate amount of the tax that will fall upon him in consequence of the expenditure. Some states (*e.g.,* Illinois and California) require that the anticipated cost of each undertaking be listed on the ballot (*e.g.,* "$12,800,000 for sewer improvements"). Of course, even when the total cost is given, the voter must depend on the newspapers to tell, or figure out for himself—if he can—how much it would increase the tax rate and how much the increased tax rate would add to his tax bill. Ohio is the only state we have studied where the voter is told on the ballot how the proposed expenditure will affect the tax rate ("17 cents per $100 valuation for each of two years"). Almost everywhere, most of the expenditure proposals are to be financed from the local property tax. Occasionally, however, a different tax (*e.g.,* the sales tax) or a different tax base (*e.g.,* the county or state rather than the city) is used. In these cases, the voter is likely to find it even harder to estimate how much he will have to pay.

We may be unrealistic also both in assuming that the voter takes only *money* costs into account (actually he may think that a proposed civic center would be an eyesore) and in assuming that the only money costs he takes into account are *taxes* levied upon him (actually, if he is a renter he may suppose—whether correctly or incorrectly is beside the point—that his landlord will pass a tax increase on to him in a higher rent).

The realism of the assumptions does not really matter. What does matter is their usefulness in predicting the voters' behavior. It is possible that voters may act *as if* they are well informed and disposed to calculate even when in fact they are neither. If we can predict their behavior without going into the question of how much or how well they calculate, so much the better.

II

On the assumptions we have made, one would expect voters who will have no tax levied upon them in consequence of the passage of an expenditure proposal to vote for it even if it will confer only trivial benefits on them. Having nothing to lose by the expenditure and something (however small) to gain, they will favor it. In the *very* low-income[1] wards and precincts of the larger cities a high proportion of the voters are in this position since most local public expenditures are financed from the property tax and the lowest-income people do not own property. We find that in these heavily non-home-owning districts the voters almost invariably support all expenditure proposals. We have examined returns on 35 expenditure proposals passed upon in 20 separate elections in seven cities and have not found a single instance in which this group failed to give a majority in favor of a proposal. Frequently the vote is 75 to 80 per cent in favor; sometimes it is over 90 per cent. The strength of voter support is about the same no matter what the character of the proposed expenditure.[2]

In all of the elections we have examined, non-homeowners show more taste for public expenditures that are to be financed from property taxes than do homeowners. Table I shows by means of product-moment (Pearsonian *r*) coefficients of correlation the strength and consistency of this relationship over a wide variety of issues in several elections in Cleveland and Chicago.[3] As one would expect, when an expenditure is to be financed from a source other than the property tax the difference between homeowner and non-homeowner behavior is reduced. This is borne out in Table II in which we have compared wards typical of four major economic groups in Cook County (Illinois) in their voting on two issues: first, a proposal to increase county hospital facilities and, second, a proposal to construct a state welfare building. The measures were alike in that they would benefit only indigents; they were different in that their costs would be assessed against different publics: the hospital was to be paid for from the local property tax, the welfare building from state sources, largely a sales tax. Middle-income homeowners showed themselves very sensitive to this difference; the percentage favoring the state-financed measure was twice that favoring the property-tax-financed one. Low-income renters, on the other hand, preferred the property-tax-financed measure to the state-financed one.

Table I. ***Relationship Between Percentage of Ward Voting "Yes" and Percentage of Dwelling Units Owner Occupied; Various Issues in Cleveland and Chicago***

Issue and Date	Simple Correlation Coefficient (r)
Cleveland (33 wards):	
Administration Building (11/59)	–0.86
County Hospital (11/59)	–0.77
Tuberculosis Hospital (11/59)	–0.79
Court House (11/59)	–0.85
Juvenile Court (11/59)	–0.83
Parks (11/59)	–0.67
Welfare Levy (5/60)	–0.72
Roads and Bridges (11/60)	–0.77
Zoo (11/60)	–0.81
Parks (11/60)	–0.57
Chicago (50 wards):	
County Hospital (1957)	–0.79
Veterans' Bonus (1957)	–0.49
Welfare Building (1958)	–0.67
Street Lights (1959)	–0.83
Municipal Building (1962)	–0.78
Urban Renewal Bonds (1962)	–0.79
Sewers (1962)	–0.79
Street Lights (1962)	–0.81

Let us turn now to the behavior of voters who do own property and whose taxes will therefore be increased in consequence of a public expenditure. One might suppose that the more property such a voter has, the less likely it is that he will favor public expenditures. To be sure, certain expenditures confer benefits roughly in proportion to the value of property and some may even confer disproportionate benefits on the more valuable properties; in such cases one would expect large property owners to be as much in favor of expenditures as the small, or more so. Most expenditures, however, confer about the same benefits on large properties as on small, whereas of course the taxes to pay for the expenditure are levied (in

Table II. ***Voting Behavior of Four Major Economic Groups Compared in Cook County***

Group	Percent "Yes" Vote: *County Hospital (1957)*	Percent "Yes" Vote: *State Welfare Building (1958)*
	(%)	(%)
*High Income Homeowners**		
Winnetka	64	76
Wilmette	55	70
Lincolnwood	47	64
Middle Income Homeowners†		
Lansing	30	54
Bellwood	21	55
Brookfield	22	51
Middle Income Renters‡		
Chicago Ward 44	65	71
Chicago Ward 48	61	72
Chicago Ward 49	64	74
Low Income Renters§		
Chicago Ward 2	88	73
Chicago Ward 3	87	76
Chicago Ward 27	87	78

*Three suburbs with highest median family income ($13,200 to $23,200) among all suburbs with 85 percent or more home ownership.

†Three suburbs with lowest median family income ($8,000 to $8,300) among all suburbs with 85 percent or more home ownership.

‡Three wards with highest median family income ($6,200 to $6,800) among all wards with less than 15 percent home ownership (none of the three wards is more than 4 percent Negro).

§Three wards with lowest median family income ($3,100 to $4,100) among all wards with less than 15 percent home ownership (Negro population of wards ranges from 59 to 99 percent).

theory at least) strictly in proportion to the value of property. The owner of a $30,000 home, for example, probably gets no more benefit from the construction of a new city hall or the expansion of a zoo than does the owner of a $10,000 one; his share of the tax increase is three times as much, however. Very often, indeed, there is an inverse relation between the value of a property and the benefits that accrue to its owner from a public expenditure. The probability is certainly greater that the owner of the $10,000 house will some day use the free county hospital (patronized chiefly by low-income Negroes) than that the owner of the $30,000 house will use it. Since normally the *ratio* of benefits to costs is less favorable the higher the value of the property, one might expect to find a positive correlation between the percentage of "No" votes in a neighborhood and the median value of homes there.

Chart 1. ***Relation between percentage voting "yes" on proposition to provide increased county hospital facilities (November 1959) and percentage of dwelling units owner-occupied in the 33 wards of Cleveland.***

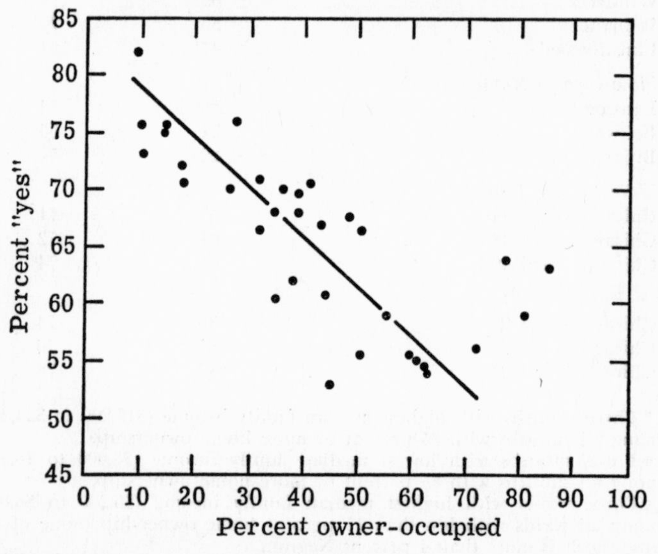

Source of housing data: U.S. Census of Housing, 1960. Figure reprinted from Edward C. Banfield and James Q. Wilson, *City Politics* (Cambridge: Harvard University Press, 1963), p. 238.

This expectation is not borne out by the facts, however. Table III gives partial correlation coefficients relating the per cent voting "Yes" in the wards of Cleveland and the suburban wards and towns of Cuyahoga County to the median family income in those wards and towns.[4] It shows that the higher the income of a ward or town, the more taste it has for public expenditures of various kinds. That the ratio of benefits to costs declines as income goes up seems to make no difference.[5]

The same pattern appears in a 1960 Flint, Michigan, vote on additional flood control facilities. This is shown graphically in Chart 3. Although there is a considerable dispersion around the line of regression, in general the higher the home value—

and accordingly the more the expected tax—the greater the support for the expenditure.[6]

Chart 2. ***Relation between percentage voting "yes" on proposition to provide additional sewer facilities (1962) and percentage of dwelling units owner-occupied in wards of Chicago.***

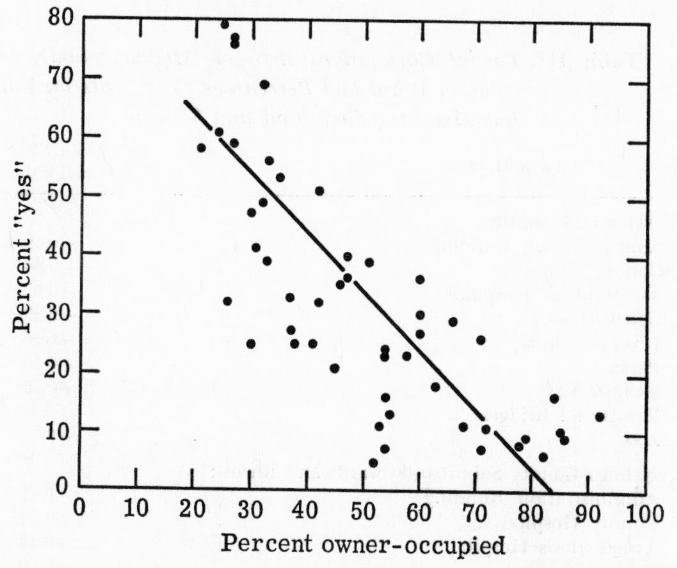

It may be argued that because of the phenomenon of the diminishing marginal utility of money these findings are not really anomalous. The richer a man is, perhaps, the smaller the sacrifice that an additional dollar of taxation represents to him. Thus, even though the well-to-do voter may get no more benefit than the poor one gets and may have to pay a great deal more in taxes, an expenditure proposal may nevertheless be more attractive to him. He may be more willing to pay a dollar for certain benefits than his neighbor is to pay fifty cents because, having much more money than his neighbor, a dollar is worth only a quarter as much to him.

Differences in the value of the dollar to voters at different income levels account in part for the well-to-do voter's relatively strong taste for public expenditures. They can hardly account for it entirely, however. For one thing, they do not rationalize the behavior of those voters who support measures that would give them only trivial benefits while imposing substantial costs upon them. The suburbanite who favors a county hospital for the indigent which he and his family will certainly never use and for which he will be heavily taxed is not acting according to self-interest narrowly conceived no matter how little a dollar is worth to him.

Table III. ***Partial Correlations Between Median Family Income of Ward and Percentage "Yes" Vote on Various Measures, Cleveland and Suburbs***

Area and Issue	Partial Correlation*
Cleveland (33 wards):	
Administration Building	+0.49
County Hospital	+0.64
Tuberculosis Hospital	+0.57
Court House	+0.49
Juvenile Court	+0.66
Parks	+0.48
Welfare Levy	+0.70
Roads and Bridges	+0.61
Zoo	+0.59
Cuyahoga County Suburbs (90 wards and towns):	
Administration Building	+0.47
County Hospital	+0.54
Tuberculosis Hospital	+0.43
Court House	+0.60
Juvenile Court	+0.59
Parks	+0.52
Welfare Levy	+0.35
Roads and Bridges	+0.60
Zoo	+0.62

*Controlling for proportion of dwelling units owner-occupied.

Moreover, if the well-to-do voter places a low value on the dollar when evaluating some expenditure proposals, one would expect him to place the same low value on it when evaluating all others. In fact, he does not seem to do so; indeed, he sometimes appears to place a *higher* value on it than does his less-well-off neighbor. Compare, for example, the behavior of the Cook County (Illinois) suburbanites who voted on a proposal to build a county hospital (an expenditure which would confer only trivial benefits on them and for which they would be taxed in proportion to the value of their

Chart 3. ***Relation between percentage voting "yes" on proposition to provide additional flood control facilities (November 1960) and median value of owner-occupied dwelling units in the precincts of Flint, Michigan.***

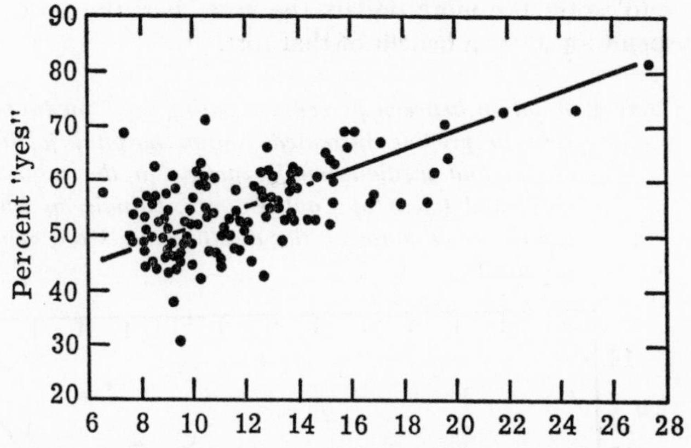

NOTE: Only property owners and their spouses could vote.
Source of housing data: U. S. Census of Housing, 1960. Figure reprinted from Banfield and Wilson, *City Politics,* p. 239.

property) with the behavior of the same suburbanites who voted on a proposal to give a bonus of $300 to Korean War veterans (an expenditure from which the well-to-do would benefit about as much as the less-well-to-do and for which they would not be taxed disproportionately, since the bonus was to be financed from state, not local, revenues, and the state had neither an income tax nor a corporate profits tax). As Charts 4 and 5 show, the higher the median family income of a voting district, the larger the percentage voting "Yes" on the welfare building (the rank-order correlation was +0.57), but the *smaller* the percentage voting "Yes" on the veterans' bonus (the rank-order correlation was −0.71).

In Cuyahoga County, Ohio, the same thing happened. There the higher the median family income, the larger the percentage voting for all the expenditure proposals except one —a bonus for Korean War veterans. On this one measure there was a correlation of −0.65 between median family income and percentage voting "Yes."

Thus, although it is undoubtedly true that the more dollars a voter has, the more he will pay for a given benefit, the principle does not explain all that needs explaining. When it comes to a veterans' bonus, for example, the opposite principle seems to work: the more dollars the voter has, the fewer he will spend for a given benefit of that sort.

Chart 4. *Relation between percentage voting "yes" on proposition to provide increased county hospital facilities (1957) and median family income in the suburban cities and towns of Cook County, Illinois, in which two-thirds or more of the dwelling units are owner-occupied.*

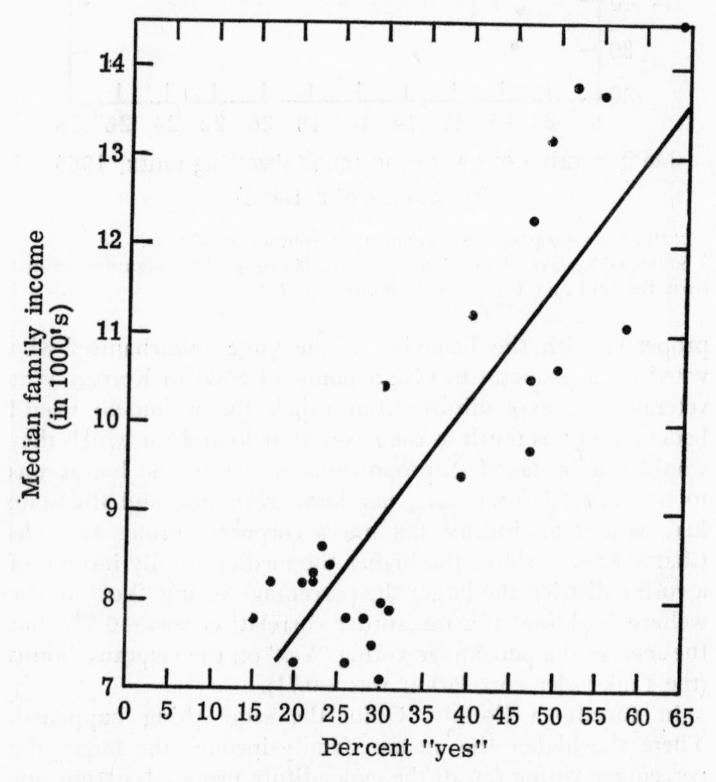

That there is a positive correlation between amount of property owned (or income) and tendency to vote "Yes" does

Chart 5. ***Relation between percentage voting "yes" on proposition to approve a $300 bonus for veterans of Korean War (1958) and median family income in the suburban cities and towns of Cook County, Illinois, in which two-thirds or more of the dwelling units are owner-occupied.***

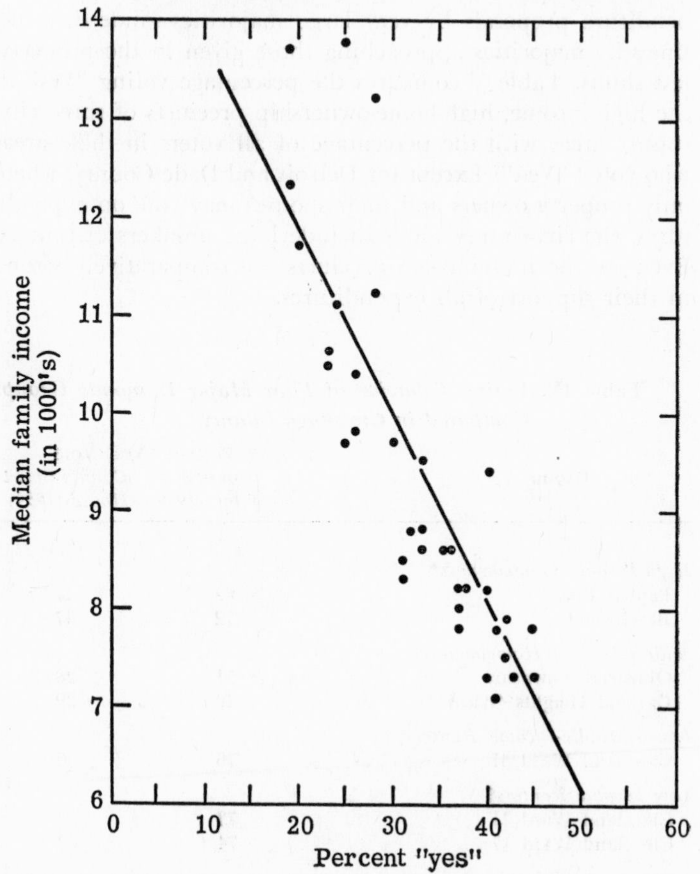

not, of course, imply that a majority of property owners at *any* income level favors expenditures: the correlation would exist even if the highest income voters opposed them, provided that at each lower level of income voters opposed them by ever-larger majorities. In fact, middle-income homeowners often vote against proposals that are approved by both the very poor (renters) and the very well-to-do (owners). Table IV gives a rather typical picture of the response of the various income groups to proposals that are to be financed from the property tax in Cuyahoga County (Ohio).

Not infrequently the highest-income districts support expenditure proposals by very large majorities—indeed, sometimes by majorities approaching those given in the propertyless slums. Table V compares the percentage voting "Yes" in the high-income, high-home-ownership precincts of three city-county areas with the percentage of all voters in these areas who voted "Yes."[7] Except for Detroit and Dade County, where only property owners and their spouses may vote on expenditures, the city-county totals include large numbers of renters. Even so, the high-income precincts are comparatively strong in their support of all expenditures.

Table IV. ***Voting Behavior of Four Major Economic Groups Compared in Cuyahoga County***

Group	Percent "Yes" Vote: *County Hospital (1959)*	Percent "Yes" Vote: *County Court House (1959)*
	(%)	(%)
*High-Income Homeowners**		
Pepper Pike	69	47
Beachwood	72	47
Middle-Income Homeowners†		
Olmstead Township	51	28
Garfield Heights (Ward 4)	48	29
Lower-Middle-Income Renters‡		
Cleveland Ward 31	76	66
Low Income Renters§		
Cleveland Ward 11	73	63
Cleveland Ward 17	74	62

*Two suburbs with highest median family income ($15,700 and $19,000) of all suburbs with 85 percent or more home ownership.

†Two suburbs with lowest median family income ($6,800 and $7,000) of all suburbs with 85 percent or more home ownership.

‡The one ward with less than 15 percent home ownership and which is less than 10 percent Negro (median income: $4,700).

§Two wards with lowest median family incomes ($3,400 and $3,600) of all wards with less than 15 percent home ownership (Negro population of wards was 90 and 97 percent).

III

When we hold constant the percentage of home ownership, percentage of nonwhites, and median family income, a negative correlation appears between the percentage of voters in the wards of Cleveland who are of foreign stock and the percentage of the total vote in those wards that is "Yes." This is shown in Column 1 of Table VI.[8] Of the many foreign stocks in Cleveland, the Poles and Czechs have the strongest distaste for expenditures. Column 2 of Table VI shows how markedly the presence of Poles and Czechs in a voting district affects the "Yes" vote.[9] In the suburbs the correlation is only slightly weaker, but significant at the .001 level in all but two cases and in these at the .01 level. The complete correlation table shows that in all but three cases the percentage of Poles and Czechs is a more important influence on voting than median family income, and is second in influence only to home ownership. In two of the three exceptional cases, indeed, it was *more* important than home ownership.

Table V. *Percentage Voting "Yes" on Expenditures in Home-Owning, Upper-Income "Oldstock" Precincts in Various Counties*

County, Issue, and Date	Percent "Yes" Vote in Upper-Income Precincts	Percent "Yes" Vote in County as a Whole
	(%)	(%)
Detroit-Wayne County		
Sewers (8/60)	83.6	64.3
Increase School tax limit	52.0	39.0
Build Schools (4/63)	52.0	33.4
Increase sales tax (11/60)	78.6	47.8
Kansas City—Jefferson County		
Increase school taxes (11/60)	68.6	54.9
Build jails (3/62)	86.3	78.0
Sewage treatment plant (11/60)	93.2	81.6
Miami-Dade County		
Highways (5/60)	71.2	53.0
Schools (1955)	90.8	92.1

Table VI. ***Partial Correlations Between Selected "Ethnic" Variables and Percentage Voting "Yes" on Expenditures in Cleveland and Cuyahoga County Wards and Towns****

Issue	Foreign Stock *City*	Foreign Stock *Suburbs*	Polish-Czech *City*	Polish-Czech *Suburbs*	Negro *City*	Negro *Suburbs*
Admin. Building	–0.40	ns†	–0.54	–0.17	ns	ns
County Hospital	ns	ns	–0.79	–0.40	ns	ns
TB Hospital	ns	–0.22	–0.74	–0.46	ns	ns
Court House	–0.47	ns	–0.58	–0.28	ns	ns
Juvenile Court	–0.46	ns	–0.74	–0.40	ns	ns
Parks (1959)	–0.41	ns	–0.62	–0.31	–0.49	ns
Welfare Levy	–0.58	ns	–0.71	–0.49	ns	ns
Roads & Bridges	–0.48	ns	–0.66	–0.40	ns	ns
Zoo	–0.62	ns	–0.71	–0.40	ns	ns
Parks (1960)	ns	ns	ns	–0.50	ns	ns

*These are partial correlation coefficients derived from a regression analysis in which home ownership, median family income, and two "ethnic" variables have been held constant.

†If the correlations were not significant at the .05 level (Student's *t*), "ns" is entered in the table. The critical values were based on 27 degrees of freedom for the city data and 84 degrees of freedom for the suburban data.

Table VII. ***Percentage of Various "Ethnic" Precincts Voting "Yes" on Selected Expenditures in Chicago***

Ethnic Group and Number of Precincts	Percent Voting "Yes" on: *Co. Hosp.* *(6/57)*	*Vet's Bonus* *(11/58)*	*Urban Renewal* *(4/62)*	*City Hall* *(5/62)*	*School* *(4/59)*
	(%)	(%)	(%)	(%)	(%)
*Low-Income Renters**					
Negro (22)	84.9	80.2	88.6	82.3	97.8
Irish (6)	61.3	55.3	45.7	46.3	79.4
Polish (26)	60.1	54.6	57.1	53.8	81.8
Middle-Income Home-Owners†					
Negro (13)	66.8	54.9	69.6	49.8	88.9
Irish (6)	54.6	44.1	22.0	27.2	64.2
Polish (38)	47.4	40.0	14.6	15.2	58.3

*Average median family income under $6,000 per year; at least two-thirds of all dwelling units renter-occupied.

†Average median family income between $7,500 and $10,000 a year for whites; over $6,000 a year for Negroes. At least 80 percent of all dwelling units owner-occupied.

Table VII. ***Percentage of Various "Ethnic" Precincts Voting "Yes" on Selected Expenditures in Cleveland and Cuyahoga County***

Ethnic Group and Number of Precincts	Percent Voting "Yes" on: *Co. Hosp.* *(11/59)*	*Court House* *(11/59)*	*Parks* *(11/59)*	*Welfare Levy* *(5/60)*	*Vet's Bonus* *(11/56)*
	(%)	(%)	(%)	(%)	(%)
*Low-Income Renters**					
Negro (16)	78.6	67.3	52.6	85.9	89.9
Italian (10)	68.8	53.3	43.5	49.9	74.8
Polish (6)	54.9	39.9	28.1	33.7	71.6
Middle-Income Home-Owners†					
Negro (8)	68.1	54.0	39.6	73.2	79.2
Italian (7)	59.3	49.7	41.1	56.8	66.8
Polish (12)	52.9	35.8	34.3	46.4	61.7
Upper-Income Home-Owners‡					
Anglo-Saxon (11)	70.6	51.4	57.2	64.8	53.7
Jewish (7)	71.7	47.1	48.4	64.5	56.8

*Average median family income less than $6,000 per year; at least two-thirds of all dwelling units renter-occupied.

†Average median family income between $7,000 and $9,000 a year for whites; over $6,000 a year for Negroes. At least 75 percent of all dwelling units owner-occupied.

‡Average median family income over $10,000 per year; over 85 percent of all dwelling units owner-occupied.

The findings in Column 3 of Table VI are surprising. We expected a positive correlation between percentage of Negroes and the strength of the "Yes" vote. Deficiencies in the data may possibly account for the absence of any correlation: there are not enough home-owning Negroes or enough very low-income whites in Cleveland to make a really satisfactory matching of wards possible.

In order to get a closer view of ethnic voting it is necessary to forego general correlations and instead to examine individual precincts known to be predominantly of a single ethnic group. In Tables VII and VIII we show how selected "ethnic" precincts belonging to two income and home-ownership classes voted in several elections in the Chicago and Cleveland areas.[10] There is a remarkable degree of consistency in the influence of both ethnicity and income or home-ownership, whether viewed on an intra- or inter-city basis. In Chicago, for example, the low-income renters in *every* case voted more favorably for expenditures than did the middle-income homeowners of the same ethnic group. Within the same economic class, however, ethnicity makes a striking difference. Low-income Negro renters are in *every* case more enthusiastic by a wide margin about public expenditures than low-income Irish or Polish renters. Middle-income Negro homeowners are in *every* case more enthusiastic about the same proposals than middle-income Irish or Polish homeowners. (In passing it is worth noting that Negroes are two or three times more favorable toward urban renewal—despite the fact that they are commonly the chief victims of land clearance programs—than Irish or Polish voters.)

Essentially the same relationships appear in Table VIII for Cleveland-Cuyahoga County. With one exception (Italians voting on the welfare levy), low-income renters in an ethnic group are more favorable to expenditures than middle-income homeowners in the same ethnic group. Low-income Negro renters are the most favorable to all proposals and middle-income Negro homeowners are more favorable to them than are the other middle-income ethnic groups. Aside from the veterans' bonus (a special case), both the "Anglo-Saxon" and the Jewish upper-income homeowners are more favorable to expenditures than any middle-income groups except the Negro.

IV

We have shown both that a considerable proportion of voters, especially in the upper income groups, vote against their self-interest narrowly conceived and that a marked ethnic influence appears in the vote. Now we would like to bring these two findings together under a single explanatory principle.

One such principle—but one we reject—is that the voters in question have acted irrationally (either in not calculating benefits and costs at all or else by making mistakes in their calculations) and that their irrationality is a function of their ethnic status. According to this theory, the low-income Polish renter who votes against expenditures proposals that would cost him nothing and would confer benefits upon him and the high-income Anglo-Saxon or Jewish homeowner who favors expenditures proposals that will cost him heavily without benefiting him would both behave differently if they thought about the matter more or if their information were better.

A more tenable hypothesis, we think, is that voters in some income and ethnic groups are more likely than voters in others to take a public-regarding rather than a narrowly self-interested view of things—*i.e.,* to take the welfare of others, especially that of "the community," into account as an aspect of their own welfare.[11] We offer the additional hypothesis that both the tendency of a voter to take a public-regarding view and the content of that view (*e.g.,* whether or not he thinks a Korean war veterans' bonus is in the public interest) are largely functions of his participation in a subculture that is definable in ethnic and income terms. Each subcultural group, we think, has a more or less distinctive notion of how much a citizen ought to sacrifice for the sake of the community as well as of what the welfare of the community is constituted; in a word, each has its own idea of what justice requires and of the importance of acting justly. According to this hypothesis, the voter is presumed to act rationally; the ends he seeks are not always narrowly self-interested ones, however. On the contrary, depending upon his income and ethnic status they are more or less public-regarding.[12]

That his income status does not by itself determine how public-regarding he is, or what content he gives to the public interest, can be shown from the voting data. As we explained above, generally the higher a homeowner's income the more likely he is to favor expenditures. This is partly—but only partly—because the value of the dollar is usually less to people who have many of them than to people who have few of them. We suggest that it is also because upper-income people tend to be more public-regarding than lower-income people. We do not think that income *per se* has this effect; rather it is the ethnic attributes, or culture, empirically associated with it. It happens that most upper-income voters belong, if not by inheritance then by adoption, to an ethnic group (especially the Anglo-Saxon and the Jewish) that is relatively public-regarding in its outlook; hence ethnic influence on voting is hard to distinguish from income influence.

In the three scatter diagrams which comprise Chart 6 we have tried to distinguish the two kinds of influence. For this figure, we divided all wards and towns of Cleveland and Cuyahoga County in which 85 or more percent of the dwelling units were owner-occupied into three classes according to median home value. Diagram 6a shows the voting where that value was more than $27,000; diagram 6b shows it where it was $19,000–27,000, and diagram 6c shows it where it was less than $19,000. The horizontal and vertical axes are the same for all diagrams; each diagram shows the relationship between

Chart 6. ***Relation between percentage voting 'yes" on proposition to provide additional zoo facilities (1960) and proportion of ward or town population which is of Polish or Czech foreign stock in Cuyahoga County, Ohio; at three median home value levels (only wards and towns with 85 percent or more owner-occupied dwellings used).***

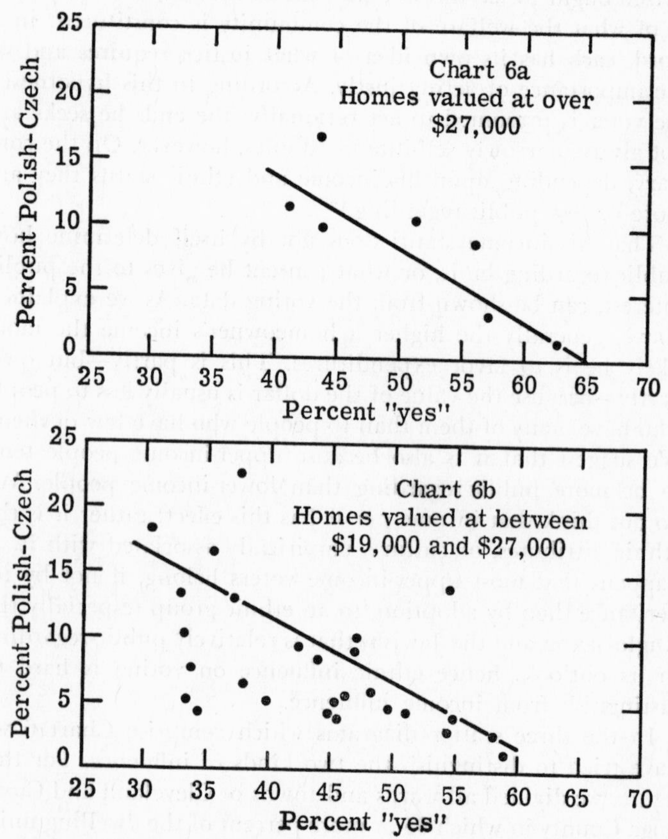

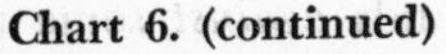

Chart 6. (continued)

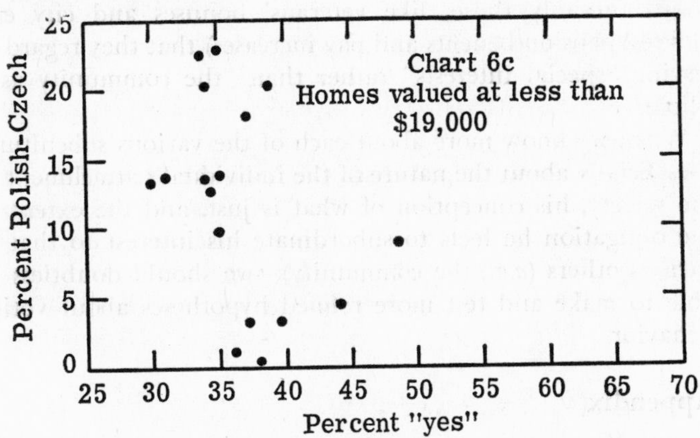

the percentage of voters in the ward or town who are Polish-Czech (vertical axis) and the percentage of "Yes" vote on a proposal to expand the zoo (horizontal axis). In the group of wards and towns having the lowest median home value (diagram 6c) the presence of Polish-Czech voters made little difference; these wards and towns were about 65 percent against the proposal no matter how many Poles and Czechs lived in them. In both groups of higher home-value wards and towns, however, Poles and Czechs were conspicuously less favorable to the proposal than were the rest of the voters. Among the non-Polish-Czech voters in these higher home-value wards and towns, Anglo-Saxons and Jews were heavily represented; therefore it seems plausible to conclude that, as compared to Poles and Czechs in these two income groups, the Anglo-Saxons and Jews were decidedly public-regarding.

Another interpretation of the behavior of the Poles and Czechs is possible, however. It may be that they had the welfare of the community in view also but defined it differently than did the Anglo-Saxons and the Jews. They may have thought that the particular expenditure proposed, or for that matter all public expenditures, would do the community more harm than good. (This would rationalize the behavior of those low-income renters—see Table VIII—who voted against proposals giving them benefits without any costs.[13]) Whatever may be true of the Poles and Czechs, it seems clear that upper-income Anglo-Saxons, and to a somewhat lesser degree Jews, tend to vote on public-regarding grounds *against* some proposals (notably those, like veterans' bonuses and city employees' pension benefits and pay increases) that they regard as serving "special interests" rather than "the community as a whole."

When we know more about each of the various subcultures —especially about the nature of the individual's attachment to the society, his conception of what is just, and the extent of the obligation he feels to subordinate his interest to that of various others (*e.g.*, the community)—we should doubtless be able to make and test more refined hypotheses about voting behavior.

Appendix

We chose the "ethnic" precincts for Tables VII and VIII by inspecting census tract data and then visiting the precincts that appeared to be predominantly of one ethnic group to get confirmatory evidence from well-informed persons and from a view of the neighborhoods. We could have used a less impressionistic method (*e.g.*, counting the proportion of ethnic names on voter registration lists), but since we wanted only to identify precincts that are predominantly of one ethnic group, not to place them on a scale of ethnicity, this did not appear necessary.

Having identified the "ethnic" precincts, we divided them into two (sometimes three) income groups on the basis of census data. As we indicate on the tables, with one exception we used the same cutting points to separate the income levels of all ethnic groups. The exception was the Negro. The income distribution among Negroes is so skewed to the low end of the scale that "middle-income" has to be defined differently for Negroes than for whites. We identified "middle-income Negro" precincts by selecting from among all precincts that were at least 85 percent Negro and had an owner-occupancy rate of at least 80 percent those few with the highest median family incomes. Some of these precincts turned out to have median incomes as low as $6,000 a year, which is about $1,000 less than any of the "middle-income white" precincts had. If we had made the cutting point higher, however, we would not have had enough middle-income Negro precincts to work with. In our opinion, Negroes with incomes of $6,000 are about as likely to "feel" middle-income as are whites with incomes of $7,000.

Notes:

1. Median family income under $3,000 per year. Needless to say, most voters in this category are Negroes.

2. The cities and elections examined are:
Cleveland-Cuyahoga County: Nov., 1956; Nov., 1959; May, 1960; Nov., 1960.
Chicago-Cook County: June, 1957; Nov., 1958; Nov., 1959; April, 1962.
Detroit-Wayne County: August, 1960; Feb., 1961; April, 1961; April, 1963.
Kansas City: Nov., 1960; March, 1962.
Los Angeles: Nov., 1962.
Miami: Nov., 1956; May, 1960.
St. Louis: March, 1962; Nov., 1962; March, 1963.

3. The degree of association was also calculated using a nonparametric statistic (Kendall's *tau*). The relationship persists but at lower values. Since we are satisfied that the relationship found by *r* is not spurious, we have relied on it for the balance of the analysis because of its capacity to produce partial correlation coefficients.

4. Only two measures of tax liability can be got from the Census: median home value and median family income. We have used the latter for the most part. The Census classifies all homes valued at over $25,000 together, thereby collapsing distinctions that are important for us. We think, too, that people are more likely to know their incomes than to know the current market value of their homes, and that therefore the Census information on incomes is more reliable. Finally, in neighborhoods populated mostly by renters, median home values are likely to be unrepresentative of the class character of the neighborhood: this is so, for example, where a few owner-occupied slums exist in a district of luxury apartments.

5. Other studies which suggest that upper-income groups may have a greater preference for public expenditures than middle-income groups include Oliver P. Williams and Charles R. Adrian, *Four Cities: A Study in Comparative Policy Making* (Philadelphia: University of Pennsylvania Press, 1963), ch. v; Alvin Boskoff and Harmon Zeigler, *Voting Patterns in a Local Election* (Philadelphia: J. B. Lippincott Co., 1964), ch. iii; Richard A. Watson, *The Politics of Urban Change* (Kansas City, Mo.: Community Studies, Inc., 1963), ch. iv; and Robert H. Salisbury and Gordon Black, "Class and Party in Non-Partisan Elections: The Case of Des Moines," *American Political Science Review,* Vol. 57 (September, 1963), p. 591. The Williams-Adrian and Salisbury-Black studies use electoral data; the Boskoff-Zeigler and Watson studies use survey data. See also Otto A. Davis, "Empirical Evidence of 'Political' Influences Upon the Expenditure and Taxation Policies of Public Schools," Graduate School of Industrial Administration of the Carnegie Institute of Technology, January, 1964 (mimeo), and William C. Birdsall, "Public Finance Allocation Decisions and the Preferences of Citizens: Some Theoretical and

Empirical Considerations," unpublished Ph.D. thesis, Department of Economics, Johns Hopkins University, 1963. A difficulty with the Davis and Birdsall studies is the size (and thus the heterogeneity) of the units of analysis—entire school districts in one case, entire cities in the other.

6. Michigan is one of the few states which restricts the right to vote on expenditures to property owners and their spouses. Because the Flint returns were tabulated on a precinct basis, demographic data had to be obtained from block rather than tract statistics; since median family income is given only for tracts, median value of owner-occupied homes had to be used.

Possibly the flood control benefits would be distributed roughly in proportion to the value of properties; about this we cannot say. However, it is worth noting that the vote in Flint on other expenditures which presumably would *not* distribute benefits in proportion to the value of properties (*e.g.*, parks) followed the same pattern.

7. We isolated all precincts in Census tracts having median family incomes of at least $10,000 a year, with at least 70 percent home ownership (the central city of Chicago was excepted here), and at least 70 percent of the population third- (or more) generation native born.

8. A person is of "foreign stock" if he was born abroad or if one or both of his parents was born abroad. We believe that the reason why a significant relationship does not appear for the suburbs is that there is a considerable number of Jews among the foreign stock of the suburbs. In the central city, there are practically no Jews. Like other Jews, Jews of Eastern European origin tend to favor expenditures proposals of all kinds. Their presence in the suburbs, therefore, offsets the "No" vote of the non-Jews of foreign stock.

9. Since no home-owning ward or town in Cuyahoga County is more than 25 percent Polish-Czech according to the 1960 Census, it may be that no inferences can be drawn from the voting data about Polish-Czech behavior. Three considerations increase our confidence in the possibility of drawing inferences, however. (1) Only first- and second-generation Poles and Czechs are counted as such by the Census, but third- and fourth-generation Poles and Czechs tend to live in the same wards and towns; thus the proportion of the electorate sharing Polish-Czech cultural values (the relevant thing from our standpoint) is considerably larger than the Census figures suggest. (2) When other factors are held constant, even small increases in the number of Poles and Czechs are accompanied by increases in the "No" vote; nothing "explains" this except the hypothesis that the Poles and Czechs make the difference. (3) When we take as the unit for analysis not wards but precincts of a few hundred persons that are known to contain very high proportions of Poles and Czechs, we get the same results. Because we are using ecological, not individual, data, we are perforce analyzing the behavior of ethnic "ghettos" where ethnic identification and attitudes are probably reinforced. Poles in non-Polish wards, for example, may behave quite differently.

10. The method by which these precincts were selected is given in the Appendix. Unfortunately, it proved impossible to identify relatively homogeneous precincts typical of other ethnic groups at various income levels and degrees of home-ownership. For example, middle-income Jews

tend to be renters, not homeowners, and there are practically no low-income Jewish precincts in either city. A complete list of these precincts is available from the authors.

11. *Cf.* Anthony Downs, "The Public Interest: Its Meaning in a Democracy," *Social Research,* Vol. 29 (Spring 1962), pp. 28–29.

12. The proposition that "subculture" can be defined in ethnic and income terms is highly provisional. We are looking for other and better criteria and we think we may find some. But so far as the present data are concerned, ethnic and income status are all we have.

13. Two other explanations are possible and, in our opinion, plausible. One is that the low-income renters may have taken into account costs to them other than taxes—*e.g.,* the cost (perhaps monetary) of changes in the neighborhood that would ensue from expenditures. (Irish objections to urban renewal in Chicago may have been due, not to a fear of higher taxes, but to fear of neighborhood "invasion" by Negroes displaced from land clearance projects.) The other is that in these precincts a much higher proportion of renters than of homeowners may have stayed away from the polls. In Cleveland (though not, interestingly, in Chicago) voter turnout is highly correlated with home ownership and almost all white renter precincts have at least a few homeowners in them. Conceivably—we think it unlikely—all those who voted in some "renter" precincts were actually owners.

Part III. The Personal Basis of Political Behavior

P*olitical behavior is personal behavior.* Human behavior is personal in that no man, no matter how similar to that of others his social or cultural environment may be, has exactly the same life experiences as any other man, and because, in addition, he brings to the experiences that he does have a variety of inherited characteristics. Therefore, individuality in political behavior cannot be ignored. The idiosyncratic variations in political conduct that are related to what one may loosely call a man's "personality" are, of course, manifold. And though these variations may be similar for certain types of personality, analysis of political behavior in terms of a person's idiosyncratic responses must assume that, in the end, there is something unique in the conduct of every man.

Uniqueness in political behavior is likely to become particularly evident as one moves from the more superficial to the deeper levels of personality. A person's perceptions and opinions are not only his most directly observable responses, but they are also likely to reveal less individuality than his attitudes. When one moves from the level of attitudes to that of motivations, direct observation becomes more difficult, the need for making inferences about psychological aspects of behavior increases, and the factor of individuality is accentuated. Although some degree of rational purposiveness is present in the motivational structure of most men, motivations are often related to unconscious psychological mechanisms that must be explored as essential aspects of an individual's total personality.

Political scientists have long been interested in the "public

NOTE: Here the student is referred to Chapter Four of *The Behavioral Persuasion in Politics,* which develops the view of a "Personal Basis of Political Behavior."

opinion" of the electorate and the "elite opinion" of high governmental decision-makers. But relatively little attention has been given to the opinions of the important stratum of political activists who perform a kind of "middleman function" in the governmental process. In "Local Party Leaders: Groups of Like-Minded Men," Thomas A. Flinn and Frederick M. Wirt explore the opinions on public issues of such political middlemen. The analysis proceeds on two levels—the immediately given level of explicitly stated opinions, and the constructed level of attitude clusters. The evidence supports the idea that local party leaders perform a middleman's function. Their attitudes on state and national issues, for instance, are positively related; furthermore, their attitudes on national issues closely resemble the attitudes of national leaders in the respective parties. As Flinn and Wirt point out, "There is in this way an informal linking of local and national parties."

But neither inter- nor intra-party differences on national and state issues are related to differences in personal characteristics or in background. Rather, these attitudes seem to be corollaries of partisan and other affective associations that either reinforce or weaken a person's stand on particular issues. "At bottom," write Flinn and Wirt, "there is in each party a distinctive issue orientation which apparently cannot be reduced to non-political variables." In other words, partisan attitude structures seem to be of sufficient autonomy and permanence to be reckoned with as quite independent variables in the political process.

The linkage function that party activists perform in the political system is established, in the Flinn and Wirt study, through comparison of relevant attitudes held by local and national leaders. The connection between public and elite attitudes is more directly tackled by Warren E. Miller and Donald E. Stokes in "Constituency Influence in Congress." This is perhaps the most elaborate attempt of its kind to study the nature of this connection and its consequences for the formulation of public policies. Miller and Stokes examine, through correlational analyses, the network of perceptions and attitudes that binds constituents and congressmen to each other, and the effects of this perceptual and attitudinal network on legislative behavior as evidenced in congressional roll calls. The analysis is based on the assumption that, even though they must take definite stands on particular matters, congressmen respond to many issues in terms of fairly broad attitudes, and that their own generalized attitudes and their perceptions of their constituents' generalized attitudes intervene between the public's preferences and their own conduct in legislative decision-making.

The linkage of perceptions, attitudes, and behavior on particular issues is often less complete, however, than the assumption would lead one to expect. It is fairly satisfactory in the case of civil rights, but much less where social welfare and foreign policy are involved. This may be largely due to the very imperfect information that congressmen have about the issue preferences of their constituents, and the limited awareness on the part of constituents about their congressman's policy stands. Nevertheless, the Miller-Stokes study demonstrates both the utility of perceptual and attitudinal research on political behavior and some of the difficulties that are encountered in doing this kind of research in the real world of politics.*

The way in which public attitudes toward politics can actually be "exploited" by the rationally calculating politician who is sensitive to them and to other motivations is suggested by Murray B. Levin and Murray Eden in "Political Strategy for the Alienated Voter." This study is of interest for a variety of reasons, only one of which is the insights it gives into the attitudes and motivations of politically alienated people. By using a sophisticated "rational" model of voting behavior, Levin and Eden show that the alienated voter's orientations and expectations, though admittedly cynical, are by no means as irrational as one might suppose; rather, this voter's attitude toward the political process is ambivalent. Even though his stance is cynical, this very cynicism implies and may actually include an element of trust. When he votes, he seems to suspend judment; his cynicism is reactivated only if a candidate, upon being elected, betrays whatever trust may have existed

*The interested student might find it worthwhile, after reading the Miller and Stokes study, to consult the detailed commentary I have written about it, in collaboration with Katherine Hinckley, "Legislative Behavior and Institutions," in James A. Robinson, ed., *Political Science Annual,* Vol. 1 (Indianapolis: Bobbs-Merrill, 1966).

when the voter went to the polls. For this reason, the rational campaign strategist is confronted with alternatives with consequences difficult to predict. Whether he should stress "style" or "program" in his campaign planning is not easily determinable, for whatever strategy he employs may well backfire because of the alienated voter's initial ambivalence and the readiness with which trust may be transformed into cynicism.

The Levin-Eden study itself may strike some students as rather cynical; yet such an evaluation would miss the study's main point, which is that a rational model of voter and candidate behavior can serve to explain what, on the surface, may appear to be irrational conduct. And the model must at no time be mistaken for the empirical reality that it seeks to explain.

If one sets the Levin-Eden study side by side with Fred I. Greenstein's "Children's Feelings about Political Authority," one is immediately struck by the contrast between juvenile and adult political attitudes. What transforms young children with the favorable attitudes toward political authority that Greenstein discovers into the rather cynical and alienated individuals Levin and Eden find in the adult mass electorate? Clearly, there is no one-to-one relationship between juvenile and adult attitudes; further, the process of transition from childhood to manhood is discontinuous. It is clear, then, that the study of early political socialization is not sufficient to explain adult political attitudes. Yet early political socialization experiences may account for a great deal of the diversity in mature political behavior.

It is now generally recognized that the term "socialization" refers primarily to the process of child development. Yet socialization, like learning, goes on throughout life. This is particularly true of *political* socialization. Greenstein, following the socialization process in some detail, suggests that the greatest change in political attitudes from childhood to adulthood takes place in adolescence. It is a period of disenchantment, resulting from the child's acquisition of increased political knowledge and his need to assume adult ways. Nevertheless, if adult political cynicism is not as widespread as it might be, it is probably due to the profound effect that early childhood experiences with political symbols have on adult political behavior. For it is in childhood that basic orientations crystallize and become part of a man's personality; once having become a part of personality, they persist through adolescence into adult life.

Cynicism is hardly a personality characteristic of political party activists. Samuel J. Eldersveld, in "Motivational Diversity in the Party Hierarchy," shows that local party leaders are motivated by a great variety of drives which may or may not be satisfied by their party activities. It is too simple to assume, as earlier studies had done, that men are driven into politics because they seek power as compensation for personal deprivations. On the contrary, it is because of the diversity of motivations that characterize political activists that the American party system is as loosely organized as it is. As Eldersveld puts it, "The party is a motivationally complex and pluralistic structure."

Although the data of Eldersveld's study are limited to Detroit and Wayne County, it is probable that replication of this research elsewhere would yield pretty much the same results. Perhaps of most interest is the finding that the great majority of precinct leaders changed motivational direction after beginning party work. Moreover, Eldersveld finds considerable inconsistency between role perceptions, goal conceptualizations, and motivational stimuli. The low salience of ideological motivations seems to be due to in-group socialization, which replaces an earlier idealism. The study provides much evidence that the attempt to reduce behavior to simple motivational formulas may seriously distort our understanding of individuality in politics. But it also shows how analysis of political motivations can tell us a great deal about the political parties as behavioral systems.

Of the studies presented here, "Psychological Dimensions of Anomy," by Herbert McClosky and John H. Schaar, searches more broadly and more deeply than any other into the psychodynamics of political behavior. More explicitly indebted to psychological and especially to psychoanalytic personality theory, the authors suggest that the view of modern society as normless, morally chaotic and purposeless—a view usually explained in terms of a person's position and role in the social matrix—is also a function of his intellectual and personality characteristics. The authors' objective is not to replace or invalidate conventional sociological explanations but to supplement them. Employing a variety of attitude scales and personality inventories, McClosky and Schaar show that anomic reactions are related to a number of other personality characteristics, such as anxiety, inflexibility, hostility, ideological extremism, and others.

In other words, anomy as a psychological attribute of the individual seems to be embedded in a complex syndrome of attitudes and motivations that must be probed more deeply than analysis on the level of interpersonal relations can do. Yet even though the data provide only indirect support, McClosky and Schaar suggest that anomy (a sense of "normlessness") is likely to be due to inadequate experiences in interpersonal relations, failures in social communication, and stulted socialization processes in early life. If so, this study would seem to complete the circle of political behavior studies. For it suggests, perhaps more fully than any other part of the research reported in this volume, that political behavior, in order to be understood in all of its complexity, requires examination on all three levels of analysis—the level of social relations, of cultural milieu, and of personality characteristics.

A. *Perceptions and Attitudes*

1 *Local Party Leaders: Groups of Like Minded Men*

by Thomas A. Flinn and Frederick M. Wirt

In the conclusion to his recent survey of opinion data V. O. Key, Jr. remarked,

> . . . as we have sought to explain particular distributions, movements, and qualities of mass opinion, we have had to go beyond the survey data and make assumptions and estimates about the role and behavior of that thin stratum of persons referred to variously as the political elite, the political activists, the leadership echelons, or the influentials. In the normal operation of surveys designed to obtain tests of mass sentiment, so few persons from this activist stratum fall into the sample, that they cannot well be differentiated, even in a status description, from those persons less involved politically. The data tell us almost nothing about the dynamic relations between the upper layer of activists and mass opinion. The missing piece of our puzzle is this elite element of the opinion system.[1]

There are, of course, some data that bear on the attitudes of the leadership stratum. Organizational leaders' attitudes toward civil rights have been studied by Stouffer. Representative role concepts have been examined by Eulau *et al.* with

Reprinted from *Midwest Journal of Political Science*, 9, 1 (February, 1965), 77–98, by permission of the authors and the Wayne State University Press.

reference to state legislators and by Miller with reference to congressmen while a survey of business attitudes of senators was made by Hacker and a survey of policy attitudes of presidential convention delegates by McClosky *et al.*[2] Still the essential correctness of Key's assessment is beyond dispute, and it is the aim of this study to provide some additional information concerning the opinion of political activists, specifically county party leaders in Ohio.[3]

In particular, we wish to describe these party leaders in terms of attitudinal characteristics on public policy issues. This section of our study is in part a replication of McClosky's using, however, a different population. For some this will be mere replication, but we trust that others will agree with us that it is important to see if we know what we think we know and to see whether what is true in one situation is true also in another. An additional objective of our inquiry is to test for the presence of attitude structures. Finally, we will make a serious effort to explain attitudinal differences between and within the parties.

Method

The data were collected by use of a mail questionnaire. In preparation for its mailing, a list was made containing the names of all the chairmen and secretaries of the county central and executive committees of the Ohio Republican and Democratic parties who were elected in 1958 or in 1960. Duplications were eliminated as were the names of officers who had cooperated with an earlier version of the study. A list of 565 remained, 298 Republicans and 267 Democrats. Several waves of questionnaires were sent to them early in 1962. Replies were received from 135 (45%) of the Republicans and from 127 (48%) of the Democrats. Respondents appeared to be representative of the original list of party officers (see the *Appendix* pp. 361–63 on the "Sample").

The questionnaire consisted of three parts, the first dealing with political career, the second with socio-economic characteristics, and the third with opinion on policy issues. The last part, which contained 35 items, provides the larger part of the data to be analyzed here. The first 24 items were the national issue items McClosky used in his study of leader-follower relations.[4] The next 4 items dealt with civil liberties and the last 7 with state government issues. The first 24 items in this series of 35 will be referred to as the national issues schedule, the next 4 as the civil liberties schedule, and the last 7 as the state issues schedule.

In the questionnaire these items were simply listed, national issues first, civil liberties second, and state government issues last. Instructions preceding the list asked respondents to indicate whether they thought government support for an issue should increase, decrease, or remain the same. The three alternative responses were then stated in the space below each listed issue. Incidentally, our instructions were identical with those used by McClosky.

For the purpose of analysis we employed two measures: (1) an "Individual Support Ratio," and (2) a "Party Support Ratio." As will appear, each permits somewhat different analyses. Every respondent received three "Individual Support Ratios" corresponding to the three schedules, and "Party Support Ratios" were computed for each item in the questionnaire. The first measure (ISR) indicates where a respondent stood over a range of topically related issues while the second measure (PSR) shows where all members of each party stood on an issue or set of issues.

As a first step in the computation of Individual Support Ratios we selected 10 items from the national issues schedule.[5] One reason for the move was to reduce the required number of computations. Another was to limit analysis to items with high salience. Determination of salience is, of course, difficult; and doubt may arise concerning the selections that were made. What we did was to choose items which we thought were issues familiar to political activists over a long period of time. Another reason for limiting this analysis to 10 items was to segregate domestic policy from foreign policy on the chance that these are different dimensions of opinion for members of our sample. All of our selected items deal with domestic matters.

The actual procedure used in scoring respondents on each schedule was as follows: every reply favoring increased governmental activity was given a value of 100; every reply favoring decreased governmental activity was given a value of 0; every reply favoring neither an increase nor a decrease was given a value of 50; failures to reply[6] were also given a value of 50. The total value of the responses in each schedule was divided by the number of items in the schedule which yielded an Individual Support Ratio for the schedule. Computation of Party Support Ratios required as a first step the grouping of all Democratic and of all Republican responses to each item in the questionnaire. For each party group replies were then scored in accordance with the procedure described above.[7]

Differences Between and Within the Parties

Our first effort was to determine the extent to which the policy views of Ohio Republican and Democratic leaders differ. The next and closely related task was to measure differences within each party. (Table I.)

Table I. ***Percentage Distribution of Individual Support Ratios by Party and by Issue Schedule***

Individual Support Ratio	National		State		Civil Liberty	
	D	R	D	R	D	R
100-80	21%	0%	14%	2%	49%	62%
79-60	48	7	40	17	26	21
59-40	23	44	36	35	9	13
39-20	6	35	7	30	10	2
19-0	1	14	3	15	5	2
	99%	100%	100%	99%	99%	100%
Mean	64	37	62	42	74	81

On national and state issues the inter-party differences are striking. On national issues, very few Republicans appear in the highest and very few Democrats in the lowest quintile; two-thirds of the Democrats have scores of 60 or more and half of the Republicans have scores under 40. On state issues, very few Republicans appear in the highest and very few Democrats in the lowest quintile; more than half of the Democrats have scores of 60 or more and almost half of the Republicans have scores under 40. The Democratic mean ISR on national and state issues is 64 and 62 respectively compared to 37 and 42 for the Republicans. Democrats are obviously much more in favor of governmental activity than Republicans, whether that government be in Washington or

Columbus. It should be added, however, that there is an area of overlap in regard to both national and state issues; that is, there are Republicans and Democrats at the center in terms of ISR scores who agree with each other despite differences in party membership.

With reference to civil liberties, members of both parties urge stronger governmental action to restrain films, teachers, and Communists, with one-half of the Democrats and three-fifths of the Republicans placing in the highest ISR quintile. At the other end of the scale, there are more Democrats than Republicans with ISRs under 40, and the Democratic mean is slightly lower than the Republican. In general, the leaders of neither party appear as libertarians although the Democratic position seems to be a little less strongly anti-libertarian than is the Republican.

Another inference which may be drawn from Table I is that a high level of intra-party agreement exists with some exceptions and qualifications. This is an inference which we cannot "prove" statistically, but we can show how we reasoned from the quantitative data to the qualitative judgment. Note that on national issues about 70% of the Democrats are in the range from 40 to 80. In other words, the large majority of the party favors the status quo or offers moderate support for increased governmental activity, which appears to us to be a narrow range of opinion. The same thing may be said of the Republicans in regard to national issues with the differences that the range of opinion in the large majority of the party is from the status quo to moderate preference for less governmental activity. On state issues the range and character of opinion in each party is much the same as on national issues with the exception that the Republicans in particular show a slightly greater range of opinion. In the area of civil liberties the Republicans are united, but the Democrats show signs of intra-party conflict. Thus we agree with McClosky's conclusion that examination "of the opinions of Democratic and Republican leaders (on national issues) shows them to be distinct communities of co-believers. . . ."[8] We would add that this statement applies only slightly less well to state issues but substantially less well to questions involving civil liberties.

Party stands on specific issues are shown by Table II.

Table II. ***Democratic and Republican Party Support Ratios, Issues Listed in Order of Greatest to Least Disagreement by Schedule***

Issue	Subject National Issues	Dem.	Rep.	D-R
1	Federal Aid to Education	76	31	45
2	Business Regulation	48	13	35
3	Social Security Benefits	86	53	33
4	Slum Clearance & Public Housing	87	59	28
5	Public Ownership of Resources	70	42	28
6	Utility Regulation	77	50	27
7	Foreign Aid	37	10	27
8	Reliance on the UN	67	40	27
9	Minimum Wages	76	49	27
10	Corporate Income Tax	54	28	26
11	Tariffs	31	54	–23
12	Farm Price Supports	38	18	20
13	Tax on Business	43	23	20
14	Tax on Large Incomes	59	39	20
15	US Participation in Military Alliances	65	47	18
16	Enforcement of Integration	65	47	18
17	Public Control of Atomic Energy	72	56	16
18	Defense Spending	54	41	13
19	Tax on Middle Incomes	36	25	11
20	Trade Union Regulation	74	66	8
21	Immigration	33	27	6
22	Restrictions on Credit	60	54	6
23	Tax on Small Incomes	13	16	–3
24	Enforcement of Anti-Trust	64	63	1
	State Issues			
25	Level of State Services	69	39	30
26	State Taxes	58	32	26
27	Unemployment Compensation	56	31	25
28	Mental Health Program	94	75	19
29	Estb State Corp. Income Tax	42	24	18
30	State Aid to Education	79	63	16
31	Estb State Individual Income Tax	37	25	12
	Civil Liberties Issues			
32	Loyalty Oaths for Teachers	66	80	–14
33	Investigation of Communism	71	85	–14
34	Enforcement of Laws Against Communism	87	96	–9
35	Motion Picture Censorship	69	68	1

The data may be more easily grasped if issues are collected in subject matter categories, and for this purpose we use the categories employed by McClosky with the addition of state and civil liberties categories. The stand of each party in each issue category is designated as the mean of all PSRs in the group. Thus we find that Democratic and Republican positions in various issue categories are as shown in Table IIa.

Table IIa. ***Democratic and Republican Party Support Ratios by Categories of Policy Issues***

	Dem.	Rep.	D-R
Equalitarianism and Human Welfare (items 1, 3, 4, 9, 16, and 21)	70	44	26
Foreign Policy (items 7, 8, 15, and 18)	56	34	22
Public Ownership (items 5 and 17)	71	49	22
Taxes (items 10, 13, 14, 19, and 23)	41	26	15
Govtl Regulation of the Economy (items, 2, 6, 11, 12, 20, 22, and 24)	56	45	11
State Issues (items 25, 26, 27, 28, 29, 30, and 31)	62	41	21
Civil Liberties (items 32, 33, 34, and 35)	73	82	–9

Mean differences are fairly large in all categories with the exception of the categories labeled "Governmental Regulation of the Economy" and "Civil Liberties"; but even in the first of these two categories there are some items on which party differences are substantial, i.e., business regulation (35 points difference), utility regulation (27 points difference), and farm price supports (20 points difference).

Additional use may be made of the data in Table II by making the rearrangement shown in Table III.

Table III. ***Distribution of Party Support Ratios on 35 Policy Issues***

Rep. PSR	Dem. PSR 0-25	26-45	46-55	56-75	76-100
0-25	1	6	1		—
26-45	—	1	2	6	1
46-55	—	1	—	3	3
56-75	—	—	—	4	3
76-100	—	—	—	2	1

NOTE: Boxed categories are those which contain issues on which Democratic and Republican PSRs fall in the same range.

An illustration may make reading of the table easier. The item which appears in the top row and in the center column is the item, "Regulation of Business" (item 2). The Democrats had a PSR of 48 and the Republicans a PSR of 13.

Proceeding now to inferences, note that only 7 of the 35

issues fall into the boxed categories. The measure is rough, but one can only conclude that the parties disagree much more than they agree. Note also that 23 Democratic Party Support Ratios fall to the right of the vertical lines and that only 10 Republican Party Support ratios fall below the horizontal lines indicating that the Democrats are much more than the Republicans in favor of governmental activity. These conclusions coincide, of course, with those made earlier on the basis of analysis of Individual Support Ratios.

So far, heavy emphasis has been laid upon inter-party disagreeements, but further analysis of the data in Table II reveals an unexpected area of agreement between the parties. The item on the national issues schedule which Ohio Democrats support most strongly is slum clearance and public housing, and their second favorite is social security benefits. Ohio Republicans also give these issues strong support relative to the support they give other issues. More systematic investigation of the order of preferences expressed by Democratic and by Republican leaders shows that there is on the national issues schedule a rank order of correlation of plus .64. On the state issues schedule there is an even higher rank order correlation: plus .80.[9] It is obvious that Democratic and Republican respondents agree fairly well on priorities although the Democrats are more in favor of government action than are the Republicans.

Attitude Structure

It is occasionally asserted that the good conservative not only opposes governmental regulation of economic relations but also governmental interference with individual non-property rights or that the true liberal favors government action to deal with economic and social problems but opposes governmental interference with freedom of speech and assembly. Stripped of their normative content, such statements are actually hypotheses concerning attitude structures; that is, they assert that attitudes on one subject predict attitudes on another due to some common underlying dimension of opinion.

One way to test for the presence of attitude structures is to correlate scores on one attitude test with scores on another attitude test, and that was done in this study. What we did, for instance, was to take the individual scores of all Democratic respondents on the 10 selected national issues and to correlate these with the scores of the same respondents on state issues and then on civil liberties issues. Results are reported in Table IV.

Table IV. ***Product Moment Coefficients Expressing Correlations Between Individual Support Ratios on Three Schedules by Party Affiliation***

	Democrats			Republicans		
	Natl.	State	Civ. Lib.	Natl.	State	Civ. Lib.
Civil liberties	−.073	−.099	—	+.077	+.025	—
National issues	—	+.525	−.073	—	+.519	+.077
State issues	+.525	—	−.099	+.519	—	+.025

It appears that ISR scores on national issues relate positively to ISR scores on state government issues and that the relationship is virtually the same for Democrats as for Republicans, .525 and .519 respectively. A party official who views national government action favorably is also favorable to state government action; the same consistency holds if one desires that government restrain its action. Party leaders in Ohio evidently do not endorse the argument that federal activities should be restrained in order to create greater opportunities for state government action. It must be added, however, that national issue positions predict state issue positions imperfectly since there is considerable unexplained variance.

Further inspection of Table IV shows that there is no relation between responses to national issues and responses to civil liberties issues no matter which party group is viewed. The same is true with regard to the relation of state issues to civil liberties issues. Evidently our respondents put the liberties questions in one compartment different from and unrelated to national and state policy questions.

We conclude that the data support the view that pro-government action views on national policy tends to predict somewhat similar views on state policy. However, the data contradict the notion that pro-government action views related to the handling of social and economic matters correlates positively and closely with civil libertarianism. These are different dimensions of opinion. It also appears that on these points opinion structure in the two major parties is essentially similar.

Sources of Opinion

So far analysis has indicated that each set of Ohio party leaders tends to be a group of "co-believers" whose outlook differs substantially from that of the opposite set of party leaders and that there are underlying ideologies. One explanation may be that Democrats, for example, agree among themselves and disagree with Republicans because of a common socio-economic background which is different from that of the Republicans; and our data permit us to test this hypothesis in several operational forms.

It is possible that inter-party disagreement arises because Republican leaders have high incomes and Democratic leaders relatively low incomes. The facts are, however, contrary to the hypothesis (See Table V). There are in each party considerable differences in the income of leaders, but the distribution of income within the respective parties is surprisingly parallel (Table V).

Table V. ***Percentage Distribution of Ohio Party Leaders by Income and by Party***

	Under $5000	$5-7500	$7500-$10,000	$10-15,000	Over $15,000	
Dems. (N = 120)*	15%	31%	27%	17%	10%	100%
Reps. (N = 125)*	21%	30%	23%	16%	10%	100%

*The number of responses reported in the table is less than the total number of respondents because a few members of each party did not reply to the income question.

Similar analyses can be made substituting other factors for income. In Table VI that is done by introduction of the variables: age, education, and occupation.

It may be seen easily that there are age, educational, and occupational differences in each party and that the distribution does not vary with party with one exception: the number of housewives and the number of hourly paid workers is somewhat greater in the Democratic group than in the

Republican group which includes on the other hand relatively more farmers; however, these occupational differences are not great. It seems fair to say that the similarities are more striking than the differences. Thus it appears that the leadership levels of the Ohio Democratic and Republican parties do not differ substantially with respect to income, age, education, and occupation.

Table VI. ***Percentage Distribution of Ohio Party Leaders by Age, Education, Occupation and by Party***

Age	26-35	36-45	46-55	56-65	65 +
Dems. (N = 126)*	6%	26%	35%	22%	10%
Reps. (N = 130)*	4%	25%	34%	18%	18%

Education	*Completed 8 Grades*	*Completed 9-11 Grades*	*Completed 12 Grades*	*Attended College*	*College Degree*	*Advanced Degree*
Dems. (N = 123)*	5%	6%	35%	21%	13%	20%
Reps. (N = 128)*	2%	5%	35%	21%	16%	20%

Occupation	*Housewife*	*Lawyer*	*Other Prof.*	*Business Self-Employed*	*Business Salaried*	*Clerical*	*Hourly Pd. Manual*	*Farmer*	*Other*
Dems. (N = 124)*	10%	18%	3%	26%	6%	4%	11%	6%	15%
Reps. (N = 126)*	5%	19%	4%	27%	5%	3%	6%	20%	11%

*The number of responses reported in the table is less than the total number of respondents since a few members of each party did not reply to one or more of the relevant items.

They do, however, differ with respect to religion. Twenty-seven per cent of the Democratic respondents who gave their religious affiliation (N = 124) were Roman Catholics, 72% were Protestants, and 1 Democrat stated that he had no religious affiliation. In contrast to the Democrats, only 8% of the Republicans who gave their religious affiliation (N = 130) were Roman Catholics and 92% were Protestants. One Republican stated that he belonged to no religious group. It is conceivable that part of the difference between Democratic and Republican policy preferences may be due to differences in religious background. Inspection of Table VII suggests no strong relationship between religious affiliation and opinion within the respective parties. The chi-square test confirms what inspection suggests: it produces no value significant at the .10 level. It is interesting to note in particular that religious affiliation does not relate significantly to leadership opinion on civil liberties, a finding which is contrary to Stouffer's finding that Roman Catholics living in the north are slightly less sympathetic to civil liberties claims than are Protestants in the same region;[10] however, not too much should be made of this point since the number of Roman Catholics in our sample of party leaders is small. The principal point to be made here is that religious affiliation does not relate significantly to intra-party difference of opinion

Table VII. ***Distribution of Individual Support Ratios Around the Party Mean by Religious Affiliation***

	Natl. ISR		State ISR		Civ. Lib. ISR	
	Mean or Above	*Below Mean*	*Mean or Above*	*Below Mean*	*Mean or Above*	*Below Mean*
Dems.						
RC	17	17	18	16	23	11
P	48	41	49	40	54	35
Reps.						
RC	4	6	7	3	8	2
P	61	58	63	56	70	49

and hence cannot explain differences between Republicans and Democrats.

Therefore, our general conclusion is that leaders of the two parties do not differ in attitudes toward public policy issues because of differences in background. It appears that the contrasting attitudes and attitude structures which divide Republicans from Democrats relate to party itself and not to some other factor lurking behind or operating through party.[11]

Not only are there differences between the parties but also within each and some effort should be made to explain their presence. It has already been stated that they do not relate to religious affiliation; but it is possible, of course, that these differences do relate to some other socio-economic or demographic factors. Evidence is provided by Table VIII.

Table VIII. ***Product Moment Correlations of Selected Variables with ISRs by Party***

	Natl. ISR		State ISR		Civ. Lib. ISR	
	Rep.	*Dem.*	*Rep.*	*Dem.*	*Rep.*	*Dem.*
Age	.03	.04	–.09	–.09	–.01	.28
Ed.	–.19	–.13	.06	.00	–.30	–.44
Inc.	–.18	–.18	–.03	–.06	–.30	–.23
% U	–.05	.11	.07	.01	–.01	–.18
% M&M	–.08	.00	.04	–.07	.00	.00
% RF	.09	.01	–.14	.06	–.02	.10
Ct. Hse.	–.05	.05	.01	.11	–.13	.04
% Dem.	.09	.07	.15	.08	.23	.01

Legend:
Age–age with values assigned from lowest to highest age category.
Ed.–education with values assigned from lowest to highest grade completed.
Inc.–income with values assigned from lowest to highest income category.
% U–per cent of county population classified urban in 1950.
% M&M–per cent of county population employed in mining and manufacturing in 1950.
% RF–per cent of county population classified rural farm in 1950.
Ct. Hse.–county court houses classified as Democratic, Mixed, and Republican according to the number of victories won by each party in 1956 and 1958 elections excepting the office of coroner; values assigned from least to most Republican.
% Dem.–county median Democratic vote for president, 1940–1956 (5 elections).

The independent variables in Table VIII are of three kinds: (1) personal, i.e., age, education, and income; (2) ecological, i.e., per cent urban, per cent mining and manufacturing, and per cent rural farm; and (3) electoral, i.e., party control of court house offices and median percentage of the presidential vote, 1940–1956. In general, no variable has a consistently close relation to attitudes in policy issues, and in no *instance* does any single variable explain more than 20 per cent of the variation in Individual Support Ratios within either party.

In the areas of state and national issues there is no relationship as strong as .2, which is very weak, of course. In regard to civil liberties, it can be noted that there are some stronger relationships. They indicate that low ISRs (i.e., the more libertarian outlook) are associated with high income, high education, and youth which is a finding consistent with Stouffer's finding that higher occupational status, higher educational achievement, and youth are positively related to tolerance[12] assuming a rough equivalence of occupational status and income. It appears also that age has a negative relation to civil liberties in the Democratic Party. The most interesting feature of this analysis is that certain personal variables operate to influence opinion most strongly in the area of civil liberties where party ideology does not run. Its absence evidently frees and permits the operation of factors associated particularly with education and income.

Another explanation for differences of opinion within the parties in addition to those explored above is that these differences relate to the personal associations of leaders, with those who associate most with persons of the same party taking policy positions most consistent with the dominant tendency in their own party. To test this hypothesis leaders of each party were divided into classes according to the politics of their friends, and mean class ISRs were computed. (Some respondents were not included in this analysis since they had failed to answer one or more questions concerning the politics of their friends.) Analysis of variance was deemed an appropriate and flexible method for determining the relation of these personal associations to attitudes.[13] Results are reported in a series of equations which are forms of the equation.

$$S = b_1A_1 + b_2A_2 + b_3A_3 \ldots$$

where S is the *actual* line of regression, b the class mean, and A_1, A_2, etc. the classes. The object is, of course, to discover how much of the variance can be accounted for by classification in terms of the specified variable; and this is expressed by R-values which if squared state the per cent of total variance which is explained.

The Republicans were divided into 6 classes with the aim being to create the largest possible number of classes without establishing classes with excessively few members. In the case of Republicans, however, it was impossible to avoid the creation of one very large class since the pattern dominant in the party was association with friends of the same party. The same thing was less true of the Democrats. Analysis of Individual Support Ratios on national issues yields the following:

$$S = 34A_1 + 38A_2 + 32A_3 + 51A_4 + 51A_5 + 38A_6$$
$$R = .402$$

where A_1 is a class whose members associate most with Republicans and A_2 is a class whose members associate next most frequently with Republicans, etc. The finding is in accord with the hypothesis. Combination of classes 1, 2, and 3 (Ns = 70, 12, and 7 respectively) and of classes 4, 5, and 6 (Ns = 7, 5, and 7) straightens the line of regression with this result:

$$S = 34A_{1\text{-}2\text{-}3} + 47A_{4\text{-}5\text{-}6}$$
$$R = .357$$

In words, Republicans who associate less with members of their own party give most support to government action, a position characteristic of Democrats; however, it should be added quickly that only a relatively small part of intra-party variance is accounted for in this way.

Analysis of Individual Support Ratios on state issues yields the following outcome:

$$S = 39A_1 + 48A_2 + 44A_3 + 45A_4 + 55A_5 + 45A_6$$
$$R = .229$$

Reduction to 2 classes (A_1 and $A_{2\text{-}6}$) which seems reasonable, given the shape of the line of regression, yields this result:

$$S = 39A_1 + 47A_{2\text{-}3\text{-}4\text{-}5\text{-}6}$$
$$R = .199$$

The outcome is in accord with the hypothesis, but the relation between the variables is very weak.

Similar consideration of individual responses to civil liberties issues produces the following result:

$$S = 80A_1 + 79A_2 + 88A_3 + 93A_4 + 80A_5 + 87A_6$$
$$R = .193$$

Reduction to 2 classes seems to be in order. Analysis produces the following:

$$S = 80A_{1\text{-}2} + 87A_{3\text{-}4\text{-}5\text{-}6}$$
$$R = .158$$

Thus, it appears that Republicans who associate less with

members of their own party support the party position more than others, a finding which is contrary to the hypothesis; however, it would be a mistake to rest much on this finding since the relation between the variables is almost negligible.

The Democrats were divided into 4 classes with the aim again being to create the largest number of classes without establishing excessively small ones. The number of members in each class is as follows: $A_1 = 41$, $A_2 = 28$, $A_3 = 24$, and $A_4 = 10$. Analysis of Individual Support Ratios on national issues yields the following:

$$S = 72A_1 + 67A_2 + 55A_3 + 55A_4$$
$$R = .473$$

where A_1 is a class whose members associate most with Democrats, A_2 is a class whose members associate next most frequently with Democrats, etc. It can be seen that Democrats whose friendships are less with other Democrats give less support to national issues, a finding which supports the hypothesis.

Analysis of Individual Support Ratios on state issues yields this result:

$$S = 67A_1 + 66A_2 + 60A_3 + 58A_4$$
$$R = .194$$

The line of regression is in accord with the hypothesis, but very little is explained by classification.

Similar consideration of individual responses to civil liberties issues produces the following result:

$$S = 77A_1 + 75A_2 + 69A_3 + 54A_4$$
$$R = .260$$

It appears that Democrats who associate more than others with non-Democrats are more favorable to civil liberties. Evidently this group of Democrats helps to give the Democratic leadership group the appearance of being slightly more libertarian than the Republican; however, it must be quickly added that the relation between the politics of friends and attitudes on civil liberties is weak even though the line of regression is consistent with the hypothesis.

To summarize this section, we can say that Republican and Democratic leaders who associate more with members of their own party have attitudes more consistent with the tendency of their party on national issues than do other leaders. The same statement may be made with reference to state issues, but the relation is substantially weaker. The relation between the politics of friends and attitudes on civil liberties issues varies in direction with party and is strong in neither case, but this is not surprising. It has been noted that civil liberties is a dimension of opinion apart from national and state issues and that party positions on civil liberties are neither distinctive nor well established. Consequently, it is reasonable to expect that the partisan preference of friends will have little to do with opinion on liberties issues.

State and National Leaders

So far our analysis has been confined to the attitudes of county party leaders in Ohio. It is possible to add another dimension by comparing their attitudes with the attitudes of national party leaders[14] as reported by McClosky. In an item by item comparison of responses to national issues Ohio Republicans show higher support ratios (PSRs) than do national Republicans on 9 items, lower support ratios on 12 items, and the same support ratio on 3 items. The median difference is 5 points. We may conclude that Ohio Republican leaders are slightly less in favor of governmental action than were national Republican leaders; however, it is the essential similarity of outlook which must be emphasized. Furthermore, issues receiving relatively strong support from one group also receive relatively strong support from the other. The order of preference shown by these 2 groups correlates with a coefficient of plus .928.[15]

Ohio Democratic leaders show higher support ratios (PSRs) than do national Democratic leaders on 17 national issues, lower support ratios on 5 national issues, and the same support ratio on 2 other national issues. The median difference is 5 points. Thus Ohio Democrats emerge as being somewhat more sympathetic to governmental action than were Democratic national leaders, but once again it is the essential similarity between the state and national groups which must be emphasized. Furthermore, issues popular with one group are popular with the other; and issues opposed by one are likely to be opposed by the other. The order of preference shown by the 2 Democratic groups correlates with a coefficient of plus .867.[16]

It is a fair inference to say that the opinions of county party leaders in Ohio are not unique. They resemble closely the opinions of national party leaders even though Ohio Democratic leaders are slightly more "liberal" than national Democratic leaders and Ohio Republican leaders, slightly more "conservative" than their opposite numbers. There is, therefore, an informal linkage between important leaders in basic units of party organization on the one hand and on the other leaders who may be identified as belonging to the national party. This is a finding which contrasts with the many facts demonstrating the federal and local character of American parties.

Summary

1. Ohio Democratic and Republican leaders differ sharply on issues involving national and state government policies with Democrats favoring relatively more governmental action than Republicans. The difference is slightly greater on national than on state issues.

2. The national issues which show the greatest inter-party conflict are such familiar items as slum clearance and public housing, federal aid to education, and social security benefits.

3. Democrats and Republicans agree on priorities or on their order of preferences concerning national and state issues despite generally different attitudes towards government action.

4. In the area of civil liberties both leadership groups strongly favor government action which has the effect of restraining the liberties involved; Democrats are, however, slightly less anti-libertarian than Republicans.

5. Each group of party leaders tends to be internally united although there are differences of opinion within each party on national, state, and civil liberties issues. Internal unity is greatest on national issues, slightly less on state issues, and least on civil liberties issues where the Democrats can hardly be said to be united at all.

6. The attitude of individual leaders to national issues relates positively to their attitudes toward state issues. Leaders

favoring federal action tend also to favor state action. There are what may be called government action and government inaction ideologies.

7. Attitudes toward civil liberties cannot be predicted, however, by attitudes toward either state or national issues. Civil liberties is a separate dimension of opinion.

8. Inter-party differences of opinion cannot be attributed to differences in the backgrounds of Democratic and Republican leaders since these differences are either non-existent or unrelated to opinion.

9. Differences of opinion within the respective parties concerning national and state issues do not relate to differences in personal background, county demography, and county politics unless some very weak relations are counted as exceptions.

10. Intra-party differences of opinion concerning civil liberties are, however, related to income, education, and age. Higher income, extended education, and youth relate positively to libertarian positions. The absence of government action ideologies in this area evidently permits operation of these factors.

11. Leaders whose friends mostly belong to their own party show on national issues attitudes more consistent with the dominant tendency of their party. The same statement may be made concerning the relation of personal associations to state issues, but the relationship is weak.

12. The partisan preferences of friends relate to opinion on civil liberties in a way which is contradictory and inconclusive, but this is reasonable since stands on these issues have little relation to party affiliation.

13. Ohio Democratic and Republican leaders have attitudes on national issues which closely resemble the attitudes of the national leaders of their respective parties. There is in this way an informal linking of local and national parties.

14. In general, there is a consistent point of view on national and state issues within each party which is shared by most of their members and which contrasts with that of the opposing party. Neither inter-party nor intra-party differences on national and state issues can be attributed to differences in personal characteristics or in background. Inter-party differences are based on attitudes which we think are corollaries of party membership and leadership, and intra-party differ-

ences are to some extent consequences of the politics of friends.

In other words, party leaders are not issue neutrals. Furthermore, their attitudes on national and state issues are not functions of social status. Rather, these attitudes may well be correlates of party itself (or of some variable which we neither locate nor suggest) and of associations which re-enforce or wear away loyalties to party stands. These statements are more true when applied to national issues than to state issues which are tied a little less closely to party. At bottom, there is in each party a distinctive issue orientation which apparently cannot be reduced to non-political variables.

Different conclusions are in order when civil liberties are considered. Both groups of Ohio party leaders are generally anti-libertarian. However, intra-party differences exist; and they relate to variables which have been found in other studies to affect attitudes on civil liberties issues. Most important for this study is the fact that views on civil liberties are not to any significant extent a part of the well-developed issue orientations which distinguish Republican leaders from Democratic leaders.

Comment

Political parties have been described in terms of the face they show the electorate. One type is the party which emphasizes policy and which seeks to clarify and perhaps to magnify differences between groups in the electorate in order to gain the cherished goal which is, of course, public office. Another type is the party which de-emphasizes policy and which seeks to blur and minimize group conflict in order to gain majority support; and this kind of party is in some circles referred to with approval as an agent of consensus, a not too well defined condition which is presumably healthy. This concept supposes relatively free manipulation of issues for electoral advantage. A closely related concept of party is that of party as the "honest broker." It maintains that party goes between competing groups, offers compromises without prejudice, and through its own electoral success or failure reflects in policy the strength of the contending groups. Another view of party, often advanced only for the purpose of presenting an error with which to contrast the truth, is that of party as a group of like-minded men banded together in order to win the offices required for the effective expression of their common convictions (the Burkean view).

Our finding is that local party leaders in Ohio tend to be groups of like-minded men whose agreement is not easily reducible to something other than membership and leadership in party itself. This lends support to the Burkean view of party, although we would not for a moment claim it is a completely adequate view since party is, after all, a complex phenomenon that varies from time to time and place to place. Conversely, our finding suggests that contrasting views of party ought not to be swallowed whole.

The fact that our party leaders are not issue neutrals suggests that they may not be able to freely manipulate issues for the sake of electoral triumph as the agency of consensus model of party activity supposes. They may well take risks for what they themselves prefer, and their preferences may prejudice what appear to be purely "practical" decisions about the use of issues. Along the same line, it is to be doubted whether parties are honest brokers; and adding an impression which is outside those suggested by our data, we doubt that many major interest groups suppose that the parties are honest brokers. We would suggest instead that, at least, the party organizations we have considered are composed of leaders who have definite policy preferences which will influence their perception of electoral necessities and their tactical decisions. A model of American party politics presuming free maneuver by leaders exclusively concerned with electoral victory is dubious. One last important implication of our findings is that party may well have the function of providing a method for the expression of ideology in political life, a function groups organized around one or a few issues cannot perform easily; and we would add that in our opinion this function may be needed in a viable democratic system.

Appendix: The Respondents as a Sample

Our respondents constituted an accidental or self-selected sample, but we are convinced that they are representative and that the sample is not seriously biased. Our reasons are as follows: (A) The whole population is homogeneous in that all members have more than usual interest and involvement in politics or, at least, that can be safely assumed. (B) Respondents were compared with non-respondents in regard to place of residence and it was found that the two groups were generally similar with reference to county demography and politics. For example, respondents were neither more nor less urban than non-respondents. (C) Attitude scores of early respondents were compared with those of later respondents. The theory was that if non-residents differed from respondents in attitude the later respondents would differ from earlier in the same way but to lesser degree. There was, however, no significant difference between early and late Democratic respondents in attitude toward any set of issues. Nor did early and late Republican respondents differ in attitude toward state and civil liberty issues; they did differ on national issues with late respondents being more in favor of government action ($X^2 = 8.8$, df = 1). However, the relation was weak (phi coefficient = .259); so we once again concluded respondents and non-respondents were probably similar. (D) A small random sample was collected (some of it as much as a year or more after the first sample) for the purpose of comparing its characteristics with those of the larger self-selected sample. Insofar as possible the two samples were compared item by item through the use of chi-square tests. We found that there was a probability of .7 or higher that differences in regard to age, place of residence, and politics of friends were due to chance. The probabilities for education were .3 and .4 respectively for the Democrats and Republicans. On the 19 national issues where it was possible to compare Democrats in the random sample and Democrats in the self-selected sample it was found that there was a probability of .9 or higher that differences on 7 items were due to chance. The probability was .7 or .8 on another 7 items, and .5 on 3 other items. On only 2 items were probabilities as low as .3. They were the items dealing with military alliances and with integration. It is possible that the former was a fairly meaningless issue and that opinion on the latter had changed. Neither of these items was used in computing Individual Support Ratios. Comparison of Republicans in the 2 samples on national issues produces the same general pattern; that is, there is a very strong probability that nearly all differences are due to chance. There are 2 exceptions. One is the item dealing with restrictions on credit, but we are confident this issue was virtually without meaning in 1962–1963. The other exception is responses to several tax items. Members of the random and later sample were significantly less in favor of tax cutting than were members of the self-selected and earlier sample. This difference may easily be attributed to changes of opinion since the clearly articulated Republican Party position in 1963 was opposition to tax cuts. Thirteen chi-square tests were run on state issues, 6 comparing the 2 groups of Republicans and 7 the 2 groups of Democrats. On 4 issues the probabilities were .9 or higher, on 3 issues .8, on 4 issues .5, and on only 2 issues lower than .5. It was not possible to run chi-square tests on Republican responses to civil liberties items, but inspection of the frequencies shows little difference between the samples. Chi-square tests were run on Democratic responses to 3 civil liberties items, and produced in each case a probability of .3. Random and later respondents were somewhat more libertarian on these issues. Differences might be due to bias, changes of opinion, or to instability of opinion. In view of the fact that the 2 samples resemble each other closely over a long range of national and state issues we are inclined to rule out bias. Evidence in this study suggests that opinion on civil liberties may not be very well organized and that instability may be the explanation. In general, we feel that our self-selected sample has the characteristics of our random sample.

Notes:

1. *Public Opinion and American Democracy* (New York: Knopf, 1961), p. 537.

2. Samuel A. Stouffer, *Communism, Conformity, and Civil Liberties* (New York: Doubleday, 1955). Eulau *et al.*, "The Role of the Representative: Some Empirical Observations on the Theory of Edmund Burke," *American Political Science Review* (Sept., 1959), pp. 742–756. Warren Miller, "Majority Rule and the Representative System," paper delivered at the 1962 APSA meeting. Andrew Hacker, "The Elected and the Anointed: Two American Elites," *American Political Science Review* (Sept., 1961), pp. 539–549. Herbert McClosky *et al.*, "Issue Conflict and Consensus Among Party Leaders and Followers," *American Political Science Review* (June, 1960), pp. 406–427.

3. The studies on which the publication is based were made under a grant from The Maurice and Laura Falk Foundation of Pittsburgh through the Eagleton Institute of Politics, Rutgers, The State University. However, the Foundation is not the author, publisher, or proprietor of this publication and is not to be understood as endorsing, by virtue of its

grant, any of the statements made or views expressed herein. Gratefully appreciated and necessary assistance has come also from the Ohio Center for Education in Politics and from a Ford Fund grant to Oberlin College for the study of public affairs.

4. McClosky *et al., op. cit.*

5. The items selected were those which appear in Table II with the following numbers: 1, 2, 3, 6, 9, 10, 12, 13, 14, 24. It may be of interest to note we have subsequently discovered that these items when applied to a population of state legislators constitute a Guttman scale.

6. Nearly all respondents completed every item in the opinion section of the questionnaire.

7. The procedure was devised by McClosky with the exception that a scale of 100 is used here while he used a scale ranging from .00 to 1.00. In a subsequent comparison of the Ohio findings with McClosky's, his scores are converted to the scale of 100.

8. McClosky, *op. cit.,* p. 426.

9. The coefficients are Spearman rank order correlation coefficients.

10. Stouffer, *op. cit.,* p. 144.

11. Note that we do not attempt to say whether the development of attitudes and ideology precede or follow identification with the party and entrance to its leadership level. One study, at least, suggests that the development of similar attitudes in a party member follows rather than precedes party "membership." Belknap and Campbell, "Political Party Identification and Attitudes Toward Foreign Policy," *Public Opinion Quarterly* (Winter, 1951–52), pp. 601–623.

12. *Ibid.,* p. 139 and pp. 89–93.

13. See A. M. Mood, *Introduction to the Theory of Statistics* (New York: McGraw-Hill, 1950), pp. 318–326.

14. McClosky defined national leaders as delegates to the 1956 national conventions.

15. The coefficient is a Spearman rank order correlation coefficient.

16. *Idem.*

2 *Constituency Influence in Congress**

by Warren E. Miller and Donald E. Stokes

Substantial constituency influence over the lower house of Congress is commonly thought to be both a normative principle and a factual truth of America government. From their draft constitution we may assume the Founding Fathers expected it, and many political scientists feel, regretfully, that the Framers' wish has come all too true.[1] Nevertheless, much of the evidence of constituency control rests on inference. The fact that our House of Representatives, especially by comparison with the House of Commons, has irregular party voting does not of itself indicate that Congressmen deviate from party in response to local pressure. And even more, the fact that many Congressmen *feel* pressure from home does not of itself establish that the local constituency is performing any of the acts that a reasonable definition of control would imply.

Constituency Control in the Normative Theory of Representation

Control by the local constituency is at one pole of *both* the great normative controversies about representation that have arisen in modern times. It is generally recognized that con-

Reprinted from *American Political Science Review,* 57 (March, 1963), 45–56, by permission of the authors and the publisher.

*The research reported here was made possible through grants of the Rockefeller Foundation and the Social Science Research Council, whose support is gratefully acknowledged. The authors are indebted also to Ralph Bisco and Gudmund R. Iversen for invaluable assistance.

stituency control is opposite to the conception of representation associated with Edmund Burke. Burke wanted the representative to serve the constituency's *interest* but not its *will,* and the extent to which the representative should be compelled by electoral sanctions to follow the "mandate" of his constituents has been at the heart of the ensuing controversy as it has continued for a century and a half.[2]

Constituency control also is opposite to the conception of government by responsible national parties. This is widely seen, yet the point is rarely connected with normative discussions of representation. Indeed, it is remarkable how little attention has been given to the model of representation implicit in the doctrine of a "responsible two-party system." When the subject of representation is broached among political scientists the classical argument between Burke and his opponents is likely to come at once to mind. So great is Burke's influence that the antithesis he proposed still provides the categories of thought used in contemporary treatments of representation despite the fact that many students of politics today would advocate a relationship between representative and constituency that fits *neither* position of the mandate-independence controversy.

The conception of representation implicit in the doctrine of responsible parties shares the idea of popular control with the instructed-delegate model. Both are versions of popular sovereignty. But "the people" of the responsible two-party system are conceived in terms of a national rather than a local constituency. Candidates for legislative office appeal to the electorate in terms of a *national* party program and leadership, to which, if elected, they will be committed. Expressions of policy preference by the local district are reduced to endorsements of one or another of these programs, and the local district retains only the arithmetical significance that whichever party can rally to its program the greater number of supporters in the district will control its legislative seat.

No one tradition of representation has entirely dominated American practice. Elements of the Burkean, instructed-delegate, and responsible party models can all be found in our political life. Yet if the American system has elements of all three, a good deal depends on how they are combined. Especially critical is the question whether different models of representation apply to different public issues. Is the saliency of legislative action to the public so different in quality and degree on different issues that the legislator is subject to very different constraints from his constituency? Does the legislator have a single generalized mode of response to his constituency that is rooted in a normative belief about the representative's role or does the same legislator respond to his constituency differently on different issues? More evidence is needed on matters so fundamental to our system.

An Empirical Study of Representation

To extend what we know of representation in the American Congress the Survey Research Center of The University of Michigan interviewed the incumbent Congressman, his non-incumbent opponent (if any), and a sample of constituents in each of 116 congressional districts, which were themselves a probability sample of all districts.[3] These interviews, conducted immediately after the congressional election of 1958, explored a wide range of attitudes and perceptions held by the individuals who play the reciprocal roles of the representative relation in national government. The distinguishing feature of this research is, of course, that it sought direct information from both constituent and legislator (actual and aspiring). To this fund of comparative interview data has been added information about the roll call votes of our sample of Congressmen and the political and social characteristics of the districts they represent.

Many students of politics, with excellent reason, have been sensitive to possible ties between representative and constituent that have little to do with issues of public policy. For example, ethnic identifications may cement a legislator in the affections of his district, whatever (within limits) his stands on issues. And many Congressmen keep their tenure of office secure by skillful provision of district benefits ranging from free literature to major federal projects. In the full study of which this analysis is part we have explored several bases of constituency support that have little to do with policy issues. Nevertheless, the question how the representative should make up his mind on legislative issues is what the classical arguments over representation are all about, and we have given a central place to a comparison of the policy preferences of constituents and Representatives and to a causal analysis of the relation between the two.

In view of the electorate's scanty information about government it was not at all clear in advance that such a comparison could be made. Some of the more buoyant advocates of popular sovereignty have regarded the citizen as a kind of kibitzer who looks over the shoulder of his representative at the legislative game. Kibitzer and player may disagree as to which card should be played, but they were at least thought to share a common understanding of what the alternatives are.

No one familiar with the findings of research on mass electorates could accept this view of the citizen. Far from looking over the shoulder of their Congressmen at the legislative game, most Americans are almost totally uninformed about legislative issues in Washington. At best the average citizen may be said to have some general ideas about how the country should be run, which he is able to use in responding to particular questions about what the government ought to do. For example, survey studies have shown that most people have a general (though differing) conception of how far government should go to achieve social and economic welfare objectives and that these convictions fix their response to various particular questions about actions government might take.[4]

What makes it possible to compare the policy preferences of constituents and Representatives despite the public's low awareness of legislative affairs is the fact that Congressmen themselves respond to many issues in terms of fairly broad evaluative dimensions. Undoubtedly policy alternatives are judged in the executive agencies and the specialized committees of the Congress by criteria that are relatively complex and specific to the policies at issue. But a good deal of evidence goes to show that when proposals come before the House as a whole they are judged on the basis of more general evaluative dimensions.[5] For example, most Congressmen, too, seem to have a general conception of how far government should go in the area of domestic social and economic welfare, and these general positions apparently orient their roll call votes on a number of particular social welfare issues.

It follows that such a broad evaluative dimension can be used to compare the policy preferences of constituents and

Representatives despite the low state of the public's information about politics. In this study three such dimensions have been drawn from our voter interviews and from congressional interviews and roll call records. As suggested above, one of these has to do with approval of government action in the social welfare field, the primary domestic issue of the New Deal-Fair Deal (and New Frontier) eras. A second dimension has to do with support for American involvement in foreign affairs, a latter-day version of the isolationist-internationalist continuum. A third dimension has to do with approval of federal action to protect the civil rights of Negroes.[6]

Because our research focused on these three dimensions, our analysis of constituency influence is limited to these areas of policy. No point has been more energetically or usefully made by those who have sought to clarify the concepts of power and influence than the necessity of specifying the acts *with respect to which* one actor has power or influence or control over another.[7] Therefore, the scope or range of influence for our analysis is the collection of legislative issues falling within our three policy domains. We are not able to say how much control the local constituency may or may not have over *all* actions of its Representative, and there may well be pork-barrel issues or other matters of peculiar relevance to the district on which the relation of Congressman to constituency is quite distinctive. However, few observers of contemporary politics would regard the issues of government provision of social and economic welfare, of American involvement in world affairs, and of federal action in behalf of the Negro as constituting a trivial range of action. Indeed, these domains together include most of the great issues that have come before Congress in recent years.

In each policy domain we have used the procedures of cumulative scaling, as developed by Louis Guttman and others, to order our samples of Congressmen, of opposing candidates, and of voters. In each domain Congressmen were ranked once according to their roll call votes in the House and again according to the attitudes they revealed in our confidential interviews. These two orderings are by no means identical, nor are the discrepancies due simply to uncertainties of measurement.[8] Opposing candidates also were ranked in each policy domain according to the attitudes they revealed in our interviews. The nationwide sample of constituents was ordered in each domain, and by averaging the attitude scores of all constituents living in the same districts, whole constituencies were ranked on each dimension so that the views of Congressmen could be compared with those of their constituencies.[9] Finally, by considering only the constituents in each district who share some characteristic (voting for the incumbent, say) we were able to order these fractions of districts so that the opinions of Congressmen could be compared with those, for example, of the dominant electoral elements of their districts.

In each policy domain, crossing the rankings of Congressmen and their constituencies gives an empirical measure of the extent of policy agreement between legislator and district.[10] In the period of our research this procedure reveals very different degrees of policy congruence across the three issue domains. On questions of social and economic welfare there is considerable agreement between Representative and district, expressed by a correlation of approximately 0.3. This coefficient is, of course, very much less than the limiting value of 1.0, indicating that a number of Congressmen are, relatively speaking, more or less "liberal" than their districts. However, on the question of foreign involvement there is no discernible agreement between legislator and district whatever. Indeed, as if to emphasize the point, the coefficient expressing this relation is slightly negative (—0.09), although not significantly so in a statistical sense. It is in the domain of civil rights that the rankings of Congressmen and constituencies most nearly agree. When we took our measurements in the late 1950s the correlation of congressional roll call behavior with constituency opinion on questions affecting the Negro was nearly 0.6.

The description of policy agreement that these three simple correlations give can be a starting-point for a wide range of analyses. For example, the significance of party competition in the district for policy representation can be explored by comparing the agreement between district and Congressman with the agreement between the district and the Congressman's non-incumbent opponent. Alternatively, the significance of choosing Representatives from single-member districts by popular majority can be explored by comparing the agreement between the Congressman and his own supporters with the agreement between the Congressman and the supporters of his opponent. Taking *both* party competition and majority rule into account magnifies rather spectacularly some of the coefficients reported here. This is most true in the domain of social welfare, where attitudes both of candidates and of voters are most polarized along party lines. Whereas the correlation between the constituency majority and congressional roll call votes is nearly +0.4 on social welfare policy, the correlation of the district majority with the non-incumbent candidate is −0.4. This difference, amounting to almost 0.8, between these two coefficients is an indicator of what the dominant electoral element of the constituency gets on the average by choosing the Congressman it has and excluding his opponent from office.[11]

These three coefficients are also the starting-point for a causal analysis of the relation of constituency to representative, the main problem of this paper. At least on social welfare and Negro rights a measurable degree of congruence is found between district and legislator. Is this agreement due to constituency influence in Congress, or is it to be attributed to other causes? If this question is to have a satisfactory answer the conditions that are necessary and sufficient to assure constituency control must be stated and compared with the available empirical evidence.

The Conditions of Constituency Influence

Broadly speaking, the constituency can control the policy actions of the Representative in two alternative ways. The first of these is for the district to choose a Representative who so shares its views that in following his own convictions he does his constituents' will. In this case district opinion and the Congressman's actions are connected through the Representative's own policy attitudes. The second means of constituency control is for the Congressman to follow his (at least tolerably accurate) perceptions of district attitude in order to win re-election. In this case constituency opinion and the Congressman's actions are connected through his perception of what the district wants.[12]

These two paths of constituency control are presented schematically in Chart 1. As the figure suggests, each path has two steps, one connecting the constituency's attitude with an "intervening" attitude or perception, the other connecting this attitude or perception with the Representative's roll call behavior. Out of respect for the processes by which the human actor achieves cognitive congruence we have also drawn arrows between the two intervening factors, since the Congressman probably tends to see his district as having the same opinion as his own and also tends, over time, to bring his own opinion into line with the district's. The inclusion of these arrows calls attention to two other possible influence paths, each consisting of *three* steps, although these additional paths will turn out to be of relatively slight importance empirically.

Chart 1. ***Connections between a constituency's attitude and its Representative's roll call behavior.***

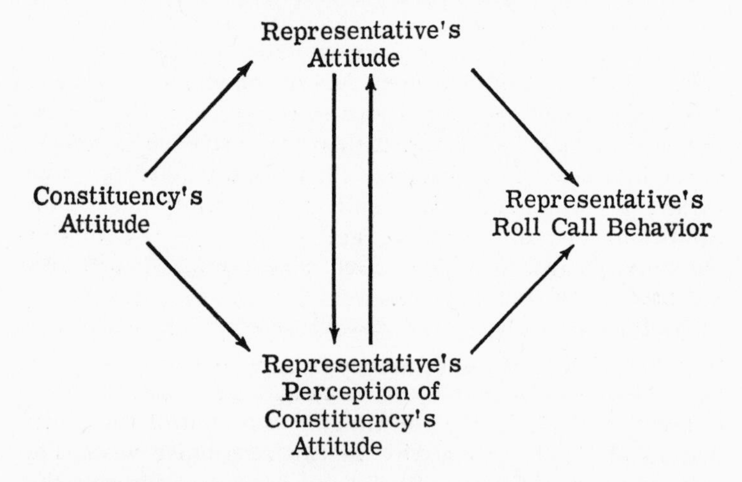

Neither of the main influence paths of Chart 1 will connect the final roll call vote to the constituency's views if either of its steps is blocked. From this, two necessary conditions of constituency influence can be stated: *first,* the Representative's votes in the House must agree substantially with his own policy views or his perceptions of the district's views, and not be determined entirely by other influences to which the Congressman is exposed; and, *second,* the attitudes or perceptions governing the Representative's acts must correspond, at least imperfectly, to the district's actual opinions. It would be difficult to describe the relation of constituency to Representative as one of control unless these conditions are met.[13]

Yet these two requirements are not sufficient to assure

control. A *third* condition must also be satisfied: the constituency must in some measure take the policy views of candidates into account in choosing a Representative. If it does not, agreement between district and Congressman may arise for reasons that cannot rationally be brought within the idea of control. For example, such agreement may simply reflect the fact that a Representative drawn from a given area is likely, by pure statistical probability, to share its dominant values, without his acceptance or rejection of these ever having been a matter of consequence to his electors.

Evidence of Control: Congressional Attitudes and Perceptions

How well are these conditions met in the relation of American Congressmen to their constituents? There is little question that the first is substantially satisfied; the evidence of our research indicates that members of the House do in fact vote both their own policy views and their perceptions of their constituents' views, at least on issues of social welfare, foreign involvement, and civil rights. If these two intervening factors are used to predict roll call votes, the prediction is quite successful. Their multiple correlation with roll call position is 0.7 for social welfare, 0.6 for foreign involvement, and 0.9 for civil rights; the last figure is especially persuasive. What is more, both the Congressman's own convictions and his perceptions of district opinion make a distinct contribution to his roll call behavior. In each of the three domains the prediction of roll call votes is surer if it is made from both factors rather than from either alone.

Lest the strong influence that the Congressman's views and his perception of district views have on roll call behavior appear somehow foreordained—and, consequently, this finding seem a trivial one—it is worth taking a sidewise glance at the potency of possible other forces on the Representative's vote. In the area of foreign policy, for example, a number of Congressmen are disposed to follow the administration's advice, whatever they or their districts think. For those who are, the multiple correlation of roll call behavior with the Representative's own foreign policy views and his perception of district views is a mere 0.2. Other findings could be cited to support the point that the influence of the Congressman's own preferences and those he attributes to the district is extremely variable. Yet in the House as a whole over the three policy domains the influence of these forces is quite strong.

The connections of congressional attitudes and perceptions with actual constituency opinion are weaker. If policy agreement between district and Representative is moderate and variable across the policy domains, as it is, this is to be explained much more in terms of the second condition of constituency control than the first. The Representative's attitudes and perceptions most nearly match true opinion in his district on the issues of Negro rights. Reflecting the charged and polarized nature of this area, the correlation of actual district opinion with perceived opinion is greater than 0.6, and the correlation of district attitude with the Representative's own attitude is nearly 0.4, as shown by Table I. But the comparable correlations for foreign involvement are much smaller —indeed almost negligible. And the coefficients for social welfare are also smaller, although a detailed presentation of

Table I. ***Correlations of Constituency Attitudes***

Policy Domain	Correlation of Constituency Attitude with	
	Representative's Perception of Constituency Attitude	*Representative's Own Attitude*
Social welfare	.17	.21
Foreign involvement	.19	.06
Civil rights	.63	.39

findings in this area would show that the Representative's perceptions and attitudes are more strongly associated with the attitude of his electoral *majority* than they are with the attitudes of the constituency as a whole.

Knowing this much about the various paths that may lead, directly or indirectly, from constituency attitude to roll call vote, we can assess their relative importance. Since the alternative influence chains have links of unequal strength, the full chains will not in general be equally strong, and these differences are of great importance in the relation of Representative to constituency. For the domain of civil rights Chart 2 assembles all the intercorrelations of the variables of our system. As the chart shows, the root correlation of constituency attitude with roll call behavior in this domain is 0.57. How much of this policy congruence can be accounted for by the influence path involving the Representative's attitude? And how much by the path involving his perception of constituency opinion? When the intercorrelations of the system are interpreted in the light of what we assume its causal structure to be, it is influence passing through the Congressman's perception of the district's views that is found to be preeminently important.[14] Under the least favorable assumption as to its importance, this path is found to account for more than twice as much of the variance of roll call behavior as the paths involving the Representative's own attitude.[15] However, when this same procedure is applied to our social welfare data, the results suggest that the direct connection of constituency and roll call through the Congressman's own attitude is the most important of the alternative paths.[16] The reversal of the relative importance of the two paths as we move from civil rights to social welfare is one of the most striking findings of this analysis.

Evidence of Control: Electoral Behavior

Of the three conditions of constituency influence, the requirement that the electorate take account of the policy positions of the candidates is the hardest to match with empirical evidence. Indeed, given the limited information the average voter carries to the polls, the public might be thought incompetent to perform any task of appraisal. Of constituents living in congressional districts where there was a contest between a Republican and a Democrat in 1958, less than one in five said they had read or heard something about both candidates, and well over half conceded they had read or heard nothing about either. And these proportions are not much better when they are based only on the part of the sample, not much more than half, that reported voting for Congress in 1958. The extent of awareness of the candidates among voters is indicated in Table II. As the table shows, even of the portion of the public that was sufficiently interested to vote, almost half had read or heard nothing about either candidate.

Just how low a hurdle our respondents had to clear in saying they had read or heard something about a candidate is indicated by detailed qualitative analysis of the information constituents *were* able to associate with congressional candidates. Except in rare cases, what the voters "knew" was confined to diffuse evaluative judgments about the candidate: "he's a good man," "he understands the problems," and so forth. Of detailed information about policy stands not more than a chemical trace was found. Among the comments about the candidates given in response to an extended series of free-answer questions, less than two percent had to do with stands in our three policy domains; indeed, only about three comments in every hundred had to do with legislative issues of *any* description.[17]

Chart 2. *Intercorrelations of variables pertaining to Civil Rights.*

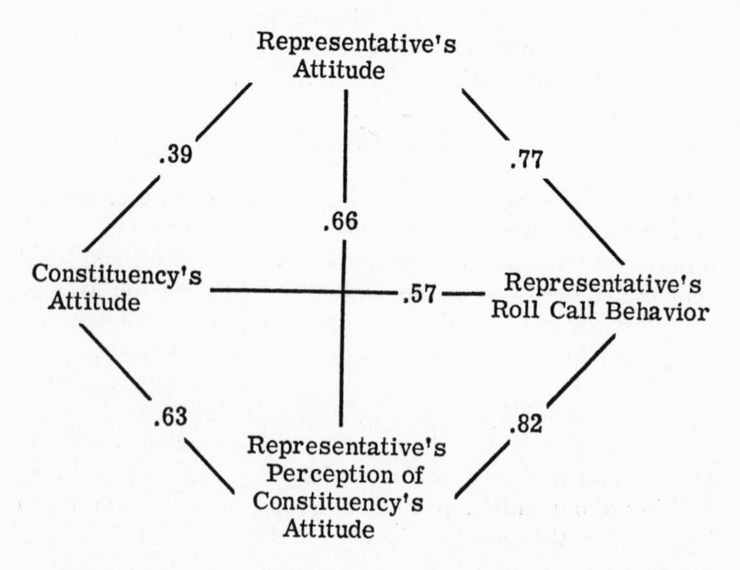

This evidence that the behavior of the electorate is largely unaffected by knowledge of the policy positions of the candidates is complemented by evidence about the forces that *do* shape the voters' choices among congressional candidates. The primary basis of voting in American congressional elections is identification with party. In 1958 only one vote in twenty was cast by persons without any sort of party loyalty. And among those who did have a party identification, only one in ten voted against their party. As a result, something like 84 percent of the vote that year was cast by party identifiers voting their usual party line. What is more, traditional party voting is seldom connected with current legislative issues. As the party loyalists in a nationwide sample of voters told us what they liked and disliked about the parties in 1958, only a small fraction of the comments (about 15 per cent) dealt with current issues of public policy.[18]

Table II. *Awareness of Congressional Candidates Among Voters, 1958*

		Read or Heard Something About Incumbent*		
		Yes	No	
Read or Heard Something About Non-Incumbent	Yes	24	5	29
	No	25	46	71
		49	51	100%

*In order to include all districts where the House seat was contested in 1958 this table retains ten constituencies in which the incumbent Congressman did not seek re-election. Candidates of the retiring incumbent's party in these districts are treated here as if they were incumbents. Were these figures to be calculated only for constituencies in which an incumbent sought re-election, no entry in this four-fold table would differ from that given by more than two percent.

Yet the idea of reward or punishment at the polls for legislative stands is familiar to members of Congress, who feel that they and their records are quite visible to their constituents. Of our sample of Congressmen who were opposed for re-election in 1958, more than four-fifths said the outcome in their districts had been strongly influenced by the electorate's response to their records and personal standing. Indeed, this belief is clear enough to present a notable contradiction: Congressmen feel that their individual legislative actions may have considerable impact on the electorate, yet some simple facts about the Representative's salience to his constituents imply that this could hardly be true.

In some measure this contradiction is to be explained by the tendency of Congressmen to overestimate their visibility to the local public, a tendency that reflects the difficulties of the Representative in forming a correct judgment of constituent opinion. The communication most Congressmen have with their districts inevitably puts them in touch with organized groups and with individuals who are relatively well informed about politics. The Representative knows his constituents mostly from dealing with people who *do* write letters, who *will* attend meetings, who *have* an interest in his legislative stands. As a result, his sample of contacts with a constituency of several hundred thousand people is heavily biased: even the contacts he apparently makes at random are likely to be with people who grossly overrepresent the degree of political information and interest in the constituency as a whole.

But the contradiction is also to be explained by several aspects of the Representative's electoral situation that are of great importance to the question of constituency influence. The first of these is implicit in what has already been said. Because of the pervasive effects of party loyalties, no candidate for Congress starts from scratch in putting together an electoral majority. The Congressman is a dealer in increments and margins. He starts with a stratum of hardened party voters, and if the stratum is broad enough he can have a measurable influence on his chance of survival simply by attracting a small additional element of the electorate—or by not losing a larger one. Therefore, his record may have a very real bearing on his electoral success or failure without most of his constituents ever knowing what that record is.

Second, the relation of Congressman to voter is not a simple bilateral one but is complicated by the presence of all manner of intermediaries: the local party, economic interests, the news media, racial and nationality organizations, and so forth. Such is the lore of American politics, as it is known to any political scientist. Very often the Representative reaches the mass public through these mediating agencies, and the information about himself and his record may be considerably transformed as it diffuses out to the electorate in two or more stages. As a result, the public—or parts of it—may get simple positive or negative cues about the Congressman which were provoked by his legislative actions but which no longer have a recognizable issue content.

Third, for most Congressmen most of the time the electorate's sanctions are potential rather than actual. Particularly the Representative from a safe district may feel his proper legislative strategy is to avoid giving opponents in his own party or outside of it material they can use against him. As the Congressman pursues this strategy he may write a legislative record that never becomes very well known to his constituents; if it doesn't win votes, neither will it lose any. This is clearly the situation of most southern Congressmen in dealing with the issue of Negro rights. By voting correctly on this issue they are unlikely to increase their visibility to constituents. Nevertheless, the fact of constituency influence, backed by potential sanctions at the polls, is real enough.

That these potential sanctions are all too real is best illustrated in the election of 1958 by the reprisal against Representative Brooks Hays in Arkansas' Fifth District.[19] Although the perception of Congressman Hays as too moderate on civil rights resulted more from his service as intermediary between the White House and Governor Faubus in the Little Rock school crisis than from his record in the House, the victory of Dale Alford as a write-in candidate was a striking reminder of what can happen to a Congressman who gives his foes a powerful issue to use against him. The extraordinary involvement of the public in this race can be seen by comparing how well the candidates were known in this constituency with the awareness of the candidates shown by Table II above for the country as a whole. As Table III indicates, not a single voter in our sample of Arkansas' Fifth District was

Table III. ***Awareness of Congressional Candidates Among Voters in Arkansas Fifth District, 1958***

		Read or Heard Something About Hays		
		Yes	No	
Read or Heard Something About Alford	Yes	100	0	100
	No	0	0	0
		100	0	100%

unaware of either candidate.[20] What is more, these interviews show that Hays was regarded both by his supporters and his opponents as more moderate than Alford on civil rights and that this perception brought his defeat. In some measure, what happened in Little Rock in 1958 can happen anywhere, and our Congressmen ought not to be entirely disbelieved in what they say about their impact at the polls. Indeed, they may be under genuine pressure from the voters even while they are the forgotten men of national elections.[21]

Conclusion

Therefore, although the conditions of constituency influence are not equally satisfied, they are met well enough to give the local constituency a measure of control over the actions of its Representatives. Best satisfied is the requirement about motivational influences on the Congressman: our evidence shows that the Representative's roll call behavior is strongly influenced by his own policy preferences and by his perception of preferences held by the constituency. However, the conditions of influence that presuppose effective communication between Congressman and district are much less well met. The Representative has very imperfect information about the issue preferences of his constituency, and the constituency awareness of the policy stands of the Representative ordinarily is slight.

The findings of this analysis heavily underscore the fact that no single tradition of representation fully accords with the realities of American legislative politics. The American system *is* a mixture, to which the Burkean, instructed-delegate, and responsible-party models all can be said to have contributed elements. Moreover, variations in the representative relation are most likely to occur as we move from one policy domain to another. No single, generalized configuration of attitudes and perceptions links Representative with constituency but rather several distinct patterns, and which of them is invoked depends very much on the issue involved.

The issue domain in which the relation of Congressman to constituency most nearly conforms to the instructed-delegate model is that of civil rights. This conclusion is supported by the importance of the influence-path passing through the

Representative's perception of district opinion, although even in this domain the sense in which the constituency may be said to take the position of the candidate into account in reaching its electoral judgment should be carefully qualified.

The representative relation conforms most closely to the responsible-party model in the domain of social welfare. In this issue area, the arena of partisan conflict for a generation, the party symbol helps both constituency and Representative in the difficult process of communication between them. On the one hand, because Republican and Democratic voters tend to differ in what they would have government do, the Representative has some guide to district opinion simply by looking at the partisan division of the vote. On the other hand, because the two parties tend to recruit candidates who differ on the social welfare role of government, the constituency can infer the candidates' position with more than random accuracy from their party affiliation, even though what the constituency has learned directly about these stands is almost nothing. How faithful the representation of social welfare views is to the responsible-party model should not be exaggerated. Even in this policy domain, American practice departs widely from an ideal conception of party government.[22] But in this domain, more than any other, political conflict has become a conflict of national parties in which constituency and Representative are known to each other primarily by their party association.

It would be too pat to say that the domain of foreign involvement conforms to the third model of representation, the conception promoted by Edmund Burke. Clearly it does in the sense that the Congressman looks elsewhere than to his district in making up his mind on foreign issues. However, the reliance he puts on the President and the Administration suggests that the calculation of where the public interest lies is often passed to the Executive on matters of foreign policy. Ironically, legislative initiative in foreign affairs has fallen victim to the very difficulties of gathering and appraising information that led Burke to argue that Parliament rather than the public ought to hold the power of decision. The background information and predictive skills that Burke thought the people lacked are held primarily by the modern Executive. As a result, the present role of the legislature in foreign affairs bears some resemblance to the role that Burke had in mind for the elitist, highly restricted *electorate* of his own day.

Notes:

1. To be sure, the work of the Federal Convention has been supplemented in two critical respects. The first of these is the practice, virtually universal since the mid-19th Century, of choosing Representatives from single-member districts of limited geographic area. The second is the practice, which has also become virtually universal in our own century, of selecting party nominees for the House by direct primary election.

2. In the language of Eulau, Wahlke, *et al.,* we speak here of the "style," not the "focus," of representation. See their "The Role of the Representative: Some Empirical Observations on the Theory of Edmund Burke," *American Political Science Review,* Vol. 53 (September, 1959), pp. 742–756. An excellent review of the mandate-independence controversy is given by Hanna Fenichel Pitkin, "The Theory of Representation" (unpublished doctoral dissertation, University of California, Berkeley, 1961). For other contemporary discussions of representation, see Alfred de Grazia, *Public and Republic* (New York, 1951), and John A. Fairlie, "The Nature of Political Representation," *American Political Science Review,* Vol. 34 (April–June, 1940), pp. 236–48, 456–66.

3. The sampling aspects of this research were complicated by the fact that the study of representation was a rider midway on a four-year panel study of the electorate whose primary sampling units were not congressional districts (although there is no technical reason why they could not have been if the needs of the representation analysis had been foreseen when the design of the sample was fixed two years before). As a result, the districts in our sample had unequal probabilities of selection and unequal weights in the analysis, making the sample somewhat less efficient than an equal-probability sample of equivalent size.

It will be apparent in the discussion that follows that we have estimated characteristics of whole constituencies from our samples of constituents living in particular districts. In view of the fact that a sample of less than two thousand constituents has been divided among 116 districts, the reader may wonder about the reliability of these estimates. After considerable investigation we have concluded that their sampling error is not so severe a problem for the analysis as we had thought it would be. Several comments may indicate why it is not.

To begin with, the weighting of our sample of districts has increased the reliability of the constituency estimates. The correct theoretical weight to be assigned each district in the analysis is the inverse of the probability of the district's selection, and it can be shown that this weight is approximately proportional to the number of interviews taken in the district. The result of this is that the greatest weight is assigned the districts with the largest number of interviews and, hence, the most reliable constituency estimates. Indeed, these weights increase by half again the (weighted) mean number of interviews taken per district. To put the matter another way: the introduction of differential weights trades some of our sample of congressional districts for more reliable constituency estimates.

How much of a problem the unreliability of these estimates is depends very much on the analytic uses to which the estimates are put. If our goal were case analyses of particular districts, the constituency samples would have to be much larger. Indeed, for most case analyses we would want several hundred interviews per district (at a cost, over 116 districts, of several small nuclear reactors). However, most of the findings reported here are based not on single districts but on many or all of the districts in our sample. For analyses of this sort the number of interviews per district can be much smaller.

Our investigation of the effect of the sampling variance of the constituency estimates is quite reassuring. When statistics computed from our constituency samples are compared with corresponding parameter values for the constituencies, the agreement of the two sets of figures is quite close. For example, when the proportions voting Democratic in the 116 constituencies in 1958, as computed from our sample data, are compared with the actual proportions voting Democratic, as recorded in official election statistics, a product moment correlation of 0.93 is obtained, and this figure is the more impressive since this test throws away non-voters, almost one-half of our total sample. We interpret the Pearsonian correlation as an appropriate measure of agreement in this case, since the associated regression equations are almost exactly the identity function. The alternative intraclass correlation coefficient has almost as high a value.

Although we believe that this analysis provides a textbook illustration of how misleading intuitive ideas (including our own) about the effects of sampling error can be, these figures ought not to be too beguiling. It is clear that how close such a correlation is to 1.0 for any given variable will depend on the ratio of the between-district variance to the total variance. When this ratio is as high as it is for Republican and Democratic voting, the effect of the unreliability of our constituency estimates is fairly trivial. Although the content of the study is quite different, this sampling problem has much in common with the problem of attenuation of correlation as it has been treated in psychological testing. See, for example, J. P. Guilford, *Fundamental Statistics in Psychology and Education* (New York, 1956), pp. 475–78.

4. See Angus Campbell, Philip E. Converse, Warren E. Miller, and Donald E. Stokes, *The American Voter* (New York, 1960), pp. 194–209.

5. This conclusion, fully supported by our own work for later Congresses, is one of the main findings to be drawn from the work of Duncan MacRae on roll call voting in the House of Representatives. See his *Dimensions of Congressional Voting: A Statistical Study of the House of Representatives in the Eighty-First Congress* (Berkeley and Los Angeles: University of California Press, 1958). For additional evidence of the existence of scale dimensions in legislative behavior, see N. L. Gage and Ben Shimberg, "Measuring Senatorial Progressivism," *Journal of Abnormal and Social Psychology,* Vol. 44 (January 1949), pp. 112–117; George M. Belknap, "A Study of Senatorial Voting by Scale Analysis" (unpublished

doctoral dissertation, University of Chicago, 1951), and "A Method for Analyzing Legislative Behavior," *Midwest Journal of Political Science,* Vol. 2 (1958), pp. 377–402; two other articles by MacRae, "The Role of the State Legislator in Massachusetts," *American Sociological Review,* Vol. 19 (April 1954), pp. 185–194, and "Roll Call Votes and Leadership," *Public Opinion Quarterly,* Vol. 20 (1956), pp. 543–558; Charles D. Farris, "A Method of Determining Ideological Groups in Congress," *Journal of Politics,* Vol. 20 (1958), pp. 308–338; and Leroy N. Rieselbach, "Quantitative Techniques for Studying Voting Behavior in the U. N. General Assembly," *International Organization,* Vol. 14 (1960), pp. 291–306.

6. The content of the three issue domains may be suggested by some of the roll call and interview items used. In the area of social welfare these included the issues of public housing, public power, aid to education, and government's role in maintaining full employment. In the area of foreign involvement the items included the issues of foreign economic aid, military aid, sending troops abroad, and aid to neutrals. In the area of civil rights the items included the issues of school desegregation, fair employment, and the protection of Negro voting rights.

7. Because this point has been so widely discussed it has inevitably attracted a variety of terms. Dahl denotes the acts of *a* whose performance *A* is able to influence as the *scope* of *A*'s power. See Robert A. Dahl, "The Concept of Power," *Behavioral Science,* Vol. 2 (July 1957), pp. 201–215. This usage is similar to that of Harold D. Lasswell and Abraham Kaplan, *Power and Society* (New Haven: Yale University Press, 1950), pp. 71–73. Dorwin Cartwright, however, denotes the behavioral or psychological changes in *P* which *O* is able to induce as the *range* of *O*'s power: "A Field Theoretical Conception of Power," *Studies in Social Power* (Ann Arbor: Research Center for Group Dynamics, Institute for Social Research, The University of Michigan, 1959), pp. 183–220.

8. That the Representative's roll call votes can diverge from his true opinion is borne out by a number of findings of the study (some of which are reported here) as to the conditions under which agreement between the Congressman's roll call position and his private attitude will be high or low. However, a direct confirmation that these two sets of measurements are not simply getting at the same thing is given by differences in attitude-roll call agreement according to the Congressman's sense of how well his roll call votes have expressed his real views. In the domain of foreign involvement, for example, the correlation of our attitudinal and roll call measurements was .75 among Representatives who said that their roll call votes had expressed their real views fairly well. But this correlation was only .04 among those who said that their roll call votes had expressed their views poorly. In the other policy domains, too, attitude-roll call agreement is higher among Congressmen who are well satisfied with their roll call votes than it is among Congressmen who are not.

9. During the analysis we have formed constituency scores out of the scores of constituents living in the same district by several devices other than calculating average constituent scores. In particular, in view of the ordinal character of our scales we have frequently used the *median* constituent score as a central value for the constituency as a whole. How-

ever, the ordering of constituencies differs very little according to which of several reasonable alternatives for obtaining constituency scores is chosen. As a result, we have preferred mean scores for the greater number of ranks they give.

10. The meaning of this procedure can be suggested by two percentage tables standing for hypothetical extreme cases, the first that of full agreement, the second that of no agreement whatever. For convenience these illustrative tables categorize both Congressmen and their districts in terms of only three degrees of favor and assume for both a nearly uniform distribution across the three categories. The terms "pro," "neutral," and "con" indicate a relative rather than an absolute opinion. In Case I, full agreement, all districts relatively favorable to social welfare action have Congressmen who are so too, etc.; whereas in Case II, or that of no agreement, the ordering of constituencies is independent in a statistical sense of the ranking of Congressmen: knowing the policy orientation of a district gives no clue at all to the orientation of its Congressman. Of course, it is possible for the orders of legislators and districts to be *inversely* related, and this possibility is of some importance, as indicated

Case I: Full Policy Agreement

	Constituencies			
Congressmen	Pro	Neutral	Con	
Pro	33	0	0	33
Neutral	0	34	0	34
Con	0	0	33	33
	33	34	33	100%

Correlation = 1.0

Case II: No Policy Agreement

	Constituencies			
Congressmen	Pro	Neutral	Con	
Pro	11	11	11	33
Neutral	11	12	11	34
Con	11	11	11	33
	33	34	33	100%

Correlation = 0.0

above, when the policy position of non-incumbent candidates as well as incumbents is taken into account. To summarize the degree of congruence between legislators and voters, a measure of correlation is introduced. Although we have used a variety of measures of association in our analysis, the values reported in this article all refer to product moment correlation coefficients. For our hypothetical Case I a measure of correlation would have the value 1.0; for Case II, the value 0.0. When it is applied to actual data this convenient indicator is likely to have a value somewhere in between. The question is where.

11. A word of caution is in order, lest we compare things that are not strictly comparable. For obvious reasons, most non-incumbent candidates have no roll call record, and we have had to measure their policy agreement with the district entirely in terms of the attitudes they have revealed in interviews. However, the difference of coefficients given here is almost as great when the policy agreement between the incumbent Congressman and his district is also measured in terms of the attitudes conveyed in confidential interviews.

12. A third type of connection, excluded here, might obtain between district and Congressman if the Representative accedes to what he thinks the district wants because he believes that to be what a representative *ought* to do, whether or not it is necessary for re-election. We leave this type of connection out of our account here because we conceive an influence relation as one in which control is not voluntarily accepted or rejected by someone subject to it. Of course, this possible connection between district and Representative is not any the less interesting because it falls outside our definition of influence or control, and we have given a good deal of attention to it in the broader study of which this analysis is part.

13. It scarcely needs to be said that demonstrating *some* constituency influence would not imply that the Representative's behavior is *wholly* determined by constituency pressures. The legislator acts in a complex institutional setting in which he is subject to a wide variety of influences. The constituency can exercise a genuine measure of control without driving all other influences from the Representative's life space.

14. We have done this by a variance-component technique similar to several others proposed for dealing with problems of this type. See especially Herbert A. Simon, "Spurious Correlation: A Causal Interpretation," *Journal of the American Statistical Association,* Vol. 49 (1954), pp. 467–479; Hubert M. Blalock, Jr., "The Relative Importance of Variables," *American Sociological Review,* Vol. 26 (1961), pp. 866–874; and the almost forgotten work of Sewall Wright, "Correlation and Causation," *Journal of Agricultural Research,* Vol. 20 (1920), pp. 557–585. Under this technique a "path coefficient" (to use Wright's terminology, although not his theory) is assigned to each of the causal arrows by solving a set of equations involving the correlations of the variables of the model. The weight assigned to a full path is then the product of its several path coefficients, and this product may be interpreted as the proportion of the variance of the dependent variable (roll call behavior, here) that is explained by a given path.

A special problem arises because influence may flow in either direction between the Congressman's attitude and his perception of district attitude (as noted above, the Representative may tend both to perceive his constituency's view selectively, as consistent with his own, and to change

Model I: A→P　　　　Model II: P→A

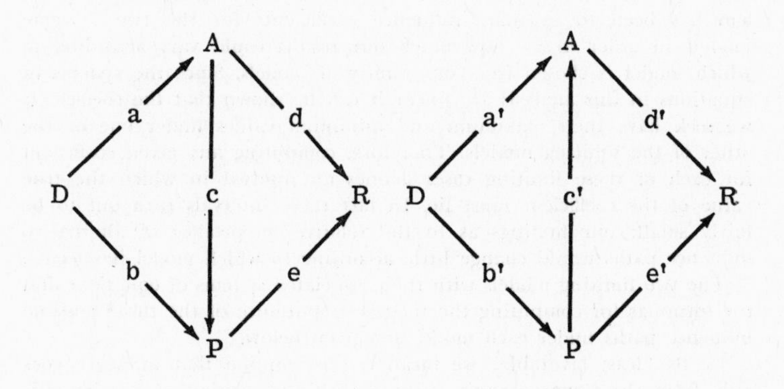

$r^2AR = d + ce$
$r^2PR = e$
$r^2DA = a$
$r^2DP = b + ac$
$r^2AP = c$

$r^2AR = d'$
$r^2PR = e' + c'd'$
$r^2DA = a' + b'c'$
$r^2DP = b'$
$r^2AP = c'$

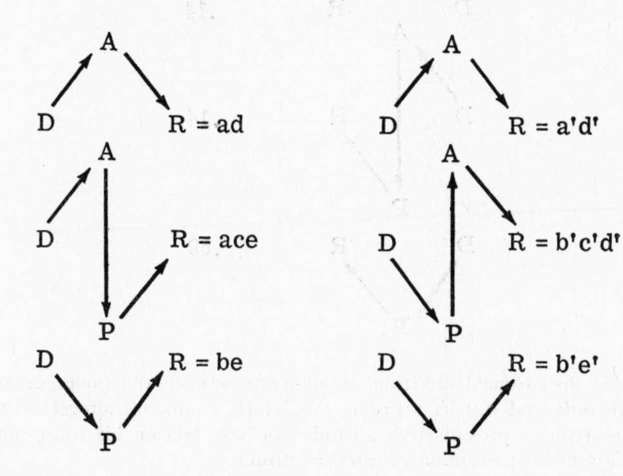

his own view to be consistent with the perceived constituency view). Hence, we have not a single causal model but a whole family of models, varying according to the relative importance of influence from attitude to perception and from perception to attitude. Our solution to this problem has been to calculate influence coefficients for the two extreme models in order to see how much our results could vary according to which model is chosen from our family of models. Since the systems of equations in this analysis are linear it can be shown that the coefficients we seek have their maximum and minimum values under one or the other of the limiting models. Therefore, computing any given coefficient for each of these limiting cases defines an interval in which the true value of the coefficient must lie. In fact these intervals turn out to be fairly small; our findings as to the relative importance of alternative influence paths would change little according to which model is selected.

The two limiting models with their associated systems of equations and the formulas for computing the relative importance of the three possible influence paths under each model are given below.

15. By "least favorable" we mean the assumption that influence goes only from the Congressman's attitude to his perception of district attitude (Model I) and not the other way round. Under this assumption, the proportions of the variance of roll call behavior accounted for by the three alternative paths, expressed as proportions of the part of the variance of roll call votes that is explained by district attitude, are these:

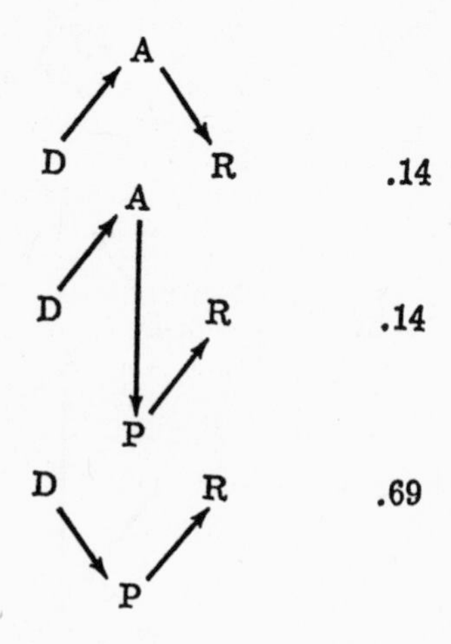

Inverting the assumed direction of influence between the Congressman's own attitude and district attitude (Model II) eliminates altogether the effect that the Representative's attitude can have had on his votes, independently of his perception of district attitude.

16. Under both Models I and II the proportion of the variance of roll call voting explained by the influence path involving the Representative's own attitude is twice as great as the proportion explained by influence passing through his perception of district attitude.

17. What is more, the electorate's awareness of Congress as a whole appears quite limited. A majority of the public was unable to say in 1958 which of the two parties had controlled the Congress during the preceding two years. Some people were confused by the coexistence of a Republican President and a Democratic Congress. But for most people this was simply an elementary fact about congressional affairs to which they were not privy.

18. For a more extended analysis of forces on the congressional vote, see Donald E. Stokes and Warren E. Miller, "Party Government and the Saliency of Congress," *Public Opinion Quarterly,* Vol. 26 (Winter 1962), pp. 531–546.

19. For an account of this episode see Corinne Silverman, "The Little Rock Story," Inter-University Case Program series, reprinted in Edwin A. Bock and Alan K. Campbell, eds., *Case Studies in American Government* (Englewood Cliffs, 1962), pp. 1–46.

20. The sample of this constituency was limited to twenty-three persons of whom thirteen voted. However, despite the small number of cases the probability that the difference in awareness between this constituency and the country generally as the result only of sampling variations is much less than one in a thousand.

21. In view of the potential nature of the constituency's sanctions, it is relevant to characterize its influence over the Representative in terms of several distinctions drawn by recent theorists of power, especially the difference between actual and potential power, between influence and coercive power, and between influence and purposive control. Observing these distinctions, we might say that the constituency's influence is *actual* and not merely *potential* since it is the sanction behavior rather than the conforming behavior that is infrequent (Dahl). That is, the Congressman is influenced by his calculus of potential sanctions, following the "rule of anticipated reactions" (Friedrich), however oblivious of his behavior the constituency ordinarily may be. We might also say that the constituency has *power* since its influence depends partly on sanctions (Lasswell and Kaplan), although it rarely exercises *control* since its influence is rarely conscious or intended (Cartwright). In the discussion above we have of course used the terms "influence" and "control" interchangeably.

22. The factors in American electoral behavior that encourage such a departure are discussed in Stokes and Miller, *loc cit.*

3 *Political Strategy for the Alienated Voter**

by Murray B. Levin and Murray Eden

On November 7, 1960, the voters of Massachusetts, despite their strong affection for John Kennedy and their customary allegiance to the Democratic Party, elected John Volpe, a Republican, as Governor of the Commonwealth. Volpe, a relatively unknown underdog, upset Joseph Ward, the Democratic candidate, by 138,485 votes, although Kennedy received a plurality in excess of half a million. Two months before Volpe's victory, Ward, who was the endorsee of the Democratic Party pre-primary convention, defeated six Democratic Party chieftains (one of whom was named John F. Kennedy) who opposed him in the primary. In November 1959 another relatively unknown underdog, John Collins, was elected mayor of Boston when he defeated John Powers, president of the state senate and one of the most powerful figures in the Democratic Party.

Although these three elections seem to have little in common—they took place at different times, in different constituencies, and involved different offices—they are, in fact, ex-

Reprinted from *Public Opinion Quarterly,* 26 (Spring, 1962), 47–63, by permission of the authors and the publisher.

*The research for this paper was made possible by grants from the Joint Center for Urban Studies of Harvard University and the Massachusetts Institute of Technology, the Citizenship Project of Massachusetts Institute of Technology, and the Boston University Graduate Research Fund.

pressions of a common phenomenon, voter cynicism, anger, and alienation.

Characteristics of the Alienated Voter

In each case public opinion studies reveal that between 20 and 50 per cent of the respondents who voted "for" the winner actually voted against the loser, that is, for the candidate perceived as "the lesser of two evils."[1] Many respondents who voted did so on the assumption that it made no difference which candidate won because both candidates were perceived as selfish or crooked.[2] In the Powers-Collins election 43 per cent of those who voted for Powers thought he would be no better than his opponent, while 57 per cent of those who voted for Collins thought he would be no better than Powers.

A study of those eligible to vote (unenrolled voters and registered Democrats) in the 1960 Democratic gubernatorial primary reveals an extremely high proportion of voters with a low sense of political efficacy. Forty-eight per cent of the respondents "agreed" with the statement, "Public officials in Massachusetts don't care what people like me think." Forty-seven per cent of the respondents disagreed with the statement, "The way people vote in Massachusetts is the main thing that decides how things are run in this state." Thirty-three per cent of the respondents disagreed with the statement, "Voting is the only way people can have any say about how things are run in Massachusetts." Forty-three per cent of the respondents agreed with the statement, "People like me don't have any say about what the state government does," while sixty-six per cent agreed that "Politics and government in Massachusetts seem so complicated that people like me can't understand it."

In each of these elections at least one-fifth of those interviewed believed that the candidates were obligated to, and dominated by, small groups of self-interested contributors. These contributors are stereotyped as buyers purchasing future political favors.[3] The contributors and the candidates in each of these elections form, in the view of many respondents, an oligarchy which controls the community in its own interest. Many respondents also complained that the candidates did not present a serious and meaningful discussion of the issues and that the rhetoric of the campaign had been reduced to mutual character assassination, which made it impossible to tell who was telling the truth. These attitudes reflect the fact that in recent years several investigations into various branches of the state government and the government of Boston have revealed pervasive conflict of interest and outright corruption.[4]

Assuming that politicians are corrupt, these citizens have concluded that voting is useless, reform impossible, and the so-called democratic process a hollow mockery of what it is supposed to be. They structure the political world in terms of a sharp dichotomy between the powerful insiders—politicians, contractors, bookies, big businessmen—and the voters, who are powerless outsiders.

They are alienated voters who believe that they are manipulated and exploited by forces that they cannot uproot or even influence. The feeling of being wrongfully excluded, powerless, and cheated of one's political birthright is the essential component of political alienation.[5] In a democratic society it may arise from (1) the disjunction between democratic values and perceived political realities—between the roles which democratic man expects he has a right to play and the role he believes he is forced to play, or from (2) actual experience with corrupt politicians.

Individuals who believe they have a right to be politically efficacious but who feel politically powerless will feel alienated. Individuals who believe that they are supposed to be able to cast a vote that is meaningful (i.e. based on adequate information) but who have cause to believe their vote is cast without the minimum amount of information will also feel alienated.[6] Individuals who expect government by due process of law but believe that they must bribe public officials in order to have influence will also feel alienated.

Alienated voters are hostile to politicians and disenchanted with the political process. They are wary of candidates who spend large sums of money during campaigns. They are skeptical of those who are endorsed by powerful "public" figures, and they tend to believe that campaign promises and platforms are empty verbiage. If they vote at all, it is against the "greater evil," against the "politician," against the well-financed, and against the powerful. They do not really vote "for" anyone.

Given this condition of extreme skepticism and hostility, or perhaps in some instances extreme sophistication, the traditional vote-getting techniques and the customary political rhetoric are likely to backfire. The candidate who campaigns in an alienated electorate must avoid the appearance of being "a politician," he must not conduct "opulent" campaigns, and he must convince alienated voters that he is not corrupt or at least less corrupt than his opponent. This is not easy to do.

Many candidates in Massachusetts know that alienated voters are plentiful and that they want information relevant to the candidate's integrity, not his program. Candidates therefore respond by proclaiming their purity while castigating the opposition. Mud slinging has become the major commodity in recent Massachusetts elections.

The candidates, however, have not appreciated the subtlety of the problem. Since they assume that the candidates are dishonest, alienated voters have no reason to believe what they say.[7] A Democratic alienated voter responded to the Democratic candidate's attack on the opposition as follows: "It takes a crook to know one." Under these conditions a candidate must re-evaluate traditional vote-getting techniques and re-examine standard political strategies.

Although the degree of political alienation in Massachusetts may exceed that in other communities, we believe that cynicism and hostility to state and local politicians are common enough to warrant an analysis of the problems faced by political strategists who seek the support of alienated voters.[8]

Theoretical Model of the Distribution of an Electorate

The theoretical model of political strategy which follows assumes a political universe of candidates and voters who are both rational and selfish. We assume, with Downs,[9] that candidates wish to be rational, that is, to utilize their scarce resources (time, manpower, and money) most efficiently so as to maximize output (votes) for a given input, or minimize input for a given output. We also assume "that politicians . . . never seek office as a means of carrying out particular policies; their only goal is to reap the rewards of holding office per se. They treat policies purely as a means to the attainment of their private ends, which they can reach only by being elected. Parties formulate policies in order to win elections, rather than win elections in order to formulate policies."[10]

We also assume, with Downs, that voters behave rationally, i.e. "that each citizen casts his vote for the party he believes will provide him with more benefits than any other party."[11] In so doing the rational citizen "compares the utility incomes (streams of benefit) he would receive were each party in office. . . . The difference between these expected utility incomes is the citizen's expected party differential. If it is positive, he votes for the incumbents; if it is negative, he votes for the opposition; if it is zero, he abstains."[12] It is likely that a citizen with a large expected party differential will be quite certain which candidate he prefers and that he will vote.

In Chart 1, *D* and *R* represent the candidates in a two-party election. A plus sign denotes a positive expectation toward the candidate, that is, a belief that one will receive benefits if the candidate is elected. A minus sign denotes a negative expectation toward the candidate, that is, a belief that one will suffer losses if the candidate is elected. Like Downs[13] we use the terms "benefit" and "loss" with reference only to the economic or political goals of citizens or parties. No doubt this usage is arbitrary, since the political behavior of many citizens is motivated primarily by psychological considerations that may have little or nothing to do with economic or political goals. For example, a citizen who expects to benefit economically or politically from a Republican victory but votes for the Democratic candidates because he is a co-religionist may be acting rationally in terms of his personality needs. However, he is acting irrationally as we have defined the term, since his decision runs counter to his schedule of economic or political goals.

All citizens who fall into quadrant II expect that they will benefit from the election of *D* and lose from the election of *R*. Conversely, all citizens in quadrant IV expect to benefit from the election of *R* and lose from the election of *D*. All citizens who fall into quadrant I expect to benefit from the election of either candidate, although they may assess the benefits of one candidate as greater than those of the other. All citizens falling into quadrant III expect to lose from the election of either candidate, although they may expect to lose more from the election of one candidate than the other. Quadrant III is the quadrant of alienation.

Chart 1.

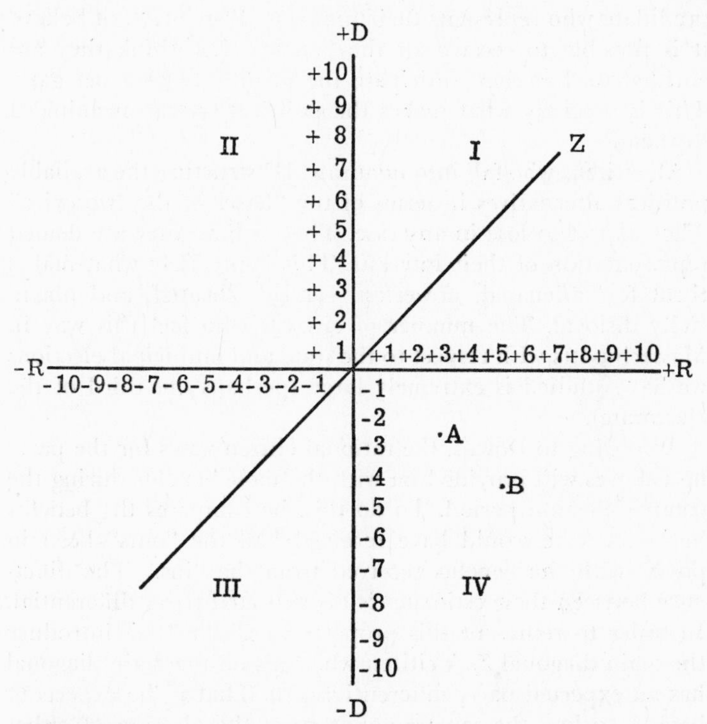

LEGEND:
D and *R* denote the candidates in a two-party election.
+ denotes a belief that the citizen expects to gain benefits from the election of the candidate.
− denotes a belief that the citizen expects to suffer losses from the election of the candidate.
A denotes one citizen.
B denotes a second citizen.

Democratic theory in its most utopian form suggests that citizens may expect to be confronted with political alternatives both of which are beneficial. If this were the case in reality, citizens would be forced to decide between the greater of two "goods." Undoubtedly, there are some citizens in some elections who see the political alternatives in these terms.[14] Nevertheless, the democratic citizen may still feel that the existing system is meaningful so long as he sees the election of one of the parties in terms of his own economic or political gain. Citizens who fall into quadrants, I, II, or IV will therefore have some commitment to the system. They believe it is possible to exercise some political power since they have a candidate who represents their interests. They may not believe it is possible to receive all the benefits they think they are entitled to, but they anticipate the possibility of a net gain. This is precisely what makes the political system meaningful to them.

All citizens who fall into quadrant III structure the available political alternatives in terms of the "lesser of the two evils." They expect to lose in any case. They believe they are denied representation of their interests. This is precisely what makes them feel alienated, powerless, cynical, cheated, and potentially disloyal. The number of citizens who feel this way in Massachusetts with respect to the state and municipal elections we have studied is extremely large (perhaps one-third of the electorate).

According to Downs, the rational citizen votes for the party he believes will provide him with the most benefits during the coming election period. To do this, he compares the benefits he believes he would have received had the "outs" been in power with the benefits received from the "ins." The difference between these estimates is his expected party differential. In order to represent this property in Chart 1 we introduce the main diagonal *Z*. A citizen who falls on the main diagonal has an expected party differential of 0. That is, he expects to benefit or lose the same amount from the election of either candidate. It is rational for a citizen in this situation to abstain. The closer a citizen is to the main diagonal the smaller is his expected party differential. For example, *A* believes he will gain 3 units of benefit from the election of *R* and lose 2 units of benefit from the election of *D*. His expected party differential is $+3 - (-2) = +5$. *B* believes he will gain 5 units of benefit from the election of *R* and lose 4 units of benefit from the election of *D*. His expected party differential is $+5 - (-4) = +9$. It will be noted that any point to the left of the diagonal *Z* represents a citizen whose expected party differential is favorable to *D* while any point to the right of the diagonal represents a citizen whose expected party differential is favorable to *R*. It should also be noted that we have extended the definition of expected party differential proposed by Downs to include differences between expected losses as well as expected benefits.

The distribution of citizens in the various quadrants will be a basic factor determining the outcome of elections. Some conjecture concerning the likely distribution in any democratic political system is in order. We suggest that a relatively small proportion of the electorate will be found in quadrant I, because a commitment to a particular party leads the citizen to find reasons for disliking the opposition. Several studies of political behavior indicate, for example, that citizens tend to pull the candidate they prefer closer to themselves and push the opposition away. They tend to "increase" the distance which separates the candidates by remembering statements made by their choice which agree with their own views and statements of their opponent which disagree with their own views.[15] This obviously makes the citizen feel more comfortable concerning his political choices. We therefore suggest that locations in quadrant I are essentially unstable and citizens who initially find themselves in this location will move either to quadrant II or IV, depending on their original political predisposition. The tendency to dislike at least one of the candidates is strengthened by the fact that in democratic societies politicians are one of the few culturally "legitimate" objects of public venom. We are taught to love our neighbors regardless of race, color, or national origin, but it is perfectly acceptable to denigrate the political opposition. The ability to release one's aggressions in the political realm is precisely what makes politics such an enjoyable spectator sport for so many citizens.

Criteria for Voting Decisions

Chart 1, which represents the distribution of voters, may serve as a starting point for analyzing problems of political strategy. Citizens who fall into quadrants I, II, and IV structure their voting decision to maximize benefits. The political strategist who wishes to act rationally will attempt to discover the distribution of voters along every particular benefit dimension, taking into account the intensity of the voters' preferences. The computation may be exceedingly difficult, but it is possible in principle for the candidate, given full knowledge, to assume those positions which will maximize his votes. However, it appears dubious to us that an approach of this kind can be politically effective in dealing with citizens who fall into quadrant III. Citizens who feel that candidates are self-interested, corrupt, incompetent, venal, and boss-controlled will not structure their voting decision in terms of issues, simply because they do not believe that the statements of candidates have any relevance to the real world. The standard clichés and the traditional vote-getting techniques will not work for the alienated. Citizens who fall into quadrants I, II, and IV have identified their well-being with at least one of the candidates. This means that they assume that at least some of the statements of their candidate are relevant. Since they interpret the political system in terms of benefits, they may regard the platforms of the candidates as pertinent data, as a relatively reliable indication of what the candidate would do if elected.

Since citizens in quadrant III are cynical and tend to disbelieve the statements of candidates, they will not regard platforms as reliable indicators of future action. However, if they are to vote they must do so in terms of some calculation which has relevance to their expected losses. The rational strategist is obliged to discover what those criteria are and to maximize their values for the alienated voter.

Two alternatives are available to alienated voters—abstention and voting for the lesser of two evils, both of which may be rational in the sense in which Downs used the term. There are several mechanisms for handling the anger and the feeling of powerlessness which are alienation, such as seeking and identifying with a charismatic leader, attempting to create new parties, or destroying the existing set of political institutions via revolution. Nevertheless, in the particular context of an election there are no alternatives other than abstention or voting for the lesser evil. It is possible to receive different kinds of gratification in taking the rational approach toward the lesser of two evils. One source of gratification is the simple fact that the economic or political losses have been minimized. We suspect that another source of gratification may stem from the reduction of anger which ensues when one "punishes" the "more evil" candidate by voting for his opponent.

Having shown the alternatives available to citizens in quadrant III, we must examine the criteria they can use to arrive at a political decision. The alienated voter discounts the statements concerning programs of both candidates. He assumes that platforms are equally attractive, equally unrealistic, and equally meaningless. If he votes at all, it will be because in his judgment one candidate is less crooked or more honest than the other. Judgments of honesty and integrity are notoriously difficult to make on an objective basis. In a large measure such judgments turn on an evaluation of the personality or character of the individual candidate. The alienated voter is forced to fall back upon intuitive feelings to make this determination. For example, the authors have found the following responses to the question: "What do you like least about ——?" "I looked in his eyes and I knew he was a crook," "too polished," "biggest stuffed shirt I've ever seen," "smug," "fat and pudgy," "looks crooked," "something about his eyes." Positive judgments are also made on this basis. For example, in response to "What do you like best about ——?" "Nice quiet manner," "he spoke to you with his heart, not his mouth," "just the way he spoke, I feel he is honest."

Strategies Available to the Rational Candidate

Thus far we have described a model of the distribution of an electorate using expected gains and losses as our measure. We have also indicated what we regard to be the criteria by which various populations determine their voting decisions. How can this model be used to guide the rational candidate in determining his political strategy? The rational candidate wishes to maximize output for a given input or minimize input for a given output. In other words, he wishes to use scarce resources most efficiently. It is a commonplace of political practice not to spend time and money in those areas which have been traditionally committed to a particular party when there is no reason to believe the situation is changing. At the beginning of the campaign, every candidate seeks information on this very point. The ability to delimit the boundaries of one's potential effectiveness is the first step toward a husbanding of scarce resources. Precinct captains and ward leaders who know their business provide a cheap means for finding those areas which are safe or hopeless, far cheaper than reliable public opinion polls.

We can use our model to illustrate the nature of this problem by partitioning the population into two groups, the committed and the uncommitted. We introduce a rectangle into Chart 2, the "bound of utility"—the area within which it may be useful to campaign.

In Chart 2 there are four segments of the population outside the bound of utility: (1) citizens whose party differential is large enough to ensure a vote for *D*, (2) citizens whose party differential is large enough to ensure a vote for *R*, (3) citizens of small party differential and great expectation of gain (the proportion of voters in this group is so small that the rational strategist wil not waste scarce resources appealing to it), and (4) citizens whose alienation is so extreme that they will not vote in any case. All citizens who fall within the bound have an expected party differential that is small enough to make them available to persuasion—thus the phrase, "the bound of utility." The rational strategist will concentrate his resources on an attempt to convert those citizens who fall within this bound. However, his approach to these citizens must vary according to whether he is attempting to convert those who fall into quadrants I, II, or IV—in which case he stresses issues—or those who fall into quadrant III—in which case he must prove his integrity.

Given his pervasive cynicism, the alienated voter tends to vote against the candidate who appears to be more experienced, well known, "professional," political, dishonest, and heavily financed. These criteria, however, have been developed by the alienated in response to feelings of powerlessness and meaninglessness. The strategist is likely to be more effective attending to the basic forms of alienation rather than to the political stereotypes of the alienated. The alienated voter, if he will respond at all, will respond to the candidate who gives him a sense of power or leads him to believe that the election is meaningful. The problem of wooing the alienated is not simply one of nominating a candidate who doesn't "smoke cigars" or who is not "fat and pudgy." The projection of the style of the candidate and the response of the electorate are not easily calculated. While one can determine the proportion of voters who can be swayed by an appeal to abolish rent control, an issue, we can suggest no method for determining whether a reserved demeanor on TV will be interpreted as "statesmanlike" or vacuous. Modern technology can provide the means for "changing" the color of a candidate's eyes ("I looked in his eyes and I knew he was a crook"); the question still remains, What color should they be? Since the political strategist must choose some alternative other than the traditional one and since the degree of uncertainty for him is so great, a bold and imaginative style is as likely to succeed as a conservative one. The choice of a bold strategy is not made for its own sake. The determinants of the strategy are still to be found in the feelings of powerlessness and meaninglessness of the alienated.

Chart 2.

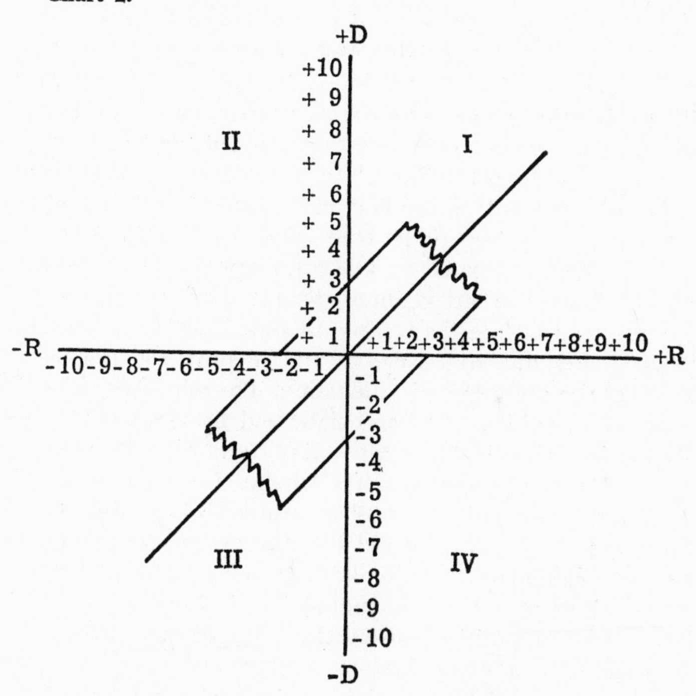

Strategies to appeal to feelings of powerlessness. Two strategies are available to the rational candidate who wishes to exploit feelings of powerlessness, both advantageous to the party that is out of power.

1. The candidate tries to enhance feelings of powerlessness by emphasizing the unchecked tyranny of the incumbents and suggesting that their hegemony is the cause of the citizen's powerlessness. A dramatic example of this strategy occurred during the Ward-Volpe contest. An advertising executive, who

had been advising candidates in Massachusetts for thirty years and who wished to take advantage of feelings of political powerlessness, suggested to a high-ranking Republican official that Volpe would benefit enormously if the party placed the following ads in newspapers throughout the state:

Negroes
Jews
Protestants
excluded from participation
in
the Democratic Party

The advertising executive was perfectly aware of the explosive character of such an advertisement, and he was concerned with the possibility of an adverse reaction. However, he argued, it would gain many more votes than it would lose because it was essentially true—the Democratic Party has traditionally nominated an all-Catholic white ticket. Such an advertisement, in his opinion, would therefore confirm or bring to the surface the feelings of powerlessness of alienated Jews, Protestants, and Negroes and identify the Democratic Party as the cause of their alienation. The effectiveness of this approach would be further heightened by the fact that the Republican slate included an Italian Catholic, a Protestant, a Jew, a Negro, and a Polish Catholic. In Massachusetts, a coalition-of-minorities strategy that succeeds in uniting Italian Catholics, Jews, Negroes, and Protestants can defeat an Irish Catholic candidate. The exploitation of racial and religious antagonisms may be unfortunate but it is a "constant" in Massachusetts politics. Given the facts of political life in Massachusetts, the nomination for the first time of a non-Protestant candidate for governor by the Republican Party was obviously a rational strategy, since for many voters the religion or the ethnic origin of the candidate is a prime consideration.

The Republican official rejected the proposal for two reasons: (1) it might boomerang (the Democrats could point to a small number of non-Catholics in their party or stress the "un-Americanism" of the advertisement); (2) it violated his sense of "the rules of the game." The former reason is rational, the latter is not unless voters believe in the same rules.

Nevertheless, the proposal is instructive. The advertising executive stressed the fact that the Massachusetts electorate, particularly the alienated, were far more sophisticated than most politicians would admit. He insisted that their feelings of powerlessness were well founded and that their image of the political system was basically accurate. This, he argued, is precisely why the old clichés will not work. Indeed, the traditional clichés may even backfire, because the candidate who uses them only fits the stereotype of the typical politician more closely.

For example, Ward has seven daughters. It seemed perfectly obvious that a candidate with seven daughters should appear on TV with them as often as possible, not only because Massachusetts is predominantly Catholic, but because many people seem to expect their candidate to be a family man. Ward accordingly played the family-man role to the hilt. He appeared on TV with his family several times and mailed thousands of multicolored postcards that showed a photograph of his family accompanied by the statement: "My 23-point program is based on the family as the fundamental unit of society." On TV Mrs. Ward said, "Joseph Ward has been a good father to his children; he will be a good father to you." No member of the Ward entourage doubted the rationality of this approach. The fact of the matter is that it angered many voters.

Respondents were asked in a post-election survey what they liked best and least about Ward and Volpe. Although those who mentioned Ward's family favorably outnumbered (4 to 1) those who were antagonized by the use to which Ward put his family, the interesting fact is that some voters reacted negatively to this standard campaign gambit. One respondent answered as follows to the question: "What do you like least about Ward?": "Nothing at all. He is doing a good job raising his large family, *but that won't benefit the state, at least not yet.*" Another respondent replied that she liked least Ward's "constant use of his wife and children as a vote-getting issue."

2. The object of the first strategy is to make the alienated voter more aware of his powerlessness by indicating to him that the incumbents are its cause. A second strategy, which is also available to the incumbents, and which takes advantage of powerlessness, offers the alienated voter a way out. In such a strategy the candidate attempts to identify himself with the alienated voter by stressing his own powerlessness. He imputes

power to the opposition or perhaps to some power elite (contractors, bookies, big businessmen, labor racketeers). This is the classic "underdog" gambit. He suggests that, by combining their small increments of power, he and the other little people may overthrow the powerful by their joint efforts. This appeal to collaboration offers them a promise of power and a feeling of participation. Collins, for example, portrayed the contest between himself and Powers as a struggle between David and Goliath—between the little people and professional power politicians. He used the slogan "Stop power politics—elect a hands-free mayor." Whenever possible he referred to his organization as a "small group of enthusiastic amateurs," at war with an army of mercenaries. He also sponsored an essay contest on the definition of "power politics." The winning essay, submitted by a fourteen-year-old girl, defined a power politician as "a man who is surrounded by political bigwigs and who administers to his and their gains first, and to the people last or not at all." One Bostonian who voted for Collins stated: "I don't like the idea that since all the big guys are for [Powers], the little people like us should be for him too."

Strategies to appeal to feelings of meaninglessness. The strategies we have described are designed to appeal primarily to feelings of powerlessness. Another aspect of the syndrome of alienation is meaninglessness, which may be experienced in two different ways. A citizen may feel that an election is without meaning because there are no real differences between the candidates, or he may feel that an intelligent and rational decision is impossible because the information he needs is lacking. If the candidates and platforms are very similar or identical, or if the voter refuses to give credence to campaign promises because he thinks the candidates are dishonest, it will be difficult to find meaningful information on which to base a voting decision.

1. A strategy that offers the alienated voter information he did not expect to receive may take advantage of feelings of meaninglessness. The alienated voter regards as meaningful information relative to the size and source of campaign expenditures. John Francis Kennedy, one of the six candidates who opposed Ward in the Democratic gubernatorial primary, made explicit use of such a strategy. He notified the public that he would not pay for TV or radio time, or newspaper ads, or

billboards, or bumper stickers, or any other form of campaigning which requires money. That he did not appear on TV or advertise in any other medium made his claim credible. With one stroke, he satisfied the syllogism of the alienated voter: Opulent campaigning is the cause of the candidate's indebtedness to his contributors. Kennedy's campaign is frugal. Therefore, Kennedy is not indebted. Kennedy's strategy, however, may have been self-defeating for those voters who were unaware of his candidacy.

2. During the primary election Endicott Peabody, another opponent of Ward's, developed a "meaningful" strategic gambit. Peabody sponsored a number of five-minute "news" broadcasts called "the Political Roundup." The format of the program was similar to that of any TV news roundup, consisting of a number of "news" clips dealing with international and national events, including clips showing Peabody campaigning. The "news" reporter, a hired employee of the Peabody organization, "reported" a ground swell for Peabody. Although the "Political Roundup" was preceded and followed by the legally required statement that "the following broadcast is sponsored by the Peabody for Governor Committee," the program appeared to be a regular news broadcast, i.e., an objective report of the Peabody ground swell. In this sense it appeared to be nonsponsored or nonpolitical and was therefore possibly more credible to alienated voters. One Boston station discontinued the "Political Roundup" because, in the words of the manager, it "confused" many voters.

3. Another strategy for taking advantage of meaninglessness is the appeal of frankness. The candidate tells the voter many "facts of political life" which are usually censored but which the alienated voter has discovered independently. In this case the alienated voter *knows* that the candidate has told the truth. This is the strongest evidence possible to establish the integrity of the candidate. For example, the candidate could boldly state that campaigns cost money and many large contributors expect special favors. He could say openly that campaigns require organization and that party workers demand patronage in return for services. He could point out that these are the facts of political life for all candidates. In other words, he could repeat the classic analysis of the distribution of power and the nature of competition in state and local government. Having established the truthfulness of his ap-

proach, he could then go on to differentiate between himself and his opponent. Whether the remainder of his argument was "true" or not would depend upon the purposes and ethics of the candidate.

4. Another strategy is available to the candidate who wishes to take advantage of meaninglessness. The alienated voter believes that candidates take care of themselves and their entourage rather than the public. Any information indicating that the candidate cares about the voter would be meaningful. A simple statement by the candidate to the effect that he is interested in the public will be worthless; evidence of another sort must be made available. During the elections we have studied, candidates spent large sums of money proclaiming their virtues on stickers, billboards, etc. Perhaps a more rational allocation of scarce resources would have been to use a more indirect and imaginative approach. For example, the candidate could send large numbers of voluntary workers to conduct opinion polls in areas defined by the bound of utility. Since this poll would not have the usual academic objectives, the criteria of sample choice would be political rather than statistical. The pollster would tell the respondent that the purpose of the poll was to inform a particular candidate (who would be named) about the desires of the electorate. The real purpose would be to show the respondent that the candidate is interested in his welfare. The incontrovertible evidence that the candidate has spent time and money attempting to find out how the voter feels is precisely the type of information which is meaningful in the assessment of the candidate's character. As a by-product, the data may furnish the candidate with useful information, but the principal purpose has been acomplished the moment the interview is completed.

Discussion

The candidate who is forced to campaign in a community where many alienated voters reside must, of course, ask himself three fundamental questions: (1) Is the proportion of alienated voters (who are likely to vote rather than abstain) large enough to warrant strategies designed especially for them? (2) What is the party identification of most alienated voters? and (3) will strategies designed for the alienated voter repel the nonalienated voter?

With respect to the second question, the candidate should realize that political alienation tends to convert party identifiers into skeptical "independents." The candidate of the minority party or the "outs" (who is likely to profit by a large turnout of "independents") has more to gain by increasing the amount of political alienation. The candidate of the party that has a "normal" majority of party identifiers (the Democrats in Massachusetts), who are disillusioned by scandals that have occurred during the most recent Democratic administration, may be wise to stress the importance of party loyalty and play down appeals to the alienated. It is instructive to note that more strategies for the alienated voter are available to the "out" party, because the alienated voter is likely to assume that the incumbents have greater opportunities to be "professional" politicians, i.e. corrupt politicians. In Massachusetts, the view is widespread that one cannot remain an honest man in politics.

With respect to the third question, it is possible that strategies designed for the alienated voter will repel the nonalienated voter. The voter who wants candidates to discuss issues (and not sling mud) may be frustrated, for example, by Kennedy's nonappearances or by Ward's use of his family. However, we do not believe that Peabody's "Political Roundup," Collins's appeal to the underdog, or the appeal of frankness will frustrate and anger the nonalienated voter. Nevertheless, the profound cynicism of the alienated voter and the intensely personal nature of the "gut reactions" he uses to decide his vote make the formulation of a political strategy for him exceedingly difficult. Some of these strategies may backfire. It is not inconceivable that an alienated voter could react to a candidate's public opinion poll by asking, "Who does he think he's fooling with that fake poll?"

Implicit in this discussion is the suggestion that it is rational for candidates who seek the alienated vote to stress style rather than content, the "correct" demeanor rather than the "correct" program. Some readers may be repelled by the Machiavellian uses to which such an approach may be put and some may conclude that the strategies we have suggested reduce the democratic process to a hideous farce. We would like to point out, however, that such is not necessarily the case. In some political situations, the views of alienated voters are correct. Their alienation is testimony to their powers of rational perception. If the candidate uses the strategies we have discussed, he must reckon with the consequences, for the alienated voter has not lost his cynicism. He is merely suspending judgment until the newly elected candidate either delivers or reneges. The alienated citizen who votes has placed some trust in his choice. If this trust is betrayed, he may recognize the perverse use to which these strategies have been put, and they will not work again with him.

Notes:

1. "I don't like the caliber of the candidates." "Of the worst he was the best. All a bunch of chiselers." "Volpe is not quite as bad as Ward. I didn't have anything better to vote for." "Not much to offer between either—almost left it blank." "Felt they were all no good." "Neither candidate appealed to me." "He was the lesser of two evils." "Collins will not steal as much." "Even Volpe is crooked. He's a contractor."

(Unless otherwise indicated, the quotations which appear in footnotes are taken from public opinion surveys relating to these elections.)

2. "Doesn't matter who wins on the state level, they are all crooks." "Things always turn out the same no matter who wins." "It makes no difference who wins, Massachusetts is just a crappy state. You can't do anything with it. There is something wrong here." "Voting wouldn't do any good—they're both no good." "Well, voting only decides between the politicians." "Once they get into office, that's the end of what we have to say." "They care only to win elections." "The vote doesn't mean anything." "We have no control at all." "I get the feeling that it's all a big hoax, especially on the state level." "Things are decided long before the vote." "Voting makes no difference. Never has before, why should it now?" "Whoever you vote for, they're going to get in and line their pockets."

3. "He has too many prior commitments. . . ." "Powers was being sponsored by too many business interests. I mean those people not concerned with social welfare of the voting public." "Too much of a politician, commitments to groups." "You can't tell me Collins didn't have one thousand people on his back." "Too many apron strings, hard to hold office without doing favors." "I felt he made deals with backers of the campaign." "They are all linked up with business and business has money." "When a politician gets through he gets a job handing out favors. You get the runaround if you don't know the politicians . . . what you need is to know the guy and have money." "Ward made too many promises." "Owes too much to too many."

4. See, for example, Anthony Lewis, "Massachusetts Aroused by Corruption Scandals," *New York Times,* June 19, 1961, p. 1.

5. For an analysis of the forms and causes of political alienation see Murray B. Levin, *The Alienated Voter,* New York, Holt, Rinehart, and Winston, 1960.

6. "He didn't have any program at all and I didn't know what to make of him other than he's done a good job to bring his family up." "All he

did was attack." "I didn't think he was telling the truth." "Didn't like his accusations—he said too much about his opponent—should have talked about himself." "I didn't like the way he handled his speeches against Volpe. I would rather see them talk about the issues that face us in the future and leave the past buried." "I didn't like those attempts to make Volpe look crooked. That literature could have been taken out in the wrong way—they could have photographed only half a letter. . . ." "His tactics during the campaign were not very nice . . . bring out skeletons from the closet, I call it—that's not the way to show you are a better man, is it?"

7. "All a pack of lies." "The TV appearances did not influence my vote because they were merely mutual character assassinations."

8. See, for example, James Reichley, *The Art of Government, Reform and Organization Politics in Philadelphia,* New York, The Fund for the Republic, 1958, and Fred J. Cook and Gene Gleason, "The Shame of New York," *The Nation,* Special Issue, Oct. 31, 1959.

9. Anthony Downs, *An Economic Theory of Democracy,* New York, Harper, 1957.

10. *Ibid.,* p. 28.

11. *Ibid.,* p. 36.

12. *Ibid.,* p. 39.

13. *Ibid.,* p. 6.

14. "They're all good men. Good luck to them."

15. See Bernard Berelson, Paul Lazarsfeld, and William McPhee, *Voting,* Chicago, University of Chicago Press, 1954, Chap. 10.

B. *Motivations and Personality*

4 *Children's Feelings about Political Authority*

by Fred I. Greenstein

Citizens' feelings about political authority have a complex and imperfectly understood, but important, bearing on the equilibrium of the body politic. People inevitably have assumptions about their leaders: assumptions about whether leaders are benign or malignant, whether they are on a plane with "the rest of us" or whether they are a higher order of being. These assumptions probably vary from one leadership role to another, and within and between societies. [Here] we shall examine their childhood antecedents.

The feelings New Haven children displayed toward political authority were striking. In some respects they resembled adult political views; in others they were distinctively childlike. Their childlike aspect was sufficiently pervasive to be elicited unexpectedly by a research procedure not primarily designed to deal with feelings toward authority. Before discussing the New Haven findings we might usefully consider *adult* feelings about political authority.

Reprinted from *Children and Politics,* by Fred I. Greenstein (New Haven, Conn.: Yale University Press, 1965), pp. 27–54, by permission of the author and the publisher.

Adult Ambivalence Toward Political Authority

Adult assessments of political leaders are curiously inconsistent. In some ways Americans seem to have an abiding distrust of politics and politicians. For example, more Americans agree than disagree with statements such as "it is almost impossible for a man to stay honest if he goes into politics," a substantial proportion of the population feels that it is at best dubious for a young man to make politics his career, and similar anti-politician attitudes often are elicited by public opinion polls. Cynical, unsympathetic images of politics and the politician also are revealed by a great many adults in responses to various questions about the individual's political efficacy, as measured for example by willingness to agree with the statement "I don't think public officials care much what people like me think."[1]

But this is not the whole story. Other studies have shown that Americans hold specific political roles—for example, senator, mayor, and governor—in exceedingly *high* esteem. Over the years, the many studies of occupational prestige have shown that people rank these roles well above all but an occasional civilian role such as physician in terms of importance and status.[2] These inconsistencies led one commentator to write of "the ambivalent social status of the American politician."[3]

Public responses to individual politicians fluctuate greatly. Perhaps the best barometer of this variation is the American Institute of Public Opinion's regular estimates of presidential popularity. Since the 1930s, countless national cross-sections have been asked, "Do you approve or disapprove of the way President X has been handling his job?" Favorable response to Roosevelt, during his term in office, ranged from 50 per cent to 84 per cent; approval of Truman from 23 per cent to 87 per cent; Eisenhower from 49 per cent to 79 per cent. Support for Kennedy, although consistently high during his administration, also was variable, ranging from a low of 57 per cent to a high of 83 per cent.[4]

One of the most substantial assets of the president evidently is the public respect for his role and his symbolic position at the pinnacle of the nation. Thus it has been shown that the mere fact of incumbency is sufficient to improve a leader's reputation with people who had previously been skeptical of him. One study of this tendency elicited statements like the following made several weeks after the 1952 election by a Stevenson supporter who had been critical of Eisenhower: "I feel a little more confident in his ability as a president. The change . . . is probably due only to the reason that he has been elected president. I can't explain myself too well, but I feel that Eisenhower is just a better man than I had imagined."[5] When a vice-president assumes the presidency unexpectedly, after the death in office of a president, this effect may be especially visible, as can be seen from the following interviews conducted in the immediate aftermath of President Kennedy's assassination.[6]

> In 1960 I came to the conclusion on the basis of very little evidence that [Lyndon Johnson] was a megalomaniac and somebody I didn't want to see in the White House. . . . I thought . . . he really wanted to hold complete power over government in his hands. . . . Immediately upon hearing that Kennedy died, I started revising my opinion and got much more temperate. . . . In about five minutes . . . I just decided that, well, you know, he's really a great tactician and we have to give him a chance and all we can do is hope for the best.
>
> We immediately began to think of Johnson in slightly better terms than we [had] before.
>
> Just the fact that he was in the presidency gave him a sort of deification.
>
> I thought [after hearing of President Kennedy's assassination], "Oh my God, what are we going to do with Johnson in there?" And then I thought and thought. Well, gee, I was kind of impressed a little earlier with him, you know, before he was vice-president I didn't think he was such a bad guy. Maybe things aren't going to be so bad after all.

The polls have generally shown a rise in the post-election poularity of reelected incumbents. They also show the striking willingness of citizens to rally around the president when his role of national leader in the international arena is emphasized—for example, during Roosevelt's period of wartime leadership, after the dispatch of troops to Korea by Truman and to Lebanon by Eisenhower, and after Kennedy's declaration of blockade during the 1962 Cuban crisis.[7]

Children's Idealization of Political Authority

The most conspicuous difference betwen adult political orientations and those of the New Haven children was in attitudes of cynicism and distrust toward politics. Virtually *no* children entertained these widespread adult views. In spite of a variety of attempts to evoke such responses during my preliminary interviewing and pretesting, for example, the references to "politician" and "bribe" in the interview with Judith, there was no evidence even of a frame of reference which would make it possible to use questionnaire items designed to evoke political cynicism. The final version of the New Haven questionnaire contained a number of items which might have evoked spontaneous references to the malignancy of politicians, but only one or two of the 659 children made statements which could be construed in this way. Instead, as we shall see, the spontaneous references to politicians had a remarkably benign quality.[8] We may now look more specifically at three classes of New Haven findings which bear on this: children's rankings of the "importance" of political leaders; their evaluations of the incumbent president, governor, and mayor; and their spontaneous statements.

THE IMPORTANCE OF POLITICAL LEADERS

New Haven children were asked to tell which of a number of adult roles are "most important." Choices offered included the president and mayor, authority figures of the immediate environment such as school principals and teachers, as well as physicians, clergymen, police chiefs, and judges. *At every age level, there were more references to the president and mayor than to any of the other roles.* Thus, although the negative side of adult images of politicians is not present in childhood, the positive side—the attribution of great prestige to specific roles—emerges early.

How early? Table I, which reports the responses of the youngest group in this sample, shows that by the age of nine the belief that the president and mayor are figures of great importance is firmly entrenched. Both political executives are mentioned by over 20 per cent more children than is the next most prestigeful individual, the physician. Indeed, there is a clear distinction in the data between estimates of the importance of the president and mayor, and estimates of the importance of the other six figures. The gap between each of the remaining roles is in no case greater than 13 per cent.

The importance of political roles clearly is learned quite early, before the age of nine. The age at which children first acquire this particular evaluation cannot be determined from the New Haven sample, but since reporting this finding in 1960, I have learned of several instances in which children of preschool age (in one case a two-year-old) showed a respectful awareness of the president, and, in the Kennedy years, of the presidential family.[9] The nine-year-olds whose responses are reported in Table I have virtually no specific *knowledge* of the presidential or mayoral roles. Children of this age (fourth graders) were uniformly aware of President Eisenhower's name (96 per cent could name him in the written questionnaire) and

Table I. ***Judgments by Fourth Grade Children of Which Adult Roles Are "Most Important"****

Roles	Per Cent Choosing Each Role
President	80
Mayor	79
Doctor	57
Police chief	51
Judge	48
School teacher	35
Religious leader	32
School principal	22
Number of cases	111

*Children were permitted four choices, so the percentages exceed 100. The mayor's prestige may be a function of the great personal popularity of New Haven's incumbent city executive.

only slightly less aware (90 per cent) of the name of New Haven's popular mayor. But, using the most generous coding standards, less than a fourth of them could describe the president's duties; about a third could make a "reasonably accurate" statement about the mayor, largely because New Haven's Mayor Lee was then engaged in a spectacular and highly publicized urban renewal program. Awareness of other aspects of the political environment (e.g. the governor and the legislative bodies at various levels of government) was nil.

The following passage from an interview with a seven-year-old (just beginning second grade) provides some insight into the character of young children's conceptions of political leaders:

> INTERVIEWER: Have you ever heard of the President of the United States?
> ROBERT: Yes.
> I: What is his name?
> R: Eisenhower.
> I: What does he do?
> R: Well, sometimes he . . . well, you know . . . a lot of times when people go away he'll say goodbye and he's on programs and they do work.
> I: What kind of work does he do? Do you know any more about it?
> R: (After thought) Studying.
> I: What sorts of things does he study?
> R: Like things they gotta do . . . like important . . . what's happening and the weather and all that.
> I: Now tell me this. Who is more important, the President of the United States or a doctor?
> R: (Pause) The President.
> I: Who do you think is more important, the President of the United States or a school teacher?
> R: (Emphatically) President!
> I: Why is the president more important?
> R: They do much more work and they're much importanter. School teacher isn't.
> I: (After being told in response to further questions that the president also is more important than a storekeeper and than a general in the army): Who do you think is more important than the president?
> R: (Long pause) Lemme see . . . I don't know.

Robert is unshakable in his assessment of the president's importance. He has acquired this assessment—as his attempt to explain the president's duties in terms of a workaday seven-year-old frame of reference shows—in the absence of even a moderately precise awareness of what the president does. The exact reason for the president's importance is one of those adult mysteries which, like the daily weather forecast, appear on the television screen in the intervals between broadcasts for children. If the president is important, he *must* do important things, as does Robert's older brother, who studies his homework.

Evaluations and "affective knowledge" about political leaders precede the factual information on which one might assume they would be based. [Later] we shall examine a quite similar pattern of development, the genesis of identification with political parties. Here also, the emotional tie to an aspect of the adult political world precedes even moderately differentiated cognitive development. Political information increases substantially over the brief age span of the New Haven sample, but the structure of factual knowledge is erected on a foundation of feelings, assessments, and opinions.

EVALUATIONS OF PUBLIC OFFICIALS

Another point at which children's orientations can be compared, at least crudely, with adult responses is in ratings of individual political leaders. Following the various information items which called, for example, for descriptions of the mayor, governor, and president, the children were asked to evaluate these leaders on a four-point scale ranging from "very good" to "bad."

Here children's responses did not merely reflect what might be expected from comparable adult samples. Their modal assessment of each of the three incumbents was in the highest possible category—"very good."[10] The New Haven survey was conducted during the period of national soul-searching which followed the long-delayed American response to the first Russian space satellite launching. Judging from the way national cross-sections of adults responded to the opportunity to rate President Eisenhower during this period, *children's views of political leaders are substantially more favorable than those of their elders.* Table II contrasts the New Haven responses with the American Institute of Public Opinion's February 1958 report of the president's popularity. Needless to say, this comparison of New Haven findings with national survey data must be treated as suggestive;[11] however, differences between adults and children in evaluation of the president are considerable. Adults were about five times more willing to criticize the chief executive. It is only during the immediately post-election honeymoon periods that the AIPO finds as few as five per cent of the adult population critical of the president.[12]

New Haven responses to items dealing with political efficacy also suggest that children are far more positive in their political orientations than adults. Less than two per cent of the children said that they would not vote when they reached twenty-one. And over two thirds agree that "it makes much difference who wins an election," in contrast to the markedly smaller proportions of adult samples making such statements.[13]

Table II. ***Children's Evaluations of Three Political Executives Contrasted with Adult Evaluations of President Eisenhower During the Same Time Period***

	Children				Adults*
	Mayor	*Governor*	*President*		*President*
Very good	62%	40%	71%	Approve	58%
Fairly good	27	28	21		
Not very good	4	2	4	Disapprove	27
Bad	1	—†	1		
Don't know	6	30	4	No opinion	15
Number of cases	651‡	643‡	649‡		

*February 1958 AIPO findings, reported in March 1958 release. These findings are based on a national sample. On their comparability with the New Haven data, see footnote 11.

†Less than 1 per cent.

‡Number of cases does not equal complete sample due to invalid responses.

THE BENEVOLENCE OF LEADERS

I have already noted that various items in the New Haven questionnaire might have stimulated spontaneous references to graft, corruption, and political immorality, if these images were important in children's perceptions of politics. References of this sort were not made. Instead a quite different set of images emerged spontaneously in response to the six open-ended items asking for descriptions of the duties of local, state, and federal executives and legislative bodies. The items were quite unstructured, simply asking, "What sorts of things does the mayor (etc.) do?" As might be expected, most of the children who were able to respond made rather straightforward factual assertions—"The mayor runs the city"; "Congress makes laws"; etc. What was surprising, however, was that a conspicuous minority of the children volunteered affective or affectively toned responses—especially in descriptions of the mayor and president. As noted above, only one or two of these statements were unsympathetic. Several classes of response are worth examining.

Services to children. About ten per cent of the responses to the mayor were to child-related portions of his role. For example:

> The mayor makes parks and swings. (Fifth grade girl.)
> The mayor repairs the parks, roads, schools, and takes the snow off the roads when it snows. (Fifth grade boy.)

It is a reasonable assumption that when a child's first image of a political leader emphasizes pork-barrel indulgences to the child, the image is favorable.

Normative role. In addition, some children explicitly characterized political leaders in positive normative terms—either as people "who do good things," or as specialists in making moral judgments:

> The president does good work. (Sixth grade boy.)
>
> The mayor sends men to build parks for us and make our city be a good one. (Fourth grade girl.)
>
> The president makes peace with every country but bad. (Fifth grade boy.)
>
> The mayor talks business to all the people and says what's wrong or bad. (Fourth grade girl.)
>
> I think that he [the president] has the right to stop bad things before they start. (Fifth grade girl.)

General benevolence. More generally, children tended to describe political leaders as "helping," "taking care of," and "protecting" people. Benevolent perceptions of this sort were especially evident in descriptions of the president and mayor, but also occasionally were apparent in descriptions of the governor and of legislative bodies. For example:

> The president deals with foreign countries and takes care of the U.S. (Eighth grade boy.)
>
> The mayor helps people to live in safety. . . . The president is

> doing a very good job of making people be safe. (Fourth grade girl.)
>
> The president gives us freedom. (Eighth grade girl.)
>
> The Board of Aldermen gives us needs so we could live well. (Fourth grade girl.)

In a few cases children went so far as to perceive political authority as a direct source of economic support:

> The mayor pays working people like banks. (Fifth grade boy.)
>
> The mayor sees that schools have what they need and stores and other places too. (Fifth grade girl.)
>
> The mayor helps everyone to have nice homes and jobs. (Fourth grade boy.)

The frequency of references to the mayor connected with services to children and of generally "benevolent" and "normative" references to the mayor and president is shown in Table III. Here we see that statements of this sort were made by some children at every age level, but that benevolent imagery declines with age. Although the total of these classes of response rarely exceeds 15 per cent in any cell of Table III, what is remarkable is that any such images are expressed in answer to such bland, unstructured stimulus questions. Moreover, additional descriptions of political leaders had favorable connotations which do not fit as readily into a few simple categories. For example, some children placed emphasis on the wisdom, capability, and solicitousness of public officials:

> The president is in charge of the United States and has many wise men to tell him what is best. (Sixth grade boy.)
>
> The president worries about all the problems of all the 48 states. Takes care of threatening wars by holding peace conferences. (Seventh grade boy.)
>
> The mayor has to keep track of everything that happens in New Haven. (Sixth grade boy.)

The spontaneous appearance of these images suggests that appropriately structured questions would show the imagery of benevolence to be considerably more common among grade school children than Table III (p. 420) indicates.[14]

The research of David Easton and Robert Hess makes it clear that this indeed is the case. At approximately the same time as the New Haven field work, Easton and Hess[15] studied the political socialization of 366 second through eighth grade children in a Chicago suburb. The Chicago study employed a number of multiple choice items specifically designed to detect idealization of authority: for example, questions asking whether the president is "the best person in the world," "a good person," or "not a good person." The findings clearly demonstrated idealization of the president by young children, and a rather complicated pattern of deidealization with age, depending upon the facet of the presidential image referred to by the child. Thus, 60 per cent of the second graders and only two per cent of the eighth graders took the hyperbolic position that the president was "the best person in the world." About

Table III. ***Children's Images of the Mayor and President, by School Year****

	School Year				
Mayor	*4th*	*5th*	*6th*	*7th*	*8th*
Benevolence: "helps us" "gives us freedom"	20%	16%	9%	3%	4%
Normative role: "does good things" "tells what is right or wrong"	7	12	13	8	12
Services to children: "makes parks and swings"	15	14	1	11	15
Number of cases	55	82	98	115	151
President					
Benevolence	26%	11%	5%	5%	4%
Normative	5	9	11	3	7
Number of cases	62	80	95	112	160

*Percentages are based on those children who were able to produce a description of the executive role, whether or not the description was "reasonably accurate" (excluding grossly inaccurate or vague statements).

three quarters of the second graders and less than half of the eighth graders agreed that the president "likes almost everybody." Comparisons of other attributes of the president with "most men" (e.g. his knowledge, "how hard" he works) also produced highly favorable responses, but in these cases the responses did not decrease—some even increased slightly—with age. A replication by Easton and Hess shortly after Kennedy's inauguration demonstrated that the findings were not simply a function of Eisenhower's incumbency; additional studies in other nations (Chile, Puerto Rico, Australia, and Japan) showed tendencies, which parallel the New Haven findings, for young children to perceive political leaders as benevolent, and for the leader's image to lose some of this positive coloration among older children.[16]

The New Haven findings may be summarized as follows: (1) children are at least as likely as adults to perceive high political roles as being important; (2) they seem to be more sympathetic to individual political leaders (and, in general, to politics) than are adults; (3) in at least some cases their actual images of political leaders are qualitatively different from the images one would expect adults to hold, especialy in the emphasis on benignness; and (4), most important, the widespread adult political cynicism and distrust do not seem to have developed by eighth grade (age 13).

Causes and Consequences of the Child's View of Political Authority

Why is the child's early view of political authority so strikingly favorable? What, if any, effect does this aspect of individual political development have on adult political behavior and on the political system? Fully convincing answers to this pair of questions (particularly the second) are not available. This is so partly because the New Haven data are limited, but also because the existing body of basic knowledge linking childhood experience and adult behavior is quite rudimentary,[17] as is our understanding of the connections between individual attitudes and behavior and the functioning of political systems.

SOURCES OF THE CHILD'S VIEW OF AUTHORITY

In hypothesizing about how children acquire their idealized conceptions of political authority, it is important to consider not only the agencies of socialization to which children are exposed, but also the socialized themselves—what children "are able to absorb and what they selectively perceive and misperceive."

As with a number of other aspects of political learning we

shall consider, conceptions of leaders seem to spring up in a singularly haphazard manner. In New Haven, at least, there is little formal adult effort to shape the political information and attitudes of grade school children. No mandatory provision for training in the subject matter once called civics exists until eighth grade. Social studies curriculum guides do not even suggest the possibility of introducing such training until sixth grade. New Haven is not unique in this respect, judging from the following report on social studies teaching:

> In most cases, the social studies program of the primary grades (K-3) focuses on the home, family, and community. In the intermediate grades, children usually study about their home states, about the United States, about some foreign countries, and sometimes about the history of the Old World. In grades seven and eight, geography or community study and the study of the U.S.A. are the general rule. Examination of materials used throughout these grades, especially in K-4, shows that study of politics and government, when included, is often incidental rather than central.[18]

The children themselves, with very rare exceptions, do not actively search for political information; at the younger age levels in the sample, in fact, few interests are evident beyond the child's immediate circle.

Nevertheless, by adolescence a large proportion of the political orientations which guide the participation of adult voters are already present. Many of these orientations are acquired during the fourth through eighth grade years covered by the New Haven study; a few, including the perception—in an idealized form—of leaders such as the president, are already evident by fourth grade.

The most important source of children's conceptions of authority undoubtedly is the civic instruction which goes on incidental to normal activities in the family.[19] Children overhear parental conversations; they sense, or are informally told of, their parents' stance toward political authority in general and partisan politics in particular. Parents are called upon to answer questions about politics just as they are called upon to answer questions about the thousand and one other aspects of society the child gradually becomes aware of. Inadvertent political learning also takes place in the schools; patriotic rituals are observed, national heroes (including Washington and Lincoln) are discussed, and, during election campaigns, partisanship, campaign buttons, and the general ballyhoo of American elections spill over not only into the classroom, but also into the peer-group, neighborhood, and—especially—the mass media, as we saw in Judith's lament about election broadcasting. Between as well as during elections, the mass media seem to be especially important agents of informal learning.[20] Children only rarely attend closely to political news (although dramatic political events, such as satellite launchings and integration crises, *do* interest children deeply). But they inevitably are exposed to reports of the adult political world and willy-nilly a rough conception of politics begins to form.[21]

There are a number of possible reasons for the peculiarly idealized character of early political images. One is the nature of the political communications adults direct to children. While there is no explicit norm in the United States that children should be "protected" from politics, it is likely that adults—even politically cynical adults—more or less unconsciously sugarcoat the political explanations they pass on to children. As Easton and Hess have suggested,[22] politics may be in the same class as sex—one of those sordid aspects of adult existence from which it is thought that young children are best shielded.

What young children are "willing" to learn is probably as important as what adults are willing to teach. Parents, teachers, and the very setting of childhood (especially dependency upon adults) provide children with something considerably more important than specific political attitudes—namely, general orientations to the adult world. Through the entirety of his experiences with adults the child acquires a frame of reference within which to place an especially important class of adult—the political leader. Having learned to see adults many times larger than life size, children are likely simply to misperceive and otherwise screen out discordant information about "corruption" and other negative aspects of the adult political environment.[23] Since it is not possible that children are completely insulated from adult attitudes of distrust toward politics, selective perception of this sort would seem to be an important explanation of the lack of political cynicism among children.

Psychoanalytic theory suggests another and deeper way in

which experiences with authority figures in the immediate environment may affect responses to authority in the wider political world. Figures in the latter setting, for instance the president, are *unconsciously* (i.e. in a way not accessible to conscious awareness) perceived as the analogues of parents and other immediate environment authorities. The public figure becomes invested with powerful private feelings; response to him assumes some of the qualities of response to family members and others in the face-to-face environment.

This notion was first advanced to political scientists by Harold Lasswell.[24] It now is quite familiar and in fact has been thoroughly vulgarized, particularly during the Eisenhower years, in the form of popular references to political "father figures." Vulgarizations notwithstanding, there may be considerable empirical substance to the thesis that private orientations to authority become channeled into public orientations. A good bit of scattered psychiatric evidence based upon patients in therapy has accumulated.[25] Further, public behavior during certain "extreme conditions," such as the unexpected death of a popular leader, is quite consistent with the hypothesis that such an unconscious analogy exists. On these occasions, not only do many citizens experience extreme grief of the sort we expect to find when a parent has died, but they also often draw this analogy themselves. Orlansky[26] reports the following reactions to Roosevelt's death:

> You expect me to say something about what happened. But I cannot speak about Roosevelt's death any more than I could speak about the death of my mother and father. (New York high school teacher to her class.)
>
> It's almost as though father had died. (Liberal newspaper editor.)
>
> He was just like a daddy to me always; he always talked to me just that way. (Democratic Representative Lyndon Johnson of Texas.)
>
> He was father and brother to us all. (Frank Sullivan.)

The death of Edward VII of England was the occasion for the following piece of popular doggerel:

> Greatest sorrow England ever had
> When death took away our dear Dad.[27]

The massive public response to the assassination of President John F. Kennedy in 1963 brought forth a variety of research reports confirming the impression that intensively felt attachments with figures in the remote environment, especially the president, are prevalent even though the presence of such attachments is not ordinarily apparent. There is a good bit of evidence that children as well as adults were emotionally affected by Kennedy's death. And at least in some specialized populations of children, namely children undergoing psychotherapy, feelings toward family members were very much implicated in responses to the President's death.[28]

For adults, as Sheatsley and Feldman comment, it was "difficult to picture the youthful, fun-loving Kennedys as serving *in loco parentis.*"[29] Nevertheless, statements such as the following (which were made by college students shortly after the assassination)[30] suggest that the magnitude of grief was as great, if not quite as enduring, as would be expected in the death of a member of the immediate family, or a very close friend.

> Well, a friend of mine [died in an accident] several years ago. We had a room near each other in the [dormitory] that year and we were real good buddies, and when he died I found out about it sort of matter of factly—somebody assumed that I already knew—and I felt sort of guilty that one of my reactions was that, well, X's gone, you know. And, in a way it was, how could he do that to me? How could he leave me? In the loss you felt that there was a personal anger . . . and this is very similar to what I felt about Kennedy, and yet with Kennedy it was not only me, but the whole country. It was not so much that Kennedy was dead, but that I was without a friend and a leader, and so was the whole country. It had become sort of queer. Well, my mother's been in the hospital recently, you know, and kind of ill. In a kind of a way I felt that it would be better if she had died rather than Kennedy.

> I had a cousin who died of sleeping sickness about three years ago, who I didn't know too well, and I didn't give a damn, actually. And I felt more strongly about this, and God knows I knew her better. I didn't know Kennedy at all—I've never met the man. I did feel some sort of identification, and I can't say why because I wasn't a rabid Kennedyite.

> The only experience I've had with death is that my grandfather died after two years of the state that Joseph Kennedy is in

> now and it wasn't pleasant. And at the time I vividly recall that I was sorry, but not upset like this, like I was Friday. . . . Somehow I felt when I heard this news like I think I might have felt if I'd been told someone real close to me had died. It's something I can't . . . I've tried to explain to myself and I can't.

The existing fragments of quantitative evidence are ambiguous on the hypothesis that citizens unconsciously link primary and secondary environment figures and respond to the latter in terms of the former. However, verification is made difficult (although not, as has been alleged, impossible) by the evident complexity of such a process and the variable forms it might take. A public figure (for example, President Kennedy) might take on the characteristics of a family member without specifically serving as a parent surrogate; he might serve as a sibling, a son, even as a composite of several family members. Furthermore, for some people, the unconscious linkage of immediate and secondary environment figures may be a simple generalization from the former to the latter, but for others there may be more devious compensatory associations. Thus, for example, for one individual, hostility toward primary group figures such as the father may lead to hostility to other authority figures such as the president. For another individual, primary group hostilities may be reacted to by idealizing public figures.[31] Research on the psychoanalytic hypotheses about authority therefore will require considerable ingenuity of conceptualization and technique. In particular, it will be important to specify and measure the conditions under which one or another type of linkage between primary and secondary environment figures takes place.[32] For the present purposes, we may simply note that one source of the imagery of benevolence, protectiveness, and extreme sagacity in children's descriptions of leaders *could* prove to be unconscious processes of the sort suggested in psychoanalytic theory.

As we have seen, the child's glowing political imagery shows signs of attrition (mainly in the use of "benevolent" language) during preadolescence. The greatest change away from political euphoria probably is in adolescence. Disillusionment, following increased realistic political understanding, might produce such changes. Another likely cause would be the adolescent's need to assume adult mannerisms, including in some cases an inside dopester's appraisal of politics. Adolescence is, at any rate, a time for felling idols and perceiving the commanding figures of one's adult enviroment in a more fallible light.

CONSEQUENCES OF THE CHILD'S VIEW OF POLITICAL AUTHORITY

How does knowledge that the political learning sequence is from childhood idealism to adult realism and cynicism add to our understanding of citizens' responses to political authority? To answer this some further remarks on adult orientations to political leaders are necessary.

The cynical imagery of Americans seems to have less effect on their political behavior than the positive side of their responses—their respect for high political leaders and roles, and their frequent willingness to hold individual leaders in great esteem. This is evident not merely from such relatively narrow phenomena as the increased esteem politicians receive once they are elected and the general willingness to accept the verdict of elections. Acceptance of, and even devotion to, authority is a pervasive phenomenon which we take for granted; it has an atmospheric ubiquity, ever-present yet inconspicuous. The oft-proclaimed stability of the American political system, in spite of a remarkably heterogeneous population, suggests that powerful psychological mechanisms encouraging political obedience are present in the citizenry. These mechanisms—along with, it should be added, the widespread disinterest of Americans in politics—may be as important as many of the more familiar historical, political, economic, and social factors that are drawn on to explain the complex phenomenon of political stability.

Favorable conceptions of political authority are an early acquisition. They emerge years before the child has more than a smattering of factual political information. Negative attitudes toward political leaders are chronologically late arrivals. Psychologists of various schools, ranging from psychoanalysis to learning theory, argue that "learning which takes place early in life should have especially great influence on lasting personality characteristics."[33] Similar conclusions have been reached by anthropologists, who hypothesize that the elements in a culture learned earliest in childhood are the elements most resistant to change.[34] It is possible, therefore, that when the adult is in conflict between his positive and negative assessments of political leaders, the longest held of these is most likely to influence his response. The hypothesis that early learning is especially potent learning also seems to fit other aspects of political development, both cognitive and affective.

"If," as Easton and Hess[35] note, "what is learned early in life is hard to displace in later years, we have here an important increment to our understanding of the sources of stability in the American political system." Early idealization of the president "should contribute to the ease with which members of the American political system develop a strong attachment to the structure of the regime." Moreover, "insofar as feelings generated with respect to the Presidency as a focal point are subsequently extended to include other parts of the political structure . . . this may well be the path through which members of the system come to value the whole structure."

Notes:

1. H. Cantril and M. Strunk, *Public Opinion: 1935–1946* (Princeton, Princeton University Press, 1951), p. 584; National Opinion Research Center, *The Public Looks at Politics and Politicians* (Report No. 20, March 1944); Angus Campbell *et al., The Voter Decides* (Evanston, Row, Peterson, 1954), pp. 187–94. Also see Robert E. Agger *et al.*, "Political Cynicism: Measurement and Meaning," *Journal of Politics,* 23 (1961), 477–506, and Edgar Litt, "Political Cynicism and Political Futility," *ibid.*, 25 (1963), 312–23.

2. See "Jobs and Occupations: A Popular Evaluation," *Opinion News,* 9 (September 1, 1949), 3–19; Mapheus Smith, "An Empirical Scale of Prestige Status of Occupations," *American Sociological Review,* 8 (1943), 185–92; Harvey C. Lehman and Paul A. Witty, "Further Study of the Social Status of Occupations," *The Journal of Educational Sociology,* 5 (1931–32); George W. Hartmann, "The Prestige of Occupations," *The Personnel Journal,* 13 (1934–35), 144–52. For an early attempt at cross-cultural study, see Jerome Davis, "Testing the Social Attitudes of Children in the Government Schools in Russia," *American Journal of Sociology,* 32 (1926–27), 947–52.

3. William C. Mitchell, in the *Western Political Quarterly,* 12 (1959), 683–98.

4. For a summary of trends in the public support of Roosevelt, Truman, and Eisenhower see the poll findings reported by Hazel Gaudet Erskine in *Public Opinion Quarterly,* 25 (1961), 135–37. Data on Kennedy's popularity may be found in subsequent installments of Mrs. Erskine's regular reports of the polls in *ibid.* and in the regular news releases of The American Institute of Public Opinion, especially the November 10 and December 15, 1963 releases.

5. I. H. Paul, "Impressions of Personality, Authoritarianism, and the *Fait Accompli* Effect," *Journal of Abnormal and Social Psychology,* 53 (1956), 343. Also see Hadley Cantril, *Gauging Public Opinion* (Princeton, Princeton University Press, 1944), pp. 37–38; Paul F. Lazarsfeld *et al., The People's Choice* (New York, Columbia University Press, 1944), pp. 37–38; Paul F. Lazarsfeld, "Public Opinion and the Classical Tradition," *Public Opinion Quarterly,* 21 (1957), 47; and V. O. Key, Jr., *Public Opinion and American Democracy* (New York, Knopf, 1961), p. 479. This seems to be a part of a more general phenomenon which has been called the *fait accompli* effect. For example, support for a bill increases after it has been passed and becomes a law and, conversely, people are less likely to support a policy if they are told it will be necessary to change a law or amend the Constitution to attain this goal.

6. Fred I. Greenstein, "College Student Reactions to the Assassination of President Kennedy," paper delivered at Conference on Children's Reactions to the Death of the President, April 1964; published in abbreviated form in Bradley S. Greenberg and Edwin B. Parker, eds., *Communication in Crisis* (Stanford, Stanford University Press, 1965). Nelson W. Polsby and I conducted the interviews quoted in the text.

7. See references in note 4. On Roosevelt, see Cantril and Strunk, *Public Opinion: 1935–1946,* p. 756.

8. This is not to say that children never develop aversions to *individual* political leaders, although as is shown below, they probably are less likely than adults to do so. One item which did evoke spontaneous negative references to individual politicians asked the child, "Name a famous person you *don't* want to be like." About 15 per cent of the respondents named a political leader of the present or of the recent past. Interestingly, more than half of these references were to foreign leaders such as Nikita Khrushchev. Follow-up interviews suggested that some of the negative references to domestic leaders were rejections of the responsibility of being (say) president, rather than personal criticisms of the leader.

9. There have been a number of popular accounts of young children's interest in President Kennedy and his family. For example, Bill Adler, *Kids' Letters to President Kennedy* (New York, Morrow, 1961).

10. For a discussion of the validity of the responses reported in Table II see Fred I. Greenstein, "The Benevolent Leader: Children's Images of Political Authority," *American Political Science Review,* 54 (1960), 937 n.

11. At least three points of noncomparability should be noted: the differences in population (New Haven versus a National sample); the differences in question wording; and the differences in response alternatives. With these major reservations in mind, the following additional AIPO findings on President Eisenhower, for the months surrounding this survey, may be noted. (AIPO releases November 1957, January and March 1958.)

	Approve	Disapprove	No Opinion
November 1957	57%	27%	16%
January 1958	60	30	10
March 1958	52	33	15

The November AIPO report, which controls for region, suggests that Southern responses may have inflated the "disapproval" column. In that month, Eastern states were reported as 65% approve, 21% disapprove, and 14% no opinion. This still is considerably more than the 5% of the New Haven children who checked the "bad" and "not very good" alternatives.

12. See notes 4 and 7. In Germany, expressions of disapproval of Adenauer never fell below 15 per cent between 1949 and 1962. Erich P. Newmann and Elisabeth Noelle, *Statistics on Adenauer* (Allensbach and Bonn, Verlag für Demoskopie, 1962), pp. 40–44.

13. For example, in the Survey Research Center's 1952 election study sample, only a fifth of the respondents claimed that "it would make a great deal of difference to the country whether the Democrats or the Republicans win the elections." Campbell *et al., The Voter Decides,* p. 38. The same reservations about comparability of samples, question wording, and response alternatives expressed in note 11, above, are also relevant here.

The Survey Research Center reports that 43 per cent of the respondents replied "some difference, minor differences." Compare a 1946 cross-section of the national population which was asked: "Do you think it makes much difference or only a little difference which party wins the elections for Congress this fall?" About half said it made "much difference," about 30 per cent "little," and the remaining 20 per cent was divided evenly between "no difference" and "no opinion." Cantril and Strunk, p. 582.

14. Another class of political imagery is worth noting. A small percentage of the respondents (but some in each of the four schools which make up the sample) coped with the problem of organizing their fragmentary political information by using hierarchical concepts. They saw politics, even in the case of individuals and institutions which are formally coordinate, in terms of a chain of command. For example: "The mayor gets orders from the president . . . The president gives orders to the governor." (Fifth grade girl.) "The mayor handles the minor problems and if it is too big he goes to the governor." (Seventh grade boy.) "The mayor takes the problems of the town. He [the governor] takes the hard problems." (Fifth grade boy.) One notably ingenious misconception combined hierarchy with benevolence. The fifth grade boy whose statement that "The mayor pays working people like banks" was cited above went on to say, "The governor pays mayors. . . . The president pays the governor." Again the appropriate instrument might reveal that this way of perceiving politics is reasonably common in childhood and, perhaps, that it is related to certain types of nonpolitical—e.g. primary groups—experiences. See note 34, below.

15. Robert D. Hess and David Easton, "The Child's Image of the President," *Public Opinion Quarterly,* 24 (1960), 632–44. For a comparison of this work with certain of the New Haven findings see Fred I. Greenstein, "More on Children's Images of the President," *Public Opinion Quarterly,* 25 (1961), 648–54.

16. Robert D. Hess, "The Socialization of Attitudes Toward Political Authority: Some Crossnational Comparisons," *International Social Science Journal,* 15 (1963), 542–59. There are interesting variations from nation to nation in the absolute levels of idealization, but the tendency for

younger children to display more idealized conceptions of leaders than do older children is consistent from nation to nation. Also see Daniel Rosenblatt's finding that American adults were more likely than a matched sample of Russians "to view the father as . . . wise and benevolent." "Responses of Former Soviet Citizens to Selected *TAT* Cards," *Journal of General Psychology,* 62 (1960), 278.

17. For a summary of this literature, see Irvin L. Child, "Socialization," in Lindzey, ed., *Handbook of Social Psychology,* 2 (1954), 655–92.

18. Gloria Cammarota, "Children, Politics, and Elementary Social Studies," *Social Education,* 27 (1963), 205. Also see Robert D. Hess and David Easton, "The Role of the Elementary School in Political Socialization," *The School Review,* 70 (1962), 257–65.

19. Cf. Hyman, *Political Socialization,* Chap. 4.

20. Cf. Fred I. Greenstein, "Children's Political Perspectives: A Study of the Development of Political Awareness and Preferences among Preadolescents" (unpublished Ph.D. dissertation, Yale University Library, 1959) for data on the political aspects of children's media behavior.

Iona and Peter Opie observe, somewhat wistfully, that English school children "undoubtedly . . . were more actively employed in nineteenth-century parliamentary elections than they are today. . . . Election time . . . used to be, and still is in the United States, a period of high spirits . . ." They record two bits of juvenile political rhyme from the Roosevelt-Willkie campaign:

Fried cats
And stewed rats
Are good enough
For the Democrats.

Roosevelt in the White House
Waited to be elected;
Willkie in the garbage can
Waiting to be collected.

The Lore and Language of School Children (Oxford, Oxford University Press, 1959), pp. 348–49.

21. For the suggestion that inadvertent political learning of the sort discussed here "is more significant than . . . formal education" because "the child hears informally . . . the real political attitudes of adults" see Gabriel A. Almond and Sidney Verba, *The Civic Culture,* pp. 325–26 and 498–99.

22. David Easton and Robert D. Hess, "The Child's Political World," *Midwest Journal of Political Science,* 6 (1962), 229–46.

23. An added element contributing to these perceptions of adults undoubtedly is the painfully benevolent portrayal of the wider environment in contemporary children's literature. Books such as *Our Friend the Farmer* and *How the Policeman Helps Us* are couched in language which closely resembles some of the preadolescent descriptions of political leaders reported above. Cf. Martin Mayer, *The Schools* (New York, Anchor Books, 1963), p. 378. Nineteenth-century children's literature evidently presented the world in far less sanguine terms. See *The* [Lon-

don] *Times Literary Supplement Children's Book Section,* June 14, 1963, pp. 421–22.

24. Harold D. Lasswell, *Psychopathology and Politics,* reprinted in *The Political Writings of Harold D. Lasswell,* p. 173 f. In addition, see Lasswell's *Power and Personality* (New York, Norton, 1948), pp. 156–57, and C. W. Wahl, "The Relation Between Primary and Secondary Identification," in Eugene Burdick and Arthur J. Brodbeck, *American Voting Behavior,* pp. 262–80.

25. Sebastian DeGrazia, "A Note on the Psychological Position of the Chief Executive," *Psychiatry,* 8 (1945), 267–72; W. R. D. Fairbairn, *An Object Relations Theory of Personality* (New York, Basic Books, 1954), pp. 223–29; Franz Alexander, "Emotional Factors in Voting Behavior," in Burdick and Brodbeck, *American Voting Behavior,* pp. 300–07; Richard E. Renneker, "Some Psychodynamic Aspects of Voting Behavior," *ibid.,* pp. 399–413.

26. Harold Orlansky, "Reactions to the Death of President Roosevelt," *Journal of Social Psychology,* 26 (1947), 235–66, esp. 243. Also see Bernard Asbell, *When FDR Died* (New York, Holt, Rinehart and Winston, 1961).

27. Kingsley Martin, *The Magic of Monarchy* (New York, Knopf, 1937), p. 19.

28. Numerous studies of public reaction to President Kennedy's assassination are reported in Greenberg and Parker, eds., *Communication in Crisis.* On the reactions of children in therapy see the papers by Augusta Alpert, Martha Wolfenstein, Joan J. Zilbach, Gilbert Kliman, and Othilda Krug in a forthcoming volume to be edited by Martha Wolfenstein and Gilbert Kliman.

29. Paul B. Sheatsley and Jacob J. Feldman, "The Assassination of President Kennedy: A Preliminary Report on Public Reactions and Behavior," *Public Opinion Quarterly,* 28 (1964), pp. 189–215.

30. Greenstein, "College Student Reactions to the Assassination of President Kennedy."

31. Judith V. Torney, in an analysis of portions of the data collected by Easton and Hess, reports findings consistent with (but not directly demonstrative of) the hypothesis that idealization of political authority is compensatory—that it forms in reaction to unsatisfactory experiences with paternal authority. "The Child's Idealization of Authority" (unpublished M.A. thesis, University of Chicago Library, 1962). She suggests a possible connection with George R. Bach's findings on "Father-Fantasies and Father-Typing in Father-Separated Children," *Child Development,* 17 (1946), 63–80. Possible reaction-formation relationships between authority experiences in the family and responses to non-family authority are suggested in Leroy S. Burwen, "A Study of Attitudes toward Authority" (unpublished Ph.D. dissertation, University of Chicago Library, 1954), and Leroy S. Burwen and Donald T. Campbell, "The Generality of Attitudes toward Authority and Nonauthority Figures," *Journal of Abnormal and Social Psychology,* 54 (1957), 24–31. John E. Teahan and Sanford Golin, on the other hand, found what seemed to be a direct generalization of attitudes in a study of reactions to President Kennedy's assassination. Among male (but not female) college

students the tendency to respond impersonally to the President's death was greater if the individual's feelings toward his father or brother were negative. "Reaction to the Death of the President as a Function of Sex, Ideology, Symbolic Significance and Perception of Family Figures," mimeographed, 1964. Also relevant are Benson H. Marsten and James C. Coleman, "Specificity of Attitudes toward Paternal and Non-Paternal Authority Figures," *Journal of Individual Psychology,* 17 (1961), 96–101; Robert A. LeVine, "The Role of the Family in Authority Systems: A Cross-Cultural Application of Stimulus-Generalization Theory," *Behavioral Science,* 5 (1960), 291–96 and "The Internalization of Political Values in Stateless Societies," *Human Organization,* 19 (1960), 51–58; Aron Wolfe Siegman, "An Empirical Investigation of the Psychonalytic Theory of Religious Behavior," *Journal for the Scientific Study of Religion,* 1 (1961), 75–78; Ross Stagner, "Attitude toward Authority: An Exploratory Study," *Journal of Social Psychology,* 40 (1954), 197–210. For an attempt to explain the idealization of political leaders by young children largely in terms of cognitive development and the child's increasingly realistic understanding of the punishments which can be administered by political leaders, see Lewis A. Froman, Jr., "Learning Political Attitudes," *Western Political Quarterly,* 15 (1962), 304–13.

32. The hierarchical imagery reported in note 14 provides an illustration of one type of linkage which may take place. In each instance the child clearly has meager factual information about the roles he is attempting to describe. His allusion to a chain of command seems to result from an attempt to organize what fragmentary information he has. This may be seen in further detail in a follow-up interview with a sixth grade boy who had responded hierarchically on his questionnaire:

INTERVIEWER: What sorts of things does Mayor Lee do?
LARRY: Well, he keeps the city together and tells them what to do.
I: Tells who what to do?
L: Well, let's see. He probably tells some of the most important people and then they tell the ones that are less important and they keep on going.
I: What kinds of people are these? Do you mean *any* people in the city?
L: No, like the police chief and the head of the schools or something.
I: What do you think the governor does?
L: Well he probably tells the mayors what to do and he probably tells other people what to do.
I: When you say "probably" does that mean you're sort of guessing about what he does?
L: Yes . . . He has to tell *somebody* what to do.
I: President Eisenhower, what does he do?
L: He probably tells the governors what to do.
I: Can you think of any other things that he might do?
L: He probably tells the people that are going to foreign countries to present a thing or something he wants that if they might be interested in. [sic]
I: What kind of thing do you mean?

L: Well, like a peace treaty or something.

That Larry turns "automatically" to hierarchy as an organizing principle suggests that his prepolitical experiences have taught him to view the world in terms of "telling people what to do." One might hypothesize, for example, that children responding in this way are more likely to come from families in which parental authority follows similar patterns.

33. Child, "Socialization," p. 678.

34. Edward M. Bruner, "Cultural Transmission and Cultural Change," *Southwestern Journal of Anthropology,* 12 (1956), 191–99; Melford Spiro, "The Acculturation of American Ethnic Groups," *American Anthropologist,* 57 (1955), 1240–52. For further discussion of the significance of early learning see *Children and Politics,* Chapter 4, pp. 79 ff.

35. Easton and Hess, "The Child's Political World."

5 *Motivational Diversity in the Party Hierarchy*

by Samuel J. Eldersveld

Crucial for the party's survival is the satisfaction of the personal needs of activists in the party structure. Motives of leaders, probably more than any other perspective, determine the character of the individual's relationship to the party, as well as the drive potential of the group collectively. Nothing is so disintegrative as leadership motives which diverge and detract from the implementation of party group goals. Ideological positions of leaders may, indeed, conflict; yet one senses that divergent issue positions are not critically dysfunctional to leadership activity. Interpretations of party goals may be contradictory or unclear; yet the activist continues to work energetically. Role perceptions may vary; yet he maintains his position, oblivious to the task definitions assumed by others. Although these perspectives are relevant to the party's organizational style as well as to the unity with which leadership cadres carry on their operations, they do not necessarily define the "meaning" of party work for the individual leader. His drive to fulfill a salient personal need, however, is a variable of greater theoretical validity for understanding his relationship with the party. [Here] we examine the kinds of needs expressed by party leaders and the extent to which leaders perceived these needs to be fulfilled. Such analysis will, it is

Reprinted from *Political Parties: A Behavioral Analysis,* by Samuel J. Eldersveld (Chicago: Rand McNally & Company, 1964), pp. 272–303, by permission of the author and the publisher.

hoped, contribute to our knowledge of the party as a viable social-psychological action system.

The data on political motivation in the party hierarchy are concerned with four major aims. First is a description of patterns of leadership motivation at one point in time for the three basic echelons in each party—precinct, executive board, and chairmen. We will relate our data to different concepts of motivation, distinguishing between the personally instrumental and exploitative and the "impersonal," socially normative, or group-value-directive. A second aim is to trace certain developmental patterns in motivation. [Elsewhere] we discussed at length the career entrance motivations of leaders in terms of the personal drives most prominent when they began party work. We seek here to analyze the extent to which these entrance motivations were continued or modified during the period prior to our interviews in 1956. Further, we are interested in the phenomenon of political socialization as it relates to motivational development, particularly party differences, organizational milieu differences, and the effect of changed party leadership status on the alteration of motivational perspectives. Third, we wish to correlate again a variety of personal and social characteristics with motivational interests, to determine the relative contribution of certain social categories and subcoalitions to the emergence of the key motivational types. Finally, we intend to examine the political party collectively as a structure of motives. The basic question here is: Does "motivational pluralism" exist, and if so does it reflect such irreconcilable demands for gratification by leaders that the party as a group cannot successfully implement these personal drives? Or does such "motivational pluralism" merely reflect a predictable and natural differentiation in human needs with which the party can cope as a balanced social group without impairing the efficient pursuit of its political goals?

Voluntarism Versus Personal Rewards

Party leaders at the lower echelons gave a great variety of answers when asked about their major satisfactions. The two state chairmen themselves, however, explained in very similar ways the motives of their activists, and in general perceived many activists as group-conscious "volunteers." One chairman said some were active out of a desire to "help shape events," others wished to associate with top politicians, and still others merely enjoyed working and associating with like-minded people. The other chairman also said that being a "part of something" and participating in the excitement of a campaign was important, emphasizing especially that for many the opportunity for meeting and working with friends was most significant. Both men felt the Democratic workers had a greater personal stake in politics than the Republicans. As one chairman commented: "Many Republicans are not hungry enough for the experience of participation in politics—they have a pretty good economic base and social life and thus have no need for the social aspect of political life. The Democrats seem to work for a political goal, and the Democratic party has worked on the psychic have-nots." Both men desired more "voluntarism" in political activity and de-emphasized the importance of patronage. One chairman claimed "there is very little patronage to dispense, and it would make very little difference if it were increased or decreased. It should be abolished as a reward for party service." For the other chairman patronage "has now only a symbolic effect; the people we appoint symbolize the party and the choice always brings out a show of force; I am not in favor of much patronage, it is a device for crystallizing groups in parties. It would not make much difference to the party if it were abolished. A little is helpful." These views were generally echoed by the county chairwomen, although one of them said, "Many people feel they should belong to a party to gain patronage. We might win more votes if there was more patronage."

This "voluntaristic" conception of party worker motivation was not unanimously shared by the men responsible for the district party machines. All of them admitted that there was patronage to be dispensed, and usually explained at some length the procedures for consultation on patronage. Almost all, however, agreed that patronage had decreased. Of interest was the fact that only one chairman spoke critically of the idea of patronage (calling it the "curse of American politics"), while seven chairmen were frankly critical of civil service and desired more patronage as a means of building up their own organizations. There was a clear-cut indication in both parties that the congressional district elite felt more people could be attracted to party work, and turnover in the precincts diminished, if party work was less altruistic and volunteer. The district chairmen were willing to admit that many people entered party work "to improve their own lot," socially or economically, and that it was difficult to satisfy these workers without more political largess to distribute. It is interesting to note in this connection that 33 per cent of the district chairmen of both parties held governmental positions in the Detroit area, 20 per cent of the executive board members did, and only 10 per cent of the precinct leaders.

A basic conflict seems to exist, then, between the "voluntaristic" ideal type of party worker conceived by the state chairmen, and the real "personal-reward motivated" person at the grass roots with whom the district chairmen perceived they had to contend. Implicit in this difference of opinion are two types of questions about party worker motivations: Are party workers involved because they see this work as "personally instrumental," as satisfying some personal interest, or are they involved impersonally for the purpose of "group realization," in order to "do a job" as a citizen or as a loyal group supporter? And if they see their work as "personally instrumental," what type of satisfactions are most prominent in their minds? The data on the various echelons of the party hierarchy will help describe the contemporary motivational patterns in the two parties in terms of these conceptual categories.

A political party machine has two tasks: keeping its hardcore activists personally satisfied, and at the same time marshalling its best efforts in mobilizing votes for support of its elective leadership. A political party which can dispense patronage, in jobs or in other forms to 100 per cent of its activists can be a highly effective political team, as other studies have shown.[1] Today, however, in most communities such a completely patronage-based machine is rare. In Detroit, patronage as a reward for party service was possible for only a small minority of activists. This created for the party the dilemma of satisfying those who seek personal rewards, while moving the party ahead toward its political objectives, and this was no mean task. In Detroit almost 50 per cent of the precinct activists in 1956 had begun work only recently; almost one-fourth had no experience prior to 1956. This high turnover underscores the problems of motivational fulfillment. Are the motivational expectations of American party workers such that their personal relationship to the party will in all probability be tenuous and short-lived? Do they enter the party with drives which are eventually unfulfilled and thus induce frustration?

The study of "motivation" is admittedly a difficult undertaking, and we should be clear about the conceptual context in which it was pursued in our study. It is difficult *for the researcher* because of the many meanings and connotations attached to the term. It is difficult *for the political leader* who is asked direct or indirect questions about motivation, either because he is unwilling to explain his motives frankly, or because he is confused about his actual primary and secondary personal interests in political party work. Which terms are most meaningful or "real" to the party worker—"aspiration," "drive," "motivation," "interest," "satisfaction," or "reward"? And what indirect evidence, admitting that all party leaders cannot be forthright and frank, is acceptable and demonstrative? Our investigation proceeds on the assumption that "motivation" is a "three-layer phenomenon." We believe, first, that every individual has deeply imbedded "needs" which he feels, with greatly varying intensity, must be fulfilled—prestige, power over others, feelings of contributing to some social goal, economic status, social interaction, etc. These "needs" lead to "drives" or determinations to satisfy these "needs," though again, with varying urgency. The consequence of the activation of these "drives" over time is a resultant feeling of some degree of fulfillment (or nonfulfillment) of needs, or "satisfaction" (dissatisfaction). In interviewing party leaders about their "motivations" we can certainly secure some evidence of whether they sense a "satisfaction," and of whether the particular substantive type of satisfaction which they claim has or has not been fulfilled. We can also attempt to deduce from this and other interview responses what the "drives" and "needs" of the party leader were, or are. But we should not delude ourselves into thinking that we have secured complete insight into the motivational orientation of the leader. The fact that he tells us he has secured a certain satisfaction from the social contacts, or economic gain, concomitant with his career in the party is not necessarily the whole motivational picture. He may hide from us the fact that there were other "needs," such as a craving for personal political recognition, evoking "drives" which were never implemented. Thus, in presenting our data on "motivation," we wish it to be understood that these data may only be describing the peak of the "motivational iceberg." We will discuss "satisfactions" or "rewards" (the things people say they would miss if they were forced to leave party politics), and these may be probes in depth of basic personality needs and drives, but we cannot be sure.

Hierarchical Differences in Work Satisfactions

What type of responses did we get from party leaders about "satisfactions" derived from party work, or what they would "miss" if forced to drop out of political activity tomorrow? As Table I reveals, the "satisfactions" differed for both parties, and by leadership status.

Table I. ***Current Satisfactions from Party Work***

	Chairmen and Executive Boards		Precinct Leaders	
	Demo-cratic	*Repub-lican*	*Demo-cratic*	*Repub-lican*
Personally instrumental satisfactions				
Social contacts	21%	34%	63%	47%
Political fun (and inside information)	4	10	12	8
Business, economic, and political gain	25	24	1	1
Group and society-related satisfactions				
Moral and philosophical satisfactions	21	17	4	3
Ideological or issue satisfactions	29	10	3	17
No satisfactions received (nothing would be missed)	0	3	15	22
Number of cases	24	29	138	143

If these data are accepted under the conditions used in securing them, and despite obvious limitations, they do show some interesting contrasts.

Precinct leaders in both parties frankly revealed the personally instrumental nature of their involvement much more readily than did leaders at the upper echelons. This was particularly distinctive in the Democratic party where 76 per cent of the precinct leaders, contrasted to 50 per cent of the upper elite, gave such responses. Precinct leaders were also willing to admit their low level of motivational fulfillment—15 to 22 per cent admitted there was nothing to be missed by leaving party work. But the upper organizational leaders were more willing to reveal a personal political or economic drive satisfied through political work—one-fourth citing this as a major satisfaction, while only 1 per cent of the precinct leaders did. Contrary to expectations, the majority of party leaders did not lapse into philosophical rationalizations in explaining their satisfactions in party work. Not all of them appeared to be hiding their motivations and gratifications. The picture that emerges is one of considerable disillusionment motivationally among precinct leaders, coupled with high personal need fulfillment (especially a desire for social contacts and association with friends), and very few ideological-philosophical gratifications. Above all, politics seemed to be socially gratifying for a large percentage of precinct activists, while social interaction was either a less dominant need for the upper organizational elite or it may have been a need, but fulfilled adequately for only a small minority.

The question can well be raised: How much evasion existed at all levels—how much unwillingness to admit they were in politics for the fulfillment of personal, economic, or political objectives? A variety of evidence suggests that the percentages in the table are too low. Thus, though only 1 per cent of the precinct leaders openly admitted such needs existed, about 17 per cent had already demonstrated some upward mobility in the hierarchy, and from 10 to 12 per cent held some type of governmental position, or their husbands did (16 per cent of the Democratic precinct leaders, 9 per cent of the Republicans). Further, 57 per cent of the precinct leaders said they might aspire to a higher party position if it was offered them.[2]

Similar data are suggestive for higher echelon leaders. Although only one-fourth of these admitted deriving satisfactions related to personal economic and political power drives, over 70 per cent might conceivably have had such drives, based on the data concerning their past, attempted, or present governmental employment (42 per cent of the Democrats, 46 per cent of the Republicans), on their aspirations for governmental careers (67 per cent of the Democrats, 46 per cent of the Republicans), plus other indications that they saw politics as a means to implement their own personal ambitions. It is extremely difficult of course clearly and confidently to deduce "motivation" from upward organizational mobility or interest in, and tenure of, a governmental patronage position. But if one uses such indirect evidence, the probable proportions of those interested in a personal economic and political power satisfaction is as shown in Table II.

Table II. ***Proportions of Leaders Interested in Personal Economic and Political Power Satisfaction***

	Democratic	Republican
Chairmen	83%	83%
Executive board	78	70
Precinct leaders		
On the basis of governmental position held	16	9
On the basis of party organization mobility	17	17

Much more decisive data are necessary before determining to what extent personal entrepreneurial ambitions were primary. It is possible to consider the responses to direct questions about satisfactions as honest. Thus, while 17 per cent of precinct leaders *may have been* personal entrepreneurs about politics, most of them realized currently that this was not their primary satisfaction nor the reason they stayed in politics. Only 1 per cent may in fact have considered this the primary satisfaction, while the others stayed in politics for the reasons they gave us, with 15–22 per cent seeing no need fulfillment whatsoever in politics. By the same token, the vast majority of upper echelon leaders may have been personal entrepreneurs about politics at one time, but in fact may have reassessed the reasons for their involvement and their satisfactions. Only 25 per cent continued in politics because of the satisfactions of personal ambition, and the remainder genuinely experienced the fulfillment of other needs, particularly sensing more philosophical and ideological satisfactions from party work than did the precinct leaders. More "depth" data on motivational drives are needed to ascertain exactly which interpretation is correct.

Noncongruences in Motivational Perceptions

Since the party is presumably an organizational team of workers, leaders' perceptions of the motivations of others, particularly in comparison with their own alleged motivations, are important, psychologically as well as politically. The two significant phenomena are, of course, "projection"—ascribing one's own motivations to others—and "incorporation"—assimilating the perceived satisfactions of others.

Table III. ***Motivational Perceptions of "Others" and "Self" (precinct leaders)***

	Self Perceptions							
	Democrats				Republicans			
Perceptions of "Others'" Motivations	*A*	*B*	*C*	*Number of Cases*	*A*	*B*	*C*	*Number of Cases*
Social contacts	87%	0%	13%	15	67%	0%	0%	18
Ideological satisfaction	68	6	9	53	43	22	6	81
Fun, excitement	40	0	0	23	56	25	0	16
	D	*E*	*F*	*Number of Cases*	*D*	*E*	*F*	*Number of Cases*
Personally instrumental	71	9	19	68	79	11	9	47
Impersonal task-oriented	82	5	11	62	51	29	20	84
Nothing—no rewards	*	*	*	6	18*	0*	82*	11

*Too few cases for reliable analysis.

Our data suggest minimal projection and incorporation (Table III). The best examples of incorporation were, first, a small minority (11 to 13 per cent) of Republicans and Democrats who thought other precinct leaders were in politics for social contacts, and from 67 to 87 per cent of these groups who said that they were also in politics because of that satisfaction. Second, a very small minority of Republicans (8 per cent) said their fellow workers got no rewards out of political work, and 82 per cent of these admitted the same disillusionment. Such coincidence was the exception, however, rather than the rule.

In fact, if we invert Table III and ask what percentage of those who repsonded about "self" in a particular way ascribed the same motivation to others (the phenomenon of "projection"), we find a very limited amount of mutuality in motivational perceptions. Thus, although 63 per cent of the Democrats claimed their main satisfaction was social contacts, only 15 per cent of the group saw this as a satisfaction for other leaders. The same was true for Republicans—48 per cent saw social contact as the major satisfaction for self, but only 18 per cent of these perceived it as a primary motivation for others. Further, only 5 per cent of Democrats and 29 per cent of Republicans who said they derived no satisfactions from political work felt this was true for other party leaders.

Particularly significant, and indicative of the frankness with which these politicians responded, was the tendency to ascribe altruistic motivations to others but deny them for themselves. Of the Democratic precinct leaders, 36 per cent said that other leaders were receiving ideological satisfactions—working for things they believed in—but only 6 per cent claimed this satisfaction personally. The percentages for the Republicans were 57 per cent ascription of this satisfaction to others, but only 22 per cent of the group declaring this to be their own satisfaction. Conversely, 76 per cent of the Democrats and not quite 60 per cent of the Republicans claimed "personally instrumental" satisfactions for themselves, but only 46 and 45 per cent of these leaders, respectively, ascribed such motivations to others.

In sum, our analysis of specific motivational perceptions for others and self reveals that 84 per cent of the Democrats and 72 per cent of the Republicans did not share motivational perceptions. There seemed to be great confusion about why the "other fellow" was involved in party work, as well as a tendency to think that he was more ideologically committed and satisfied than was one's self, and than was realistically the case. Whether this condition resulted from misperceptions of reality, or from difficulty in generalizing about the satisfactions of others, the finding points to the incohesiveness of the party group as an action system. The existence of "motivational pluralism" in the organization has been demonstrated. We now find, in addition, the existence of marked confusion about why one's fellow workers were involved in political life. The resulting impression is that the local party organization was not a tightly knit associational team, but consisted, rather, of a set of individuals pursuing particular needs and deriving satisfactions, irrespective of the motivation of other workers. The party was a tangled web of personal motivational relationships between activists and the group, with a minimal amount of awareness by each activist of the motivations that drove his political confreres on with party work.[3] These findings are highly supportive, of course, of the "stratarchical" model of the party structure.

Career Factors as Explanations of Motivational Differences

As noted before, a high percentage of precinct leaders seemed to derive personal, social gratification from politics, with one-tenth seeing ideological-philosophical satisfactions as primary, and almost 20 per cent sensing no motivational fulfillment. Differentiations in terms of career tenure appeared, however, for the precinct leaders of both parties (Table IV, p. 446).

One set of differences emerged when precinct leaders were grouped by the era in which they began party work. The recent joiners, since 1952 in the Republican party and since 1955 in the Democratic, seemed to be the most frustrated and at a loss to discuss their satisfactions with party work. Further, it is clear that long-time members were much more likely to be impersonally motivated and satisfied ideologically with party work. Over 40 per cent of the Republicans who began in party work before 1940 did not have a personal entrepreneurial motivational perspective, as was the case for one-fourth of the Democrats who began before 1932. Either of two explanations may hold: the old-timers may have been transformed into task-oriented ideologues over the years and thus lost a personal entrepreneurial approach to politics, or contemporary party leadership elites have been unable to recruit, educate, or transform the activist cadre, in keeping with their "voluntaristic" and "idealistic" model of the party organization.

A further analysis of precinct leaders by career status, using the categories suggested in an earlier chapter, indicates the relevance of this status to personal motivational relationships to the party, (Table V). Two characterizations are determined from these data. One concerns the top organizational mobiles (precinct leaders who have been conspicuously active, moved upward in the hierarchy, and aspire to higher positions). This group placed the highest premium on social contacts as a personally instrumental type of satisfaction most important for them. They were also the least disillusioned about party work (only 4 per cent in both parties said they would miss nothing if they had to leave party work). On the other hand, the noncareerists stood in sharp contrast. They were the most disillusioned (36–44 per cent), and they had a relatively low proportion deriving social gratifications from politics. Aside from these findings, the differences are not generalizable for both parties. For example, the Democratic potential careerists were a socializing group, while the Republican potential careerists had a relatively high proportion of ideologues. The Republican nonmobile regulars were rather disillusioned, while the Democratic regulars still viewed party work in terms of personal rewards. These variations in the extent and type of satisfaction derived from party activity suggest, then, that career status differences may determine one's motivational

Table IV. ***Era of Career Origin and Current Satisfactions (precinct leaders)***

Career Era (first campaign)	Social Contacts	Other Personally Instrumental Satisfactions	Impersonal Satisfactions	No Satisfactions	Number of Cases
			Democrats		
1956	53%	6%	0%	38%	32
1952–55	59	17	10	10	29
1940–51	73	10	3	13	30
1932–39	70	22	0	4	27
Before 1932	60	10	25	5	20
			Republicans		
1956	53%	19%	16%	9%	32
1952–55	42	0	17	42	36
1940–51	54	21	8	18	39
1932–39	40	0	47	13	15
Before 1932	48	0	38	14	21

emphasis, and, further, that generally only certain types of individuals with particular drives will succeed to top party career positions.

Table V. *Motivations of Precinct Leaders by Career Status*

	Instrumentalists Social-izers	Others	Ideologues and Philos-ophers	Disillu-sioned	Num-ber of Cases
			Democrats		
Top organizational mobiles	83%	4%	9%	4%	23
Informal influentials	76	8	0	16	37
Nonmobile regulars	52	29	10	5	21
Potential careerists	59	25	3	13	32
Noncareerists	40	0	16	36	25
			Republicans		
Top organizational mobiles	67%	0%	29%	4%	24
Informal influentials	63	32	5	0	19
Nonmobile regulars	39	2	20	39	44
Potential careerists	35	18	30	15	40
Noncareerists	56	0	0	44	16

Motivational Reorientation

The foregoing leads into a discussion of developmental patterns in party worker motivations. We are, on the one hand, interested in the contemporary structure of political motivations in party organizations. We are also concerned with the modification and transformation of motivational perspectives in the party worker from the time he joined the party to the present. Is the party worker "socialized" over time, and do his personal needs, drives, and satisfactions change? Or does he come into the party with certain needs and motives which remain constant throughout his career and whose fulfillment condition his tenure in the organization? Since we asked party leaders why they first became active, as well as about their current satisfactions from party activity, a developmental analysis, though only suggestive, is possible.

Upper echelon party leaders were quite frank in admitting that they began their careers with a desire to fulfill personalized drives, and maintained this drive perspective, or changed to another personalized motivational orientation. The reverse tended to be true for the precinct leader (Table VI). The elite leader wanted something personal out of politics when he became involved initially, or he was soon socialized to this expectation. The precinct leader ordinarily did not assert that he thought in terms of personal gain when he began party work. However, the grass-roots activist soon took on personalized motivational perspectives, if he did not start out with them. This observation is borne out by our data: 60 per cent of the top elite began with personalized motivations and 79 per cent held such motivations currently, while only 21 per cent of the precinct leaders began with personal political drives and 68 per cent were thus motivated currently. In Detroit this was somewhat less true for the Republican precinct leaders—60 per cent were currently preoccupied with personal satisfactions as against 76 per cent of the Democrats. There was less tendency for the Republican precinct leader to discard his ideological-philosophical and task motivations.

Table VI. ***Changes in General Motivational Orientations During Party Career***

	Upper Echelons		Precinct Leaders	
	Democrats	*Republicans*	*Democrats*	*Republicans*
Began with personalized motivation	67%	45%	26%	15%
Remained unchanged	75	92	97	57
Changed to or toward impersonal orientation	25	8	0	24
Became disillusioned	0	0	3	19
Began with impersonalized motivation	33%	55%	74%	85%
Remained unchanged	37	50	12	22
Changed to personalized motivation	63	50	68	57
Became disillusioned	0	0	20	21
Total percentage changing motivational direction	38%	31%	66%	73%
Number of cases	24	29	136	137

It is also significant that the upper echelon leader did not vacillate, motivationally, during his career as much as the precinct leader. Only one-third of upper echelon leaders said that the satisfactions currently derived from politics differed from their original drives, while two-thirds of the precinct leaders said they had changed. This seemed to be related to hierarchical status or to other characteristics, and not to lengthy tenure in party service, since precinct leaders who began party work before 1940, but who had not become members of the elite corps, changed motivational orientation almost as much as did other precinct leaders (see Table VII).

The differences in motivational development by time period of entrance into party work are interesting. The old-timers (began party work before 1940) actually were more "personal-drive-conscious" when they began their work than those who began after 1940 (especially the "newcomers" group of 1952–56). But they tended to change more away from this personalized perception of relation to the party, or changed less to personalized motivations from impersonal motivations (the Republicans accounted for almost all of the difference here). Thus only 46 per cent of the old-timers were currently (in 1956) motivated by overt self-interest, while 62 per cent of the newcomer group and 83 per cent of the group joining the party cadre in the 1940–51 period were so motivated. Recent precinct leaders were much more likely to begin with idealistic motivations (from 73 to 94 per cent since 1940), but they took on personal motivations and left idealism behind much more than those with 15 to 30 years of party service.

Especially noticeable is the large number of idealistic recent joiners who became disillusioned. The "realists," except for Republicans who joined from 1940 to 1951, gave no inkling of disillusionment comparable to the feeling of dissatisfaction among those with impersonalized motivational directions.

We have noted before that at least 55 per cent of precinct leaders currently reported their primary satisfaction was social contacts and friendships. In one sense this is strange, because only 5 per cent reported this as the initial reason they began to work. What were the initial drives and what happened to them in the course of their careers (Tables VIII and IX)? Those who began with a desire to influence governmental policies (21 per cent of the sample) seem to have turned to personalized satisfactions. No Democrats, and only one-fourth of the Republicans remained ideologues. Those who began work because of a desire to help a candidate friend (12 per cent) were the most disillusioned group in the sample—over 50 per cent in both parties reported no current satisfactions.

Table VII. *Motivational Constancy and Change by Era of Entrance into Party Career (precinct leaders only)*

	Era of Career Origin					
	1952–56		*1940–51*		*Before 1940*	
	Democrats	*Republicans*	*Democrats*	*Republicans*	*Democrats*	*Republicans*
Began with personalized motive*	14%	6%	27%	18%	40%	32%
Remained unchanged	100	100	100	43	94	50
Changed to impersonalized motivation	0	0	0	0	0	50
Became disillusioned	0	0	0	57	6	0
Began with impersonal motive	86%	94%	73%	82%	60%	68%
Remained unchanged	9	17	5	10	20	47
Changed to personalized motivation	61	56	77	81	75	29
Became disillusioned	30	27	18	9	5	24
Percentage changing						
From one specific motive to another†	96	77	53	91	74	65
From one category of motivation (personal, impersonal) to another‡	78	78	70	85	51	52
Number of cases	59	67	30	39	45	31

*The *N*'s in the subcells of this group were very small and the results are therefore suggestive only.

†The *N* used here is smaller than the total *N* indicated, because not all responses could be placed in precisely comparable categories.

‡Includes changes to disillusionment ("nothing would be missed," etc.).

The philosophers, both those who said they began because "politics is part of my way of life" (11 per cent) or because they had to "fulfill a sense of community obligation" (20 per cent), were highly socialized in the direction of social contact and other personal satisfactions, with the Republicans tending to become quite disillusioned, and only a small percentage of these two categories combined remaining philosophical about politics (16 per cent Democrats, 12 per cent Republicans). One of the highly disillusioned groups was the "party loyalists," who began because of their belief in the party. From one-fifth to one-third of these were currently dissatisfied, and most had also become socialized in the direction of personalized expectations about politics. On the other hand, the Democrats who reported frankly that party work was for them meaningful from the outset in terms of a personal need or drive, overwhelmingly remained committed to this perception. This was not as true for the Republicans, as noted earlier, many of whom became dissatisfied (24 per cent) and some of whom shifted to an ideological motivational direction (24 per cent).

These patterns of motivational stability and change are indeed significant. They suggest that while grass-roots workers and leaders may have been recruited under the guise of the "voluntaristic-idealistic-impersonal-task-oriented" concept of party work outlined earlier by the two state chairmen, these precinct leaders in large numbers changed motivational direction during their careers. Many became disillusioned; the majority soon articulated personal demands, needs, and satisfactions to be derived from party activity. In reality this means that the majority of precinct leaders changed their motivational relationship to the party. This is perhaps not unexpected, but the changers did not move in the direction of ideological rationalizations of party activities (except perhaps the old-timer Republicans who joined before 1940). Nor did they even become philosophical generalists about their tasks. They either became disillusioned, or they conceptualized their relationship in terms of social friendship satisfactions (66 per cent of the Democrats, 49 per cent of the Republicans), a desire to be "in the know" and gain prestige in the neighborhood (4 per cent of the Democrats, 6 per cent of the Republicans), or they saw other personalized satisfactions such as the enjoyment of the "fun and excitement" of a cam-

Table VIII. ***Change and Stability in Specific Motivational Perspectives (precinct leaders)***

Original Perceived Motive	Current Satisfactions					
	Ideological Achievement	*Other Impersonal Philosophical Satisfactions*	*Social Contacts*	*Other Personalized Satisfactions*	*No Satisfactions*	*Number of Cases*
Policy influence						
Democrats	0%	0%	58%	23%	19%	26
Republicans	26	12	44	14	3	34
Candidate friendship						
Democrats	0	0	38	0	56	16
Republicans	11	0	37	0	53	19
Philosophical orientation ("politics is part of my way of life")						
Democrats	9	23	59	9	0	22
Republicans	10	0	30	40	20	10*

Original Perceived Motive	Current Satisfactions					
	Ideo-logical Achieve-ment	*Other Imper-sonal Philo-sophical Satis-factions*	*Social Con-tacts*	*Other Per-sonalized Satis-factions*	*No Satis-factions*	*Num-ber of Cases*
Sense of community duty						
Democrats	0	0	77	14	5	22
Republicans	15	0	58	3	24	33
Party loyalty						
Democrats	13	0	33	13	33	15
Republicans	10	5	48	19	19	21
Personal drives: social contacts, fun, political position, business contacts, desire to be close to important people, recognition in community						
Democrats	0	0	81	15	3	35
Republicans	24	0	48	5	24	21

*Too few cases for reliable analysis.

NOTE: When the total percentages do not add up to 100%, the balance represents those who were unclear or unascertainable on current motivations.

paign (6 per cent of the Democrats, 4 per cent of the Republicans).

Table IX. ***Current Motivation of all Those Changing Motivational Direction, by Era of Career Origin***

Current Satisfaction	Era of Career Origin						Total	
	1952–56		*1940–51*		*Before 1940*			
	D	*R*	*D*	*R*	*D*	*R*	*D*	*R*
Ideological	5%	3%	0%	5%	3%	44%	3	12
Other impersonal	0	8	0	0	0	0	0	4
Social contacts	56	49	73	57	80	36	66	49
Other personalized	12	10	9	19	11	0	11	11
No satisfaction	27	30	18	19	6	20	18	24
Number of cases	57	61	22	37	36	25	115	123

Inconsistency in Perspectivist Patterns

Not only was there great "mobility" in the precinct leader's motivations during his career, but his current perspectives toward party activity exhibited considerable disjunction. One might expect a certain consistency in the concentrations of activists in the perspectivist categories used in preceding chapters. The person who perceived his role as "ideological mentor," for example, and the person who was consistently liberal or conservative on public issues might be expected to give motivational responses indicating he derived the greatest satisfaction in party work from promotion of ideological causes. But this is not the case (Table X). Less than one-fifth of the consistent ideologues in both parties seemed motivated and satisfied by ideological or philosophical interests. Less than one-tenth of the Democrats and only 30 per cent of the Republicans who defined their role ideologically derived their greatest satisfaction from the party ideologically. Further, only small percentages (6 per cent Democrats, 22 per cent Republicans) of those who saw the party's goal as fighting on the issues and problems of the day, related themselves personally to the party in these terms. Thus, the political orientations of party leaders were multidimensional, and their orientations toward the party were separable, not cumulative.

The one striking consistency of perspectives emerging from this analysis is that those activists who were unable to articulate the goal of the party, and those who had no clear perception of their own role, were definitely inclined to be disillusioned motivationally. Otherwise there seems to be a limited correlation between perspectives. The inconsistent ideologically were no less "socializers" than the consistent ideologues. The power salients, who saw the party's goal clearly in terms of winning elections and power, were distributed motivationally very similarly to those who had no such goal orientation for the party. Two general conclusions are suggested, then: (1) the particular content of a person's ideological position, or conception of what the party should be fighting for, or his own role in the party structure, was not necessarily related to the satisfaction he derived from party work. *Goal, role,* and *ideology* might be in one compartment, motivation in another. (2) The "social contacts" type of motivational response was so frequent and normal, particularly in the Democratic party, that even though a precinct leader clearly understood the party task to be winning power, and his own task to be mobilization of votes, yet his satisfaction was inclined to be highly personalized and instrumental. The *party* was striving for power. The majority of individual leaders were striving for social gratifications and personal status.

Analysis of current motivations by the social strata and social characteristics of precinct leaders gives us clues about the types of individuals in both parties who derived particular motivational fulfillment (Table XI). First, these data suggest that the disillusioned minority originated in politically deviant social sectors. One-half of the wealthy Democrats would miss nothing if they had to step out of party work; there was a similar slight tendency for those among the lower-income Republican leaders to be disillusioned. Republican Catholics had a high percentage of disillusioned (47 per cent) and up to 50 per cent of the leaders in both parties whose family origin was in eastern and southern Europe were motivationally unhappy. Second, the ideologically motivated leaders came from different social sectors for both parties. For the Democrats the highest percentages were found among those in the lower income brackets and the college-educated, but they were only one-fifth in each such demographic category. The Republicans with ideological motivation were distributed in a less discernible pattern of regularities. Besides the college-educated, who were one-third ideological, the women leaders were also relatively high in this respect. But all Republican

Table X. *Congruence of Personal Party Perspectives (precinct leaders)*

Categories of Other Perspectives	Motivational Perspectives									
	Democrats					Republicans				
	Instrumentalists		*Ideologues-Philosophers*	*Disillusioned*	*Number of Cases*	*Instrumentalists*		*Ideologues-Philosophers*	*Disillusioned*	*Number of Cases*
	Socializers	*Others*				*Socializers*	*Others*			
Ideology:										
Consistently liberal	63%	14%	13%	8%	63	*	*	*	*	9*
Consistently conservative	*	*	*	*	6*	41%	16%	16%	25%	32
Middle of the road (not consistent)	67	14	2	17	42	48	9	22	22	69
Party goal orientation:										
Power salients	72	16	6	5	85	43	17	26	14	42
Power latents	50	13	13	25	24	64	8	19	8	36
Idealists	82	6	6	0	17	50	8	22	18	50
Unoriented	0	0	0	90	12	13	0	0	87	15
Personal role perceptions:										
Vote mobilizer	58	19	8	15	62	59	14	19	8	63
Ideological mentor	61	12	9	15	33	48	0	30	18	33
Welfare promoter	90	7	3	0	30	60	5	10	25	20
No role	33	0	0	58	12	6	24	6	65	17

*Too few cases for analysis.

social groups with few exceptions, the most notable being the lowest income group, tended to exhibit more ideological motivation than did the Democrats.

A third question is, Which social strata produce the "socializers"? The most significant concentrations in both parties were found among the Negroes and the Protestants. The Catholics were particularly low in this satisfaction in the Republican party, where, as noted previously, almost half were disillusioned about satisfactions received from party work. It is interesting to note also that there was a great percentage difference in social gratifications among the upper and low income groups in the Democratic party, and to a lesser extent in the Republican party, with the findings somewhat reversed for the two parties. That is, low-income Democrats were "social-contact conscious" while low-income Republicans were not; but in both parties fewer of the wealthy were in politics for social rewards. Women differed also by party in this respect—Democratic women were much more likely to be socializers than their Republican counterparts. The same was true for the older leaders, those with an elementary education, and those with a northwestern European family origin. Thus, while race and religion may have been common social-group factors for both parties, there is evidence that other social factors were not generalizable, and that the differences in motivational perspectives for population subgroups stemmed from internal party conditions and environmental factors.

Motivational Variations Within District Organizations and Precinct Types

The pluralistic motivational structure of the party elites has been apparent in the analysis presented thus far. The question remains as to whether there is more homogeneity within the party if we look at the "party," not as a mammoth county hierarchy, but as a series of fairly autonomous districts and precincts. The distribution of motivations and satisfactions by the six congressional districts is presented in Table XII, and it can be seen that precinct leaders may vary considerably by district.

The 1st District of Congressman Machrowitz, made up primarily of Negroes and Poles, included a high proportion (82 to 95 per cent) of "socializers" in both parties. The 17th

Table XI. ***Current Motivations by Social Strata (precinct leaders)***

	Democrats					Republicans				
	Instrumentalists		*Ideolo-gues-Philos-ophers*	*Disillu-sioned*	*Num-ber of Cases*	*Instrumentalists*		*Ideolo-gues-Philos-ophers*	*Disillu-sioned*	*Num-ber of Cases*
	Social-izers	*Others*				*Social-izers*	*Others*			
Income (family)										
Under $4,000	80%	0%	20%	0%	10	33%	43%	0%	24%	21
$4–6,000	70	27	0	3	37	41	0	28	31	29
$6–10,000	72	2	10	14	58	72	8	8	11	36
Over $10,000	29	8	4	50	24	44	4	28	24	50
Race										
Negro	81	3	3	13	32	74	22	4	0	23
White	58	16	8	16	106	43	8	22	26	120
Sex										
Female	67	33	0	0	21	36	25	32	4	28
Male	62	9	8	18	117	50	6	17	26	115
Age										
Under 30	*	*	*	*	7	40	16	24	20	25
30–59	59	16	6	18	112	56	2	17	24	89
60 and over	84	0	11	0	19	34	22	27	17	29
Education										
Elementary	60	15	5	15	20	25	25	25	25	16
High school	65	14	0	20	81	60	2	2	36	53
College	59	21	22	5	37	43	12	32	11	74

	Democrats					Republicans				
	Instrumentalists		*Ideolo-gues-Philos-ophers*	*Disillu-sioned*	*Num-ber of Cases*	*Instrumentalists*		*Ideolo-gues-Philos-ophers*	*Disillu-sioned*	*Num-ber of Cases*
	Social-izers	*Others*				*Social-izers*	*Others*			
Religion										
Catholic	60	14	6	15	65	29	16	15	47	34
Protestant	77	6	6	10	62	56	12	19	13	97
Nationality										
Northwestern European	56	11	13	18	45	27	9	29	33	45
Central European	63	23	2	10	41	59	3	15	24	34
Eastern and southern European	40	10	0	50	10*	28	0	28	44	18

*Too few cases for analysis.

District of Congressman Martha Griffiths, a more marginal area, had a relatively low proportion of "socializers" (38 to 39 per cent) in both parties, more activists (particularly among the Democrats) who were interested in other kinds of personal aims, Republican ideologists, and a larger percentage of disillusioned precinct leaders (particularly among the Republicans). Other districts were outstanding in other respects, although the reason for this is not so readily apparent. Why should 50 per cent of the Republicans in the heavily Negro 13th District have been ideologically motivated, with practically a total absence of Democratic ideologists in the same district? Why should there have been such a high proportion of disillusioned Republicans in the 15th District? These and other differences hint again at such possible controlling factors as the conditions of party competition, top elite recruitment of precinct leaders, and organizational morale as basic to understanding the motivational structure of the party, a structure which is geographically and organizationally nonmonolithic.

If our precincts are divided on the basis of competitive status, we derive some help in explaining differences in motivation (Table XIII), but these differences occurred by party. It is true that sure Republican and Democratic precincts had the highest percentages of "socializers," but the differences (particularly among Republicans) were not significant. Also, the marginal precincts seemed to have the highest proportions of ideologically motivated, but again the Republican differences were small. Marginal areas may have had few or no disillusioned workers (Democrats) or a relatively high percentage (31 per cent among the Republicans). The differences, thus, seemed to be within party by type of precinct, rather than generalizable for both parties. The Republican picture was quite disorderly; the Democrats revealed more uniformities. Their sure districts were heavily composed of "socializers," the opponents' sure districts included Democrats relatively disillusioned, and the marginal districts found Democrats more ideologically motivated and apparently fairly well satisfied about their personal motivational relationship to the party.

Some patterns are also observable if we divide the precinct by turnout level. Those areas where the voters were apathetic tended to be neighborhoods where the precinct leaders enjoyed

Table XII. ***Motivations Within the District Hierarchies (precinct leaders only)***

	Democrats					Republicans				
	Instrumentalists		*Ideologues-*	*Disillu-*	*Number*	*Instrumentalists*		*Ideologues-*	*Disillu-*	*Number*
Districts	*Socializers*	*Others*	*Philosophers*	*sioned*	*of Cases*	*Socializers*	*Others*	*Philosophers*	*sioned*	*of Cases*
1st	82%	0%	6%	6%	17	95%	0%	0%	5%	20
13th	68	0	0	21	19	28	22	50	0	18
14th	35	30	10	25	20	46	25	21	8	24
15th	67	6	6	22	18	35	6	0	59	17
16th	77	2	9	9	43	44	0	24	29	41
17th	38	43	5	14	21	39	13	22	26	23

Table XIII. ***Motivational Patterns by Precinct Types***

	Democrats					Republicans				
	Instrumentalists		*Ideolo-gues-Philos-ophers*	*Disillu-sioned*	*Num-ber of Cases*	*Instrumentalists*		*Ideolo-gues-Philos-ophers*	*Disillu-sioned*	*Num-ber of Cases*
	Social-izers	*Others*				*Social-izers*	*Others*			
Competitive status of precincts										
Sure Democratic	80%	3%	1%	15%	79	51%	13%	20%	16%	69
Sure Republican	34	25	7	31	29	46	11	17	23	35
Marginal	47	33	20	0	30	44	2	23	31	39
Turnout level of precincts										
High	47	21	11	18	74	46	9	15	29	79
Medium and low	81	4	2	13	64	50	11	27	13	64

social gratification from party work, where the Republicans were ideologues but the Democrats were not, and where there tended to be fewer disillusioned party leaders. On the other hand, in high-turnout areas, Democrats and Republicans expressed the greatest dissatisfaction with party work, perhaps because so many of them were seeking social contacts and the character of the party operation was less conducive to promotion of this type of satisfaction. A somewhat paradoxical situation obtained, therefore: where voter interest and participation were high, partly due no doubt to the hard work of the party machine, in such neighborhoods party activists' satisfactions with party work were low!

Conclusions

Here we have documented certain prominent aspects of the motivational structure of the party. It seems clear that the party structure comprehends leaders with a great variety of drives which may or may not be satisfied. The party is a motivationally complex and pluralistic structure. We have seen how these satisfactions differed for the top elite and the grass-roots actives. Among the latter motivation might differ by type of district or neighborhood in which one worked, by tenure and career status in the organization, as well as by the type of social strata in which one has been reared.

Aside from this diversity in motivational patterns hierarchically, areally, and organizationally, great perceptual confusion was displayed among party leaders as to why their colleagues were involved in party work. Fully three-fourths of precinct leaders ascribed motivations to others different from their own, and not borne out by reality.

A further analysis which complicates the picture is the considerable movement and change in motivation from the time of career origin to the present. The great majority (over two-thirds) of precinct leaders changed motivational direction after beginning party work, whether they began before 1940 or after.

Finally, the disjunction and noncongruence of motivations in relation to other personal political perspectives adds to the puzzle. There seems to be considerable inconsistency between role perception and goal conceptualization for the party when placed alongside motivation. But it is important to realize that what the individual personally felt he got out of politics may be one thing, while what he realized was his role, and what the party's goal was, might be quite other matters. Personal goals and group goals, as perceived by the party leader, did not often coincide.

That no more than 10 per cent of the precinct leaders of the parties (actually only 3 per cent of the Democrats) were ideologically motivated in their work may be a disturbing fact, but it is a fact which should be clearly recognized. A party is a social group, and the personal motivational relationship in the party is basically the same, apparently, as in other social groups. Social friendships, rewards, and other personally instrumental satisfactions were most salient in the minds of the precinct activists, as well as in the minds of the top organizational mobiles and those who had arrived in the top elite positions. They may have started out as idealists (especially those who were at the lower echelons and non-mobile), but they were soon acclimated and socialized to expect personal satisfactions and to stay in party work because of them. Though party work was "voluntaristic," since there were few real patronage jobs to dispense, it was not "ideological" as those with reformist visions might have hoped. The political party unites an agglomeration of people with a rich variety of motivations, drives, and needs. As such it is a very incohesive team of leaders and workers. But it is clear that the vast majority of these people sought some personalized satisfaction—whether good fellowship, excitement, social recognition, prestige, money, or friendship. In a broader sense, this is the "patronage" they expected, and this "patronage" produced not only personal contentment but probably also induced them to continue work, be maximally productive in their roles, and inspired the fight for higher status in the party machine.

Notes:

1. See for example, Harold F. Gosnell, *Machine Politics: Chicago Model* (Chicago, 1937); D. H. Kurtzman, *Methods of Controlling Votes in Philadelphia* (Philadelphia, 1935); Peter H. Rossi and Phillips Cutright, "The Impact of Party Organization in an Industrial Setting," in M. Janowitz, ed., *Community Political Systems* (Glencoe, Ill., 1961), pp. 81–116.

2. Using "aspiration" as a clue to "motivation" seems highly ques-

tionable. A person may be willing, even eager, to move to more responsible positions in the hierarchy, and yet his personal linkage to the party and the satisfactions he derives or expects from party work may be other than personal political gain.

3. When asked whether the party workers of the opposition differed "at all in the rewards and satisfactions which they got out of political activity," 53 per cent of all precinct leaders said there were no differences (65 per cent of the Democrats, 41 per cent of the Republicans), with about 10 per cent in both parties uncertain.

6 *Psychological Dimensions of Anomy**

by Herbert McClosky and John H. Schaar

Since Merton's seminal contribution of 1938, around 35 scientific papers have appeared on the subject of anomy,[1] most of them since 1950. In addition, the concept has been used in a large number of books and essays and applied to discussions of an astonishing variety of topics, ranging from delinquency among the young to apathy among the old, and including along the way such matters as political participation, status aspirations, the behavior of men in prisons, narcotics addiction, urbanization, race relations, social change, and suicide.

Virtually all of this work has employed a single explanatory model for the analysis of anomy: a specified social-cultural condition gives rise to specified feelings in individuals which in turn result in specified behaviors. Different writers have worked variations on this scheme, but nobody has challenged the scheme itself or attempted a fundamental revision of it.

Reprinted from *American Sociological Review,* 30 (February, 1965), 14–40, by permission of the authors and the American Sociological Association.

* This is publication A34 of the Survey Research Center, University of California, Berkeley. The data presented in the paper have been prepared and analyzed under grants from the Rockefeller Foundation and the Social Science Research Council. A fellowship to the senior author by the Center for Advanced Studies in the Behavioral Sciences was of great value in processing the Minnesota study. This investigation was supported in part by Public Health Service Research Grant MH-05837, from the National Institutes of Health.

Since it is our purpose in this paper to offer such a revision, we shall begin by showing the main ways in which the model is used in the recent literature. Even a brief review will demonstrate that while the variations have been many, the theme remains the same, with the result that the literature of anomy is much more heterogeneous in appearance than it is in fact.

Most of the variations have taken place in the first component of the sequence, the social condition that triggers the subsequent responses. To Durkheim, anomy meant a condition of de-regulation or relative normlessness in a social group. In his view, anomy was endemic in modern societies, and especially virulent in the economic sector where all the customary restraints and moral limits on men's aspirations were being undermined by the capitalist ethic of greed and gain. This weakening of restraints gave men a feeling of wandering through an empty space with no landmarks from which to take a bearing and set a course. Society imposed no limit on man's "insatiable and bottomless" cravings for wealth, prestige, and power, and when a man's goals are infinite, his strivings are futile. "Those who have only empty space above them are almost inevitably lost in it, if no force restrains them." [2] Each step upward only discloses to the climber the infinite reaches beyond; each success turns into another failure. In the end, "reality seems valueless by comparison with the dreams of fevered imagination; reality is therefore abandoned. . . ." [3] Finding no fixed reference points by which to locate itself, the soul tires of its wanderings through a social landscape desolate of norms. The struggle seems futile, life itself loses value, and the result for many is anomic self-destruction.

Except for his passionate rhetoric, all the elements of Durkheim's treatment still remain in the recent literature, albeit in different proportions and vocabularies. Most importantly, the categories of his explanatory model are unchanged.

Merton's work illustrates this.[4] Discarding Durkheim's concept of man as a bundle of passions which can be tamed only by social restraints, he examines the actual social pressures upon persons to violate the accepted codes. He retains Durkheim's definition of anomy as a condition of relative normlessness in a society, but offers a revised statement of its causes. Whereas Durkheim held specifically that anomy was produced by an economic ethic that removed all limits from greed, Merton sees anomy as the result of "a breakdown in the cultural structure, occurring particularly when there is an acute disjunction between the cultural norms and goals and the socially structured capacities of members of the group to act in accord with them. . . . When the cultural and the social structure are malintegrated, the first calling for behavior and attitudes which the second precludes, there is a strain toward the breakdown of the norms, toward normlessness." [5]

But when Merton applies this general conception to a specific social setting, the results are quite similar to Durkheim's. Merton believes that modern American society has placed a tremendous emphasis on the goal of success, which means "accumulated wealth," without a corresponding insistence on pursuing that goal by legitimate means. Where Durkheim says greed, Merton says success. But do the two really mean different things? [6] For both writers, the basic point is that in some societies certain goals, which are in their nature unlimited, have been pursued so fervently that the appropriate normative restraints have virtually collapsed. The result is "a strain toward anomie and deviant behavior." [7]

Merton's analysis of the behavioral consequences of anomy is more complex than Durkheim's. Merton does not deal with a single action, such as suicide. Rather, noting that the malintegration of cultural goals and institutionalized means falls with different impact upon persons located at different points in the social structure, he constructs a typology of modes of adaptation and offers some arguments and evidence to suggest which of the modes will typically be followed in given social groups. In Merton's scheme, then, while anomy produces a strain toward deviant behavior, the content as well as the incidence of that behavior varies among groups differently located in the social system. In other words, deviant behavior, which takes a number of forms, is the final indicator of anomy—although Merton concedes that not all deviant behavior is produced by malintegration and anomy.[8] He offers no tests, however, for telling which is and which is not.

In sum, Merton's fundamental logic is Durkheim's: social condition→psychological state→deviant behavior. The content of each category is different, but the categories themselves and the relations between them are the same. Moreover, both writers focus on the two outside links of the causal chain and have little to say about the link in the middle. In this sense, their orientation is sociological rather than psychological.

In addition to the manifestly sociological work, there is a large body of writing that appears to be psychologically oriented. It focuses on the middle link in the same causal chain: anomy is conceptualized as a state of mind rather than as a state of society. MacIver, for example, defines anomy as "the state of mind of one who has been pulled up by his moral roots. . . . The anomic man has become spiritually sterile, responsive only to himself, responsible to no one. He lives on the thin line of sensation between no future and no past." [9]

The most important work here is that of Leo J. Srole.[10] Srole conceptualized anomy as a psychological state which refers to "the individual's generalized, pervasive sense of 'self-to-others belongingness' at one extreme compared with 'self-to-others distance' and 'self-to-others alienation' at the other pole of the continuum." [11] He then postulated five attitudinal-ideational components of the anomic state of mind, and devised a five-item scale to measure them.[12] The scale has been employed in a large number of investigations. Srole's scale and Merton's typology of modes of adaptation are the two most widely used research instruments in the study of anomy.

In his earliest work, Srole used the standard explanatory model in which social malintegration stands as the independent variable and the mental state of anomy as the dependent variable. He theorized that "to a large degree the state of anomia in an individual is dependent upon and determined by the condition of sociological integration at the points of the social system concurrently occupied by him." [13] In his later work, however, Srole broadened this formulation to include the possibility that anomy might be a function not only of social conditions but also of personality factors. In Srole's words, "the original emphasis on the sociogenesis of the anomic state has been refined to include psychogenic personality factors in an interactive relationship with elements of dysfunction and malintegration in the social system." [14]

However plausible this broadened formulation may seem, it appears in Srole's paper only as an assertion, not as a proposition grounded in psychological theory. Nor has this broader conception yet given birth to much research on the psychogenesis of anomy. In a recent exploration of the relations between anomy and various degrees of mental disturbance, Srole tested the general proposition that anomy is positively correlated with mental disturbance and found that the relation held only between anomy and "severe" disturbance.[15] He also found (as all other investigators have) that anomy is inversely related to social and economic status independently of the mental disturbance factor. Therefore, he concluded, social dysfunction, by which he meant low status, was the independent variable: "Both anomia with psychopathology and anomia without psychopathology are postulated as consequences of social dysfunction. Both combinations stand in a strong inverse linear relationship with socio-economic status. This fact would indicate that our social class system is a major axis of differential concentrations of dysfunctional elements in the moving social settings of people's life histories." [16]

As this account shows, Srole has not gone beyond the basic theoretical framework established by Durkheim and Merton. For him as for them, the psychological state of anomy reflects economic and social conditions. This is true not only of Srole's own work, but also of the many other studies in which his scale has been used. Virtually all of these studies have examined the sociostructural foundations of anomy. They have, in the main, tried to find out where the anomic individuals are located in the social structure, though a few have investigated the relations between anomy and such other attitudes as authoritarianism and prejudice.

No writer known to us has specifically explored the relations between anomy and various dimensions of personality. Nor has anyone tried to assess the contributions various psychic states may make to anomy *independently* of the person's social status. No study has attempted to revise even in a modest way the thesis that certain objective social conditions cause anomy and that, conversely, individuals' anomic feelings may be taken as evidence that those objective social conditions exist. We hope to take a few steps toward these ends. Before that, however, there are still some preliminary questions.

One who reads the modern literature of anomy senses, beneath the dispassionate scientific method and vocabulary, passions no less intense than Durkheim's, and moral concerns not too different from his. Its authors are interested in something more than the advancement of science. They are involved in a question that troubles everyone who gives serious thought to the quality of modern life: the question of community and purpose. Does our society show signs of moral breakdown? Are we adrift, wandering without clear goals, out of touch with the cherished values that make up our heritage? Are the ties that bind us together in networks of mutual care and sympathy dangerously strained and weakened?

These are fashionable themes today, the *leitmotifs* of social and political criticism. They appear in the discussion of a thousand questions—juvenile delinquency, family relations, unemployment, economic growth, education, political reform, foreign policy—and in a variety of forums, including professional journals of social science. We do not mean to dismiss these themes nor to belittle this literature, but we do suggest that these discussions are embarrassed by problems that resist scientific analysis and by assumptions that are hard to defend in scientific terms.

Sometimes the assumptions are explicit, as they are when a writer states that "man is a creature who must avoid competing loyalties." [17] Usually, however, they are implicit. There is an assumption in much of the literature, for example, that men find it extremely difficult to function under conditions of normative uncertainty and conflict. But how much uncertainty and conflict, and whether the limits are the same for all men—these decisive questions are nowhere squarely confronted. Instead, one encounters only vague warnings that men need secure moral codes, and cannot function effectively unless their society is "well integrated." What Americans once considered their greatest challenge to the past and promise to the future—the affirmation that men could freely assume responsibility for their own lives, that they would flourish in the open spaces cleared of the walls and towers of dogmatic codes, fixed statuses, and entrenched authorities—appears in this literature as our greatest vulnerability. Perhaps this is as much a manifestation of a failure of nerve as an exercise in scientific analysis.

All these writers assume, and many of them state explicitly, that anomy is a "problem" in our society, that our society suffers to a substantial degree from disintegration of the norms. But by what standard can this be judged? On the crucial questions of the "anomicity" of this society as compared with others, and of how much anomy can be safely tolerated, we can say little that is scientifically grounded without evidence from cross-cultural studies of great depth and scope. Lacking such evidence, we can only worry and argue. On *a priori* grounds one can argue that modern society, with its intricate division of labor, pluralism, rapid change, high mobility, weakening of traditional institutions, and so forth, is highly susceptible to normative uncertainty, conflict among men, and strain between cultural goals and institutionalized means. But whether these things in fact produce anomy, or whether anomy is more pervasive today than in previous societies, cannot be said with much confidence. Many forces that appear on *a priori* grounds to produce anomy may be effectively counteracted by, for example, the prodigious advances in communication, education, literacy, and economic well-being. In short, we must acknowledge complexity, and concede that many of the social conditions that are loosely thought to be destroying norms may simultaneously be welding the population into a stronger and more coherent value community than existed in the past. There may be a "selective fallacy" at work in much of the literature of anomy, as suggested by the fact that while normlessness is one of the *leitmotifs* of contemporary American social critcism, conformity is another. We are simultaneously said to be plagued by lack of shared norms and threatened by too much agreement on norms. Something has been left out of each picture.

Two kinds of evidence are currently offered to support the thesis that ours is an anomic society. Critics of modern society frequently cite rates of crime, delinquency, divorce, and so on as evidence of moral breakdown. But these and other presumed signs of anomy are very complex phenomena which may or may not reflect anomy, and which may themselves be produced by factors that have little to do with the general state of the norms.

Similar considerations apply to the other type of evidence. Many investigators who have administered the Srole scale to various samples report that a large proportion of respondents score "high" on the scale,[18] and this finding is then sometimes said to indicate a high degree of anomy in the society itself.

Srole, for example, writes that his scale, along with other techniques, permits us to gain knowledge of "one of the most pervasive and potentially dangerous aspects of Western society, namely, the deterioration in the social and moral ties that bind, sustain and free us." [19]

The logic of psychological scale construction, however, will not support inferences from scale scores to the state of the society, because the distribution of scores is a function of the difficulty of the scale items themselves. One could construct an anomy scale composed of such "easy" items that almost everyone would score "anomic;" one could also construct a scale consisting of such "difficult" items that almost nobody would score "anomic." From the findings yielded by the easy scale we might infer that the society is highly anomic, whereas we might infer from the difficult scale that the society is happily free of anomy. Obviously, the procedure is fallacious. An ordinal scale permits many kinds of comparison among the people who respond to it, but it permits no statements about the absolute magnitude of the property it purports to measure.

Moreover, the leap from the subjective feelings expressed by individuals to statements about objective social conditions is a perilous one. What people believe about a society may or may not be an accurate reflection of its nature; perceptions and feelings are never a literal copy of what is "out there" but are always powerfully shaped by the needs, motives, attitudes, and abilities of the observer. Hence, we can never confidently assume that because some people feel anomic the society is anomic. Moreover, even if one could establish that some members of a society report strong anomic sentiments, one could label the society anomic only after systematically comparing that society with others. No one, including Durkheim, who came closest, has done this.

More than that, the findings already available concerning the location of anomic individuals in the social structure raise some difficult questions both for the standard explanatory scheme and for the notion of the anomic society. Investigators who have administered the Srole scale to various samples have uniformly reported that anomy is highest among certain sectors of the population: old people, the widowed, the divorced and separated, persons of low education, those with low incomes and low prestige occupations, people experiencing downward social mobility, Negroes and foreign-born, farmers and other rural residents.[20] The tendency to perceive the society as anomic depends very much on one's location in the social structure.

All the groups just mentioned have one thing in common: they are outside the articulate, prosperous, and successful sectors of the population. Anomic feelings appear most frequently and most strongly among those who, for whatever reason, are stranded in the backwaters of the symbolic and material mainstream, those whose lives are circumscribed by isolation, deprivation, and ignorance. Persons who do not share in the life of the articulate and active community are prone to confusion about the norms. In comparison, the relatively successful, well-educated, articulate and aware groups show little difficulty in finding order and meaning in society. Although their society is undergoing rapid change, contains competing value systems, and is increasingly urban and secular, they do not seem especially perplexed and uncertain. They do not report strong feelings of aimlessness, drift, and confusion, and they score low on measures of anomy. It appears, then, that anomy in part reflects patterns of communication and interaction that reduce opportunities to see and understand how the society works, and what its goals and values are.

We have tried to clear the ground. Hopefully, we have established two modest conclusions: virtually all studies of anomy have employed the same explanatory model; and it is extremely difficult at present to say anything scientifically persuasive about the question of the anomic society. It should be clear that we are not addressing the substantive question of whether or not our society is predominantly "healthy" or anomic. We merely suggest that the standard explanatory model is both oversimplified and over elaborate: many of the empirical findings concerning anomy cannot be understood within the terms of the model; and many of the findings can be explained without recourse to the elaborate notions of dysfunction and malintegration employed in the model. Given these considerations, we propose to revise the model so as to approach anomy as a set of learned attitudes and to make more adequate provision for the contribution of psychological factors independently of social structure.

Personal Factors in Anomy

We propose to conceptualize anomy as a state of mind, a cluster of attitudes, beliefs, and feelings in the minds of individuals. Specifically, it is the feeling that the world and oneself are adrift, wandering, lacking in clear rules and stable moorings. The anomic feels literally *de*-moralized; for him, the norms governing behavior are weak, ambiguous, and remote. He lives in a normative "low pressure" area, a turbulent region of weak and fitful currents of moral meaning. The core of the concept is the feeling of moral emptiness.

The norms of a society are, of course, learned; so too are the anomic feelings that there are no norms. What is learned is a function of many things: what is actually "out there" to be learned; the nature and quality of the teaching process; the learner's own ability and motivation; the strength and frequency of reinforcement; the amounts and kinds of impediments to learning, and so forth.

From the basic proposition that anomic feelings are learned, there follows a more specific proposition that applies with special force to the theory of anomy: whatever interferes with learning the norms of a society tends to increase anomic feelings among its members. This proposition is also supported by empirical findings, some of which were mentioned above. First of all, persons who are in an effective social position to learn the norms do not report a high incidence of anomic feelings. This suggests that the norms are in fact "out there" and can be "seen" by those who are in a position to see them. The conclusion is fortified by a small number of studies dealing with the question of "consensus" in American society. These studies have uniformly found that the values usually considered fundamental to our way of life (e.g., belief in freedom, democracy, constitutional and procedural rights, tolerance, human dignity) are shared more widely and held more strongly among people in positions of leadership, influence, and high status than among the less favored classes.[21] Conversely, those who occupy social positions remote from the mainstream exhibit a high incidence and intensity of anomic feelings. Because of poverty, or little education, or the conditions of their employment or residence, these people are relatively isolated from the cultural mainstream. This condition reduces communication and impairs their ability to learn the norms of the larger community which, in turn, gives rise to feelings of normlessness. In short, whatever interferes with one's ability to learn a community's norms, or weakens one's socialization into its central patterns of belief, must be considered among the determinants of anomy.

Some of these determinants are obviously sociological in the sense that certain roles, statuses, and social settings impede the learning process. Others, however, are psychological and personal; if this were not the case, we would expect all persons in a given role or social setting to be anomic. But this is clearly not the fact.

The two sets of determinants sometimes act together, and sometimes independently of each other. People who share the same social circumstances within a given society do not all react to the society in the same way. The same holds for those who have similar psychological and intellectual characteristics. We would suppose, however, that certain personality types (say, highly anxious persons) in certain social circumstances (say, low status and education) in certain societies (say, pluralistic and rapidly changing) would be highly susceptible to anomy, while self-confident persons of high status in a relatively simple and stable society might be virtually immune. The important point is that anomic feelings are not necessarily produced by a single cause or factor, or even by a cluster of factors all of which are on the same level of analysis, but are likely to appear whenever learning of the norms is severely impeded. Impediments may arise from an individual's social setting, from his personality characteristics, or from both.

The theory of anomy on which we shall proceed can be summarized by Chart 1. In the present paper we are not concerned with all the elements in this causal pattern. Our primary intention is to identify and to explain some of the personality and cognitive factors that contribute to anomy. We also offer some suggestions concerning the interrelations between personality factors, social-cultural conditions, and anomy. Examination of the other links in the model will be left for subsequent publications. Hopefully, this exploration of the psychological dimensions of the anomic state of mind will direct attention to some important but neglected factors in the study of anomy.

Chart 1.

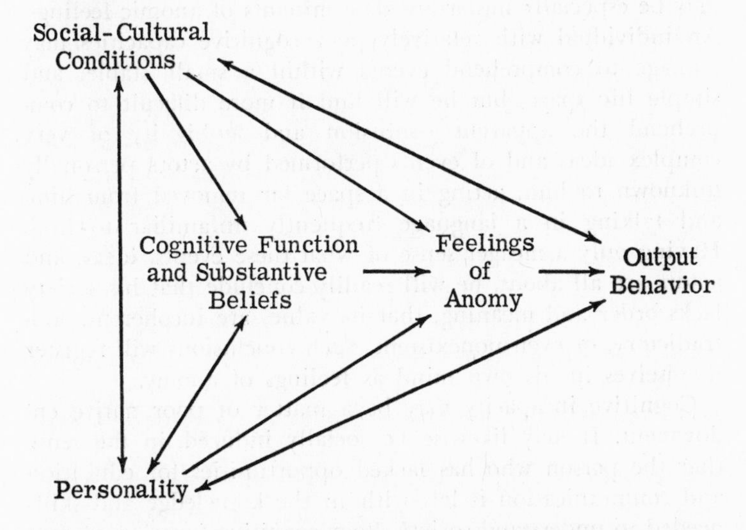

The personal factors that impair learning and socialization may be divided into three categories: (1) *Cognitive factors* that influence one's ability to learn and understand; (2) *Emotional factors* that tend to lower one's ability to perceive reality correctly; (3) *Substantive beliefs and attitudes* that interfere with successful communication and interaction. There might well be other such categories; and surely these three are not as independent of each other in reality as they are in our list. Still, the list provides a satisfactory base from which to open an exploration of the psychological dimensions of anomy.

Cognitive factors. The maxim has it that ignorance is bliss. A host of considerations suggest that the contrary is more likely the case. Those whose intellectual or cognitive equipment lacks power and efficiency find it difficult to organize and understand the events and ideas they encounter, and this difficulty apparently produces, not security and confidence, but bewilderment and anxiety. Those who cannot think clearly or relate events to each other, or organize their observations and experiences into meaningful structures, are most prone to be confused about their society's values and to see the society itself as lacking in order and meaning. In modern, rapidly changing, complex societies, such incapacities may be especially important determinants of anomic feelings. An individual with relatively poor cognitive capacities may manage to comprehend events within a small, stable, and simple life space, but he will find it more difficult to comprehend the apparent confusion and ambiguity of very complex ideas and of events performed by actors personally unknown to him, acting in a space far removed from him, and talking in a language frequently unfamiliar to him. Having only a meager sense of what these events, ideas, and actors are all about, he will readily conclude that his society lacks order and meaning, that its values are incoherent, contradictory, or even nonexistent. Such conclusions will register themselves in his own mind as feelings of anomy.

Cognitive incapacity may be a matter of poor native endowment. It may likewise be socially induced, in the sense that the person who has lacked opportunities for education and communication is left without the knowledge and skills needed to understand society. Poor cognitive functioning may also result from various psychological disorders that interfere with rational and realistic thought. Whatever its origin, we expect persons with low cognitive capacity to be more susceptible to anomy than persons with high cognitive capacity. This hypothesis will be tested below.

Emotional factors. What we have in mind here are a variety of psychological states that warp perception, interfere with cognitive functioning, or render one very uncomfortable in the face of ambivalence and ambiguity. These mental states may produce a tendency toward anomy in a number of ways. Some psychic states directly distort perception. Others so impair cognitive functioning that the person is unable to structure the world realistically. Still others so reduce his ability to interact successfully with his fellows that he fails to learn what they believe and value. This failure of learning may be especially important in the growth of anomy. One does not learn values and norms in precisely the way one learns facts: one is "socialized" into them through numerous interactions—living, working, and talking with others—repeated over time and in a variety of contexts.

Some psychic states (e.g., extreme hostility toward others) reduce one's ability to interact, and therefore prevent one from becoming well-acquainted with society's norms and values, leading one to see the society as anomic. This proposition, which will be refined and tested below, is also relevant to the third cluster of personal factors that encourage anomy.

Substantive beliefs and opinions. A person's opinions and values have a considerable effect on the way he is received by a community or group. Newcomb showed in the Bennington study that persons who had acquired the "proper" values and beliefs were more readily accepted by the members of a group and more easily attained prestige positions within the group.[22] Moreover, once a person has learned and accepted a group's values to the extent necessary to secure acceptance, his very participation will reinforce its values in his mind. Many studies of small groups have shown that group leaders, who, of course, participate most fully in the group life, are more devoted than the average member to the group's values.[23] Partial acceptance of the rules will get one into the club; once inside, the processes of indoctrination and absorption can be carried much farther.

On the other hand, persons who fail to learn the dominant values of a group, or who hold beliefs and opinions not widely shared, are not likely to be well received by group members. This in turn reduces communication and makes socialization into the group even more difficult. A deviant lacks the intimate, vital experience of participation which is essential to full appreciation of the group's norms and values. His knowledge of those norms may be abstract and "theoretical," insensitive to subtle shadings of mood and meaning—a caricature rather than an accurate portrait. In addition, since the deviant sees a group that has rejected him only from the outside, he may also see its activities as senseless and incoherent.

The connection between the holding of deviant beliefs and the feeling that society is anomic is in some instances dependent on certain personality states. A substantial body of evidence indicates that many persons who hold extreme views on political, economic, and social questions feel an unusually keen need for order and certainty in their lives.[24] This need is served by passionate attachment to a belief system. Because these people cannot gain the psychological security they crave unless they see their own beliefs embodied in the world outside, they easily come to feel that a social order not arranged along the lines of their own belief systems is really no order at all.

We shall formulate some of the general hypotheses just proposed more specifically and submit them to tests of verification after we have described the samples, questionnaires, and attitude scales employed in the present study.

Procedures

The data were collected from two general population samples: one, a cross section of the population of Minnesota (N=1082), and the other a cross section of the national population (N=1484). The Minnesota survey, done in 1955, was conducted with the cooperation of the Minnesota Poll, which designed the sample and selected the respondents. The sample for the national survey, carried out in 1958, was drawn by the Gallup Poll, which also administered the questionnaire. In both surveys, the interviewers explained how the questionnaire should be filled out and then left it with the respondent, who completed and returned it by mail. Although this departs from the more standard methods—a departure dictated by the great length and unusual content of the questionnaires—the characteristics of the samples are very close to those of the populations sampled.[25] The Minnesota survey, which was designed primarily to investigate various forms of extreme or "marginal belief," is called the Marginal Believer (MB) study, while the national survey, which focused on political affiliation, activity, and belief, is called the Political Activities and Beliefs (PAB) study.

The questionnaires for both studies, though different in some respects, had similar basic formats. Both were of the self-administering type. Both contained questions about the respondent's personal and social characteristics, group memberships and identifications, and political attitudes, interests, and activities. Both also contained a large number of attitude and personality scales, each typically composed of nine agree-disagree items. The MB questionnaire had 512 such items, randomly presented but in reality divided into 63 scales. The PAB questionnaire contained 390 items composing 47 scales, many of which had also been used in the MB study. These extensive questionnaires provide a vast amount of information on large samples drawn from different populations at different times. With this base, not only can one assess the relations between anomy and many other attitudes and personal characteristics, but one can also replicate the inquiry by comparing the results of the two studies.

The construction and testing of the large inventory of scales in these questionnaires took about two years and required the preliminary sampling of 1200 residents of the Minneapolis-St. Paul community.[26] The responses of this sample were scored and analyzed by face inspection and modified Guttman procedures to ascertain their internal consistency, their face relation to the attribute being measured, and their unidimensionality. For some scales, empirical validation was achieved through the use of criterion groups; for others, a panel of judges was used to ascertain validity; for still others more emphasis was placed on internal consistency and reproducibility. One or more procedures for estimating validity were carried out for each scale in both studies.

The Anomy scale was one of a set designed to measure response to the social and political community. Other measures in this set included bewilderment, pessimism, alienation, and sense of political futility. The definition of anomy employed in the construction of the scale is consistent with the definition already indicated, placing primary emphasis on feelings of normlessness and de-regulation.

Like the other scales, the Anomy scale began as a large pool of items, each of which was designed to assess one or another facet of the anomic state of mind. Through preliminary screening and pre-testing, the initial pool was cut to 11 items, which were then submitted to a sample of 273 Minnesota adults. Their responses were scrutinized for internal consistency, subjected to a Guttman reproducibility procedure, and finally reduced to the nine items presented in order of item difficulty in Table I.

The validity of the scale can be assessed by several different criteria. One criterion is face validity: Do the scale items appear to express the sentiments and beliefs that constitute the anomic state of mind? This is an important test in this case, because the people we designate as anomic are those who say precisely the sorts of things and display precisely the sorts of feelings that these items express. In short, the items define, by their content, our conception of anomy.

Table I. ***The Anomy Scale: Items and Level of Item Difficulty (PAB sample—N=1484)****

	Per Cent Who Agree	Per Cent Who Disagree
1. With everything so uncertain these days, it almost seems as though anything could happen.	82.3	17.7
2. What is lacking in the world today is the old kind of friendship that lasted for a lifetime.	69.3	30.7
3. With everything in such a state of disorder, it's hard for a person to know where he stands from one day to the next.	50.0	50.0
4. Everything changes so quickly these days that I often have trouble deciding which are the right rules to follow.	48.5	51.5
5. I often feel that many things our parents stood for are just going to ruin before our very eyes.	47.6	52.4
6. The trouble with the world today is that most people really don't believe in anything.	44.1	55.9
7. I often feel awkward and out of place.	37.3	62.7
8. People were better off in the old days when everyone knew just how he was expected to act.	27.4	72.6
9. It seems to me that other people find it easier to decide what is right than I do.	27.1	72.9

*Since the logic of this type of scale construction forces the respondent to agree or disagree, the proportion of "No Answers" is very small—about 1 per cent on the average. These have been omitted from the tabulation.

We are satisfied that the scale passes this test. With the possible exception of number 7, each item manifestly expresses one or another dimension of the anomic mentality. The items express the feelings that people today lack firm convictions and standards, that it is difficult to tell right from wrong in our complex and disorderly world, that the traditional values which gave meaning to the individual and order to the society have lost their force, and that the social ties which once bound men together have dissolved.

Do the items express what other students mean by anomy? To answer this question we submitted the items to several groups of graduate students in political science and psychology, and to some 40 Fellows at the Center for Advanced Study in the Behavioral Sciences. In every instance, the proportion who judged the statements as expressing some aspect of anomy was high enough to satisfy us that the scale items do in fact embody the feelings and beliefs associated with the concept.

A second method of assessing the scale's validity is to observe its relation to other attitudes that one would expect, on theoretical grounds, to find associated with feelings of anomy. One would expect an anomic person to feel lonely and distant from his fellows, to be confused and bewildered by events in his society, to report a strong sense of political futility, to feel pessimistic about himself and the future, and to display cynical attitudes toward the men and practices governing society and the state. All these expectations are clearly borne out by the correlations between Anomy and the variables just mentioned, as can be seen from Table II. The magnitude and direction of these correlations assured us that the Anomy scale is located in the proper attitude domain.

Table II. ***Correlations Between the Anomy Scale and Selected "Validating" Scales****

	Alienation	Bewilderment	Pessimism	Feelings of Political Impotence	Political Cynicism	Life Satisfaction
Sample:						
PAB: N=1484	+.60	NA†	+.50	+.54	+.59	−.41
MB: N=1082	+.58	+.62	+.43	+.55	+.62	−.39

*All figures are Pearson product-moment correlations and all are significant beyond the .01 level.

†NA = Not Available.

A third way to assess scale validity is to apply the usual technical tests for unidimensionality. Although this test matters, it is less important than the validity measures already discussed. Indeed, no one can be certain that anomy should be thought of as a unidimensional attitude: much evidence suggests, as we will show, that it is only one facet of a many-sided sense of malaise or distress.

These demurrers made, we can still report that the scale exhibits a fair degree of unidimensionality. Reproducibility procedures carried out on both the PAB general population sample and on a national sample of 3020 political influentials produced coefficients of reproducibility of .80 and .83, respectively. Observe also that all the items but one fall into the second and third quartiles of item difficulty: hence, the reproducibility coefficients are not factitiously increased by the use of items of very high or very low difficulty. The scale, then, achieves a satisfactory degree of internal cohesion and unidimensionality.

Although a nine-item scale cannot be expected to produce an extremely high reliability score, the split-half reliability coefficient as corrected by the Spearman-Brown formula is a satisfactory .76. An alternative computation utilizing a formula presented by L. J. Cronbach[27] yields a reliability coefficient of .77. Additional evidence of the stability (if not, technically speaking, the reliability) of the scale can be gleaned from a comparison of the Anomy correlations in the MB and PAB studies. The relation of Anomy to a subset of 41 variables was tested in the MB study and, in effect, retested in the PAB study. Although to correlate the two sets of correlations may in some quarters be considered unorthodox, it is nevertheless worth noting that the correlation in this case was an astonishingly high .98. Thus, people in the PAB sample who possess certain social, attitudinal, or personality characteristics register scores on the Anomy scale that are very similar to the scores made by their counterparts in the MB sample.

The criteria of face validity, correlation with related scales, reproducibility, and reliability, are the appropriate tests by which to judge the quality of the Anomy scale. Other tests might be proposed, but they are not appropriate in this case. For instance, one common validation procedure is to check respondents' scale scores against some independent and external criterion (preferably behavioral) which assesses the same dimension that the scale seeks to measure. But for anomy, no feasible criterion is available. Obviously, there is no recognizable group of anomics to whom one might turn to validate an anomy scale, as one can turn to groups of liberals or right-wing extremists to validate a liberalism or fascism scale. Rates of divorce, crime, delinquency, alcoholism, suicide, and so on, are also inappropriate criteria; for it is by no means certain that anomy typically produces these consequences or that a large proportion of them are caused by anomy. When a particular attitude has known, measurable behavioral consequences, as is the case, for example, with ethnocentrism, these consequences can serve as indicators that the attitude is present. When the consequences of an attitude are not really known, the best indicators of the presence of the attitude are the scale items themselves.

Another external criterion suggested by the literature is the observed level of agreement on basic norms. Although this mode of validation flows logically from the standard sociological theory of anomy, we doubt its utility. For one thing, which values should be used to measure the level of agreement? Americans, for example, agree more about liberty than about equality. They agree more about freedom in the abstract than about freedoms in the particular. For another thing, disagreement about values is known to be a function of social position. In the face of such facts, how can agreement on values be used to assess anomy?

There are still other difficulties. Men might agree about what they actually believe and still feel a strong sense of anomy. Conversely, men might disagree sharply and not feel anomic. Plainly, what matters in conceptualizing anomy is not the actual state of agreement on norms but the feelings men have about the state of the norms. Otherwise, any society pervaded by sharp disagreement over basic values would have to be considered an anomic society, and a society with few such differences would have to be considered non-anomic. But that conception appears nonsensical when one recognizes that even in the "consensual" society many people feel aimless and adrift.

A word about analysis procedures before turning to the findings. For convenience, we have broken all the scale distributions into approximate thirds, which meant in the case of Anomy that those who scored 6–9 were considered highly anomic, those who scored 3–5 were designated as the middle group, and those who scored 0–2 were classified as low or non-anomic. We shall report the data principally in percentage form, comparing the high, middle, and low anomics on a number of dimensions. Wherever parallel sets of data exist for both the MB and PAB samples, they will be presented.

We have also carried out a number of procedures to control for possible "contaminating" factors. Thus, we have run the Anomy scale against the other scales with education, socioeconomic status, and acquiescence controlled, among others.

In addition, we have analyzed the relations between anomy and certain personality and attitude dimensions in samples matched for seven social and demographic characteristics.

Findings

In this section we shall test the general hypotheses stated above, as well as some specific hypotheses derived from them.

Cognitive factors. A society's norms must be learned, and one of the factors determining ability to learn them is cognitive capacity. A person who finds it extremely difficult to grasp the relations among ideas and events, to reason from effects to causes and to organize his thoughts and perceptions into coherent wholes, is likely to see the social world as confusing and confused. Thus, our hypothesis is that level of cognitive functioning and anomy are inversely related.[28]

The most widely used measure of level of cognitive functioning is, of course a standard intelligence test, but it was impossible to administer such a test, in the present study. This, however, does not jeopardize our purposes. There is a great deal of "slippage" between cognitive capacity, as measured solely by intelligence test scores alone, and the level of cognitive functioning at which an individual actually conducts his life. Cognitive functioning is a composite made up of a number of dimensions, and to get at these, other measures than a standard intelligence test are needed. Our questionnaires contained a number of measures that tap various recognizable dimensions of cognitive behavior. Taken together, they provide a fairly accurate profile of a respondent's level of cognitive functioning. Specifically, we have five such measures:

1. The usual data on years of formal schooling completed were collected. While education is primarily a "social" variable, it has also repeatedly been shown to provide an indirect measure of the knowledge-and-skills aspect of cognition. Plainly, persons with little or no education are likely to lack much of the knowledge and many of the tools necessary for effective cognitive functioning and for coping with the social world.

2. The "Intellectuality" scale measures one's orientation toward and participation in intellectual and cultural activities.

3. The "Awareness" scale is a rather simple information

test. It provides a useful brief measure of the respondent's knowledge of some basic features of the political and social system. A person who scores poorly on this test will scarcely be able to perform effectively as a citizen, for he lacks even an elementary knowledge of how the system works.

4. The "Mysticism" scale measures belief in such things as spiritualism, necromancy, astrology, and the prophetic portent of various kinds of signs and wonders. Essentially, an individual's score reflects his conviction that strange and supernatural forces move among men and hover over their affairs. It therefore measures the degree to which one is attracted by magical rather than rational and scientific explanations. Note that the scale gets at something different from mere feelings of ignorance or inability to comprehend complex phenomena. It taps the feeling that many events are inherently inexplicable by the ordinary methods of reason and proof because the events themselves are the products of extraordinary and mysterious forces beyond the understanding of mere men. The person who holds such beliefs has largely abandoned the rules of logic and evidence in the search for meaning.

5. An "Acquiescence" measure, consisting of 19 pairs of contradictory items, was included for the usual purpose of gauging and controlling for response set. This measure, however, does more than improve the analyst's confidence that the relationships he has discovered among a number of variables are not merely artifacts of the tendency to acquiesce; it also discloses something about the quality of the respondent's intellectual life. Specifically, the tendency to acquiesce reflects an undiscriminating and illogical mind, one that works carelessly and makes few and superficial intellectual demands on perceptions and cognitions within a stimulus field. The Acquiescence scale measures the consistency-logicality dimension of cognitive functioning.

Table III provides the material for testing the hypothesis that level of cognitive functioning is inversely related to anomy, and it shows that the hypothesis is overwhelmingly confirmed. For example, a person who scores high on the Mysticism scale is nearly seven times as likely to score high on Anomy as a person who is low on Mysticism. Similar ratios obtain in the comparisons between persons who score high and low on Intellectuality, Awareness, Education, and Acquiescence. In both samples and on all five dimensions of cognitive functioning the results run uniformly and powerfully in the predicted direction.

Additional evidence for the hypothesis was obtained from a procedure designed to measure the consistency with which a person reasons from a general principle to a particular application. Fourteen pairs of items were constructed, each pair composed of a general statement of an idea and a particular application of that idea. In both samples, and for almost every pair of items, the highly anomic were less consistent than the non-anomic.

Emotional factors. We have suggested that the ability to comprehend a society's norms depends in considerable degree on the individual's personality. Certain personality states can lower the level of cognitive functioning, distort perception, interfere with social interaction and communication, and generally impair the ability to sort out and make coherent connections among the diverse elements of the social world. We shall examine four interrelated personality clusters which produce a tendency toward anomy: psychological inflexibility, anxiety, low ego strength, and generalized anger and aggression.

1. Inflexibility. The line of reasoning followed so far suggests that one of the personality states most conducive to anomy is psychological inflexibility. This condition is characterized by unusual rigidity in the employment of defense mechanisms. Highly inflexible persons tend toward premature cognitive closure and are inclined to restrict the range of alternatives they consider relevant to the handling of a problem. They hang tightly to their established perceptual and cognitive structures and resist changes in their set ways of thought and action; trial-and-error behavior, for example, is difficult for them. The psychologically inflexible also have a low tolerance for ambiguity. They crave order, fixed patterns, clear and simple alternatives.

The contingencies and diversities of a complex and changing society are highly unsettling to such people, and they tend to extend their need for order and predictability to the society at large. Their urge to assert rigid control over the forces affecting their personal lives registers itself in the wish to bring the community itself under firm control. Only then

Table III. ***Level of Cognitive Functioning and Anomy***

(in percentages)

	National Sample Anomy				Minnesota Sample Anomy			
	High	*Middle*	*Low*	*(N)**	*High*	*Middle*	*Low*	*(N)†*
Education								
High	13.9	41.5	44.5	(402)	8.2	34.6	57.2	(292)
Middle	35.5	40.4	24.0	(757)	26.7	34.1	39.2	(498)
Low	60.6	30.3	9.1	(320)	49.7	32.1	18.2	(280)
Intellectuality								
High	15.0	38.5	46.4	(532)	8.4	31.2	60.4	(369)
Middle	40.5	40.9	18.6	(555)	26.6	36.3	37.1	(388)
Low	54.6	35.2	10.2	(392)	51.7	33.2	15.1	(325)
Awareness‡								
High					8.1	30.9	61.0	(295)
Middle					23.6	33.6	42.8	(381)
Low					46.3	35.7	18.0	(406)
Mysticism‡								
High					47.2	33.7	19.1	(413)
Middle					21.9	39.9	38.2	(406)
Low					6.8	24.0	69.2	(263)
Acquiescence								
High	64.6	29.9	5.5	(492)	57.5	32.6	9.9	(334)
Middle	28.1	48.1	23.8	(530)	22.8	40.7	36.5	(359)
Low	11.7	36.8	51.5	(462)	7.2	28.0	64.8	(389)

*In this and most subsequent tables, the National Sample N is 1479 instead of the 1484 actually in the original sample because five persons did not report education.

†Of the 1082 persons in the Minnesota Sample, 12 did not report education.

‡Not available for the Minnesota Sample.

can they feel at home in the world. Furthermore, persons in the grip of a powerful need for certainty are likely to see the world around them as less orderly than it may in fact be. Blind to the continuities and stabilities, and hyper-sensitive to the novelties and instabilities, such persons cannot perceive what many observers have reported, namely that beneath the changes in the face of America, a remarkably stable core of values and beliefs has endured.[29]

To test the hypothesis that inflexibility produces a tendency toward anomy, we included three measures of inflexibility in the study design. The three were also combined into a summary measure, which we have called the "Inflexibility Index." Table IV, in which the relations between these measures and anomy are presented, shows a very strong connection between inflexibility and anomy. For example, 67 per cent of those in the national sample who score high on the Inflexibility Index also score high on Anomy, whereas only 13 per cent of low scorers on the Index are high on Anomy. The disproportion is almost equally large for the Minnesota sample, running from 48 to 12 per cent. Similar results obtain for each of the component measures. Thus, in the national sample, one who scores high on Intolerance of Ambiguity is almost five times as likely to score high on Anomy as one who scores low on Intolerance of Ambiguity; in the Minnesota sample the ratio is four to one.

These powerful correlations are all the more impressive and theoretically meaningful when one considers that the three inflexibility variables represent genotypic psychological states. The scales tapping them draw on personality material exclusively and are free of social or political content. A typical item from the Intolerance of Ambiguity scale: "I am the sort of person who likes to know just where he stands on everything." From the Obsessiveness scale: "I honestly believe I have more persistence than most people." From the Rigidity scale: "It bothers me when something unexpected interrupts my daily routine." Clearly, there is no connection between the face content of the items in these scales and that of the Anomy items. Hence, Table IV shows two sets of variables distinct in nature and content, yet highly correlated with each other. Inflexibility reduces one's capacity to accommodate to diversity and contingency, and limits one's ability to perceive the uniformities that may underlie diversity. Faced by com-

Table IV. *Psychological Inflexibility and Anomy*
(in percentages)

	National Sample Anomy				Minnesota Sample Anomy			
	High	*Middle*	*Low*	*(N)*	*High*	*Middle*	*Low*	*(N)*
Intolerance of Ambiguity								
High	55.5	35.3	9.2	(578)	45.3	34.8	19.9	(417)
Middle	31.4	42.4	26.2	(474)	22.0	37.2	40.8	(341)
Low	11.5	38.6	49.9	(427)	11.7	28.4	59.9	(324)
Rigidity								
High	51.9	34.2	13.9	(632)	39.5	35.9	24.6	(418)
Middle	28.0	43.7	28.3	(375)	21.7	39.7	38.6	(290)
Low	18.2	40.3	41.5	(472)	19.8	26.5	53.7	(374)
Obsessiveness								
High	46.0	36.0	18.0	(594)	34.1	36.3	29.6	(419)
Middle	31.9	42.1	26.0	(373)	25.9	33.6	40.5	(301)
Low	24.8	38.9	36.3	(512)	22.4	30.7	46.9	(362)
Inflexibility Index								
High	67	27	6	(250)	48	41	11	(157)
Mid-high	43	39	18	(466)	34	35	31	(325)
Mid-low	26	45	29	(417)	23	35	42	(346)
Low	13	38	49	(346)	12	27	61	(242)

plex stimuli from the social world, inflexible persons are easily overwhelmed. Their anxiety is aroused, they become confused, and they register intense feelings of anomy.

2. Anxiety. Persons who suffer from a high degree of anxiety are also likely to exhibit anomic feelings. The chain between these two states has a number of links. Since an inverse relationship exists between level of cognitive functioning and anomy, anything that impairs the quality of cognitive functioning thereby heightens the tendency toward anomy. That anxiety has a crippling effect on the cognitive process is not only established in numerous experiments but is apparent as well from everyday observation. Second, persons who feel generally anxious about themselves—about their health, their achievements, their strength and worth—also typically feel anxious about the external world. Their inner anxiety spills over onto the outer world, and they tend to project upon the external world the doubts and fears that dominate their own mental life. They see the society as uncertain, confused, lacking in clear standards and direction—in short, as anomic. Third, intense anxiety sometimes leads its victims to withdraw from reality, or at least to retreat from contacts with the outside. Obviously, this reduces socialization and learning, and thus indirectly increases the tendency toward anomy.

The MB study offers three scales for testing the hypothesis that anxiety increases anomy. The Manifest Anxiety scale measures generalized or "constitutional" anxiety. Its items refer to restlessness, high state of excitation, hysteria, susceptibility to loss of consciousness, and the like. The Stability-Disorganization scale assesses such characteristics as inability to concentrate, proneness to debilitating worry, and indecisiveness. A Bewilderment scale gauges a respondent's tendencies to regard the external world as unfathomable, complicated, and upsetting. Although some of the items in the Bewilderment scale express sentiments similar to some of those in the Anomy scale, the first two are close to being pure, clinical-type measures, and thus are especially useful for testing the hypothesis.

Table V shows that the hypothesis is strongly confirmed. For example, the probability of being anomic is over four times as great when one scores high on Manifest Anxiety as when one scores low. Similar results appear for the other two scales.

3. Low Ego Strength. This label refers to generalized feelings of personal inadequacy and self-contempt. We have in mind here people who feel psychologically maimed, crippled, and therefore unsightly in their own and others' eyes. Typically a person with low ego strength lacks self-confidence, gains little satisfaction from life, and is pessimistic about the future. He often bears a heavy burden of guilt, oppressive for its very vagueness and pervasiveness. Haunted by the fear that others will discover his unwholesome thoughts and acts, he urgently tries to keep his inner self inviolate. For him, the conviction that the society is anomic may be psychologically functional; his anomic feelings serve as a part of his system of self-defense and self-justification. One who feels inadequate, guilty, unhappy with the way he has managed his life, and uncertain of his worth may find it important to blame his malaise on the system rather than on himself. Not he, but the society is confused, chaotic, and sullied; being itself disordered, society has made him its victim. Thus we hypothesize that persons who possess low ego strength are likely to score high on anomy.

Table V. ***Anxiety and Anomy***

(*in percentages*)

	Minnesota Sample Anomy			
	High	*Middle*	*Low*	*(N)*
Manifest anxiety				
High	52.4	35.1	12.5	(248)
Middle	26.4	35.5	38.1	(533)
Low	10.3	29.2	60.5	(301)
Stability-disorganization				
High	51.8	32.6	15.6	(365)
Middle	21.6	36.7	41.7	(393)
Low	8.6	31.2	60.2	(324)
Bewilderment				
High	61.0	26.9	12.1	(331)
Middle	22.9	43.0	34.1	(393)
Low	2.8	29.6	67.6	(358)

Both studies included a number of measures designed to assess particular dimensions of ego strength. Compared to "pure" personality variables, such as hostility or paranoia, some of the variables in this cluster contain a larger component of "social" influences. One scale measures psychological guilt, another self-confidence. A third, Need Inviolacy, probes the depth of the respondent's fear of being unmasked, having his wishes and thoughts disclosed. An Alienation scale taps the feeling of loneliness and the yearning for supportive primary relationships. Two scales, Life Satisfaction and Status Frustration, assess the respondent's feeling that he has managed his life satisfactorily and has achieved the success he had hoped for and thought he deserved. Two others, Pessimism and Political Futility, measure respectively one's hopes and fears for the future, and the degree to which one feels capable of directing future events toward satisfactory outcomes. The Dominance scale gauges the subject's security in social relationships, his self-assurance, and his forcefulness and ability to influence others. Finally, a Social Responsibility scale measures adequacy of social adjustment and personality integration. This battery of instruments permits a broad appraisal of the main components of ego-strength. Table VI shows their relations with anomy.

Each of the ego-strength variables is related to Anomy in the direction predicted by the hypothesis. Furthermore, the connections are in each case linear and very powerful. Although a few of the correlations are slightly inflated by the similarities in content between several of the Anomy items and several items in the ego-strength scales, the correlations remain so large and consistent for all scales and individual items in this group as to leave no doubt that the weaker the self-image, the stronger the feelings of anomy.

4. Generalized Aggression. Both controlled experiments and daily observation indicate that persons in the grip of powerful, generalized emotions of rage and fear are often unable to separate their internal feelings from objective reality. The storm within boils over and damages the world without. Such persons tend to see events as caught up in the same whirlwind that buffets them. They are inclined to blame their own misfortunes on forces outside themselves, and to wish to punish others for the injuries that have been worked on them. Attributing malevolent intentions to the forces pressing upon them from the outside, they are likely to hate society for what they believe it has done to them. To judge the society as anomic is a way to express anger at it and simultaneously to make it responsible for the wrath one feels within.

Rage can lead to anomy by still another route. Persons high in hostility tend to be judgmental and severe in their attitudes toward others, and deficient in the capacity for sympathetic and trusting responses; their personal relationships are often tense, insecure and unrewarding. Through feedback, the turmoil they stir up around themselves intensifies the needs and feelings that produced the turmoil in the first place. Under these conditions, the uncertainty and instability in one's personal relationships are easily equated with the presumed uncertainties of the larger social order. Such persons perceive the world as uncertain and unreliable—anomic.

Four measures were used to tap various dimensions of generalized aggression. The questionnaires included scales, basically clinical in nature, of Hostility and Paranoia. Two other scales assess the tendency to be judgmental and severe in one's orientation toward others, to be intolerant of their weaknesses, and unforgiving of any trait or behavior that does not seem "strong" or "tough." One of these scales was called "Intolerance of Human Frailty," and the other "Contempt for Weakness." The connections between these four variables and Anomy are presented in Table VII, and in every instance the results support the hypothesis. The two clinical variables, Hostility and Paranoia, show extremely powerful correlations with Anomy. The correlations on the other two are not quite as high, perhaps because they are really projections onto external objects of personal hostility and self-doubt, and there is always some slippage between a genotypic personality state and its manifestation in the social world.

Substantive Beliefs and Opinions. We have now seen that many psychological states, because they impair social interaction, and hence impede perception and learning, indirectly give rise to anomic feelings. A person's substantive views about what the world is like may produce the same results, especially if his values, beliefs about people, and opinions on public questions are so extreme as to be unsettling to others.

Individuals whose beliefs deviate widely from those commonly held are not likely to be wholly accepted into the community, for extreme views typically express, implicitly or explicitly, rejection not only of the commonly held beliefs but also of those who hold them. Thus, deviant beliefs constitute barriers to effective interaction, and therefore to the kind of learning that requires close and repeated association with others.

An individual whose deviant and extreme opinions bar him

Table VI. *Ego Strength and Anomy*

(in percentages)

	National Sample Anomy				Minnesota Sample Anomy			
	High	*Middle*	*Low*	*(N)*	*High*	*Middle*	*Low*	*(N)*
Guilt								
High	64.0	30.4	5.6	(431)	51.7	35.1	13.2	(296)
Middle	34.5	46.9	18.6	(467)	30.3	39.2	30.5	(370)
Low	14.1	37.9	48.0	(581)	8.9	27.6	63.5	(416)
Self-confidence*								
High					13.4	33.9	52.7	(336)
Middle					28.1	34.7	37.2	(449)
Low					44.1	31.7	24.2	(297)
Need Inviolacy								
High	62.1	30.8	7.1	(491)	50.1	32.7	17.2	(355)
Middle	36.3	45.0	18.7	(380)	25.8	42.1	32.1	(252)
Low	12.5	40.8	46.7	(608)	12.4	29.9	57.7	(475)
Life-satisfaction								
High	18.3	37.7	44.0	(459)	13.0	30.6	56.4	(369)
Middle	33.3	42.3	24.4	(496)	27.5	37.2	35.3	(374)
Low	51.5	35.7	12.8	(524)	44.6	33.0	22.4	(339)
Alienation								
High	62.0	32.6	5.4	(497)	59.2	26.4	14.4	(284)
Middle	32.5	46.6	21.0	(539)	28.7	41.0	30.3	(380)
Low	8.1	35.4	56.4	(443)	6.0	31.8	62.2	(418)
Status frustration								
High	61.0	32.1	6.9	(305)	56.1	27.8	16.1	(180)
Middle	37.1	42.2	20.7	(593)	30.4	38.8	30.8	(418)
Low	19.5	38.2	42.3	(581)	15.3	31.4	53.3	(484)

	National Sample Anomy				Minnesota Sample Anomy			
	High	*Middle*	*Low*	*(N)*	*High*	*Middle*	*Low*	*(N)*
Pessimism								
High	60.3	32.8	6.9	(436)	55.0	29.8	15.2	(198)
Middle	30.9	42.7	26.4	(709)	28.8	37.7	33.5	(539)
Low	11.1	37.1	51.8	(334)	11.0	29.6	59.4	(345)
Political futility								
High	62.4	31.3	6.3	(447)	61.3	27.4	11.3	(266)
Middle	32.4	44.1	23.5	(549)	26.7	41.2	32.1	(408)
Low	12.8	38.9	48.2	(483)	7.4	30.1	62.5	(408)
Dominance								
High	18.0	37.8	44.3	(551)	7.6	30.6	61.8	(424)
Middle	32.8	44.0	23.2	(457)	31.7	35.2	33.1	(335)
Low	57.3	34.2	8.5	(471)	50.8	35.9	13.3	(323)
Social responsibility								
High	12.0	40.3	47.6	(382)	5.0	28.7	66.3	(282)
Middle	29.5	44.4	26.1	(583)	21.4	37.8	40.8	(439)
Low	58.6	30.5	10.9	(514)	53.7	32.4	13.9	(361)

*Not available for the National Sample.

from full participation in the larger society will very likely be imperfectly aware of what other members of that society believe and value, and he may easily confuse his ignorance of the norms with the conviction that no norms exist. Or, because his own strong beliefs deviate so radically from those held by others, the extreme believer may be inclined to think that other, more moderate persons really have no worthwhile values at all. What appears to the moderate as realistic good sense strikes the extremist as wishy-washy confusion masquerading as moderation.

Finally, our own data show that holding extreme views is associated with various psycho-pathological states, such as intense anxiety, hostility, and inflexibility. Here the extreme substantive views are really expressions—almost symptoms—of the underlying psychological state, and may be functionally important in satisfying the needs of the personality system. Often, these psychological disturbances themselves greatly impede interaction; when the disturbance expresses itself in radically deviant substantive views, the barriers to successful interaction grow even higher. Inability to surmount those barriers produces feelings that the society itself is disordered and confused.

For these reasons, we expected to find the holding of deviant beliefs positively associated with Anomy. A number of scales in our study tapped respondents' commitments to various deviant ideologies and attitudes. Data on these scales are presented in Table VIII. The Totalitarianism scale measures the degree to which one is prepared to sacrifice human values to an overriding political objective. The Left Wing and Right Wing scales draw their items directly from the writings produced by political movements of the extreme left and right. The Fascism scale is not the familiar California F Scale, but a measure composed of items drawn mainly from the political texts of Fascism. Our general hypothesis predicts that persons who score high on these scales are likely to be anomic.

The findings in all cases run powerfully in the predicted direction. The high correlations between Anomy and extreme substantive beliefs strengthen our thesis that Anomy reflects a failure of socialization all along the line. Not only does the anomic feel confused and normless, but he also leans toward values and opinions that are rejected in his society. Both the feeling of emptiness and the leaning toward extreme opin-

Table VII. ***Aggression and Anomy***

(in percentages)

	National Sample Anomy				Minnesota Sample Anomy			
	High	*Middle*	*Low*	*(N)*	*High*	*Middle*	*Low*	*(N)*
Hostility								
High	62.0	32.5	5.6	(413)	53.3	33.3	13.4	(246)
Middle	32.9	46.2	20.9	(632)	29.1	38.0	32.9	(495)
Low	12.7	33.2	54.2	(434)	7.9	27.6	64.5	(341)
Paranoia								
High	63.1	32.5	4.4	(567)	56.8	31.2	12.0	(391)
Middle	27.8	48.5	23.7	(443)	19.0	44.1	36.9	(331)
Low	8.1	36.5	55.4	(469)	4.7	26.6	68.7	(361)
Intolerance of human frailty								
High	54.3	34.2	11.5	(582)	46.3	34.6	19.1	(272)
Middle	27.2	44.3	28.6	(637)	26.4	36.6	37.0	(546)
Low	11.5	34.2	54.2	(260)	12.1	26.5	61.4	(264)
Contempt for weakness								
High	56.9	33.6	9.5	(390)	49.5	35.7	14.8	(305)
Middle	32.2	42.0	25.7	(735)	23.9	34.9	41.2	(478)
Low	17.0	36.7	46.3	(354)	12.4	29.4	58.2	(299)

ions are two aspects of an underlying failure to assimilate the modal values of a society in a balanced, concrete, accurate way.

So far, our data have referred to substantive beliefs and opinions about actual objects in the social environment, and about questions concerning the way social, economic, and political affairs are and ought to be handled. We now turn to a different kind of belief, namely, attitudes about people. Certain beliefs about people can have the same negative effects on interaction and learning as the substantive views just discussed. Here we refer to a cluster of attitudes which might for convenience be called misanthropy. Included under this heading are feelings of generalized mistrust and suspiciousness toward people, a readiness to find fault in others and to be harshly judgmental toward them, an unwillingness to extend sympathy, a conviction that if people are having trouble they probably deserve it, and a tendency to reject out of hand and under stereotyped slogans members of groups other than one's own.

The questionnaires contained a number of scales that tap these attitudes. The Calvinism scale, in setting forth the values of the Protestant Ethic, measures the tendency toward judgmentalism and severity in one's demands upon others. The other labels, listed in Table IX, adequately convey the attitudes being measured.

The first two scales in Table IX (Tolerance and Faith in People) measure a receptive orientation toward people, while the other three assess various dimensions of a rejective orientation. The relation between Anomy and each of the scales in both sets runs massively in the predicted direction. Persons who are highly tolerant of others and who have strong faith in the abilities and virtues of their fellow men are much less likely to score high on the Anomy scale than are persons who are not receptively oriented. On the three rejective variables, the direction is reversed: persons who score high on them are much more likely to score high on Anomy as well.

The Question of Spuriousness

To complete our presentation of the data, we must address one final question. Are the reported correlations between various personality states and anomy genuine and autonomous, or

Table VIII. *Extreme Beliefs and Anomy*

(in percentages)

	National Sample Anomy				Minnesota Sample Anomy			
	High	*Middle*	*Low*	*(N)*	*High*	*Middle*	*Low*	*(N)*
Totalitarianism								
High	64.6	30.0	5.4	(500)	47.5	34.2	18.3	(480)
Middle	29.3	28.5	22.2	(559)	15.5	40.2	44.3	(368)
Low	7.6	35.5	56.9	(420)	7.3	22.2	70.5	(234)
Fascist* values								
High					58.2	26.8	15.0	(194)
Middle					31.4	39.3	29.3	(417)
Low					12.3	31.4	56.3	(471)
Left wing								
High	72.7	24.9	2.4	(410)	68.5	24.2	7.3	(232)
Middle	32.8	49.8	17.4	(488)	31.3	44.2	24.5	(310)
Low	10.5	38.7	50.8	(581)	8.5	31.7	59.8	(540)
Right wing								
High	71.2	26.1	2.7	(490)	69.8	25.9	4.3	(212)
Middle	27.7	51.6	20.7	(560)	30.9	42.8	26.3	(434)
Low	3.5	35.7	60.8	(429)	4.6	28.2	67.2	(436)

*Not available for the National Sample.

are they epiphenomenal, the secondary products of environmental forces that underlie the psychological states?

This is a critical question, for personality and culture are, after all, elaborately intertwined, and the possibility must be faced that we are attributing to the one a power that properly belongs to the other. If, as some students believe, personality expresses the social setting so closely as to be inseparable from it, it obviously cannot play the independent, and often decisive, role we have assigned to it in our explanatory model. That social learning is vital to the formation of personality and that different social settings give rise to different modal personality configurations can scarcely be doubted.[30] But the matter, so far as it bears on the explanation of anomy, does not end there. For one thing, the social forces that have most to do with fashioning personality (e.g., primary influences in early childhood) are not necessarily the same forces that are alleged to induce anomy (e.g., status frustration, malintegration, conflict between social goals and means, etc.). For another, although persons from the same social settings resemble each other more closely on the average than they resemble persons from other social settings, they nevertheless vary widely in their personality patterns. They also vary in their response to the social norms—a variation that appears to follow closely the variations in their personalities.

We are convinced—and we believe the data will confirm it—that the principal source of anomic feeling resides for some people in their social settings; for others in their individual personalities; and for still others, in a combination of the two. This means that a person can express anomic feelings without possessing the personality traits (or alternatively, the social characteristics) that are correlated with anomy. It also means that either of those major determinants may be sufficient to evoke anomic responses, regardless of the contribution of the other. Extremely inflexible persons, for example, are significantly more anomic than flexible persons in every sample (including our elite sample of political influentials), and in every social, economic, or educational setting in which we have compared them. But it also means that someone can possess the "appropriate" personality (or social) characteristic *without* being anomic. In other words, whether the personality genotype gives rise in every individual to identical phenotypic manifestations may in part depend on the environment (which

Table IX. *Misanthropy and Anomy*

(in percentages)

	National Sample Anomy				Minnesota Sample Anomy			
	High	*Middle*	*Low*	*(N)*	*High*	*Middle*	*Low*	*(N)*
Tolerance								
High	21.6	40.6	37.8	(638)	18.1	32.1	49.8	(414)
Middle	36.0	39.1	24.9	(350)	24.0	31.8	44.2	(267)
Low	51.9	35.4	12.6	(491)	40.7	36.4	22.9	(401)
Faith in people*								
High					6.3	29.7	64.0	(300)
Middle					26.0	39.4	34.6	(439)
Low					49.3	29.7	21.0	(343)
Calvinism†								
High	46.7	42.3	11.0	(437)				
Middle	35.8	38.7	25.5	(695)				
Low	19.0	33.4	47.6	(347)				
Elitism, inequalitarianism								
High	50.2	36.4	13.5	(572)	46.4	34.0	19.6	(291)
Middle	32.2	41.7	26.1	(575)	28.6	39.7	31.7	(413)
Low	14.2	36.8	49.1	(332)	13.0	26.7	60.3	(378)
Ethnocentrism								
High	57.5	35.2	7.3	(640)	54.4	34.1	11.5	(261)
Middle	27.4	46.1	26.5	(412)	28.2	39.8	32.0	(462)
Low	8.9	36.3	54.8	(427)	8.4	25.4	66.2	(359)

*Not available for the National Sample.
†Not available for the Minnesota Sample.

can be taken to include not only the broad social conditions and the immediate life space of the individual, but also the salience of the norms, their clarity, complexity, and accessibility, and so forth). Some social conditions combine with personality to intensify the anomic response, while others combine to diminish it. Thus, the mean Anomy scores of persons with, say, extreme anxiety, will be higher among the poor than among the wealthy, among the uneducated than among the educated, among those in unskilled occupations than among those in the professions.

To satisfy ourselves that the correlations between assorted psychological states and Anomy are genuine, we carried out a number of procedures to control for such variables as education and occupation, both of which correlate significantly and negatively with Anomy (Anomy correlates −.43 with education, −.37 with occupational status). Since the responses to the Anomy items are also affected by acquiescent response set, controls for this factor were also introduced. Limitations of space prohibit a full presentation of these data, but Table X illustrates them by showing the effects of occupational status and acquiescence.

The correlations between Anomy and representative personality variables remain strong and significant when these variables are controlled; and the results are essentially the same when these controls are applied to the correlations between Anomy and all the other personality and attitude variables treated in this paper. Similar conclusions emerge when education is controlled.

These tests, however, still leave the possibility that the variations in Anomy were produced, not by a single social factor, but by a combination of several. To explore this possibility, the data were put to the more demanding test of controlling simultaneously for seven of the major sociological variables that were correlated with both Anomy and personality factors.

The national sample of 1484 adults was first broken into two groups: those who scored at the upper end (scores 6–9), and those who scored at the lower end (0–3) of the Anomy scale. Those who fell in the middle range were excluded from this procedure. We then drew randomly from these two groups every person whose particular combination of sociological characteristics was matched by a person from the other group. Our objective was to identify high and low anomics who possessed the same pattern of sociological characteristics. The seven sociological variables were education, age, size of community, occupational status, race, sex, and region.[31]

Table X. ***Mean Scores on Representative Personality Scales for High, Middle, and Low Anomics, with Occupational Status† and Acquiescence Controlled****

	Dominance	Hostility	Paranoid Tendencies	Intolerance of Ambiguity
High occupation				
High anomy	3.3	4.1	4.9	5.7
Middle anomy	4.4	3.3	3.5	4.6
Low anomy	5.7	2.2	1.8	3.1
Middle occupation				
High anomy	3.1	4.3	5.5	6.2
Middle anomy	4.0	3.6	3.8	4.7
Low anomy	4.8	2.3	2.0	3.4
Low occupation				
High anomy	2.4	4.3	5.6	6.0
Middle anomy	3.3	3.3	3.6	4.8
Low anomy	4.2	2.4	2.2	3.7

	Intolerance of Human Frailty	Rigidity	Responsibility	Sense of Political Futility
High acquiescence				
High anomy	5.2	4.0	4.7	4.6
Middle anomy	4.6	3.5	5.8	3.8
Low anomy	4.0	3.3	6.0	2.7
Middle acquiescence				
High anomy	4.3	3.4	5.6	4.2
Middle anomy	3.8	2.8	6.5	3.3
Low anomy	3.4	2.5	6.9	2.4
Low acquiescence				
High anomy	4.0	2.7	6.1	3.8
Middle anomy	3.5	2.8	6.7	2.8
Low anomy	2.9	2.2	7.4	2.0

*National Sample; N = 1484

†The occupational breaks were as follows: High=professional, managerial and upper white collar; Middle=clerical, skilled, and lower white collar; Low=unskilled workers and farmers.

This procedure yielded a total of 275 matched pairs, i.e., 275 high anomics whose individual social characteristics were specifically matched by those of 275 low anomics. The responses of the two groups of matched pairs on all scales in the PAB questionnaire were then compared. The findings for the main personality variables treated in this paper appear in Table XI. For the sake of brevity, those who scored at the "middle" level on the personality variables have been omitted from the table.

The overall result is clear: when high and low anomics are simultaneously matched on the seven social characteristics, high anomics continue to differ from low anomics on the same psychological variables we have been analyzing. Furthermore, the differences remain in every instance large enough to leave no doubt that personality factors determine Anomy independently of social influences. A person who scores high on the Anomy scale, for example, is five times as likely to score high on Hostility as his "sociological twin" among the low anomics. The ratio for Guilt is over seven to one, and for Paranoia almost five to one.[32]

These findings confirm the argument we presented at the outset. So powerful, and so clearly independent of social influences, are the correlations between certain personality states and anomy, that they cast much doubt on the adequacy of the standard sociological explanation of anomy.

The standard explanation raises another, related question of spuriousness. Basic to that explanation is the proposition that anomy results from "the conflict between culturally accepted values and the socially structured difficulties in living up to these values. . . ."[33] Our culture, according to Merton, prescribes success as a goal for all Americans, but the social system imposes barriers to the achievement of the goal, so that it is easier for some to follow the prescription than for others. When the social structure bars persons located at certain points within it from moving upward toward the goal of wealth and higher status, the result is "a strain toward . . . normlessness."[34]

This is the theoretical foundation of a large body of writing which has either implicitly assumed or explicitly asserted that persons who have lost out in the race for wealth and status show a high incidence of anomic feelings *because* they have lost the race. In this view, a felt discrepancy between status aspiration and actual achievement is the direct and most basic cause of the anomic mentality. This is probably the most widely accepted generalization in the sociological literature of anomy.

As usually presented, this explanation either ignores personality factors or plays them down. If it mentions them at all, it treats them merely as secondary variables that derive from status frustration or from similar forms of social disjunction.

Table XI. ***Matched Samples of Anomics and Non-Anomics Compared on Selected Variables.****

(*in percentages*)

	Alienation		Contempt for Weakness		Conventionality	
	High	*Low*	*High*	*Low*	*High*	*Low*
High anomy	59	8	39	13	35	24
Low anomy	8	56	15	31	8	48
	Dominance		Ethnocentrism		Guilt	
	High	*Low*	*High*	*Low*	*High*	*Low*
High anomy	22	51	50	9	52	16
Low anomy	48	17	13	42	7	64
	Hostility		Human Frailty		Intellectuality	
	High	*Low*	*High*	*Low*	*High*	*Low*
High anomy	47	13	58	7	21	36
Low anomy	9	46	24	31	46	18
	Intolerance of Ambiguity		Life Satisfaction		Need Inviolacy	
	High	*Low*	*High*	*Low*	*High*	*Low*
High anomy	59	11	17	51	52	20
Low anomy	23	44	48	22	14	65
	Need Status		Obsessiveness		Paranoid Tendency	
	High	*Low*	*High*	*Low*	*High*	*Low*
High anomy	34	22	53	26	66	9
Low anomy	9	56	27	45	13	57
	Pessimism-Optimism		Rigidity		Tolerance	
	High	*Low*	*High*	*Low*	*High*	*Low*
High anomy	51	8	59	19	31	46
Low Anomy	11	41	28	44	50	22

*The N for each matched sample is 275. Persons who scored in the middle range of either the Anomy scales or the personality scale are omitted from this table. Percentages are computed horizontally and would sum to 100 if the middle group were included. Computing the percentages horizontally rather than vertically—reversing the direction of the computations shown in previous tables—was made necessary by the prohibitive cost of running 18 separate matched sample procedures, one for each of the independent variables. While the present table gives essentially the same results, it unfortunately makes comparison with previous tables difficult. Note that the 0–3 cutting point used here to identify non-anomics differs—for reasons of sample size—from the 0–2 classification used earlier.

Hence, the observed relation between personality and anomy is considered by many sociologists to be spurious, a mere artifact of their supposedly common ancestry.

We cannot hope, in a brief discussion, to resolve an issue of such magnitude and complexity. We can, however, present evidence directly relevant to it, based on three scales in our study. One is a scale of "Material Aspirations" which measures the hunger for wealth and for the coveted objects that wealth can purchase. A second, labelled "Aspiration-Ambition," assesses the strength of a person's actual commitment to the values of success and prestige, and his yearning for achievement and reputation. Neither of these measures is significantly correlated with the Anomy scale: the correlation for the first is .07, and for the second, .01.

The third measure, Status Frustration, has already been mentioned (see Table VI), and its correlation with Anomy is a significant .42. This scale, however, differs from the other two precisely in its stronger expression of "frustration"—it expresses envy of those "born into a higher position in life," deference (and resentment) toward those who enjoy good breeding, wealth, better education, or other marks of superiority, and a sense of shame and self-doubt because of low birth or failure to have risen higher. This scale, in short, reflects several of the key emotional elements that we have already shown to be major determinants of anomy. A genuine measure of status frustration, clearly, is bound to be as heavily infused with psychological elements as with sociological ones. It is equally plain that its relation to anomy is weaker than that of many of the personality variables we have considered. Nor is there any evidence that it is a more specific "cause" of anomy than the other factors we have observed.

Suppose, however, that for the moment we consider status frustration as a purely sociological measure and as a decisive influence upon anomy. If we were to remove status frustration from the phenomenal field, would personality continue to exert the influence we have attributed to it? In Table XII we present the correlations between anomy and selected personality variables before and after status frustration has been partialed out. The zero-order correlations are, to be sure, diminished by this procedure, but so modestly as to have no substantial effect on either their magnitude or their statistical significance. Such reductions as do occur, furthermore, are doubtless related in part to the affective elements that the Status Frustration scale has in common with the personality scales.

Table XII. ***Correlations Between Anomy and Selected Personality Variables Before and After the Effects of Status Frustration Are Removed***

Anomy	Dominance	Guilt	Hostility	Intolerance of Ambiguity	Intolerance of Human Frailty	Need Inviolacy	Paranoid	Rigidity
Original Zero-order correlations	–.47	.59	.53	.51	.45	.56	.66	.41
First-order Partial correlations with status frustration held constant	–.42	.51	.45	.43	.41	.48	.58	.34

Hence we conclude that the psychological variables operate independently. While status frustration is related to anomy, it is only one of many forces capable of producing anomic responses. Not only does it fail to eliminate the correlations between anomy and personality factors, but it may itself be an aspect, or product, of the sense of generalized malaise and dissatisfaction with oneself that is characteristic of the anomic state of mind.

Summary and Concluding Remarks

We have attempted in this paper to show that the tendency to perceive the society as normless, morally chaotic, and adrift —in a word, anomic—is governed not only by one's position and role in the society but also, in no small measure, by one's intellectual and personality characteristics. Anomic feelings, we have said, result when socialization and the learning of the norms are impeded. Some impediments to learning are social, but others are personal and psychological. Thus, persons whose cognitive capacity is for some reason deficient are more likely to view the society as disorderly and bewildering, and to deplore the incoherence of its value system. Similarly, persons strongly governed by anxiety, hostility, and other aversive motivational and affective states suffer not only from impaired cognitive functioning but also from a tendency to distort their perceptions of social "reality," to accommodate poorly to social change, complexity, and ambiguity, and—through the projection of their anxieties, fears, and uncertainties—to perceive the world as hostile and anxiety-ridden. These personality dispositions also reduce their chances for effective interaction and communication, hampering further their opportunity to learn the norms and to achieve a more coherent sense of how the society works. A further hindrance to effective interaction and socialization results from the holding of extreme or deviant views.

Contrary to Srole's claim that anomy reflects mental disturbance only when the latter is "severe," and that social dysfunction is the independent variable producing anomy both with and without psychopathology, we found that personality factors are correlated with anomy at all levels of mental disturbance, and that they function independently to produce anomy among people in all educational categories and in all sectors of society.

Although we have focused in this paper on individual and personality factors as determinants of anomy, we have never suggested that sociological factors play no part. We have claimed, rather, that the bulk of writing on anomy to date has, by its almost exclusive focus on sociological variables, failed to take account of the type of influences we have examined here, and by virtue of that failure has also failed to give a correct account of the sociological influences. By forcing all determinants into a single analytic category—by, so to speak, pouring everything into the same container—nothing can be seen clearly. Far from denying the existence of sociological factors, an attempt to assess the contribution of personality to anomy is a necessary step toward clarifying their real significance.

While recognizing that social influences are important in bringing about anomic feelings, we are inclined to question whether the standard explanatory concepts employed so far, such as social dysfunction, malintegration between culturally approved goals and institutionalized means, discrepancy between aspiration and achievement, the limitless nature of the success imperative, or the presumed human need for clear limits, are necessary or sufficient conditions for anomy, or even whether they are the most appropriate concepts for explaining it. Apart from the difficulty of operationalizing these notions, little convincing evidence—in the form of "hard" data—has been presented to show that they play the role commonly attributed to them. We have suggested that an alternative and possibly more useful approach might be to regard anomy as a by-product of the socialization process—as a sign of the failure of socialization and of the means by which socialization is achieved, namely, communication, interaction, and learning —and we have presented data that furnish at least indirect support for this view.

To avert misunderstanding, we also want to point out that we have not directly addressed the substantive question of the alleged anomic condition of modern society. Our society may be more or less anomic than it used to be, or than other, simpler societies are now. About that we know very little. We have suggested that much of the discussion of this topic rests on questionable assumptions and proceeds by dubious methods. Our main concern has been to show that within the same society some people are highly resistant to anomy while others are highly vulnerable, and that one's susceptibility may be determined by personality factors quite apart from the state of the society or one's position in it.

One final observation. In most of the scientific literature, anomy is conceptualized either as a particular kind of response arising from a particular state of society, or as a particular state of society itself. For the most part, we too have treated anomy as a particular moral-psychological state, but we have also intimated that it may not be a specific and isolable condition clearly distinguishable from other moral-psychological states. It may, rather, be one dimension of a many-sided malaise. We found, for example, that persons who score high on the Anomy scale also score high on scales measuring pessimism, bewilderment, alienation, anxiety, hostility, and sense of political futility. High anomics also express extreme attitudes on authoritarianism, totalitarianism, chauvinism, political cynicism, and the like. That these symptoms of distress are so often found together in the same persons suggests that those persons are afflicted by a complex and pervasive malaise.

This is not to say that anomy is identical with any one or

all of these other components. Each component was individually defined, tested and validated, and each is conceptually different from the others. What it does suggest is that while it is defensible to approach anomy as a variable in its own right, and while it is possible to distinguish a state of normlessness from other states of moral-psychological disturbance, it may not be defensible to conceptualize anomy as a unique disease that afflicts men in certain kinds of societies. Anomy, in sum, may be only one of many symptoms expressing a negativistic, despairing outlook both on one's own life and on the community in which one lives. Whether these symptoms are reducible to a common core, whether they are mainly symptoms of underlying aversive personality states, or whether they truly reflect the condition of modern society and are themselves the "disease," are among the urgent questions to which future research might usefully be addressed.

Notes:

1. The word is Greek in origin. It was transliterated into Latin as *anomia* and into English as anomy. In that spelling the word was frequently used by 17th-century writers. Durkheim transliterated the word into French as anomie, and recent American writers have adopted his usage. Since the concept now enjoys full recognition in the vocabulary of American social science, we thought it appropriate to restore the word in its English spelling.
2. Emile Durkheim, *Suicide* (1897), trans. John A. Spaulding and George Simpson, Glencoe, Ill.: Free Press, 1951, p. 257.
3. *Ibid.*, p. 256.
4. Robert K. Merton, *Social Theory and Social Structure* (rev. ed.), Glencoe, Ill.: Free Press, 1957, pp. 121–194.
5. *Ibid.*, pp. 162–163.
6. See *ibid.*, esp. pp. 136–139.
7. *Ibid.*, p. 157.
8. See *ibid.*, p. 177.
9. Robert M. MacIver, *The Ramparts We Guard,* New York: Macmillan, 1950, p. 84.
10. Srole's work on anomy, to our knowledge, consists of these items: "Anomie, Authoritarianism and Prejudice," *American Journal of Sociology,* 62 (July, 1956), pp. 63–67; "Social Dysfunction, Personality and Social Distance Attitudes," unpublished paper read before the American Sociological Society, Chicago, 1951; "Social Integration and Certain Corollaries: An Exploratory Study," *American Sociological Review,* 21 (December, 1956), pp. 709–716; and "Interdisciplinary Conceptualization and Research in Social Psychiatry," unpublished paper read before the American Sociological Society, Detroit, 1956. A few pages in Srole, *et al., Mental Health in the Metropolis,* New York: McGraw-Hill, 1962,

touch on anomy but do not add to his previous published work on this subject.

11. Srole, "Social Integration . . . ," *op. cit.*, p. 711.

12. Both the components of anomy and the scale items are in *ibid.*, pp. 712–713.

13. Srole, "Interdisciplinary Conceptualization and Research . . . ," *op. cit.*, p. 3.

14. *Ibid.*, pp. 4–5.

15. *Ibid.* The study rested on a probability sample of 1660 individuals, aged 20–59, and living in "Midtown." These persons were given a questionnaire of some 400 items, about one-third of which related to psychological and social role functioning. Psychiatrists on a hospital staff made the "mental disturbance" ratings on the basis of these data.

16. *Ibid.*, p. 15.

17. Sebastian de Grazia, *The Political Community: A Study of Anomie*, Chicago: University of Chicago Press, 1948, p. 154.

18. "High" is usually defined as responding in an anomic direction to three or more of the items in Srole's five-item scale. The percentage of "highs" in eight studies that have used the scale ranged from 28 to 39.

19. "Social Integration and Certain Corollaries . . . ," *op. cit.*, p. 716.

20. Our own findings, based on broader samples and employing a different measure of anomy than any other study of the topic to date, follow the same pattern. These findings will be reported in subsequent publications.

21. See, for example, Samuel A. Stouffer, *Communism, Conformity, and Civil Liberties*, New York: Doubleday, 1955; James W. Prothro and Charles M. Grigg, "Fundamental Principles of Democracy: Bases of Agreement and Disagreement," *Journal of Politics*, 21 (1960), pp. 276–294; Seymour Martin Lipset, *Political Man*, New York: Doubleday, 1960, Ch. 4; and Herbert McClosky, "Consensus and Ideology in American Politics," *American Political Science Review*, 58 (June, 1964), pp. 361–382.

22. Theodore M. Newcomb, *Personality and Social Change*, New York: Holt, Rinehart and Winston, 1943, esp. Ch. 8.

23. See George C. Homans, *The Human Group*, New York: Harcourt, Brace, 1950.

24. See, e.g., T. W. Adorno, *et al.*, *The Authoritarian Personality*, New York: Harper, 1950; and Milton Rokeach, *The Opera and Closed Mind*, New York: Basic Books, 1960. Our own data, to be published subsequently, provide further support for this observation.

25. For the details, see McClosky, *op. cit.*, pp. 380–382.

26. Twenty of the scales were developed by McClosky alone. The Dominance and the Social Responsibility scales were constructed in collaboration with Harrison Gough and Paul E. Meehl. All the others were developed in collaboration with Kenneth E. Clark and Paul E. Meehl. Arnold Rose was a member of the research team at an early stage.

27. *Essentials of Psychological Testing* (2nd ed.), New York: Harper and Row, p. 141.

28. This is not the place to enter the nature-nurture debate. Suffice it to say that both hereditary and environmental factors affect the level

of cognitive functioning. Social scientists are familiar enough with the findings on the impact of sociological factors on intelligence test performance. Perhaps they are less familiar with the findings on the relations between genotypic similarities and similarity of performance on intelligence tests. A recent survey of 52 studies conducted over the past 50 years concluded that "a marked trend is seen toward an increasing degree of intellectual resemblance in direct proportion to an increasing degree of genetic relationship, regardless of environmental communality. Furthermore, for most relationship categories [e.g., parent-child; one-egg twins] the *median* of the empirical correlations [between genetic relation and performance on mental tests] closely approaches the theoretical value predicted on the basis of genetic relationship alone." L.Erlenmeyer-Kimling and Lissy F. Jarvik, "Genetics and Intelligence: A Review," *Science,* 142 (December 13, 1963).

We cite these findings because they suggest how important it is in social science inquiry to acknowledge, in both theory and method, the existence of factors operating at the genetic-psychological level. The standard theory of anomy incorporates a "uniformitarian" perspective: it takes no systematic account of individual differences. Any full explanation must give due consideration to both sets of factors. This is basic to the present paper. In principle, this inquiry into personality factors should be pushed back to genotypic differences, on the premise that they produce differences in behavior potentials, while environmental differences produce different performances. Work on the genetic bases of psychological variations has barely begun, however, so we cannot push the inquiry back that far. But we can insist that an appreciation of the causal role of personal factors is essential to a comprehensive theory of anomy.

29. See, e.g., Clyde Kluckhohn, "Have There Been Discernible Shifts in American Values During the Past Generation?" in Elting E. Morison (ed.), *The American Style: Essays in Value and Perspective,* New York: Harper, 1958, pp. 145–217.

30. See, for example, August B. Hollingshead and Frederick C. Redlich, *Social Class and Mental Illness,* New York: Wiley, 1958.

31. Sub-classifications employed within each category were: Education —11th grade and below, 12th grade and above; Age—under 35, 35–54, 55 and over; Size of community—rural, urban; Occupational status—3 levels derived from an index combining occupation and income; Race —white, non-white; Sex—male, female; Region—north, south.

32. We are aware that the matched-sample procedure does not include all the possible combinations in the same frequency with which they appear in the population. A sufficient number and variety of combinations are present, however, to warrant confidence in the results. This confidence is increased by the magnitude of the differences between the high and low groups, and by the fact that no matter which of the particular social variables we control, the results are essentially unchanged.

33. Merton, *op. cit.,* p. 191.

34. *Ibid.,* p. 163.

Bibliography

Political Behavior: General

Dahl, Robert A. *Modern Political Analysis*. Englewood Cliffs, N.J.: Prentice-Hall, 1963.

Eulau, Heinz. *The Behavioral Persuasion in Politics*. New York: Random House, 1963.

Eulau, Heinz, Samuel J. Eldersveld, and Morris Janowitz. *Political Behavior*. New York: The Free Press, 1956.

Fiszman, Joseph R. *The American Political Arena*. Boston: Little, Brown and Company, 2nd ed., 1966.

Polsby, Nelson W., Robert A. Dentler, and Paul A. Smith. *Politics and Social Life: An Introduction to Political Behavior*. Boston: Houghton Mifflin Company, 1963.

Ranney, Austin. *Essays on the Behavioral Study of Politics*. Urbana: University of Illinois Press, 1962.

Ulmer, S. Sidney. *Introductory Readings in Political Behavior*. Chicago: Rand McNally and Company, 1961.

Political Behavior: Theory

Buchanan, James M., and Gordon Tullock. *The Calculus of Consent*. Ann Arbor: University of Michigan Press, 1962.

Dahl, Robert A. *A Preface to Democratic Theory*. Chicago: University of Chicago Press, 1956.

Dahl, Robert A., and Charles E. Lindblom. *Politics, Economics, and Welfare*. New York: Harper and Brothers, 1953.

Deutsch, Karl W. *The Nerves of Government*. New York: The Free Press, 1963.

Downs, Anthony. *An Economic Theory of Democracy*. New York: Harper and Brothers, 1957.

Easton, David. *The Political System*. New York: Alfred A. Knopf, 1953.

Easton, David. *A Framework for Political Analysis*. Englewood Cliffs, N. J.: Prentice-Hall, 1965.

Easton, David. *A Systems Analysis of Political Life*. New York: John Wiley and Sons, 1965.

Lasswell, Harold D., and Abraham Kaplan. *Power and Society*. New Haven, Conn.: Yale University Press, 1950.

Lindblom, Charles E. *The Intelligence of Democracy*. New York: The Free Press, 1965.

Mitchell, William. *The American Polity*. New York: The Free Press, 1962.

Riker, William H. *The Theory of Political Coalitions*. New Haven, Conn.: Yale University Press, 1962.

Political Behavior: Comparative

Alford, Robert R. *Party and Society*. Chicago: Rand McNally and Company, 1963.

Almond, Gabriel A., and James S. Coleman. *The Politics of the Developing Areas*. Princeton, N. J.: Princeton University Press, 1960.

Almond, Gabriel, and Sidney Verba. *The Civic Culture*. Princeton, N. J.: Princeton University Press, 1963.

Apter, David E. *Ideology and Discontent*. New York: The Free Press, 1964.

Apter, David E. *The Politics of Modernization*. Chicago: University of Chicago Press, 1965.

Jacob, Herbert, and Kenneth N. Vines. *Politics in the American States*. Boston: Little, Brown and Company, 1965.

Lerner, Daniel. *The Passing of Traditional Society*. New York: The Free Press, 1958.

Lipset, Seymour M. *Political Man*. Garden City, N. Y.: Doubleday and Company, 1960.

Individual Behavior

Davies, James C. *Human Nature in Politics*. New York: John Wiley and Sons, 1963.

Greenstein, Fred I. *Children and Politics*. New Haven, Conn.: Yale University Press, 1965.

Hyman, Herbert. *Political Socialization*. New York: The Free Press, 1959.

Lane, Robert E. *Political Life*. New York: The Free Press, 1959.

Lane, Robert E. *Political Ideology*. New York: The Free Press, 1962.

Lasswell, Harold D. *Psychopathology and Politics*. New York: McGraw-Hill, 1930.

Lasswell, Harold D. *Power and Personality*. New York: W. W. Norton and Company, 1948.

Marvick, Dwaine, *Political Decision-Makers*. New York: The Free Press, 1961.

Milbrath, Lester W. *Political Participation.* Chicago: Rand McNally and Company, 1965.

Pye, Lucian W. *Politics, Personality, and Nation Building.* New Haven, Conn.: Yale University Press, 1962.

Group Behavior

Golembiewski, Robert T. *The Small Group.* Chicago: University of Chicago Press, 1962.

Verba, Sidney. *Small Groups and Political Behavior.* Princeton, N. J.: Princeton University Press, 1961.

Community Behavior

Agger, Robert A., Daniel Goldrich, and Bert Swanson. *The Rulers and the Ruled.* New York: John Wiley and Sons, 1964.

Banfield, Edward C. *Political Influence.* New York: The Free Press, 1961.

Dahl, Robert A. *Who Governs?* New Haven, Conn.: Yale University Press, 1961.

Janowitz, Morris. *Community Political Systems.* New York: The Free Press, 1961.

Jennings, M. Kent. *Community Influentials: The Elites of Atlanta.* New York: The Free Press, 1964.

Polsby, Nelson W. *Community Power and Political Theory.* New Haven, Conn.: Yale University Press, 1963.

Presthus, Robert. *Men at the Top.* New York: Oxford University Press, 1964.

Wildavsky, Aaron. *Leadership in a Small Town.* Totowa, N. J.: Bedminster Press, 1964.

Williams, Oliver P., and Charles R. Adrian. *Four Cities: A Study in Comparative Policy Making.* Philadelphia: University of Pennsylvania Press, 1963.

Electoral Behavior

Berelson, Bernard R., Paul F. Lazarsfeld, and William N. McPhee. *Voting.* Chicago: University of Chicago Press, 1954.

Burdick, Eugene, and Arthur J. Brodbeck. *American Voting Behavior.* New York: The Free Press, 1959.

Campbell, Angus, Philip E. Converse, Warren E. Miller, and Donald E. Stokes. *The American Voter.* New York: John Wiley and Sons, 1960.

Eulau, Heinz, *Class and Party in the Eisenhower Years.* New York: The Free Press, 1962.

Janowitz, Morris, and Dwaine Marvick. *Competitive Pressure and Democratic Consent,* second edition. Chicago: Quadrangle Books, 1964.

Jennings, M. Kent, and Harmon Zeigler. *The Electoral Process*. Englewood Cliffs, N. J.: Prentice-Hall, 1966.

Key, V. O., Jr. *Public Opinion and American Democracy*. New York: Alfred A. Knopf, 1961.

Legislative Behavior

Barber, James D. *The Lawmakers: Recruitment and Adaptation to Legislative Life*. New Haven, Conn.: Yale University Press, 1965.

MacRae, Duncan. *Dimensions of Congressional Voting*. Berkeley: University of California Press, 1958.

Matthews, Donald R. *U. S. Senators and Their World*. Chapel Hill: University of North Carolina Press, 1960.

Truman, David B. *The Congressional Party*. New York: John Wiley and Sons, 1959.

Wahlke, John C., and Heinz Eulau. *Legislative Behavior*. New York: The Free Press, 1959.

Wahlke, John C., Heinz Eulau, William Buchanan, and LeRoy C. Ferguson. *The Legislative System*. New York: John Wiley and Sons, 1962.

Administrative Behavior

Kaufman, Herbert. *The Forest Ranger*. Baltimore: The Johns Hopkins University Press, 1960.

March, James G., and Herbert A. Simon. *Organizations*. New York: John Wiley and Sons, 1958.

Marvick, Dwaine. *Career Perspectives in a Bureaucratic Setting*. Ann Arbor: Bureau of Government, University of Michigan, 1954.

Meyerson, Martin, and Edward C. Banfield. *Politics, Planning, and the Public Interest*. New York: The Free Press, 1955.

Peabody, Robert L. *Organizational Authority*. New York: Atherton Press, 1964.

Simon, Herbert A. *Administrative Behavior*. New York: The Macmillan Company, 1947.

Judicial Behavior

Becker, Theodore L. *Political Behavioralism and Modern Jurisprudence*. Chicago: Rand McNally and Company, 1964.

Pritchett, Herman. *The Roosevelt Court*. New York: The Macmillan Company, 1948.

Schmidhauser, John R. *The Supreme Court: Its Politics, Personalities and Procedures*. New York: Holt, Rinehart and Winston, 1960.

Schubert, Glendon, *Quantitative Analysis of Judicial Behavior*. New York: The Free Press, 1959.

Schubert, Glendon, *Judicial Decision-Making.* New York: The Free Press, 1963.

Schubert, Glendon. *Judicial Behavior.* Chicago: Rand McNally and Company, 1964.

Shapiro, Martin. *Law and Politics in the Supreme Court.* New York: The Free Press, 1964.

Party Behavior

Cotter, Cornelius P., and Bernard C. Hennessy. *Politics Without Power: The National Party Committees.* New York: Atherton Press, 1964.

Eldersveld, Samuel J. *Political Parties: A Behavioral Analysis.* Chicago: Rand McNally and Company, 1964.

Heard, Alexander. *The Costs of Democracy.* Chapel Hill: University of North Carolina Press, 1960.

Key, V. O., Jr. *Southern Politics in State and Nation.* New York: Alfred A. Knopf, 1949.

Key, V. O., Jr. *American State Politics.* New York: Alfred A. Knopf, 1956.

Leiserson, Avery. *Parties and Politics.* New York: Alfred A. Knopf, 1958.

Sorauf, Frank J. *Party and Representation.* New York: Atherton Press, 1962.

Wilson, James Q. *The Amateur Democrat.* Chicago: University of Chicago Press, 1962.

Interest Group Behavior

Bauer, Raymond A., Ithiel de Sola Pool, and Lewis A. Dexter. *American Business and Public Policy: The Politics of Foreign Trade.* New York: Atherton Press, 1963.

Cohen, Bernard C. *The Press and Foreign Policy.* Princeton, N. J.: Princeton University Press, 1963.

Huntington, Samuel P. *Changing Patterns of Military Politics.* New York: The Free Press, 1962.

Lipset, Seymour M., Martin Trow, and James Coleman. *Union Democracy.* New York: The Free Press, 1956.

Masters, Nicholas A., Robert H. Salisbury, and Thomas E. Eliot. *State Politics and the Public Schools.* New York: Alfred A. Knopf, 1964.

Milbrath, Lester W. *The Washington Lobbyists.* Chicago: Rand McNally and Company, 1963.

Truman, David B. *The Governmental Process.* New York: Alfred A. Knopf, 1951.

Zeigler, Harmon. *Interest Groups in American Society.* Englewood Cliffs, N. J.: Prentice-Hall, 1964.

International Behavior

Guetzkow, Harold, Chadwick Alger, Richard A. Brody, and Robert C. Noel. *Simulation in International Relations.* Englewood Cliffs, N. J.: Prentice-Hall, 1963.

Kelman, Herbert C. *International Behavior: A Social-Psychological Analysis.* New York: Holt, Rinehart and Winston, 1965.

Rosenau, James N. *International Politics and Foreign Policy.* New York: The Free Press, 1961.

Singer, J. David. *Human Behavior and International Politics.* Chicago: Rand McNally and Company, 1965.

Index

Contributors

EDWARD C. BANFIELD. Professor of Urban Government, Harvard University. Author of *Government Project* (1951), *The Moral Basis of a Backward Society* (1958), *Political Influence* (1961), and *Big City Politics* (1965); co-author of *Politics, Planning, and the Public Interest* (1955) and *City Politics* (1963); editor of *Urban Government* (1961).

GORDON BLACK. Research Fellow, Institute of Political Studies, Stanford University. Author of *The Arena of Political Competition* (forthcoming).

WILLIAM BUCHANAN. Professor of Political Science, Washington and Lee University. Author of *Legislative Partisanship: The Deviant Case of California* (1963); co-author of *How Nations See Each Other* (1953) and *The Legislative System* (1962).

ROBERT A. DAHL. Professor of Political Science, Yale University. Former Fellow, Center for Advanced Study in the Behavioral Sciences. Author of *Congress and Foreign Policy* (1950), *A Preface to Democratic Theory* (1956), *Who Governs?* (1961), and *Modern Political Analysis* (1963); co-author of *Politics, Economics and Welfare* (1953).

MURRAY EDEN. Professor of Electrical Engineering, Massachusetts Institute of Technology. Author of numerous articles in scientific journals.

SAMUEL J. ELDERSVELD. Professor of Political Science, University of Michigan. Former Fellow, Center for Advanced Study in the Behavioral Sciences. Author of *Political Affiliation in Metropolitan Detroit* (1957) and *Political Parties: A Behavioral Analysis* (1964); co-editor of *Public Opinion and Propaganda* (1954) and *Political Behavior* (1956).

HEINZ EULAU. Professor of Political Science, Stanford University. Former Fellow, Center for Advanced Study in the Behavioral Sciences. Author of *Class and Party in the Eisenhower Years* (1962), *Journeys in Politics* (1963), and *The Behavioral Persuasion in Politics* (1963); co-author of *The Legislative System* (1962) and *Lawyers in Politics* (1964); co-editor of *Political Behavior* (1956) and *Legislative Behavior* (1959).

RICHARD F. FENNO, JR. Professor of Political Science, University of Rochester. Author of *The President's Cabinet* (1959) and a forthcoming book on the Appropriations Committee of the U.S. House of Representatives.

LEROY C. FERGUSON. Professor of Political Science, Michigan State University. Author of *How State Legislators View the Problem of School Needs* (1960), and co-author of *The Legislative System* (1962).

ALAN FIELLIN. Assistant Professor of Political Science, City College of The City University of New York. Author of several studies on legislative behavior in political science journals.

THOMAS A. FLINN. Professor of Political Science, Oberlin College, Author of *Governor Freeman and the Minnesota Budget* (1961) and of studies on party politics and political behavior in political science journals.

WAYNE L. FRANCIS. Assistant Professor of Political Science, Syracuse University. Author of studies on political behavior in political science journals and of *A Comparative Analysis of Legislative Issues in the 50 States*.

ROBERT S. FRIEDMAN. Professor of Political Science, University of Michigan. Author of *The Michigan Constitutional Convention and Administrative Organization* (1963) and "State Politics and Highways," in H. Jacob and K. N. Vines, eds., *Politics in the American States* (1965).

FRED I. GREENSTEIN. Professor of Government, Wesleyan University. Former Fellow, Center for Advanced Study in the Behavioral Sciences. Author of *The American Party System and the American People* (1963) and *Children and Politics* (1965); co-author of *An Introduction to Poltical Analysis* (1962).

JOHN G. GRUMM. Professor of Political Science, University of Kansas. Author of studies on legislative behavior in political science journals.

ALLAN KORNBERG. Assistant Professor of Political Science, Duke University. Author of several articles on political and legislative behavior in political science journals.

MURRAY B. LEVIN. Professor of Government, Boston University.

Author of *The Alienated Voter* (1960) and *The Compleat Politician* (1962).

HERBERT MCCLOSKY. Professor of Political Science, University of California. Former Fellow, Center for Advanced Study in the Behavioral Sciences. Author of numerous articles on political behavior in political science journals, and co-author of *The Soviet Dictatorship* (1960).

CARL D. MCMURRAY. Coordinator of Federal Programs for the state of Idaho. Author of *The Impeachment of Circuit Judge Richard Kelly* (1964) and a study of roll-call factor analysis in the *American Behavioral Scientist* (1963).

WARREN E. MILLER. Professor of Political Science, University of Michigan. Former Fellow, Center for Advanced Study in the Behavioral Sciences. Co-author of *The Voter Decides* (1954), *The American Voter* (1960), and *Elections and the Political Order* (1966).

MALCOLM B. PARSONS. Professor of Government, Florida State University. Author of articles on legislative politics and budget performance in political science journals.

ROBERT H. SALISBURY. Professor of Political Science, Washington University. Co-author of *State Politics and the Public Schools* (1964) and *American Government: Problems and Readings in Political Analysis* (1965).

JOHN H. SCHAAR. Professor of Political Science, University of California at Berkeley. Author of *Loyalty in America* (1957) and *Escape from Authority* (1961).

PAUL A. SMITH. Associate Professor of Political Science, Harpur College of the State University of New York. Author of *Proceedings of the Democratic National Convention 1960* (1964), and co-editor of *Politics and Social Life* (1963).

DONALD E. STOKES. Professor of Political Science, University of Michigan. Co-author of *The American Voter* (1960) and *Elections and the Political Order* (1965).

SIDNEY VERBA. Professor of Political Science, Stanford University. Former Fellow, Center for Advanced Study in the Behavioral Sciences. Author of *Small Groups and Political Behavior* (1961); co-author of *The Civic Culture* (1963); co-editor of *The International System* (1961).

JOHN C. WAHLKE. Professor of Political Science, University of Iowa. Co-author of *The Legislative System* (1962), and co-editor of *Legislative Behavior* (1959) and *Government and Politics: An Introduction to Political Science* (1966).

JAMES Q. WILSON. Professor of Government, Harvard University.

Author of *Negro Politics* (1960) and *The Amateur Democrat* (1962); co-author of *City Politics* (1963).

FREDERICK M. WIRT. Professor of Political Science, Denison University. Author of a forthcoming book on the political sociology of American suburbia.